Women Writers of Spain

Women Writers of Spain

An Annotated Bio-Bibliographical Guide

EDITED BY CAROLYN L. GALERSTEIN

NON-CASTILIAN MATERIALS EDITED BY
KATHLEEN McNERNEY

BIBLIOGRAPHIES AND INDEXES IN WOMEN'S STUDIES, NUMBER 2

GREENWOOD PRESS
NEW YORK • WESTPORT, CONNECTICUT • LONDON

Library of Congress Cataloging-in-Publication Data

Women writers of Spain.

(Bibliographies and indexes in women's studies,
ISSN 0742-6941 ; no. 2)
  Bibliography: p.
  Includes index.
  1. Spanish literature—Women authors—Bio-bibliog-
raphy. 2. Catalan literature—Women authors—Bio-
bibliography. 3. Gallegan literature—Women authors—
Bio-bibliography. I. Galerstein, Carolyn L., 1931-
II. McNerney, Kathleen. III. Series.
Z2693.5W6W65 1986   [PQ6055]   016.86'09'9287   86-379
ISBN 0-313-24965-2 (lib. bdg. : alk. paper)

Library of Congress Catalog Card Number: 86-379
ISBN: 0-313-24965-2
ISSN: 0742-6941

First published in 1986

314027

Greenwood Press, Inc.
88 Post Road West, Westport, Connecticut 06881

Printed in the United States of America

∞

The paper used in this book complies with the
Permanent Paper Standard issued by the National
Information Standards Organization (Z39.48-1984).

10 9 8 7 6 5 4 3 2 1

CONTENTS

ACKNOWLEDGMENTS

I wish to express my deepest appreciation to:

Kathleen McNerney for editing the entries on Catalan and Galician writers

Barbara Geiger for preparing the camera-ready copy

J. C. Tupper for secretarial assistance

Antonio González for preparing the Title Index

Delfina Bedarte for research assistance

All the contributors for all their efforts

Carolyn L. Galerstein

PREFACE

This volume is intended to familiarize readers, however briefly, with the content and meaning of selected works by 300 women writers of Spain. Writers are entered in alphabetical order, according to the Spanish alphabet, and are provided with succinct biographical data. For each author, major literary works follow alphabetically with selective annotations. For a chronological list of authors, see Appendix I.

Please note that authors who write exclusively or primarily in Catalan are marked with an *. As CH and LL are not separate letters in Catalan as they are in Castilian, Catalan writers whose names begin with CH or LL are listed in regular alphabetical order within the C's or L's. A list of Catalan authors who appear in this work is to be found as Appendix II. Authors who write exclusively or primarily in Galician are marked with **, and a list of Galician authors who appear in this work is included as Appendix III.

Compilation of this volume involved the contributions of 79 specialists in Spanish literature. The initials of the researcher who prepared the entry appear at the end of that author's entry. In cases where the biographical note was written by a contributor other than the person who prepared the annotations, those initials appear at the end of the biographical note. Entries in which works of one author were annotated by more than one contributor include the initials of the particular contributor at the end of each work. To identify the initials, refer to the list of contributors which follows the Introduction.

Because it is the hope of the editors and contributors that non-Spanish readers will also be interested in learning about the contribution of women to the literature of Spain, we have written the annotations in English and have provided English translations of any quotations that appear in the annotations. We have not translated the titles of works, but we do include, as Appendix IV, an index to translated titles that are noted in the bibliography. This is not intended to be a comprehensive list of the many foreign translations of works by women authors of Spain that have been published. Nor is it an attempt to duplicate the more complete list of recent English translations found in <u>Women Writers in Translation: An Annotated Bibliography, 1945-1982</u> (New York and London: Garland Press, 1984) edited by Margery Resnick and Isabelle de Courtivron. Over the centuries since their publication, the works of Santa Teresa have been translated into many languages, but we list only a few recent English translations; and we have not attempted to list the translations of such frequently translated authors as Emilia Pardo Bazán. Appendix IV does not include works written in Catalan or other languages and then translated into Castilian; nor does it contain Catalan translations. In the body of the bibliography it is sometimes mentioned that a work is available in translation into Russian, Czech, Danish or some other language, but if the translated title and publication data are not included in the bibliography, the work is not listed in the Appendix.

Women Writers in Translation: An Annotated Bibliography, 1945-1982, includes translations of only 12 authors of Spain.   According to this bibliography, only 20 individual works, and two translations of Santa Teresa's complete or collected works, have been translated into English since 1945.   Two works are by the seventeenth-century mystic Sor María de Agreda; one is a collection of stories by Zayas y Sotomayor; and there are ten translations of six individual works of Santa Teresa.   The nineteenth century is represented by one new translation of Fernán Caballero's La Gaviota, a new translation of Pardo Bazán's Los Pazos de Ulloa and a selection of poems by Rosalía de Castro.
Considering the prolific accomplishments of women writers—novelists, poets, playwrights and essayists—since the end of the Spanish Civil War, it is astonishing and reprehensible that only seven works by six authors published since 1945 have been translated into English.   This is symptomatic of the lack of attention paid not only to Spain's women writers but also to Spanish literature, particularly of the Franco period, in general in the United States. Resnick and Courtivron's guide grew out of a panel of the Division on Women's Studies in Language and Literature of the Modern Language Association.   It was to be the first in a series of annotated bibliographies which would also include untranslated works by the women writers of various countries.
Women Writers of Spain: An Annotated Bio-Bibliographical Guide is an additional result of that initial interest on the part of the Modern Language Association.   Two subsequent volumes, on women writers of Spanish America and of the German-speaking countries are currently in preparation, to be published by Greenwood Press.
Women Writers of Spain provides, for the first time, an extensive and comprehensive list of Spanish women authors of the twentieth century and of Catalan and Galician authors, as well as an expansion on earlier studies of nineteenth-century authors.   In Apuntes para una biblioteca de escritoras españolas desde el año 1401 al 1833 (Madrid: Sucesores de Rivadeneyra, 1903-05) Manuel Serrano y Sanz presented an all-inclusive bio-bibliography of earlier authors.   Authors listed in Serrano y Sanz are not included in this work, except in those cases where some new information on the author or the work, or a more recent edition of a work, can be added.   There are a number of authors studied by Serrano y Sanz whose work bears reevaluation and careful scrutiny, and we regret that space limitations have prevented their inclusion. Many of the works listed by Serrano y Sanz cannot be located in the United States, and many cannot even be found in the Biblioteca Nacional in Madrid. However, a number of the manuscripts listed may now be available in microform. Interested researchers may contact the Dupre Library, University of Southwestern Louisiana, Lafayette, LA 70504, for more information.
Women Writers of Spain: An Annotated Bio-Bibliographical Guide is primarily an effort to evaluate the contribution made by each author and her work to the development of a particular genre and to the literary representation of the historical period in which she wrote.   To the extent possible, each literary work of an author is summarized and analyzed.   We have also emphasized feminist elements within the works, commenting upon the author's presentation of the psychology of women and their role in Spanish society.
This bio-bibliographical guide does not include women, such as Catalina Erauso, who were born in Spain but who did all, or almost all, of their writing and publishing in Spanish America.   Conversely, we do not include Spanish American women who began their work in their homeland, and even established their reputations there, but who also, like Gertrudis Gómez de Avellaneda lived and published in Spain.   Such writers will be annotated in a succeeding volume of this series, Women Writers of Spanish America: An Annotated Bio-bibliographical Guide.   Writers who were born in Spain, but who went into exile after the Civil War of 1936-39 are another group that defies categorization.

Many who established their reputations prior to the war are included, even though they may have published the bulk of their work in Mexico or Argentina. A few of these authors returned to Spain at the end of the Franco era and have resumed publication there.   An excellent example is Dolores Ibarruri "La Pasionaria," who returned to Spain in 1975 after 28 years of exile in the Soviet Union. There are also many writers who left Spain as children and who grew up and wrote exclusively in Spanish America. They are not included here but will be found in the subsequent volume on Spanish American women writers.

An excellent source for information on living authors is Quien es quien en las letras españolas, published most recently in 1979 in Madrid by INLE (Instituto Nacional de Letras Españolas).   Although some of the publication information listed here is incorrect, it is a fairly comprehensive compilation of the women writers living in Spain in that year. In cases where we could add no information beyond that in Quien es quien, the author has been omitted.

Except for the Catalans and Galicians, we do not include women whose names we found on some list or other or who appeared in some catalogue but for whom we had perhaps only one title and on whom we could track down no biographical information, and whose work we could not obtain either. There are other authors whose works could not be obtained, but whom we list, giving at least the biographical and bibliographical information. Many older catalogues list authors by last name followed by the first initial only. One cannot help but wonder how many of these are also women who did not use their tell-tale first name in order to remain anonymous. It is regrettable that these women and the many others who used pseudonyms may remain forever unknown.

We have also omitted authors who have not written "creative" works. Therefore, we include almost exclusively poets, novelists and dramatists. There are some essayists, and we do include literary critics if they have published major works and are known more as essayists than "book reviewers." We do not include writers who are exclusively journalists, sociologists or historians. There are no biographers, unless the work also is considered to have literary value or is of an important female historical or literary figure. Nor do we include psychologists unless they have contributed substantially to women's studies. We have made a special effort to include women who have contributed to the contemporary feminist movement or who were noted feminists in the past. We do not include writers who publish juvenile works exclusively, although in some cases we include the juvenile works of authors who are otherwise noteworthy. We also do not include writers whose sole output is the novela rosa, the very popular light novels which can be compared to the "romance" novels so popular in the United States and Great Britain. We have made one or two exceptions in the case where the novela rosa treats themes of importance to contemporary women, or where the popularity of the works implies that they may have some influence on the development of social ideas in young women.   Because complete data on each author and work were not always available, we hope that this guide will be considered only a beginning, and that subsequent supplements will add new works and bring new information to light. We also hope that our survey will bring the accomplishments of the women writers of Spain to the attention of the Spanish-speaking and English-speaking worlds and that their works will be studied and valued in the future.

                                                            Carolyn L. Galerstein

INTRODUCTION

Throughout the history of Spanish literature, there have been women writing and publishing poetry, fiction, drama and essays. Many of these were obscure nuns who wrote verses in praise of the Virgin; others have attained fame both inside and outside of Spain and some have received Spain's most prestigious literary prizes. Still, the average reader of the Spanish language, and even some experts in Spanish literature, are unaware of the enormous contribution which some authors have made to the development of peninsular literature and thought.

The average English-speaking reader is hardly aware of the contribution to European letters made by Spanish authors, and is even less aware of the contributions of women writers. The average reader of Spanish might have heard the names of Santa Teresa and Pardo Bazán but might not be familiar with their works. Those are about the only two women writers who would appear in histories of Spanish literature and anthologies which the average undergraduate major in Spanish would have studied. More and more Spanish programs are offering courses in contemporary literature, and here a student might read Nada by Carmen Laforet or perhaps one other well-known novel by a woman of the post-war (but probably not post-Franco) period. Graduate students are likely to read a complete novel by Pardo Bazán, but again, unless the student or the professor has a particular interest in contemporary literature, they will encounter few women. Students, scholars, and the general reader miss a great deal because they are unfamiliar with the extensive and high-quality output of women writers over the centuries.

From the beginnings of literature in the vernacular on the Iberian peninsula, women have been writing works of lasting value, often anonymously, or signed with male pseudonyms, because of the strictures against women publishing their writings. The delightful Jarchas of the eleventh century, written in archaic Castilian mixed with Hebrew and Arabic, may have been composd by women, as their lovely lyrical qualities and the expressions of pining away for the male lover would indicate.

The late Middle Ages and the Renaissance included women who participated in the development of new literary forms, and the Golden Age included its share of dramatists. The towering figure of Santa Teresa de Avila captured the imagination and reverance of all of Spain, and to this day her writings are among the best known spiritual works in the Western world. In the nineteenth century Emilia Pardo Bazán held her own creatively and intellectually with the great realistic novelists of the period and helped introduce Naturalism into Spain.

The twentieth century has witnessed an explosion in the number of literary works by women in Spain. A great deal of this work is of the highest quality and has garnered well-deserved prizes and popularity. On the other hand, much of what has been published since the Spanish Civil War is not of the quality

that could warrant inclusion in a college course or research by graduate
students.   Yet, the lesser authors have also made a contribution to the
flourishing of fiction and poetry in this century, and the fact that they were
able to publish during the censorship of the Franco regime is a tribute to their
perseverance and often to their artistry. Recently the Civil War and the exile
so many Spaniards experienced subsequently have been important themes in the
works of many women authors. There have always been feminist authors, and
their perspectives on their period, society, and the roles of women have been a
valuable   source   of   understanding   Spanish   society   and   culture.   In the
post-Franco period a new, more militant feminism has been demonstrated in the
works of many women.
    The purpose of this annotated bibliography is to create a survey of Spanish
women writers' accomplishments as well as to provide brief biographies and a
comprehensive list of the authors and their works. However, we are not the
first scholars to undertake such a task. Manuel Serrano y Sanz, in his Apuntes
para una biblioteca de escritoras españolas desde el año 1401 al 1833
presented the fruits of a monumental effort at tracking down the biographical
data on and manuscripts of the works of nearly 1100 authors. Many of these
authors noted by Serrano y Sanz are acknowledged as writers of enduring
literary value. In the eighteenth century, María Rita de Barrenechea y
Morante de la Madrid, Condesa del Carpio (1750-1795) wrote plays during a
period when the spanish theatre was dominated by French imports. Another
important figure is María de Zayas y Sotomayor (1590-1661?), one of the
earliest Spanish novelists, referred to by one contemporary critic as "The Tenth
Muse of the Age." While many of the works cited exhibit little or no literary
value, there are numerous poems and plays which may be judged as excellent
examples of the literature of their age, yet have received no attention. They
are buried in the archieves of convents and libraries, never reprinted in recent
times, and read only by the most specialized scholars. They should instead be
available to general readers and students of Spanish literature, to whom they
could well appeal, and to whom they could speak as women, as members of
Spanish society, and as artists.
    In Literatas españolas del siglo XIX: Apuntes bibliográficos (Madrid:
Imprenta de Antonio Pérez Dubrull, 1889) Juan Pedro Criado y Domínguez
lists 390 women authors categorized as dramatists, lyric poets, novelists,
writers. The largest category is that of the lyric poets, with 85 authors,
followed by novelists, of whom there are 60. He also lists pseudonyms used by
the women, some of which are women's names, some men's; others are obvious
pseudonyms, like "La Peregrina", used by Gómez de Avellaneda.
    In the dedicatory to Queen Isabel II, his patroness, Criado y Domínguez
says the work is consecrated to the perpetuation of the triumphs and merits of
Spanish women writers, a group he esteems highly as "nuestras insignes
literatas." In the introduction he admits that there is no nineteenth-century
writer to equal Santa Teresa, or several other illustrious writers of the past.
However, he believes that la Avellaneda, Fernán Caballero, Concepción
Arenal, Carolina Coronado and Pardo Bazán are certainly notable authors. He
also notes that Dolores Martí and Angela Grassi have received prizes abroad
and that Pilar Sinués was also receiving critical attention.
    Criado y Domínguez comments that women writers of the century have
developed in particular the genres of subjective poetry and the novel. He believes that la Avellaneda and Carolina Coronado wrote some of the best lyric
poetry of the century, of any country. To him the lyric is the mirror of the
soul of woman. He ponders the question of women as poets, wondering whether
the better she is as a poet, the less she is a woman, and he quotes Grassi as
saying that women should not try to be like men. He also mentions 12 women

who write religious material exclusively, but he feels they cannot compare with the great religious writers of the past. The novels of the period are a product of Catholicism; they propound a moral and present a picture of the times. In previous centuries only María de Zayas and Mariana de Carvajal appreciated the possibilities of the genre of the novel, but the nineteenth century spawned a plethora of novelists. However, only Fernán Caballero and Pardo Bazán attained critical acclaim outside of Spain. In addition, Criado y Domínguez finds Aroníz, Grassi, Biedma, Coronado, Sinués and Saez meritorious for their originality.

The first Spanish woman dramatist was Portuguese-born Paula Vicente, daughter of Gil. The sixteenth and seventeenth centuries abounded in women dramatists. Criado y Domínguez cites Galvez de Cabrera as one dramatist of the early nineteenth century who attempted to free the theatre from its French shackles. Other noteworthy dramatists are Gallego, Navarro, Medrano, Medinabeitia, Grassi, López de Madariaga, Coronado, Cabrera y Heredia and Vera, many of whom translated works from the French and Italian.

Criado y Domínguez lists 18 periodicals of the period directed by women, and these run the gamut from fashion magazines to literary and legal journals. Journalists were a new breed in the nineteenth century, and he points out some of the outstanding women in this occupation.

Criado y Domínguez also praises those who are teachers, and those who write on juridical questions, particularly Concepción Arenal, and even María Josefa de la Piedra, who writes about agriculture and agronomy. He notes that some women are great philologists and linguists, and commends them as translators of foreign literary works. There is also reference to Spain's first woman doctor, Doña Martina Castell y Ballespi, who received an M.D. degree from the University of Madrid in 1882.

Another merit of women writers, as far as Criado y Domínguez is concerned, is that, in addition to their fidelity to Catholic doctrine, they have distanced themselves from politics. He is glad they stay out of it, because it is a messy business. However, considering that Queen Isabel patronized this work, he is careful to add that women do have the ability to help men with the arduous enterprise of governing.

A more recent reference work on the nineteenth century is Juan Ignacio Ferreras' Catálogo de novelas y novelistas españoles del siglo XIX (Madrid: Ediciones Catedra, 1979). He lists 83 women novelists, 63 of whom are in Criado y Domínguez. Ferreras indicates that he cannot identify several of the women listed in Criado y Domínguez or elsewhere, most likely because a woman used a fake female name in order not to bring embarrassment to her family, and after a century, it is impossible to track her down.

Recently there have been a number of anthologies of women writers of the twentieth century, but none as comprehensive as Antología biográfica de escritoras españolas by Isabel Calvo de Aguilar (Madrid: Biblioteca Nueva, 1954). It includes 85 contemporary writers, with a one-page biography of each, and a short selection (article or short story) by each. There is no poetry. Some authors are the best known of the generation: Carmen Conde, Concha Espina, Carmen Laforet, Ana María Matute, Carmen Martín Gaite.   Many went on to have respectable literary careers and are included in this volume: Ballesteros, Barberá, Cajal, Medio, Icaza, Mulder de Daumer, Vázquez, Zardoya. Many were hardly heard from again.

The bibliographies and anthologies mentioned above do not include authors whose works are exclusively or primarily in Catalan and Galician. In addition to its purpose of bringing surveys of Spanish women writers up to date, Women Writers of Spain: An Annotated Bio-Bibliographical Guide is the first effort to include in a compilation of Spanish women writers a list of Catalan and Galician authors. Their importance is analyzed in the following section.

Carolyn L. Galerstein

Introduction to Catalan and Other Non-Castilian Authors

When this project first came to my attention, I was pleased that such useful work was being done; at the same time I noticed with dismay that only one
Catalan writer appeared on the preliminary list. It seemed that this lack was a
result of a habit of the exclusion of Catalans among Hispanic writers, somewhat
analogous to the systematic exclusion of women from literary histories,
anthologies and bibliographies—a situation this project was designed to correct.
When the opportunity to include Catalan writers was presented, the re-
quests for annotators among Catalan specialists was quick and gratifying. However, there were many difficulties. No lists of Catalan women writers existed; I
began compiling names by searching through the Diccionari de Literatura Catalana for women's names, the Serrano y Sanz bibliography for Catalan names,
indexes of anthologies, histories of literature and critical works for names
which might be both Catalan and female. A first such list cannot hope to be
definitive, though my inclination was to include as much information as possible.
The greatest problem after compilation was distance and the lack of
access to materials. Collaborators with appropriate expertise were found in
Barcelona, and new authors and more works were added to the list. Still it was
impossible to complete an annotation of every work. Therefore, this bibliography includes names of people on whom there is very little information. In
some cases there was so little information, or the source of the information did
not inspire confidence in its accuracy, and so the name was simply left out.
However, I tried to avoid exclusion and to emphasize the gathering of data,
believing that an incomplete entry could at least be the starting point for a
better, more leisurely search at some future date. Rather than apologize for
the lacunae, I would like to think of this as an on-going project and would
welcome new or additional information from anyone, with the hope of revising
and amplifying this bibliography in the future. It is important that readers
interested in European literature be made aware of the contribution to that
literature of Catalan authors.
With the exception of the long period of "Decadence," from the end of the
fifteenth century to the end of the nineteenth, Catalan literature has followed
a course roughly parallel to the literatures of other Western European countries: early historical treatises and lyric poetry from the Middle Ages,
developing into a flourish of prose and poetry in the fifteenth century. After
the virtual silence of three centuries, a new Renaissance took root in the last
third of the nineteenth century, first in poetry and later in the narrative. With
an interruption during the Franco regime, Catalan literature has maintained its
strength in our day.
An unfortunate part of this parallel is that the work of women has been
neglected, and often presumed not to exist. Very little is known of the early
period; we have some of the work of the Reina de Mallorca, but are not even
sure of her identity. As in other literatures, Anonymous was a woman, and a
few poems written from a clearly female point of view are extant. In the
fifteenth century, Isabel de Villena wrote a treatise on the life of Christ; and
in the sixteenth, Estefania de Requesens wrote copious letters to her mother.
Toward the end of the period of silence, women's voices began to be heard
alongside those of their male colleagues, simultaneously with the early feminist
movements. There is a considerable body of literature by women in the late
nineteenth and early twentieth centuries, but most of these works are out of
print and difficult to find. Edicions LaSal is making an effort to solve this
problem by republishing the works of these "lost" women and has made available
new editions of several older texts.
The best known Catalan writer of the early years of this century is
Catarina Albert (1869-1966). Like some of her counterparts in other countries

and the rest of Spain, she used a male pseudonym, Víctor Català, in her case reflecting identification with her homeland as well. Her work was admired when it frst came out and her identity was unknown, but caused a scandal when people realized that the author was a woman.

The most widely-read contemporary Catalan prose writer is Mercè Rodoreda (1909-1983). She wrote prolifically before the outbreak of the Civil War and lived in exile in Geneva for decades. In 1957 she broke a 20-year silence with a volume of short stories. It was a new beginning for her and she continued to write steadily until her death. La Plaça del Diamant (1962), generally considered to be her masterpiece, is now in its 25th edition in Catalan. It has been translated into at least ten languages, and made into a popular film of the same title.

Twelve editions of Rodoreda's novel came out during the Franco period in spite of attempts to suppress the Catalan language and culture. Maria-Aurèlia Capmany (1918-), too, continued her voluminous production through those oppressive times. But, in general, it was difficult to publish in Catalan during that 40-year period, and it is not surprising that 1975 marked a flourishing of Catalan culture and literature. What is new is that such a great deal of this recent literature, especially the narrative, has been written by women. Montserrat Roig, Carme Riera, Olga Xirinachs and others have won important literary prizes recently, and many women, now in their thirties and forties, continue to have their works reprinted year after year. Responding, perhaps, to the marketplace, criticism is finally beginning to take their work seriously, and some publishers are now eager for their new manuscripts. Many of these women—Maria-Antònia Oliver, Helena Valentí, Isabel-Clara Simó, Antònia Vicens, to name only a few—deal frequently with themes of interest to feminists: the treatment of older women in society, female adolescence, flexible relationships, careers, the isolation and solitude of women. Poetry is also represented, and beautifully so, by writers such as Marta Pessarrodona and Maria-Mercè Marçal. It is indeed gratifying to see the proliferation of works by women, about women, and of high literary quality, coming into the mainstream.

,The problems besetting the Catalan section of this bibliography were multiplied tenfold in the Galician section. I had not planned to do anything about the lack of Galician writers on the list, though I felt it was a shame that their work was not represented. Then I met a Galician graduate student, married to a Catalan who was already working on my section, and he offered to make the connections necessary to get at least some minimal information about women writing in Galician. Alberto Moreiras established a collaboration with Camiño Noia Campos in Galicia, who furnished him with enough data to list the names of several important Galician writers, to indicate the type and genre of their work, and to place them within the context in Galician letters.

As for the other minority group in Spain, the Basques, we could only include Arantxa Urretavizcaya, some of whose work has been translated into Catalan or Castilian—an inevitable result of the newness of the literary tradition in Basque as well as the difficulty of the language itself.

These sections, too, can be viewed as on-going, developing work, to which we would like to add information in the future.

I would like to heartily thank all who collaborated on this project by analyzing the works of Catalan women writers. A work such as this must necessarily be a joint effort as well as a continuing project. I would especially like to thank those who helped me in Barcelona and who continued to send me information, articles and books after my return: Isabel Segura, Maria-Antònia Oliver, Anna Sallés, and the people at the Arxiu de la Corona d'Aragó. I would also like to thank, for encouragement, moral support and other kinds of help, Anna Maria Saludes, Carme Riera, Montserrat Roig, Isabel-Clara Simó,

Helena Valentí, Judith Stitzel, Alex Susanna, Joan Oleza, Joan Rende and Xavier Tudela.

Kathleen McNerney

CONTRIBUTORS

Contributors to this volume are listed here alphabetically by surname. To identify a contributor from the initials appended to the entries, refer to the last initial (or the last two initials in cases where they are hyphenated), and search the short list of initials ending with this letter in the left-hand column below. This list contains only those publications of contributors that concern women authors of Spain.

C A   Alborg, Concha. Asst. Prof. Saint Joseph's U. (Philadelphia). Ph.D. Temple U., 1982. "El lenguaje teresiano en la obra de Jesús Fernández Santos," in Santa Teresa y la literatura mística hispánica, Madrid: EDI, 1984, 793-99.

A M A   Aldaz, Anna-Marie. Asst. Prof. Northern Arizona U. Ph.D. U. Oregon, 1969.

C G B   Bellver, Catherine G. Prof. U. Nevada, Las Vegas. Ph.D. U. California, Berkeley, 1972. "The Language of Eroticism in the Novels of Esther Tusquets," Anales de la Literatura Española Contemporánea, 9, No. 1-3 (1984), 13-17. "Two New Women Writers from Spain," Letras Femeninas, 8, No. 2 (1982), 3-7. "Carmen Martín Gaite As a Social Critic," Letras Femeninas, 6, No. 2 (Fall 1980), 3-16.

M B   Bieder, Maryellen. Assoc. Prof. Indiana U. Ph.D. U. Minnesota, 1972. "Capitulation: Marriage. Not Freedom. A Study of Memorias de un solterón de Emilia Pardo Bazán and Tristana de Benito Pérez Galdós," Symposium, 30, 1976. "The Woman in the Garden: The Problem of Identity in the Novels of Mercè Rodoreda," Actes del segon Colloqui d'Estudis Catalans a Nord America, 1979. "Cataclysm and Rebirth: Journey to the Edge of the Maelstrom: Mercè Rodoreda's Quanta, quanta guerra..." Actes del Tercer Colloqui d'Estudis Catalans a Nord America, 1983.

H P B   Boyer, H. Patsy. Prof. Colorado State U. Ph.D. U. New Mexico, 1967. "A Feminist Reading of 'Los ojos verdes'" in Cortensayas Methods of Literary Criticism, 1981. "La visión artística de María de Zayas" in Estudios sobre el Siglo de oro, Madrid: Catecha, 1983, pp. 253-264.

M E B   Bravo, Maria-Elena. Asst. Prof. U. Illinois at Chicago. Ph.D. U. Madrid, 1974.

M L B   Bretz, Mary Lee. Assoc. Prof. Rutgers U. Ph.D. U. Maryland, 1973. Concha Espina, Boston: G. K. Hall, 1980.

JL B   Brown, Joan Lipman. Assoc. Prof. U. Delaware. Ph.D. U. Pennsylvania, 1976. Secrets from the Back Room: The Fiction of Carmen Martín Gaite, University, MS, 1984. "Tiempo de silencio and Ritmo lento: Pioneers of the New Social Novel in Spain," Hispanic Review, 50, No. 1, 1982. "A Fantastic Memoir: Technique and History in El cuarto de atrás," Anales de la novela española contemporánea, 6, 1981.

NLB   Bundy, Nancy L.   Asst. Prof. Frostburg State C.   Ph.D. U. Oklahoma, 1977.
FLC   Cabello, Francisco L. Lecturer, Homboldt State U. Ph.D. U. California, Davis, 1985.
AC   Callejo, Alfonso.   Teaching Fellow, U. Pittsburgh.   "Corporeidad y escaparates en La Plaza del Diamante de Mercè Rodoreda," Butlletí de la NACS, No. 16, Tardor, 1983, 14-17.
RC   Cantavella, Rosanna.   Facultad de Filologia i Lettres, U. Valencia. Articles on Isabel de Villena and Estefania de Requesens.
KHC   Cárdenas, Karen Hardy.   Assoc. Prof. U. South Dakota.   Ph.D. U. Kansas, 1973.
HC   Cazorla, Hazel. Assoc. Prof. U. Dallas.
VC-E   Codina-Espurz, Victoria. Grad. Student, West Virginia U.
JSC   Conde, Judith S. Assoc. Prof. Asbury C. Ph.D. U. Kentucky, 1977.
FADA   de Armas, Frederick A.   Prof. Louisiana State U.   Ph.D. U. North Carolina, 1969. The Invisible Mistress: Aspects of Feminism and Fantasy in the Golden Age, Charlottesville, 1976.
EMD   Dial, Eleanor Maxwell.   Iowa State U. Ph.D. U. Missouri-Columbia. Two Dream Weavers: Carlota O'Neill's Circe and Buero Vallejo's Penelope, Mexico: Costa-Amic, 1976. "'Una Mexicana en la Guerra de España': Memorias y teatro," in Carlota O'Neill, Romanzas de las rejas, Mexico: Costa Amic, 1978, 48-52 (with John E. Dial). "Brechtian Aesthetics in Chile: Isidora Aguirre's 'Los papeleros'," in Latin American Women Writers: Yesterday and Today, Eds. Yvette E. Miller and Charles Tatum, Pittsburgh: Latin American Literary Review Press, 1977, 85-90.
JED   Dial, John E.   Marquette U.   Ph.D. U. Missouri-Columbia.   "'Una Mexicana en la Guerra de España': Memorias y teatro," in Carlota O'Neill, Romanzas de las rejas, Mexico: Costa-Amic, 1978, 48-52 (with Eleanor E. Dial).
DD   Donahue, Dorothy. U. Wisconsin-Madison.
EE   Espadas, Elizabeth.   Prof. Wesley C.   Ph.D. U. Illinois at Urbana-Champaign, 1972. "The Short Fiction of Carmen Martín Gaite," Letras Femeninas, 4, No. 1 (Spring 1978), 3-19. "Women's Experience and Images of the City in the Works of Carmen Laforet, Mercè Rodoreda, and Mercedes Salisachs," in Proceedings of the Indiana University of Pennsylvania Ninth Annual Conference on Hispanic Literatures.
AMF   Fagundo, Ana María.   Prof. U. California, Riverside.   Ph.D. U. Washington, 1967.
EFC   Fernández de Cambria, Elisa. Cleveland State U. Ph.D. City U. of New York.
EF-D   Fonseca-Downey, Elizabeth. Sam Houston State U.
CF   Frechon, Carole. Grad. Assistant, West Virginia U.
CLG   Galerstein, Carolyn L. Assoc. Prof. U. of Texas at Dallas.   Ph.D. U. Maryland, 1965. "Carmen Laforet and the Spanish Spinster," Revista de estudios hispánicos, May, 1977, 303-15. "Bibiana: A Plea for the Liberation of Spanish Women," Letras Femeninas, VIII, No. 1 (1982) 3-8. "Spanish Women Novelists and Younger-Generation Writers in Exile and Return: Outsiders or Insiders?" in European Writers in Exile in Latin America, H.B. Moeller, ed., Heidelberg: Winter Verlag, 1983, 137-48.   "The Spanish Civil War: The View of Women Novelists," Letras Femeninas, X, No. 2 (Fall, 1984), 12-19. "The Second Generation in Exile," Papers on Language and Literature.

DRG Gerling, David Ross. Asst. Prof. U. of Southwestern Louisiana. Ph.D. U.
     Arizona, 1975.
SMG González, Shirley Mangini. Assoc. Prof. Yale U. Ph.D. U. New Mexico,
     1979.
PF-CG Greenwood, Pilar F.-Cañadas.   Postdoctoral Associate Cornell U.
     Ph.D. Cornell U., 1981.
MLG-E Guardiola-Ellis, María Louisa. Lecturer, U. Pennsylvania.
EH Hernández, Edmée. Inst. Kearney State C. Ph.D. Cornell U., 1982.
NH Hernández, Nicolás. Asst. Prof. Kearney State C. Ph.D. Cornell U.,
     1982.
LJH Hutton, Lewis J. Prof. U. Rhode Island. Ph.D. Princeton, 1950.
PI Irvin, Paula. Grad. Student, U. Oregon.
MJ Jacobson, Margaret. Asst. Prof. Illinois Wesleyan U. Ph.D. U. Iowa,
     1980.
MCJ Jiménez, María C.   Assoc. Prof. Sam Houston State U.   Ph.D. U.
     Michigan, 1972.
RJ Johnson, Roberta. Assoc. Prof. Scripps C. Ph.D. U. California, Los
     Angeles, 1971. Carmen Laforet, Boston: Twayne, 1981.
MEWJ Jones, Margaret E. W. Prof. U. Kentucky. Ph.D. U. Wisconsin, 1963.
     The Literary World of Ana María Matute, Lexington: University of
     Kentucky Press, 1970. Dolores Medio, Boston: G. K. Hall, 1974.
RRK Keenan, Richard. Asst. Prof. U. Idaho. Ph.D. U. Missouri, 1980.
JBL Landeira, Joy Buckles. Editor, U. Wyoming. Ph.D. U. Colorado-Boulder,
     1981.
LL-B Lee-Bonanno, Lucy. Asst. Prof. Asbury C. Ph.D. U. Kentucky, 1984.
LGL Levine, Linda Gould. Assoc. Prof. Montclair State C. Ph.D. Harvard U.,
     1973. Feminismo ante el franquismo (with Gloria Waldman), Miami:
     Ediciones Universal, 1980. "The Censored Sex: Woman as Author and
     Character in Franco's Spain," in Women in Hispanic Literature: Icons
     and Fallen Idols, ed. Beth Miller, Berkeley: University of California
     Press, 1983, 289-315.
RL Lundelius, Ruth. U. Georgia.
MJM Manier, Martha J. Asst. Prof. Humboldt State U. Ph.D. U. Colorado,
     1976.
KNM March, Kathleen N. Asst. Prof. U. Maine at Orono. Ph.D. SUNY at
     Buffalo. "A figura femenina na poesia de preguerra de Ricardo
     Carballo Calero," Grial, 74 (xaneiro-mar. 1982), 18-34. Elena Quiroga
     entry, Gran Enciclopedia Gallega.
HPM Márquez, Hector P. U. Redlands
EM-L Mas-López, Edita. Assoc. Prof. Queens C. CUNY. Ph.D. U. Havana,
     1943.
BDM May, Barbara Dale. Assoc. Prof. U. Oregon. Ph.D., U. Utah, 1975.
     "Female Choice and Destiny in Maria Aurèlia Capmany's La color
     más azul," Letras Femeninas, 1986.
TM McNally, Tara. Student, Boston College.
KM McNerney, Kathleen. Assoc. Prof. West Virginia U. Ph.D. U. New
     Mexico, 1977. "La identitat a La Plaça del Diamant, Supressió i
     Recerca," Actas del Quart Col.loqui d'Estudis Catalans, Barcelona:
     l'Abadia, 1985.
NJM Membrez, Nancy Jane. Visiting Lecturer, U. California, Santa Cruz.
     Ph.D. U. California, Santa Barbara, 1985.
JSM Merrell, Judith S. Prof. Hobart and William Smith C. Ph.D. Harvard U.,
     1956. "Symbolism in El chico, a Novel by Mercedes Ballesteros,"
     Letras Femeninas, IX, 3-10.

MM   Misiego, Miquela. Assoc. Prof. Rutgers U. Ph.D. U. Barcelona, 1968.
        "The Status of Women in Contemporary Spain," in Libro Memoria de
        Casa Galicia," New York: 1972.
AM   Moreiras, Alberto. Grad. Student, U. Georgia.
GM   Morocco, Glenn. Asst. Prof. La Salle U. Ph.D. U. Pennsylvania, 1974.
MBM   Movassaghi, Maizie B. Asst. Prof. U. Southwestern Louisiana. Ph.D.
        Louisiana State U., 1978.
EDM   Myers, Eunice D. Asst. Prof. Wichita State U. Ph.D. U. North Carolina,
        Chapel Hill, 1977.   "Estación, ida y vuelta: Rosa Chacel's
        Apprenticeship Novel," Hispanic Journal, 4 (Spring 1983), 77-84.
        "Modern Man's Quest for Identity in Rosa Chacel's La sinrazón,"
        Perspectives on Contemporary Literature, 8 (1982), 85-90. "Four
        Female Novelists and Spanish Children's Fiction," Letras Femeninas
        (Spring 1985).
MCNC   Noia Campos, María del Camiño. Prof. Colegio Universitario de Vigo.
        Ph.D. U. Santiago, 1980.
DJO   O'Connor, D. J.   Asst. Prof. U. New Orleans. Ph.D. U. California,
        Berkeley.
PWO   O'Connor, Patricia W. Prof. U. Cincinnati. Ph.D. U. Florida, 1962.
        Gregorio and María Martínez Sierra, Boston: Twayne, 1977.
        "Spain's First Successful Woman Dramatist: María Martínez Sierra,"
        Hispanófila, 1978.
JP   Pérez, Janet. Prof. Texas Tech U. Ph.D. Duke U., 1962. Ana María
        Matute, Boston: Twayne, 1969.   Novelistas femeninas de la
        postguerra española, Madrid: Porrúa, 1983.
RDP   Pope, Randolph D. Prof. Vassar C. Ph.D. Columbia U., 1973.
AR   Rey, Arsenio. Assoc. Prof. U. Alaska, Anchorage. Ph.D. New York U.,
        1974.
RR   Rodríguez, Rodney. Assoc. Prof. Rider C. Ph.D. Northwestern U.,
        1974.
PS   Sáenz, Pilar. Assoc. Prof. George Washington U. Ph.D. U. Maryland,
        1966.
UMS   Saine, Ute M. Asst. Prof. Northern Arizona U. Ph.D. Yale U., 1971.
ASR   Sánchez Rué, Anna M. Teaching Assistant, U. Virginia.
DES   Schmiedel, Donald E. Assoc. Prof. U. Nevada, Las Vegas. Ph.D. U.
        Southern California, 1967.
ISS   Segura i Soriano, Isabel. U. Barcelona. Ph.D. U. Barcelona, 1977.
        Revistes de dons (with Marta Selva), Barcelona: Edhasa, 1984.
        Historia gráfica de la dona a Catalunya, 1850-1900, Barcelona:
        Altafulla, 1985.
SLS   Slick, Sam L. Assoc. Prof. Sam Houston State U. Ph.D. U. Iowa, 1974.
JMS   Sobre, Josep-Miquel. Assoc. Prof. Indiana U. Ph.D. U. Oregon, 1972.
        "L'artifici de La Plaça del Diamant, un estudi lingüistic," in In
        Memoriam Carles Riba: 1959-1969, Barcelona: University of
        Barcelona-Ariel, 1973, 316-328.
LAS   Sponsler, Lucy A. Assoc. Prof. U. New Orleans. Ph.D. Yale U., 1969.
        Women in the Medieval Spanish Epic and Lyric Traditions, Lexington:
        University Press of Kentucky, 1975. "The Status of Married Women
        Under the Legal System of Spain," Journal of Legal History,
        University of London, 3, No. 2 (Sept. 1982), 125-52. "Women in Spain:
        Medieval Law vs. Epic Literature," Revista de estudios hispánicos,
        VII, No. 3 (Oct. 1973), 427-48.
ES   Starčević, Elizabeth. Assoc. Prof. City College of the City U. of New
        York.   Ph.D. City U. of New York, 1977.   Carmen de Burgos,
        defensora de la mujer, Almería: Librería-Editorial Cajal, 1976.

"Carmen de Burgos: esbozo biográfico de una feminista española,"
Revista de la Casa de la Cultura de Ecuador, 20 (Nov. 1980), 119-47.

NMV   Valis, Noël M. Assoc. Prof. U. Georgia. Ph.D. Bryn Mawr C., 1975.

T-VS   Vilaròs-Soler, Teresa. Grad. Student, U. Georgia.

NV   Vogeley, Nancy. Assoc. Prof. U. San Francisco. Ph.D. Stanford U., 1980.
"Diario y cartas de la cárcel," Vórtice, 2 (Primavera 1978), 103-05.

GFW   Waldman, Gloria Feiman. Assoc. Prof. York C., CUNY. Ph.D. City U.
New York, 1978. Feminismo ante el franquismo (with Linda Levine),
Miami: Ediciones Universal, 1979. Teatro Contemporáneo (with
Elena Paz), Boston: Heinle & Heinle, 1983.

EW   Wright, Eleanor. Asst. Prof. Vanderbilt U. Ph.D. U. Michigan, 1980.

PZ   Zatlin, Phyllis. Prof. Rutgers U. Ph.D. U. Florida, 1965. Elena Quiroga,
Boston: G. K. Hall, 1977. "The Theater of Ana Diosdado," Estreno,
3, No. 1 (1977), 13-17. "Divorce in Franco Spain: Elena Quiroga's
Algo pasa en la calle," Mosaic, 17, No. 1 (1984), 129-38.

Women Writers of Spain

ABARCA DE BOLEA, Ana Francisca (1623 or 1624-late 17th century).
Born in the town of Casbas of noble parents, she entered the
Cistercian convent at the age of three and took solemn vows at a very
early age, then served as Abbess from 1672 to 1676. She maintained
literary correspondence with scholars and writers and was esteemed as a
poet and intellectual. In addition to her one religious-pastoral novel
she wrote lives of saints, recorded the miracles of Nuestra Señora de
la Gloria, venerated by her order, and composed a sonnet on the death of
Prince Baltasar Carlos.

Vigilia y octavario de San Ivan Baptista. Zaragoza: Pascual
Bueno, 1679, 241 pp.
A religious-pastoral novel, the vague plot, a gathering of
shepherds in Moncayo to celebrate St. John's eve, serves as vehicle
for a description of the countryside. Includes a short novel: Fin
bueno en el mal principio, an apologue: La ventura en la desdicha,
and poetry, some of it curious: "Liras a unas viruelas" and "Romance
en lengua popular." The novel is preceded by several letters on
literary and moral topics and a prologue to the reader. Very rare.
DES

*ABELLO I SOLER, Montserrat (1918-).
A poet, born in Tarragona, she spent her childhood in the south of
Spain and England. She came to Barcelona to study and was caught there
by the Civil War. After the war she exiled herself to France, then to
England and finally to Chile where she married and had a daughter and
two sons. In 1960 she returned to Barcelona and published Vida Diària,
her first book of poems, in 1963. She combines teaching, writing and
translating, this latter a field in which she excels. She is known as
one of the best translators in Catalan now, and she has just finished
working on the poems of Sylvia Plath. Interested in women's themes, she
participates in the feminist movement and collaborates with the
Editorial laSal, a feminist publishing house.

Vida Diària. Barcelona: Joaquim Horta, 1963, 47 pp.
In his prologue to this collection of poems, Joan Oliver says that
"the magic of these little poems is transparent, the style economic."
The economy of language in her poetry gives emphasis to certain words
and enhances their impact.

Vida Diària, Paraules no dites. Barcelona: laSal, 1981, 108 pp.
    This book contains the poems of her first book and others
previously unpublished. It is illustrated with drawings by her
friend and companion in exile, Roser Bru, and the prologue is by
Marta Pessarrodna. I quote a poem from the second part which I find
illustrative of her poetry and the themes she deals with: "Everything
seems so simple. Four walls/ make a house. A man and a woman/ a
child. A table, four chairs,/ and a bed for sleeping, being born,
dying./ It all seems so simple, if it were so!"

                                                                    ISS

ACUÑA Y VILLANUEVA DE LA IGLESIA, Rosario de (1851-1923),
Pseud. Remigio Andrés Delafón.
    With the première of each of her dramas, Rosario de Acuña created a
sensation with her controversial ideas such as civil marriage. In 1884,
"Kasabal" wrote of her in the Revista de Madrid: "La señora Acuña es
para los hombres una literata, y para las mujeres una librepensadora, y
no inspira entre unos y otras simpatías." She also wrote articles,
stories, and several studies on Spanish rural life. The Ateneo's pedagogical section honored this Madrid native at an evening session in
1933, ten years after her death.

    Amor a la patria. Madrid: Imprenta de J. Rodríguez, 1877, 34 pp.
       Drama trágico en un acto y en verso. This verse play is a
    tribute to the heroism of the Saragossan people, particularly of all
    the women patriots such as Agustina Zaragoza who died defending Spain
    against the 1808 Napoleonic invasion. The action centers on Inés,
    her daughter María and wayward son Pedro. Returning furtively to
    his homestead, he reveals that in his nine-year absence he has made
    his fortune soldiering in France and is an officer with the invading
    force. He has come to rescue his family before they are caught in
    the cross-fire. His mother, horrified and ashamed, attempts to
    persuade him to join the resistance, but he refuses. Maria enters
    and, not recognizing her brother in a French uniform, shoots him
    dead. With his dying words he repents as his mother, sister and the
    rest of the town head for the barricades.

    La casa de las muñecas. Madrid: Imprenta de Ramón Angulo, 1888.

    Consecuencias de la degeneración femenina.
       Conferencia dada en el Fomento de las Artes de Madrid el 21 de
    Abril de 1888.

    Cosas mías. Tortosa: Monclús, 1917?, 62 pp.
       Cosas mías contains three diverse essays: "Algo sobre la mujer,"
    "El primer día de libertad (Memorias de un canario)" and "Los inter-
    mediarios", which were originally published as newspaper articles.
    The first declares her absolute conviction of male-female equality,
    demolishing anti-feminist arguments but simultaneously rejecting
    emancipation as unnecessary and even counterproductive. True
    equality, she asserts, will arise naturally from women's improved
    education. The second essay, an allegory, describes a canary's first
    day of freedom--which is also his last, for ignorant of the wide
    world, he is unable to survive. The third essay is a deadpan satire
    on cursis, whom she theorizes are intermediate beings on the
    evolutionary scale between apes and humans.

El crimen de la calle de Fuencarral; odia el delito y compadece al delincuente. Madrid: Casa Editorial de J.M. Faquineto, 1880?

Ecos del alma. Poesías. Madrid: Imprenta de A. Gómez Fuentenebro, 1876, 216 pp.

La herencia de las furias o misterios de un granero. Madrid, 18--.

El hijo de los pueblos rurales. 1882.

Influencia de la vida del campo en la familia. 1882.

Morirse a tiempo. Ensayo de un poema, imitación de Campoamor. Zaragoza: Ventura, 1880.

El padre Juan, drama en tres actos y en prosa. Madrid: R. Velasco, 1891, 88 pp. 2nd ed. corregida y aumentada, Madrid, R. Velasco, 1891, 89 pp.
    This anticlerical play, whose theme is religious fanaticism, created a scandal when it was first performed. The plot concerns padre Juan's grip on an Asturian town, although only the character's shadow actually appears. Ramón--wealthy hero, free-thinker, atheist and handsome engineer--tries to enlighten his people by buying and tearing down the local shrine, establishing a health spa and marrying the beautiful, pure and pantheistic Isabel in a civil ceremony. At the padre's urging, however, the villagers first shun the couple and later precipitate Ramón's murder. Mad with grief, Isabel discovers that the hypocritical padre is in fact Ramón's natural father. The play ends with her shriek of "murderer" as the padre's shadow is seen against the moon.

Rienzi el tribuno, drama trágico en dos actos y epílogo, original y en verso. Madrid: Imprenta de J. Rodríguez, 1876, 76 pp.
    This is the historical play in verse for which Acuña is best known. Set in the fourteenth century, it concerns tribune Nicolás de Rienzi's (Cola di Rienzo) efforts to unify Rome by ending the nobles' blood feud. Pedro Colonna, the sinister antagonist, threatens the peace and attempts to dishonor Rienzi's wife, the virtuous María who has only recently discovered she is Colonna's cousin. By the end of Act II the triumphant Rienzi has achieved his peace pact. However, the epilogue tells a different tale. Seven years later the treacherous nobles led by Colonna have incited the people to rebel against the just Rienzi. Rienzi is beheaded by the mob and María stabs herself rather than submit to Colonna.

Sentir y pensar, poema cómico. Madrid: Tello, 1884, 50 pp.

La siesta, colección de artículos. Madrid: Tipografía de G. Estrada, 1882, 244 pp.

Tiempo perdido, cuentos y bocetos. Madrid: M. Minuesa de los Ríos, 1881.

Tribunales de venganza, drama trágico-histórico en dos actos y epílog, original y en verso. Madrid: J. Rodríguez, 1880, 86 pp.

La voz de la patria, cuadro dramático en un acto y en verso, original. Madrid: R. Velasco, 1893, 31 pp.
    Patriotism is the theme of this play which centers on the desperate efforts of an Aragonese mother to prevent her son's return to military service. Her pregnant prospective daughter-in-law joins her, realizing that bearing an illegitimate child will ruin her. The son is therefore caught between saving his or his bride's honor--but he makes his choice when at last he hears the "voz de la patria." The play ends with the whole company singing a rousing patriotic hymn. From the conclusion it is obvious that the play was written to whip up public sentiment in favor of the war in Melilla. It debuted at the Teatro Español on December 20, 1893.

NJM

AGREDA, María de Jesús de (1602-1665).
    Born as María Coronel to a wealthy and religious family, she became a nun when she was 17 years old and soon was chosen to head her convent. She was famous for her piety and writings, and had as correspondent Philip IV, who consulted with her during 22 years about government affairs. She was investigated by the Inquisition and was absolved of all accusations, even if the Sorbonne condemned some of her affirmations as heretical. Her book on the life of the Virgin Mary had great influence in other writers, such as Osuna.

Altíssimos documentos y exercicios, para la buena muerte. Valencia: Pablo Fernández y Lorenzo Messier, 1686, 249 pp.

Cartas de la Venerable Madre Sor María de Agreda y del Señor Rey Don Felipe IV. Edited by Carlos Seco Serrano, Biblioteca de Autores Españoles, vols. 108-109. Madrid: Atlas, 1958, 2 vols.: 477 and 459 pp.
    The Seco edition contains 614 letters dated from October 4, 1643 to March 27, 1665; an introduction by Seco, "Política y mística: el perfil histórico de Sor María de Agreda;" and adds as an appendix several other works by María de Agreda. None of them can be considered "creative," but they reveal great imagination and a subtle rhetoric.

Cartas de Sor Maria de Agreda, y del señor Rey D. Felipe IV. Edited by D. Francisco Silvela. Madrid: Sucesores de Rivadeneyra, 1885-1886, 2 vols.: I, 462 pp.; II, 794 pp.

Ejercicio cotidiano y doctrina para hacer las obras con la mayor perfección. Barcelona: Librería y Tipografía Católica, s/a but after 1900.

Ejercicios espirituales de retiro. Palma de Mallorca: José Guasp, 1676. There are several later editions, the latest in Vich: Viuda de Juan Dorca, circa 1800, 220 pp.

Escala para subir a la perfección. Barcelona: Herederos de Juan Gili, 1915, 128 pp.

Leyes de la Esposa, entre los hijos de Sion. Barcelona: Herederos de Juan Gili, 1916, 99 pp. Several editions, most recent in Madrid, Sucesores de Hernando, 1934.

Leyes segundas de la Esposa, conceptos y suspiros del corazó.
Barcelona: Herederos de Juan Gili, s/a but after 1900.

Mystica Ciudad de Dios, milagro de su omnipotencia, y abismo de la
gracia. Historia divina y vida de la Virgen Madre de Dios, Reyna y
Señora nuestra María Santíssima. Madrid: Bernardo de Villa-
Diego, 1670, 3 vols.: I, 436 pp.; II, ?; III, 522 pp. There are
over 30 Spanish editions of the complete text, plus many abridged
versions. The most recent complete text was printed in Barcelona:
Herederos de Juan Gili, 1911-14, in 5 volumes.
     This is mostly the life of Christ as told from the perspective of
the Virgin Mary. The length and the many pious meditations make it
today the reading of believers or specialists, but many details of
the everyday life of the Holy Family as revealed by the writer are
imaginative and controversial. This book was accused of being
heretical. An abridged edition, Vida de la Virgen Maria (Barcelona:
Montaner y Simón, 1899) has a prologue by Emilia Pardo Bazán.
City of God. . . the Divine History and Life of the Virgin Mother of
God Manifested to Mary of Agreda for the Encouragement of Men.
Translated from the Original Spanish by Fiscar Marison (pseud. for
the Rev. George J. Blatter). So. Chicago, Ill.: The Theopolitan,
1914, 4 volumes. There are many reprints and later editions of this
book.

Observaciones y modo que han de guardar en los exercicios de Retiro y
otras devociones, los Religiosos de Agreda. Zaragoza, 1676.
                                                              RDP

AGUIRRE, Francisca (1930-).
     Aguirre began her career within the group of poets which cultivated
denunciatory themes during the 1950's and 1960's, but from the start her
production shows an intimate thrust. It reflects a desolate world
tempered by a stubborn longing for solidarity, and by a shadow of
tenderness. Her poetic space, a reflection of her own life, shows the
scars of the unforgotten suffering caused by the Civil War during her
childhood and adolescence. Mostly self educated, she has a vast
knowledge of poetic tradition which she transforms into a unique style.
She attributes this eclecticism to the influence of Luis Rosales.

     Itaca. Colección Poética Leopoldo Panero. Madrid: Cultura
Hispánica, 1972. This book is out of print.
     The book is divided into two related sections. The first,
"Itaca," consists of a series of poems centered around the Ulysses
myth as seen from Penelope's perspective; they are reflections on
marriage, fidelity, and betrayal. Constant in the poems are desolation and solitude along with the weight of a past relationship as a
ray of hope, uncertain but persistent. The sea is interlocutor and
background simultaneously hostile and receptive. The second part "El
desván de Penélope," consists of productions from early years where
autobiographical echoes are clear; they insist on aspects of death,
solitude, and the futility of memory.

<u>La otra música</u>. Madrid: Cultura Hispánica del Centro
Iberoamericano de Cooperación, 1977, ISBN 84-7232-160-6, 58 pp.
     If music expresses sentiments without analytic or rational con-
siderations, poetry as created by Aguirre offers the possibility of
expressing a sentiment, but it also often reflects upon itself in
this her latest book which shows an enlargement of the poetic world
of its author. Like music this poetry is a torrent of feelings, and
its words examine a divided universe: bitterness as a lucid
realization of the darker side of mankind, and a desperate craving
for companionship and love. Aguirre's enlarged perspective continues
to be full of <u>chiaroscuro</u>.

<u>Los trescientos escalones</u>. San Sebastián: Caja de Ahorros
Provincial de Guipuzcoa, 1977, ISBN 84-7231-376-x.
     This book also has an autobiographical projection. Aguirre
examines her roots as a mature woman, roots that spring from a
painful childhood which appears as a shadow in the poems, sometimes
openly, at others in the background. She looks at her universe, her
relationship to others, to history and gives a transcendental account
where both confrontation and solidarity are present. When alone, the
poet struggles for clarity and faith in a space of darkness and
silence. Echoes of Vallejo and Machado are perceptible. Aguirre's
poetic energy is vital but has a dark streak to it.

M-EB

ALACSEAL, Virgili. See ALBERT, Caterina.

ALBERCA LORENTE, Luisa (1920-).
     Luisa Alberca was born in Alcázar de San Juan (Ciudad Real). She
studied in the Escuela de Comercio de Alicante. She currently holds the
position of Funcionario del Cuerpo General Administrativo del Ejército
del Aire (Official of the General Administrative Corps of the Air
Force). She is the author of numerous novels, radio scripts, children's
stories and several theatrical pieces. Though much of her work was
originally written as radio script, it has been converted into novel
form. She has been a script writer for Radio Madrid since 1950 and has
formed part of the Red de Emisoras del Movimiento (Network of Broad-
casters of the Movement) since 1957. She has received on various
occasions the Premio Nadal for novels and the Concha Espina prize for
her short stories. Much of her work has been translated into
Portuguese.

<u>Al regresar de las sombras</u>. Madrid: Cid, 1963, 192 pp.

<u>Amor en Paris</u> (with Guillermo Sautier Casaseca). Barcelona:
Pentágono, S.A., 1959, ISBN A60-2363, 350 pp.
     This <u>novela rosa</u> is the story of a selfish woman, Julia, who seems
unable to resolve her own problems. While her husband slowly loses
his mind she begins a tourist trip to Paris. The trip by bus lasts
several days and various characters are intimately introduced. The
opposition and interaction of the characters allow for an examination
of the themes of love, relationships, money, sex, etc. The main
character finally reaches her goal. Here she had planned on
borrowing some money from her in-laws to help her family. She
realizes her incapacity and her ability to overcome them brings the
novel to its happy ending. This work by Alberca and Casaseca is a

particularly interesting study of Spanish customs and values, especially in reference to women, women working, supporting their families and female relations with other males besides their husbands. It examines these problems in a contemporary light and despite its shortcomings it does so successfully. The book is available in hardback through interlibrary loan.

El camino solitario. Madrid: Cid, 1966, Vol. 1, 144 pp.; Vol. 2, 144 pp.

Campo de sangre. Madrid: Cid, 1967, 280 pp.

Cera fundida. Barcelona: Bruguera, S.A., 1962, 122 pp.

La Dama de Verde (with Casaseca). Madrid: Cid, 1958, 298 pp.

!Detrás esta la vida! Madrid: R.E.M., 1958, 217 pp.
     A novel written by Luisa Alberca based on the dramatic comedy of the same title written by Fernanco Martínez Beltrán which narrates the story of a young woman's fight to overcome the loose and carefree lifestyles of her parents. Again the themes of relationships between parents and children are of primary interest here. In addition, the themes of moral ethics and religion are dealt with. This is one in a series of paperbacks I received from the author.

Dina. Madrid: Cid, 1965, 284 pp.

En nombre del hijo (with Casaseca). 2nd ed. Madrid: Cid, 1957, 255 pp.
     The themes of love relationships between husband and wife and children and parents is thoroughly examined in this work of the novela rosa genre. There are two opposite perspectives. The authors examine the constant fighting, role playing and selfish love between a daughter and her parents. This view is opposed to a strong family whose parents love and respect each other even in the face of certain unforseeable events. The setting spans a 20- to 30-year-period and is contemporary, though of little socio-historical importance. It is a thorough portrayal of current Spanish values and mores and perhaps from this angle would warrant some interest. The book is in hardback form and is not easily available through interlibrary loan.

Extraño poder. Madrid: Cid, 1969, 205 pp.

Fijaos en los lirios. Madrid: Cid, 1963, 282 pp.

Historia de una mujer; Rosa Maria (with Casaseca). Madrid: Cid, 1964, 265 pp.
     During a world war in an imaginary country a young girl, Rosa María, encounters hate, death and treason. She escapes with members of her family to the border only to have to face betrayal again and again. Though the setting and events of this novela rosa are not realistic they are contemporary. Alberca and Casaseca treat the themes of war, oppression, love, hate, relationships and even indirectly communism. The book ends on an optimistic note with the beginnings of a new relationship between the heroine and a young man,

Sergio Mercié, who will become the hero of the sequel of this work, Historia de un hombre; Rosa Maria. The book is available in hardback through interlibrary loan.

Historia de un hombre; Rosa María (with Casaseca). Madrid: Cid, 1964, 270 pp.
    In this sequel to Historia de una mujer; Rosa María, Alberca and Casseca examine the effects of war on a devastated nation as well as its people. At the beginning of the novela rosa Sergio Mercié, introduced in the former work, has lost Rosa María to the enemy forces. He returns to his country, with a foreigner presumably an American, to begin to reconstruct his nation and the people. The themes of love, death, alcoholism and defeat, and relationships are examined in various perspectives through the juxtapositions of each of the characters with different people in their lives. Eventually after much sorrow and reevaluation Sergio and Rosa María are reunited. This novel offers a particularly interesting study of Spanish "traditional" views as opposed to American "contemporary" views, as viewed through the authors. It is available through interlibrary loan in hardback.

La Isla de Adriana. Madrid: Cid, 1965, Vol. 1, 144 pp.; Vol. 2, 144 pp.
    The characters of this novela rosa have already been introduced in a previous Alberca novel, Dina. In this story a young girl of dubious origins is raised by Dina and her second husband. After their death she undergoes a series of harsh experiences before realizing her true origins and ultimately all ends well, including her marriage to a "prince charming." All of the typical novela rosa themes are dealt with in each of the two volumes, the second volume being more of the same problems already encountered in volume one. These volumes are from the series of paperbacks received from the author.

Lo que no muere. Madrid: Imprenta Sáez, 1953, ISBN 54-28734, 474 pp. The book includes a collection of 10 pulp-novelas (folletines) each of which ranges from 45 to 48 pages. Each novela is introduced by a cover photography and biography-interview of the performers or the authors. This work has also been made into a film.
    This book, of the novela rosa type, originally appeared as a radio-novela. Two brothers have been separated and raised under a different set of values. One brother represents a traditional and patriotic viewpoint while the other practices the virtues of communism. Their recurring conflicts and reunions highlight the themes of love, relationships, family and ideals. Though the actions are contemporary to the time period in which it was written the obvious slant of the authors eliminates any import of social-historical value. This book seems to be of limited significance, though its appeal to the Spanish public might allow a more thorough understanding of the Spanish mind. It is available in hardback, as a collection of bound pulp-novelas, through interlibrary loan.

Lo que nunca somos. Barcelona: Luis de Caralt, Editor, 1952, ISBN A52-6632, 278 pp.
    This book by Alberca and Casaseca genre is an interesting study of the themes of love, relationships, destiny in that the majority of the action occurs in the United States though the characters are

typically Spanish. Alberto Lopez, a sentimental Spanish, becomes
embittered after having made unusual sacrifices only to lose his love
to another. His experiences lead him to New York where he becomes
heavily involved in the drug trade. Though he does not partake of
his trade it becomes obvious that he cares for no one or nothing,
though the reader begins to realize that a very strong sense of
Spanish morals keep him from sinking completely into despair.
Eventually he is able to escape his ambience and after a series of
coincidental happenings he flees with his true love to find their
destiny. Though this book is of very little social historical
importance there is an interesting portrayal of American society. We
meet Mister Grub, the leader of the drug trade and a plastic surgeon,
a very rich prostitute who has been able to make it big, a Spaniard
and his wife who have become Americanized to the point of ridicu-
lousness, a black housekeeper, etc. This book is available through
interlibrary loan in hardback form.

Los mensajeros del diablo. Madrid: R.E.M., 1958, 163 pp.
    This book, unlike Alberca's other works, is a children's story
(cuento infantil original) dedicated to her two daughters. Through a
series of interrelated tales the story narrates the struggle between
the forces of good and evil. Each of the individual narratives is a
story that one man, who must repay his debts to the Fairy of Youth,
experiences or hears on his quest to overcome evil. In each instance
one of the seven capital sins is treated as the topic of the tale.
There is a mixture of humor, wisdom and doom beautifully illustrated
in pen and ink drawings in each of the seven parts of the book. Los
mensajeros del diablo is well written, entertaining and delightful.
It is in hardback and is one of the many works received from Alberca.

La otra justicia. Madrid: Imprenta Frama, 1960, ISBN 65-54764,
177 pp.
    Once again the themes of love relationships, and values are
treated. This is the story of two sisters, Susana and Regina. The
latter is found dead after a series of strange incidents and the
former believes she was led to her death. After some detective work
she discovers her sister led a secret life and Susana becomes heavily
involved with the family to whom her sister was attached. She
marries one of the sons only to discover that he was responsible for
her sister's death. Her reactions, as well as those of her family
and the implicated family allows a glimpse into Spanish values
concerning love, marriage and God. This novela is of no social
historical significance though it might prove an interesting study of
Spanish contemporary society. It is available through interlibrary
loan in hardback.

Pacto peligroso. Madrid: Cid, 1964, 159 pp.

Palabras en la tierra. Madrid: R.E.M., 1958, 204 pp.
    The themes of love and relationships are examined from all angles
in this novela rosa. Palabras en la tierra is the story of one
family's struggle for survival. The father of the family, a very
brutal and miserly man, is constantly abusing his wife and children.
How each one deals with the father is an interesting examination of
the facets of love. Extra-familial relationships are included in

this examination, making this novel a fascinating study of human relations. This is one in a series of paperbacks received from the author.

Patricia Rilton. Madrid: Imprenta Sáez, 1950, 285 pp.
     In another novel characteristic of the novela rosa genre Alberca writes of one woman's struggle to reconcile her desires of womanhood with those of motherhood. Throughout the novel one sees how her relationship with her children is affected by her love for a man, whom she ultimately marries. The basic themes of love, relationships and a woman's role in society are reflected in this work. This is one in a series of paperbacks received from the author.

Pleito de amor. Madrid: R.E.M., 1958, 144 pp.
     This is another study of the relations between husband and wife, mother and children, parents and children, brothers, etc. It is the story of two brothers of opposite personalities who seek the one woman they love and the ensuing conflicts. This is one in a series of paperbacks received from the author.

La segunda esposa with Casaseca. Sixth ed. Madrid: Cid, 1956, 303 pp.
     Alberca and Casaseca once again treat the themes of love, hate, relationships and sex in this novel of murder. The death of the first wife and other three children affects each in a different way and the manner in which they deal with their lives and new stepmother is examined. As the setting is contemporary one might be able to study Spanish customs in regard to family, women, and the law though the work is of little socio-historical value. Perhaps studied as a collective work Alberca's novels could provide some insight into the Spanish popular culture. The book is available in hardback through interlibrary loan.

La última dicha (novela corta). Madrid: Cid, La novela de sábado, 1954, 64 pp.
     This abbreviated form of the novela rosa, novela corta, appeared as one in a series of publications by Ediciones Cid called "la novela del sábado". It is the story of a family, father, mother and daughter, separated from each other by the mother's ambition. After many years and much success the mother returns to her hometown where she meets her husband again. On the verge of death she retells her life and begs his forgiveness so that she might die in peace. Once again, the basic themes of love, death, power and relationships characteristic to the novela rosa genre are discussed. Annotator has a mimeographed copy received from the author.

Sombras de muerte. Madrid: Cid, 1966, 288 pp.

EF-D

*ALBERT I PARADIS, Caterina (1873-1966), Pseud. Victor Català.
She was born in a well-to-do family of Northeastern Catalonia and
enjoyed economic independence for a lifetime. Confined for a year by
the mourning of her father when she was 19, Caterina Albert developed
her artistic talents, first painting, then writing. She never married,
traveled a little, but mostly spent her time between her native village
and Barcelona. She produced two novels and six collections of short
stories about the harsh life of men and women in rural Catalonia. Her
depictions deliberately avoid easy sentimentality; her stern themes and
style may have prompted the early pen name she kept throughout her
career.

                                                                    JMS

Caires vius. Barcelona: 1907, pages 595-727 of the Obres completes.
    Victor Català's third collection of short narratives preceded by
a long foreword, "Pòrtic," by the author which is her meditation on
the role of literature in the modern Catalan cultural revival. The
stories in this collection break away from the pattern established by
her Drames rurals; some of the stories have now explicit mythological
and legendary subject matter.

                                                                    JMS

El cant dels mesos. Barcelona: 1901; later republished with a
foreword by the author from 1948, pages 1423-1437 of the Obres
completes.
    A collection of 12 poems, one on each month of the year. These
are short, metrically regular pieces of a laudatory, optimistic
character.

                                                                    JMS

Drames rurals. Barcelona: 1902, pages 431-556 of the Obres
completes.
    It is a collection of 12 short stories between 5 and 20 pages in
length. The themes of these powerful stories are rural and desolate.
The many characters are plagued by poverty, violence and alcoholism.
In a disingenuous foreword ("Prec") the author, under her male
identity warns "sensitive urban damsels" to stay away from "his" book
and wait for something mellower. The black realism of the narrative
established Victor Català's early reputation and set her on a style
and theme she would keep throughout her career.

                                                                    JMS

Drames Rurals. Caires Vius. Barcelona: Edicions 62, 1982,
ISBN 84-297-1880-X, 345 pp. Prologue by Carme Arnau.

                                                                     KM

Un film. Barcelona: 1920 with the subtitle 3,000 metres, dated
1918-1920, pages 169-427 of her Obres completes. It appeared
originally as a series of contributions to the journal Catalana under
the title of ***(3,000 metres), un film. It is the second and last
novel by Victor Català.
    This novel was a critical flop. It portrays the reality not of
rural Catalonia, as most of her narrative work, but of Barcelona
life. The analogy with the film medium (the novel was inspired by
the serial films of the time) is seen as a justification for
narrative objectivity. It is a climax-less naturalistic picaresque

novel where a large number of characters are called forth around the
figure of Nonat, an ambitious orphan who ends up as a criminal.

JMS

La infanticida i altres textos. Barcelona: LaSal, 1984.
Col.lecció Clàssiques Catalanes, ISBN 84-85627-24-5, 156 pp.
    This recent re-issue was edited and introduced by Helena Alvarado
i Esteve, who also supplied notes and a bibliography. The collection
contains, in addition to the title piece, "Les cartes," "Ombres,"
"Carnestoltes," "La pua de rampí," and "Pas de comèdia."

KM

Llibre blanc. Barcelona: 1951, in the first edition of the Obres
completes, pages 1439-1503 of the second edition.
    It gathers the remainder of the poetic output of Víctor Català.
The collection of short, metrically regular lyrical pieces with the
subtitle "Policromi-tríptic" has as an appendix a few "Poesies
disperses."

JMS

Mosaic. Barcelona: 1946, with the subtitle "Impressions literàries
sobre temes domèstics," pages 1306-1420 of the Obres completes.
    It gathers several intimate, lyrical essays on everyday topics:
her home, her room, garden, town ... and even the weather and
relatives. The collection is divided in three parts: "Facècies i
coses," "Amics i parents," and "Girades."

Obres completes, Biblioteca perenne vol. 28. Barcelona: Selecta,
1951; 2nd ed., 1972, 1872 pp. Illustrations. Unless otherwise
indicated, all entries refer to the second edition.
    This collection contains, besides the previously published work by
"Víctor Català," a preface: "L'obra de Víctor Català" by Manuel
de Montoliu (pp. ix-ixiii), and an epilog: "Els silencis de Caterina
Albert" by Maria Aurèlia Capmany (pp. 1851-1868). It also contains
her two academic speeches, her 11 journalistic articles, five
prefaces to other writers, and a sampling of her correspondence with
several well-known figures of the Catalan literary scene.

JMS

Ombrivoles. Barcelona: 1904, pages 557-594 of the Obres completes.
    A collection of four short stories. It continues the style and
themes of Drames rurals. Normally reprinted with the original short
preface and with a foreword "Les ulleres," by Victor Català added in
April 1948.

JMS

Quatre monòlegs. Barcelona: 1901, pages 1505-1563 of the Obres
completes.
    It gathers the early production of Víctor Català which was
intended for the stage in the Renaixença style of Angel Guimerà.
These four monologs are all in verse. In "La tieta" a woman
reminisces about her life; in "Pere Màrtir" a servant, Pere Màrtir,
talks to two silent characters; in "La Vepa" the actress represents a
working-class woman; finally "Germana Pau" is a nun in a sanatorium
speaking with a fellow nun at the door of her cell.

JMS

The second edition of the Obres completes also published four
short plays two of which were written before the turn of the century;
these were first published as Teatre inèdit in Barcelona (1967).
Three are monologs: one in verse ("La infanticida") and two in prose
("Les cartes," "Verbagàlia"), the last one is a one-act prose play,
"L'alcavota" with seven characters.

JMS

Solitud. Barcelona: 1905. Most of this novel first appeared in
successive issues of the periodical Joventut in 1904. It is now
normally reprinted, as in the Obres completes, with the author's
preface to the fifth reprinting (1945), pages 3-168 of the Obres
completes.
        It is considered Victor Català's best work and is the most widely
read, reprinted, and commented upon of her works. The novel tells
the story of Mila, a young woman married to a ne'er-do-well who takes
her to his job as keeper of a remote mountain hermitage. There she
leads a hard life watching her husband disintegrate under the
influence of a demonic character called Anima. When an eruption of
violence rocks the hermitage, Mila faces her loneliness and
liberation. Solitud is a powerful narrative fraught with symbolic
vision and characters but the novel never strays from the path of
realistic verisimilitude.

JMS

Solitud. Barcelona: Selecta, 1983, ISBN 84-298-0108-1, 305 pp.,
prologue by Manuel Montoliu.

KM

Other collections of short stories are:
La mare-balena, 1920, seven stories, pages 729-780 of her Obres
completes; Marines, 1928, two chapters of an incomplete novel, pages
781-811; Contrallums, 1930, 11 stories, pages 813-963; Vida mòlta,
1950, 13 stories, pages 965-1090; and Jubileu, 1951, 11 stories,
pages 1091-1285.
        Perhaps with the exception of Jubileu, marked by a milder
subject-matter, all these collections are variations on the themes of
Drames rurals. The author's fatalistic beliefs dominate over her
comic vein which appears now and then and even predominates in a few
of her stories. The Obres completes also include five "Narracions
disperses" never gathered in a volume before 1951; pages 1287-1306.

JMS

*ALBO, Núria (1930-).
        Born in la Garriga, where she eventually became mayor, she taught for
many years. As a writer, she started out as a poet and more recently
has prolifically written prose.

Agapi Mou. Barcelona: Pòrtic, 1980.

Desencís. Barcelona: La Magrana, 1980.
        A novel that looks for reality in the Catalonia between two recent
sets of elections - the municipal and the Parliament. She explores
the existences of several people who are tender, intelligent, sometimes lucid, but also conformist and passive - contradictory. This
novel won the Premi Vila d'Arenys.

Diptic with Maria Angels Anglada. 1972.

L'encenedor verd. Barcelona: Vosgos, 1980.
    Poetry.

Fes-te repicar. Barcelona: Destino, 1970.

La mà pel front. 1962.
    Poetry.

Tranquil, Jordi, tranquil. Barcelona: Pòrtic, 1984.

KM

ALBORNOZ, Aurora de (1926-).
    Aurora de Albornoz was born in Luarca, Asturias, and has been living
in Puerto Rico since 1944. She received a degree in humanities at the
University of Puerto Rico, and afterwards took some courses in Comparative Literature at the Sorbonne in Paris. Currently she is a professor
of Spanish language and literature at the University of Puerto Rico.
She has written several collections of poetry including Brazo de niebla
1955, an amplified collection published in Spain in 1957, also called
Brazo de niebla, Prosas de Paris 1959, Poemas para alcanzar un segundo
1961, and Por la primavera blanca (fabulaciones) in 1962. In addition,
she has also written Poesías de guerra de Antonio Machado 1961 and La
prehistoria de Antonio Machado 1961.

    Brazo de niebla. San Juan de Puerto Rico: Coayuco, 1955.
        In this collection of nine poems the author discusses the conflict
    created by her solitary condition as one human being and her desire
    to express herself as a poet. Poems I-V emphasize her aloneness and
    her inability to let her expressions escape through the repeated use
    of images of color, fog, nothingness, and suppressed shouts. In Poem
    VI she is no longer able to contain her shouts or feelings. The
    image of a sheet of paper floating from one corner of her head to
    another in Poem VII allows the shout to escape in Poem VIII. The
    last poem is dedicated to Antonio Machado. Brazo de niebla appears
    to be the author's first collection of poetry. Besides expressing
    her uncertainty as a poetess, these poems hint of things to come in
    Albornoz's future poetry. It is available through interlibrary loan.

    En busca de esos niños en hilera. Santander: La Isla de los
    Ratones, 1967, 65 pp.
        This book contains a collection of 25 poems, a prologue, and an
    epilogue which revolve around the theme of childhood memories.
    Whether the memories are bad, suppressed or just vignettes of an
    uncomfortable past time, each poem includes a longing to recapture
    the fleeting moments of youth. In the prologue a dedication is made
    to "all who once suffered the pain of lost time." The first seven
    poems discuss youth's unawareness of the passage of time from an
    adult's perspective. The poems that follow are descriptions of
    traumas, fears and possible instances of adult cruelty toward
    children, as well as a lack of understanding between an adult's
    perception of events and a child's. Poem 25 discusses the death of

childhood. The author writes in free verse style with recurring
images throughout the poems. This text is available in hardback
through interlibrary loan.

Poemas para alcanzar un segundo. Madrid: Rialp, S.A., 1961, 87+ pp.
     The poems in this book are divided into a prologue and six
sections, each dealing with a different time in the author's life.
The prologue is a possible justification for what will follow. The
author has already reached her 30th birthday and wonders who she is
or where she is going. "En el fondo del tiempo," the title of the
first section of four different poems, discusses significant childhood memories having to do with the Civil War in Spain. Section II,
"Metal y sombra," are poems referring to the author's time spent in
Paris and her experiences, emphasizing the passage of life to death.
In Section III, "Aquí. Ahora," poems discussing feelings of whom am
I, inadequacy as a poet, and the conflict between feelings, memories
and their expression are included. "Apuntes literarios," Section IV,
are poems dedicated to four women, a sister Sonia, Emma Bovary, Ana
Karenina and Ophelia, important to the author. "Entonces" is divided
into three poems analyzing the existence of God. Section VI, "Poemas
para alcanzar un segundo," include poems in which the author justi-
fies her poetry. She closes this collection of poetry saying "Pero
acaso hay segundos que justifican una vida." This book is available
through interlibrary loan.

Por la primavera blanca (fabulaciones). Madrid: Insula, 1962,
51 pp.
     This book is a collection of ten sketches or vignettes,
"fabulaciones" as the author calls them. Each "fabulación" discusses a feeling brought about by the remembrance of a person or
event or the contemplation of an object. Each sketch is similar to
Albornoz's poetry, though written in prose form. This book is
available through interlibrary loan.

                                                              EF-D

ALFARO, María (1900-).
     A native of Gijón, she began in 1934 to publish articles of literary
criticism for Madrid's El Sol. She has traveled to France, the United
States, and Latin America. In Paris she directed a literary segment for
Radio Mundial and later was a correspondent in Spain for Les Nouvelles
Litteraires. Besides being an accomplished poet and novelist, she has
published numerous critical essays in various journals. She has also
translated several of Corneille's plays and two Mark Twain novels into
Spanish.

Poemas del recuerdo. Madrid: Imprenta de I. Mendez, 1951, 22 pp.

Poemas líricos: selección, versión, y prólogo. Madrid:
Hispánica, 1945.

Memorias de una muerte. Spain: n.p., n.d.

Teatro mundial. 2nd ed. Madrid: Aguilar, 1961, 1272 pp.
                                                              RK

ALONSO, María Rosa.

A native of Tenerife (Spain), María Rosa Alonso has devoted her attention to the art, history and literature of that island. More than a novelist, she is an essayist, philologist and scholar. From 1942-54 she held the post of professor of literature at the University of La Laguna (Tenerife) and after her self-exile, for political reasons, she taught Spanish philology at the University of Los Andes (Mérida, Venezuela). Since her return to Spain in 1968 she has been contributing articles and essays to important Spanish newspapers. In addition to the works below, she has published works on Spanish linguistics.

Colón en Canarias y el rigor histórico. Las Palmas de Gran Canaria: El Museo Canario, 1960, 12 pp.

Comedia de Nuestra Señora de la Candelaria. Edición, Prólogo y Notas de María Rosa Alonso. Madrid: Consejo Superior de Investigaciones Científicas, 1943, 165 pp. 2nd ed., Madrid: Consejo Superior de Investigaciones Científicas, 1979, 165 pp.

Con la voz del silencio. Las Palmas: Colección bibliófilos, 1945, 15 pp.

En Tenerife, una poetisa. Victorina Bridoux y Mazzini (1835-1862). Santa Cruz de Tenerife: Librería Hespérides, 1940, 117 pp.

Manuel Verdugo y su obra poética. La Laguna de Tenerife: Instituto de Estdios Canarios, 1955, 174 pp.

Otra vez .... Santa Cruz de Tenerife: Goya-Ediciones, 1951, 152 pp.
    Otra vez, María Rosa Alonso's only novel, was written during the author's university days and reflects that ambience well. Alonso uses the literary device of claiming that the novel consists of memoirs left to her by a young man who met an early death. The title, "Otra vez," refers to the fact that in his romance, the protagonist repeats the same pattern (and with a girl from the same family) as an older friend of his. The novel may be classified as a "Bildungsroman" since it initiates the protagonist into love and suffering. (No accompanying material; out of print; copy available only from the author.)

Papeles tinerfeños. Santa Cruz de Tenerife: Nuestro Arte 197, 298 pp.

El poema de Viana. Estudio histórico-literario de un poema épico del siglo XVII. Madrid: Consejo Superior de Investigaciones Científicas, 1952, 697 pp.

Pulso del tiempo. La Laguna de Tenerife: Universidad La Laguna, 1955, 284 pp.
    Essays.

Residente en Venezuela. Mérida: Universidad de los Andes, 1960, 291 pp.

San Borondón, signo de Tenerife. Ensayos. Santa Cruz de Tenerife, 1940, 96 pp.

ALONSO I MANANT, Cecilia (1905-1974), Pseud. **Cecília A. Màntua.**
Born in Barcelona, she dedicated herself to the theater. The
Institut de teatre has most of her work.

La cançó de la florista, 1959.

La cinglera de la mort, 1955.

Història d'un mirall, 1966.

Maria Cural, 1961.

Pepa Maca, 1959.

Princesa de Barcelona, 1959.

KM

ALOS, Concha (1922-).
Born in Valencia and of working-class background, Concha Alós first
became a schoolteacher, then began contributing pieces to various
newspapers and journals. In 1957 her short story, "El cerro del
telégrafo" was awarded a prize by the Mallorcan magazine Lealtad. In
1959 she came to Barcelona, where she resides today. Her early novels
are good examples of Spanish social realism, rooted in the miseries and
deprivations of the lower classes and of women in particular. Os habla
Electra (1975), however, signals a radical departure from conventional
linear narration and character construction. Both character and plot
are, instead, "deconstructed." Argeo ha muerto, supongo, though much
less experimental in technique, continues with the same emphasis on
fragmentation of personality and the insertion of a dream world into
ordinary reality.

Argeo ha muerto, supongo. Barcelona: Plaza y Janés, 1982,
ISBN 84-01-30357-5, 244 pp. Also: Barcelona: Ediciones G.P., 1983,
ISBN 84-01-43664-8, 239 pp.
The author writes that this novel was born out of the desire to
explore "esa barrera que existe entre el mundo secreto de los adultos
y el mundo secreto de la niñez." A first-person linear narration,
Argeo ha muerto, supongo delves into the themes of childhood as a
lost paradise, identity confusion and fragmentation of personality,
the loss of illusion and first love. Haunted by the sense of the
past, the narrator/protagonist Jano finds herself floating somewhere
between reality and the dream world she has constructed out of a
frustrated passion for her foundling brother Argeo. Paper, in print.

El caballo rojo. Barcelona: Planeta, 1966, ISBN 84-320-5005-9,
266 pp. Also: Barcelona: Círculo de Lectores, 1970, ISBN
84-226-0162-1, 190 pp.; Barcelona: Plaza y Janés, 1972, ISBN
84-01-44063-7, 203 pp.; Madrid: Círculo de Amigos de la Historia,
1976, ISBN 84-225-0101-5, 256 pp.
For her fourth novel, Alós drew heavily, she says, on personal
experience suffered in the last year of the Spanish Civil War when
she and her family, who lived in Castellón de la Plana, fled from
the approaching Franquist forces to Lorca. Dedicating her book to
all those young people whose lives the war destroyed, Alós continues
to favor the style of social realism and the technique of alternating

the story line from one character to another. At war's end, El caballo rojo seems to presage better days ahead for the Félix Alegre family, with the last phrase: ". . . y volveremos a empezar." But Félix, remembering Franquist revenge, also thinks: "No quiere pensar en el futuro que teme. No quiere." Hardbound and paper.

Los cien pájaros. Barcelona: Plaza y Janés, 1963, 247 pp. Also: Barcelona: Ed. G.P., 1967; 1972; 1975, Libros Reno, no. 215, ISBN 84-01-43215-4, 282 pp.
    Alós's second novel is another example of social realism, focusing this time on the coming of age of a young girl, whose working-class origins and doubtful parentage foster feelings of insecurity and inferiority. Disabused of her romantic and social pretensions by a short-lived affair with a señorito, Cristina, pregnant and unmarried, will choose independence over security and comfort. Rather than a bird in hand, a hundred in flight: "Un pájaro, cien pájaros. Lo seguro, lo incierto." Hence the title. The theme of liberation from male dominance and faulty social values is handled through a simply written, first-person narrative. Paper.

Los enanos. Barcelona: Plaza y Janés, 1962, 319 pp. Also: Esplugas de Llobregat, Barcelona: Ediciones G.P., 1963, 1965, 1967, 1973, 1974, 1975, 317 pp.
    Winner of the 1962 Planeta Prize, the novel had to be withdrawn from the competition because of a prior publishing agreement. Using a "Ship of Fools" framework by setting the novel in a modest boarding house, Alós presents a variety of characters living on the edge of poverty, or worse, through contrapuntal narrative techniques. None of the characters can be conceived of separately from the others in this gritty and despairing picture of a life spent in unremitting dependence upon a series of impersonal forces greater than individual personalities. If men are dwarfs, Alós writes, then the world is a giant. Paper.

Las hogueras. Barcelona: Planeta, 1964, 277 pp. Also: 30th ed., 1982, ISBN 84-320-0013-2.
    Winner of the 1964 Planeta Prize, Las hogueras explores the absence of love and the unequal relationships between men and women through three plot lines: a disintegrating marriage between a self-absorbed ex-model Sibila and a self-made but reflective businessman; a passionate if ultimately meaningless love affair between Sibila and a rather brutal day laborer; and the frustrating spinster life of the school teacher Asunción. Alós' characters seem to suffocate in the dense smoke of their boredom, loneliness, and incommunication. With probable literary echoes of Moravia and Carson McCullers. Hardbound and paper.

La madama. Barcelona: Plaza y Janés, 1969, 279 pp. 2nd ed., 1970, ISBN 84-01-30058-4. Also: Barcelona: Ediciones G.P., 1973, 1974, ISBN 84-01-43452-1, 248 pp.
    Set in Spain's immediate post Civil War years, Alós' harsh novel alternates between the bitter, first-person account of prison life by a former Republican soldier Clemente, and the third-person, hence distanced, narration of the daily struggle for survival and ultimate prostitution of Clemente's family. Thus Alós juxtaposes two different worlds, an inside (the prison) and an outside (the town),

suggesting, however, that the outside world too is little better than a prison. Hardbound and paper.

Os habla Electra. Esplugas de Llobregat (Barcelona): Plaza y Janés, 1975, ISBN 84-01-30152-1, 219 pp. Also: 2nd ed., 1978, ISBN 84-01-44220-6, 187 pp.
   Os habla Electra represents a significant change in style, technique and theme for Alós. Concentrating on the thematic dichotomy between fertility and the threat of universal destruction, the novelist outlines a story of mythic and archetypal proportions, in particular, the struggle between patriarchal and matriarchal modes of being, in which the female--Electra, all Electras--strives to regain a sense of wholeness and personal identity. Weaving deftly between the real and the imaginary, with a series of oneiric images and a fragmented, often deliberately confusing narrative structure, Alós has moved far beyond the limits of social realism found in her earlier novels. Hardbound and paper.

Rey de gatos (Narraciones antropófagas). Barcelona: Barral Editores, 1972, ISBN 84-211-0256-7, 139 pp. Also: Barcelona: Plaza y Janés, 1979, ISBN 84-01-44223-0, 159 pp.
   This is a collection of nine short stories: "La otra bestia," "Rey de gatos," "Cosmo," "El leproso," "Los pavos reales," "Mariposas," "'Sutter's Gold'," "Paraíso," and "La coraza." Many are narrated in first person, thus facilitating an acute psychological analysis of characters torn by anguish, uncertainty, and an obscure sense of fear. Such themes as the war between the sexes, jealousy, alienation, and crises of identity are emblematic of a cannibalistic universe in which the loss of the human is paramount. Surreal and hallucinatory touches in Rey de gatos seem to anticipate Os habla Electra. Paper.

NMV

ALVAREZ DE TOLEDO, (Luisa) Isabel. Duchess of Medina Sidonia. (1930-).
   Alvarez de Toledo's work focuses on social and humanitarian issues, notably the plight of the economic underclass in rural and urban settings, while her portrayal of the affluent classes is highly critical. Each of her novels is an exposé of a deficiency of one sector of Spanish society. Her activism led her to defend the villagers of Palomares after a hydrogen bomb accident, for which she was jailed (March-November 1969). Her prison experience was a powerful shaping force on her subsequent writings, particularly in reference to the treatment of working-class women in Spanish society and the need for reform of women's prisons.

La base. Paris: Bernard Grasset, 1971, paperback, 220 pp.
   Set in the fictionalized village of Trujena, La base reflects the experiences of the Infantes family resulting from the establishment of a joint U.S.-Spanish base fully armed with modern weaponry in their midst. The focus is on the conflicting cultural and economic values, such as the change in moral standards (particularly for women); the decline in self-image when the small farmers are stripped of their land, then forced to work on it as day laborers at the base; the conversion of local residents into an underclass, with the collusion of Spanish authorities; the materialistic ambitions and corruption produced by the contact with American affluence, etc. The

novel concludes with a nuclear accident that destroys the region and the flight of the Minister abroad to safety. Of interest to specialists in twentieth-century literature, especially social realism.

La cacería. Barcelona-Buenos Aires-México: Grijalbo, 1977, ISBN 84-253-0917-4 paperback and 84-253-0938-7 hardback, 247 pp.
La cacería utilizes the frame of the upcoming annual hunt enjoyed by the Madrid elite in a southern Spanish village to show the moral decay of both the traditional aristocratic class and the nouveau riche. Using diverse narrative threads that explore the interrelationship of the various social strata and the manipulation and exploitation of the lower classes, she demonstrates the social injustice of the later years of the Franco regime. Of interest to scholars in literature, particularly in the area of social literature, and to social scientists for its analysis of contemporary problems and society.

La huelga. Colección Ebro; Serie Novela nueva. Paris: Librairie du Globe, 1967, 287 pp. 2nd edition: Colección Ebro; Serie Novela nuva, Bucarest, 1970, 284 pp. 3rd edition: Colección Fuera de serie, Buenos Aires: Schapire Editor, 1974, 284 pp. 4th edition: Colección Fuera de Serie, Buenos Aires: Schapire Editor, 1975, 284 pp.
The Strike. A Novel of Contemporary Spain. Trans. by William Rose. New York: Grove Press, 1971, 312 pp.
La huelga (1967) is a thesis novel that conclusively demonstrates that Andalusian workers are treated arbitrarily, unjustly and even brutally by the power structure (landowners and police, with the collusion of the Church). Neither workers nor landowners are idealized; most of the latter are parvenu rather than true aristocrats, and, as such, are treated less kindly. The view of society is critical, focusing on the social problems broadly characteristic of the Spain of the 1950's (opportunism, corruption, promiscuity, forced emigration of workers to Europe). The work is of interest to scholars of contemporary Spanish literature and to social scientists for its perspective on Spanish society.

My Prison. Trans. by Herma Briffault. New York, Evanston, San Francisco and London: Harper & Row, 1972, ISBN 06-010098-2, 169 pp. With a "Calendar of Events" and "Author's Foreword."
My Prison (1972) is an expanded version of the memoirs published in Sábado gráfico immediately following her release from prison in 1969. She served an eight-month sentence for planning a demonstration on behalf of the village of Palomares at the U.S. Embassy. The memoirs include her autobiographical account as well as extensive observations on the prison system and its administrators, fellow prisoners (political and criminal) and the nature of Spanish society. Of interest to scholars in literature and the social sciences in reference to autobiography, women's studies, Spanish society, criminal justice, and prison reform.

EE

ANDREIS, Ester de.
Andréis is a poet who also has published lives of saints and
translations from the French.

Pastor en Morea. Madrid: Insula, 1961.
    Poems.

San Juan. Barcelona: Destino, 1967.

Santa Clara. Barcelona: Herder, 1959.

                                                                CLG

ANDRES, Elena (1931-).
Andrés poetry could be situated in the mainstream of the surrealistic trend that permeates Spanish verse from the generation of 1927 on.
Although the poetry of Andrés shows, at times, a certain social
concern, her main interest is the transcendental meaning of being.
Thus, her poetry, although rooted in the here and now, has, nonetheless,
a sort of cosmic dimension, a limitless quality that sets this poetry
apart from the rest being produced by other poets at the same time.
Andrés' poetry is one of the most important in her generation for her
depth of vision, her unique expressiveness and her intensity.

El buscador. Madrid: Agora, 1959, ISBN 5046, 82 pp.
    In this book of poems Andrés begins her poetic search for
humanity's significance in a universe that is, both, real and unreal.
It is precisely this mixture of familiarity and strangeness that
pervades the poems of this book and makes it so unique. This
particular quality of Andrés' poetic vision is present throughout
her poetry. This book stands apart from what was being published in
Spanish poetry during the decade of the 1950's. The social concern
that pervades most of the poetry of that epoch is not important in
the case of Andrés' poetry. Of interest to any reader of poetry.
Available in paperback. It contains an index of the poems, a quote
from Thomas Mann and a biographical note about the poet.

Desde aquí mis señales. Salamanca: Collección Alamo, 1971,
190 pp.
    In this book of poems Andrés continues her search for humanity's
ultimate meaning in the universe but, now, with a notorious
difference from previous books of poems. In this work, the poet
describes the immediate and everyday reality as if she were trying to
proclaim the joys and pains of existence and to accept them as a way
to understanding man's significance. This poetry is now immersed in
a certain historical time and place: Spain in the early 1970's. In
this way then, this book is more a poetic biography of humanity
rather than an intellectualization of the human predicament in a
mysterious universe. Of interest to any reader of poetry. Available
in paperback. The book contains an index of the poems, a drawing and
biographical note of the poet.

Dos caminos. Madrid: Rialp (Adonais), 1964, ISBN 3640, 75 pp.
    This book of poems received the second poetry prize Adonais for
1963. For the audacious expression and the richly suggestive surrealist mood, this book is one of the best of this poet. Ms. Andrés
situates her constant search for humanity's meaning on this earth

between an exploration of the ancestral past and the mysterious future. Thus, human beings are perceived between two awesome vorteces: the limitless past and the limitless future. Of interest to any reader of poetry. Available in paperback. The book is dedicated to the composer Ramón Barce, Andrés' husband at the time. The book contains an index of the poems and a biographical note about the poet.

Eterna vela. Madrid: Rialp (Adonais), 1961, ISBN 12.470, 64 pp.
    Through a poignant remembrance of the past and a lucid analysis of the present, Andrés attempts in this book of poems to proclaim the presence and the victory of human beings over the deterioration and nothingness of life. Recreating intense reality, the poet attempts to annul the sense of nothingness that permeates conscious perception. Of interest to any reader of poetry. Available in paperback. It is dedicated to Vicente Aleixandre and contains a biographical note about the poet.

Trance de la vigilia colmada. Barcelona: Ambito Literario, 1980, ISBN 84-7457-087-5, 113 pp.
    This book received the second poetry prize "Ambito Literario." Andrés continues the exploration of humanity's significance in a universe that appears sinister and mysterious, trying to find meaning in the strangeness that lies in the depth of human perception. Thus, many times the poems reveal a nightmarish quality that one cannot quite apprehend. The tone of the entire book is of cosmic irreality and anguishable nothingness as if the poet has plunged herself in a domain beyond the real. Of interest to any reader of poetry. Available in paperback.

AMF

*ANGLADA, Maria Angels (1930-).
    Born in Vic, she has written poetry, novels and short stories.

Les closes. Barcelona: Destino, 1979.
    This novel won the Premi Josep Pla in 1978. It tells the story of Dolors Canals and her society of the late nineteenth century, particularly the difficult period preceding the revolution of 1868. The narrator is her great-granddaughter, and time is not always chronological. There are several points of view, which together create an overview.

Díptic, with Núria Albó, 1972.
    Poetry.

Kyaparíssia. Barcelona: La Magrana, 1980.
    A book of poetry with constant references to the classical world and to the Mediterranean world. We find in her verses a people, a landscape, and a language. Words, language and the atmosphere are a constant motif, and a reason for hope. Her land is her major theme.

No em dic Laura. Barcelona: Destino, 1981.
    Stories.

*ARDERIU I VOLTAS, Clementina (1899-1976).
Born in Barcelona to a traditional Catalan family, this poet studied music and languages. She published her first book of poems in 1919, and the same year married Carles Riba. Best known as Riba's wife, yet an excellent poet in her own right, she shared her literary interests with him without being overly influenced by his poetry. Before the Spanish Civil War she traveled through Europe and finished two more books. Exiled to France in 1939, she crossed the border with Riba and with Antonio Machado. She returned to Catalunya in 1943 and collaborated in the reconstruction of Catalan literary and artistic life. She published four more books before her death in 1976.

L'alta llibertat. Barcelona: Catalana, 1920, 85 pp.; rep. in Poemes, La Mirada, Barcelona: Proa, 1936, pp. 61-131; rep. in Poesies completes, Barcelona: Selecta, 1952, pp. 61-118; rep. in Obra poètica, Barcelona: Edicions 62, 1973, pp. 43-84.
Although the poems are obviously more mature and elaborate than those in her first book, they keep the naive and apparently simple word which was to become a permanent feature of Arderiu's writing. Again a small collection, it deals with facts of everyday life or with her personal past in a concise, direct way. She continues to use mostly short verse, and borrows effectively from the popular tradition. The poems transmit a pervasive sense of joy and hope.

Antologia. Proleg de J. M. Capdevila. Tria de Tomàs Garcés. Els poetes d'ara. Barcelona: Lira, 1923, 60 pp.
First anthology of Arderiu's poems from Cançons i elegies and L'alta llibertat. An introduction by J. M. Capdevila. Very difficult to find.

Antologia. Maurici Serrahima, ed. Lírics catalans, 9. Barcelona: La rosa dels vents, 1938, 84 pp.
Second anthology of Arderiu's poems from Cançons i elegies, L'alta llibertat and Cant i paraules. An introduction by Maurici Serrahima. Out of print, very difficult to find.

Antologia poética. Texto bilingüe. José Corredor Matheos ed. Adonais. Madrid: Rialp, 1961, 119 pp.; 2nd enlarged ed. Barcelona: Plaza y Janés, 1982, ISBN 84-01-80972-X, 197 pp.
The first translations published in book form of some of Arderiu's more representative poetry. A few of her poems that had appeared in anthologies of Catalan poetry were already translated. The translations into Castilian are accurate and retain a considerable amount of Arderiu's unique charm. The second, enlarged edition anthologizes L'esperança encara, naturally not included in 1961. Corredor has prepared a good introduction to the selections. Bilingual edition, and particularly useful for the non-Catalan reader.

Cançons i elegies. Barcelona: La Revista, 1916, 72 pp.; rep. in Poemes, La Mirada, Barcelona: Proa, 1936, pp. 11-58; rep. in Poesies completes, Barcelona: Selecta, 1952, pp. 19-57; rep. in Obra poètica, Barcelona: Edicions 62, 1973, pp. 17-42.
Arderiu's first book, it is a small, somewhat eclectic collection of poems. They deal with religious experience, love, and everyday life. Unequal in aesthetic value, they still have the charm and softness characteristic of Arderiu's later work. There is an

intimacy of tone that Arderiu herself associates with what she considers her "womanliness:" a quality which must be emphasized as distinctive in her work.

Cant i paraules. Barcelona: Lira, 1923, 60 pp. Pròleg de J. M. Capdevila. Biobibliography, p. 7.
    Poems.

Es a dir. Pròleg de Joan Fuster. Els llibres de l'Ossa Menor, 38. Barcelona: Ossa Menor, 1959, 53 pp.; rep. iñ Obra poètica, Barcelona: Edicions 62, 1973, pp. 161-178.
    Es a dir won the "Ossa Menor" Prize in 1958, was published in 1959 and was awarded "La lletra d'or" in 1960. Many poems are descriptions of nature, the sea, towns and places in Catalunya. However, the reader soon perceives that these topics are the pretext or the mask for a deeper search into the poet's own life and memory. There is in this book a new sense of time gone and going by. No longer a young woman, Arderiu turns to a questioning of temporality in direct, urging terms. Includes an introduction by Joan Fuster.

L'esperança encara. Pròleg de Joaquim Molas. Antologia catalana, 55. Barcelona: Edicions 62, 1969, 63 pp.; rep. in Obra poètica, Barcelona: Edicions 62, 1973, pp. 181-208.
    This is the only book published after her husband Carles Riba's death. A fear of finding herself alone was already present in Arderiu's former books. Her husband's death, and the experiences of war and exile, had proved life to be not as kind to her as she had anticipated when young. But she fights against despair. As the title of the book suggests, she finds hope - and she finds it in Christian faith and tradition.

Obra poètica. Pròleg de Joan Teixidor. Cara i creu, 19. Barcelona: Edicions 62, 1973, ISBN 84-297-0943-6, 208 pp.
    The apparently definitive edition of Arderiu's complete works, including a short introduction by Joan Teixidor. The coherence and homogeneity of a poetry written throughout the poet's whole life make themselves felt, just as much as the continuous development of her themes and fundamental insights.

Poemes. La Mirada. Barcelona: Proa, 1936, 211 pp.; rep. in Poesies completes, Barcelona: Selecta, 1952, pp. 121-176; rep. in Obra poètica, Barcelona: Edicions 62, 1973, pp. 85-122.
    Poemes contains Arderiu's first two books (Cançons i elegies and L'alta llibertat) plus the first edition of Cant i paraules. Arderiu is coherent with her former work in expressing specifically feminine experiences like giving birth, love for a son or husband, etc. However, these experiences are in themselves problematized and looked at in wonder and awe, never taken for granted. Arderiu's "womanliness" is the object for poetic investigation and insight, not the result of them. She sees herself more and more as a "house," an enclosed, private space which needs to be shared.

Poesies completes. Pròleg de Salvador Espriu. Barcelona: Selecta 1952, 245 pp.
    This collection of Arderiu's complete work up until 1952 is introduced by the poet Salvador Espriu. The volume includes Cançons i

elegies, L'alta llibertat, Cant i paraules and Sempre i ara. Sempre
i ara has been enlarged with one poem in "Estampes," three in
"Sentiment d'exili," and ten in "Sempre i ara."

Sempre i ara. Litografies d'Olga Sacharoff. Barcelona: Societat
Aliança d'Arts Gràfiques, 1946, 79 pp.; rep. in Poesies completes,
Barcelona: Selecta, 1952, pp. 181-245, rep. in Obra poètica,
Barcelona: Edicions 62, 1973, pp. 123-160.
    Sempre i ara won the "Joaquim Folguera" Prize in 1938, but it
could not be published until 1946, in a semi-clandestine edition.
The poems in it express Arderiu's characteristic everyday world, but
a new experience has been added to it: war. Sadness and melancholy
spread over the verses. Old anguishes and fears show up with a more
vivid face. The poet fights them off by attempting to shut herself
to them. She finds or wants to find in solitude the peace and
strength she needs.

                                                              TMV-S

ARENAL, Concepción (1820-1893).
    Arenal, born in Galicia, wrote some fiction and translated at least
two French novels into Castilian, but her principal contribution was her
work as a penologist and sociologist. She was an outspoken aboli-
tionist. She was also concerned with the status of women, advocating
educational reform in particular and balking at the notion of complete
equality between the sexes. Arenal was considered "one of the most
eminent of modern Spanish women" by Havelock Ellis, an appraisal shared
by most Spanish contemporaries as well as by many foreign admirers of
her contributions to international journals.

    Cuadros de guerra. Madrid: 1874.
        Arenal witnessed some conflicts of the last Carlist War as a Red
Cross observer. Her approach resembles that of the modern journalist
who composes meaningful vignettes, sacrificing chronology and an
analysis of particular economic, political or social problems to the
desire to capture what is universally experienced by ordinary people
in times of war. Arenal wanted to show that war, unless it is a
defensive struggle against aggressors, constitutes an attack on the
laws of the land. The individual suffering she depicted illustrates
all the possible ruptures of bonds that should normally hold a
society together. Available through interlibrary loan and of
interest to scholars.

                                                              DJO

ARENYS, Teresa d'.
    Author of two books of poetry and untiring cultural activist of the
Maresme.

    Aor. Barcelona: Parròquia de Sant Medir, 1976.
        This book of poetry was not offered for public sale. Winner of
the Premi Amadeu Oller, 1976.

    Onada. Vilassar: Quaderns de la Font del Cargol, 1980.
        A volume of poetry inspired by the death by drowning of a beloved
person. This book follows a long silence after the publication of

her first poems in 1976. The poetry is full of sentiment, and often has the sea as protagonist. This short but intense book merits attention.

KM

*ARITZETA I ABAD, Margarida (1953-).
A novelist, born in Valls, she has also written stories, articles and history books. She participates in a cultural program on the radio and works at the Escola Universitària de Tarragona. She has a degree in history and philology, and is working on her doctoral thesis on Josep Lleonart.

Conte d'hivern. Valencia: Prometeo, 1980.

Un febrer a la pell. Barcelona: Edicions 62, "El balancí," 1983, ISBN 84-297-1989-X, 187 pp.
    The setting of this novel is the infamous February 23, 1981, and the attempted coup. A man disappears, and the protagonist, realizing that this is not a "normal" disappearance, tries to figure out what happened, reconstructing the last days of the disappeared. We are offered a gallery of personages and events that form a puzzle for our times. The movement of the normal, working man to the individual capable of breaking with everything around him, including becoming sexually different, gives rise to both comic and serious reflexion. The mystery is maintained until the end, and the ending is open enough for us to imagine indifferent conclusions. Winner of the Sant Jordi prize.

Grafèmia. Barcelona: Laia, "El nus," 1981.

Quan la pedra es torna fang a les mans. Barcelona: Selecta, 1981. Winner of the Víctor Català prize in 1980.

Vermell de cadmi. Barcelona: Laia, "El mirall," 1984, ISBN 84-7222-431-7, 242 pp.
    Fantastic and realistic at the same time, this novel includes political cover-ups, deceptions and blunders, and manipulations of the press, as well as physical transformations of certain people into invisible beings, persons whose gender changes and who age rapidly. The journalist Bruna Bononi sometimes cannot tell whether the things related to her by Llorenç Grasses are real or dreamed. At times approaching science fiction, this novel is also a platform to examine government control of our lives and sexism seen through the eyes of people who have known both genders.

KM

*ARMENGOL DE BADIA, Agnès (1852-1934).
    Born of a wealthy family in Sabadell, Barcelona, Armengol studied in a prestigious French school where she made her first literary contacts. It was homesickness for her country that inspired her to write. Upon returning to Catalonia, she compiled songs her grandmother had sung to her and gave them to her teacher, Pelay Briz, who included them in his collection Cançons de la Terra. An intensely emotional poet with a vigorus style, she devoted her work to the search of traditions, tales and dances. She became a noteworthy pianist and composer. From 1900 to 1902, she addressed her Manifest to Catalan women, encouraging them to support the Unió Catalanista.

Els dies clars. Petits Poemes. Biblioteca Sabadellenca. Volum VII.
Sabadell. Tallers de Joan Sallent. 1926, 195 pp.
    Preface by Anton Navarro. Portrait frontispiece. Collection of
poems grouped under five sections: "Petits Poemes," "Balades,"
"Amoroses," "Amicals," and "Recordances." The author exalts the
majesty of the mountains, the colorful harmony of the nature, and the
clarity of daybreak.

Lays in Joan Roca i Bros' Volum Rimas. Barcelona: Espanyola, 1879.
    Compilation of the following poems: "Balada," "Timidesa,"
"Intima," "Lo Mas de las alsinas," "A la Verge de Montserrat,"
"Serenata," "Nit d'oratge," "A una margaridoya," "Dorm," "A un
poblet," "A Francesch y Trinitat," "Barcarola," and "Los manaments de
la música."

Poesies. Lectura Popular. Biblioteca d'autors catalans. Volum IX.
Barcelona Ilustració Catalana. 544 pp. (Armengol, pp. 353-384.)
    Compilation of some of the poems that appear in her book
Sabadellenques. The book is an anthology in which her work occupies
pages 353-384.

Ramell de Semprevives. Poesies. Sabadell. Imprenta y Litografia de
M. Torner. 1891, 80 pp.
    The book contains a dedication to her cousin Rosa Coromines de
Soler. A picture of her mother Da Eulalia Altayó i Pla de Armengol,
to whom the book is dedicated, is included also. It contains a total
of 35 poems among which stand out "Adeusiau," "Mirant el seu retrat,"
etc. All the poems also appear in her book Sabadellenques.

Redempció. Poema. Biblioteca Sabadellenca. Volum IV. First ed.
1914? Sabadell: 1925, 168 pp.
    Preface by Josep Lleonart. The poems are grouped in four
sections: "Redempció," which is an introduction; "Cant Primer,"
"Cant Segon," and "Cant Tercer." The style is clear and simple, with
a neoclassic discretion and erudite theme. The book is a treasure of
beauty, faith and feeling.

Rosari Antic, Tradicions i records. Biblioteca Sabadellenca. Volum
X. Sabadell: 1926. Tallers de Joan Sallent. 1926, 245 pp.
    A collection of poems based on memories, with a prologue by Anton
Busquets i Punset and a biography. The book is divided into five
mysteries: "De ma infantesa," "Cançonetes" which were put to music
by the writer; "Tradicions" which includes a very interesting legend
of Barbarà, el mercat del rams and 3 Sabadellenques; "Religioses"
treated with discretion and elegance; and "Varia" which includes
joyful poems about nature. Rosari Antic is a poem about living from
memories.

Sabadellenques i altres poesies. Biblioteca Sabadellenca. Volum
III. Joan Costa i Deu and Joan Sallarés, editors. Sabadell: 1925.
Oradors de Joan Sallent. 192 pp.
    Sabadellenques is a series of poems published by the Lliga
Regionalista. One notes a melancholy remembrance of things past,
especially Catalan traditions. The book is divided into six parts.
The first, "Sabadellenques" masterfully reflects the past customs and

the traditional aspects of Sabadell. The second, "Danses" includes
poems describing traditional dances, such as "Dansa catalana de
Castelltersol," which is the dance of the Fiesta Mayor. The third,
"Nupcials" are poems dedicated to young couples to be married.
"Cançons" is the fourth section. The fifth is "Endreces," poems
dedicated to specific individuals. The sixth is "Ramell de
Semprevives."

VC-E

*ARQUIMBAU, Rosa Maria. (1910-). Also: **Rosa de sant Jordi.**
     Born in Barcelona, she started to write tales when she was 14.
Afterwards, she collaborated in many leftist publications. She also
wrote several short plays. The documental character of her work is of
great interest. She belongs to the 1930's period, characterized by a
difficult diffusion of Catalan literature for political reasons. The
civil war and the exile have influence but the tendency of this period
is to escape from reality and analyze characters out of specific time.

40 anys perduts. Barcelona: Club de novelistes. Editor Biblioteca
catalana de novela, 67, 1971, 190 pp.
     A young dressmaker, working in the popular neighborhood Onda in
Barcelona, suddenly becomes famous and decides what is fashionable
for the aristocratic society. The protagonist, with great natural-
ness, manages to combine her new condition with her proletarian
origins.

Es rifa un home. Barcelona: La escena Catalana, 414, Editor
Bonavia, 1935, 12 pp.

Historia d'una noia i vint braçalets. Barcelona: Llibreria
Catalonia, 1934, N.A.G.S.A., 102 pp.
     A novel of a young girl who is sent to Barcelona by her family to
study. All the events of her life are determined by the people she
meets. Each of the 20 bracelets she wears is a symbol of a special
event in her life; they lead us to discover this interesting
character.

Home i dona. Barcelona: Quaderns literaris, 116, 1936, 26 pp.
     Several letters written by a woman to her best girlfriend reveal
to us her effort to live her own life now that she is separated from
her husband. She is a very liberated woman considering the strict
moral patterns that governed the Spanish society in 1936.

L'inconvenient de dir-se Martines. Barcelona: Premi Joan de
Santamaria, 1957, pp. 87-108.

La pau es un interval. Barcelona: Collecció Llibre de butxaca,
18, 1970, Editor Portic, 130 pp.

CF

B

BADELL, Ana María (1932-).
A native of Santander, she majored in Agriculture while at the university and later worked for the Instituto de Investigaciones Agronómicas. In 1956 she received a degree in landscaping from the Colegio de Arquitectura. In 1957 she married Miguel Fisac. Besides writing novels, she has contributed many articles to various newspapers and journals.

¡Hasta mañana, dolor! Madrid: Editorial Dólar, 1977, 301 pp.

Historia de un perro. Madrid: Iberoamericanas, 1969, 108 pp.

Jesús Niño. Madrid: Editorial Religión y Cultura, 1955.

Las monjas: esas mujeres. Madrid: Rollán, 1966, 413 pp. 4th ed. Madrid: Iberoamericanas, 1968, 415 pp.

Monte de piedad y caja de ahorros. Spain: n.p., 1977.

Las nuevas colegialas. Madrid: Iberoamericanas, 1968, 276 pp.

Sor Ada. Madrid: Iberoamericanas, 1967, 289 pp.

RK

BALLESTEROS DE GAIBROIS, Mercedes (1891-). Pseud. **Baronesa Alberta.**
Born in Madrid and married to the well-known playwright and director Claudio de la Torre, Mercedes Ballesteros has enjoyed a long and distinguished literary career as playwright, novelist, short story writer, and essayist. She is a winner of the premio Tina Gascó for her play Las mariposas cantan and of the premio Novela del Sábado for her novel Eclipse de tierra, which has been translated into English and German. Her novel Taller was a finalist in the 1959 premio Eugenio Nadal competition. A sensitive and perceptive observer of the human condition, Mercedes Ballesteros is at her best and is best known for her portrayal of children.

Así es la vida. Barcelona: José Janés, 1953, 215 pp.
A collection of brief, witty essays that touch upon the minutiae of daily life that in toto comprise the fabric of human existence. The topics range from cocktail parties to pediatricians to the many faces of love. This collection was followed by others of like nature. See entries under Este mundo, Invierno, Verano, and El personal.

La cometa y el eco. (Coleccion Autores españoles contemporáneos.)
Barcelona: Planeta, 1956. 2nd edition, 1967, 320 pp.
    A major work of the author, this novel, set in the years just
preceding and following the Spanish Civil War, follows the protagonist, Augusta, from her late teens to her mid-thirties. Her
loneliness, in large part self-imposed, and her detachment from life
serve as foil and backdrop for the other women of the novel, from the
grandmother with her nineteenth century view of women's subservient
role in society to the young social climber who marries the grandson.
The sea is an ever present part of the background, and its eternal
ebb and flow symbolizes the ebb and flow of he family blood passing
endlessly from generation to generation. A thoughtful and complex
work with close parallels to Azorín's concept of the eternal return
and repetition of time.

El chico. (Ancora y Delfín 284.) Barcelona: Destino, 1967,
185 pp. El Chico, pp. 9-107. Eclipse de tierra, pp. 111-185.
    El Chico. A poetic and sensitive novel in which the author
describe with pathos an illegitimate 12-year-old boy, who, living
first in the squalor of Madrid's slums and later in the squalor of a
village hamlet, is the personification of goodness. Nowhere is the
author's sympathetic understanding of children more evident than in
her portrayal of el chico. The boy, who is never named, is a unique
individual and yet, at the same time, he is the embodiment of all
children as they take their first hesitant steps into the adult
world.

Eclipse de tierra. (La novela del sábado, año 2, núm. 44.)
Madrid: Tecnos, 1954, 64 pp. Rpt. Barcelona: Destino, 1967. See
entry under El chico.
Nothing is Impossible. (Eclipse de Tierra.) Trans. by Frances
Partridge. London: The Harvill Press, 1956, 96 pp.
    A novelette which centers around the boarding school escapades of
Andrés, a strange little boy with a degree of perception and insight
bordering on the supernatural. He is a delightfully magical combination of naive little boy and sage possessed of the wisdom of the
ages. The poetic and gentle tone of protagonist and ambience makes
this work very similar to El chico.

Este mundo. (El Club de la Sonrisa 12.) Madrid: Taurus, 1950,
283 pp. Rpt. Barcelona: Ediciones G.P., 1959. See entries under
Invierno and Verano.
    A collection of very brief essays which view people, customs,
places, and attitudes with whimsical sarcasm. The essays are grouped
into the four categories of Winter, Spring, Summer, Fall, and the
topics touched upon range in all directions and cover such diverse
subject matter as shopping, fate, baldness, and the sins of modern
educational systems. The style, acuity of perception, and the humor
are reminiscent of the essays of Larra.

Invierno. (Libros de humor "El Gorrión" 48.) Barcelona: Ediciones
G.P., 1959, 128 pp. Rpt. of the first half of Este mundo, i.e., the
sections entitled Invierno and Primavera.
    Brief sketches about the world and its people. See entry under
Este mundo.

Lejano pariente sin sombrero. (Colección Teatro 501.) Madrid:
Alfil, 1966, 72 pp.
  A three act play set in the present. A long lost uncle arrives on
the doorstep of a family mired in a spiritless existence. Because of
his supposed wealth he is welcomed at first with open arms; his idio-
syncrasies are tolerated. When his penniless state becomes apparent,
he is rudely asked to leave. In spite of this, he remains loyal to
the family, and, by manipulation and machination, he manages to
change for the better the lives of his nieces and his nephew. In the
end, the family realizes that Uncle George, without even a hat to his
name, has left them far more than money. The dialogue is clever; the
action is well paced; and the characters are clearly delineated.

Mi hermano y yo por esos mundos. (Ancora y Delfín 227.) Barcelona:
Destino, 1962, 217 pp. Part I: No Fuimos a Mesopotamia. Part II:
El perro del extraño rabo.
  Mi hermano is a novel written in the first person by a never named
little girl of about ten. As stated in the prologue, this book does
not conform to the usual exigencies of the novel form. It has no
clear development of theme or character, nor does it reach a structurally or psychologically appropriate conclusion. It seems,
instead, rather like randomly extracted parts of a diary, and,
lacking a true beginning or end, it resembles life in which,
according to the author, "no se ata ningún nudo, no se concluye
nada." The author is here at her best. The situations into which
the precocious narrator and her brother blunder make delightful
reading.

El perro del extraño rabo. (La novela del sábado, año I, núm.
19.) Madrid: Tecnos, 1953, 62 pp. Rpt. Barcelona: Destino, 1962.
See entry under Mi hermano y yo por esos mundos.
  The adventures of a pre-teen brother and sister while visiting
relatives in Italy, this work was later published as the second half
of a longer novel. See entry under Mi hermano y yo por esos mundos.

El personal. (Ancora y Delfín 476.) Barcelona: Destino, 1975,
ISBN 84-233-0926-6, 223 pp.
  Following the format and style of Este mundo, El personal is a
collection of brief essays through which passes a parade of persons,
situations, places, and things. All is described with the wisdom and
humor typical of the author. New Year's Eve in a neighborhood bar,
literary trends, and masculine preference for fat women are just a
few of the many and diverse topics.

Quiero ver al doctor (with Claudio de la Torre). (Colección Teatro
81.) Madrid: Alfil, 1953, 63 pp.
  A three act play set in the present. With its debut in 1940 it is
the author's earliest work and the only one which represents a collaborative effort. It is a lively play in which a couple, separated
on their wedding day because of a misunderstanding, are reunited
after 19 years. The traditional values of marriage and family are
expounded as husband and wife admit that her world traveling and his
successful medical career have not afforded them happiness. The play
moves smoothly to its inevitable and predictable conclusion. Quiero

ver al doctor gives a hint of the philosophical depth which was destined to add more texture and richness of fabric to the subsequent plays.

La sed. (Ancora y Delfín 264.) Barcelona: Destino, 1965, 197 pp.
   A contemporary novel about the struggle of one woman to come to terms with her barrenness. As the character of Justa unfolds, it becomes clear that she is barren in body and spirit. Her thirst is not for motherhood or mothering; rather, it is a yearning for identity and self-knowledge, a desire to feel herself a link in the flow of time and of generations. A sensitive and poignant psychological portrait.

Taller. (Ancora y Delfín 192.) Barcelona: Destino, 1960, 197 pp. Adaptation for stage. Luca de Tena, Juan Ignacio. Las chicas el taller. Madrid: Editorial "Prensa Española," 1963, 197 pp.
   A contemporary novel set in an elegant dress salon in Madrid. The main characters, all women, are the owner and her seamstresses. The novel is a realistic and sensitive portrayal of frustration, despair, and ultimately, resignation, as the women deal with problems ranging from abortion and homosexuality to the subtly destructive challenges of loneliness, rejection, and deep-rooted feelings of inadequacy and inferiority. The character depiction is excellent. Each protagonist, with her own story, stands out clearly and yet blends into the overall fabric of the novel.

Verano. (Libros de humor "El Gorrión" 46). Barcelona: Ediciones G.P., 1959, 128 pp. Rpt. of the second half of Este mundo, i.e., the sections entitled Verano and Otoño.
   Brief sketches about life and human nature. See entry under Este mundo.

JM

BARBERA, Carmen.
   Born in Cuevas de Vinromá (Castellón de la Plana) this author has written both novels and poetry. She has twice been a finalist in the competition for the Premio Ciudad de Barcelona and her writing has merited her the Premio Ondas (1958) and the Premio Ateneo de Tortosa (1963).

Adolescente. Barcelona: J. Janés, 1957, 339 pp. (Colección Doy fé, 2.)

Al final de la ría. Madrid: CID, 1958, 279 pp.

Cartas a un amigo. San Juan, Puerto Rico: Cordillera, 1965, 148 pp.

La colina perdida. Barcelona: Car, 1961, 78 pp. (Colección El Juglar y la luna, 9.)

Debajo de la piel. San Juan, Puerto Rico: Rumbos, 1959, 243 pp. (Colección El Doncel.)

Despedida al Recuerdo. Barcelona: Rumbos, 1955, 79 pages.

Las esquinas del alba. Barcelona: Luis de Caralt, 1960, 226 pp.
(Colección Gigante.)

Tierras de luto. Barcelona: Planeta, 1976, ISBN 84-320-5353-8,
297 pp. (Autores españoles e hispanoamericanos.)
    Eleven years of silence transpired between Cartas a un amigo, a
work of poetry, and this rich and complex novel. Set in the town of
Nijven, in Holland, the novel deals with the theme of survival. The
central character, Saskia Van Tellen, survives in spite of intense
loneliness and the suicidal depression which the coastal winters
bring. Her nephew Claus survives the death of his parents and is
motivated by a desire for revenge. The novel's many characters offer
images of strength in the face of difficulty.
                                                                  KHC

BARBERO SANCHEZ, Teresa, also Teresa Barbero (1934-).
    Born in Avila, Barbero was one of the originators of the "El Cobaya"
literary group in 1953. In 1959 she moved to Madrid and began
publishing poetry. She then established her reputation as a novelist.
                                                                  CLG

Apenas llegue el buen tiempo. 1964.
    Novel, Premio Sésamo finalist.
                                                                  CLG

Gabriel Miró. Madrid: Epesa, 1974, 194 pp. (Colección Grandes
escritores contemporáneos.)
                                                                  KHC

Una manera de vivir. Madrid: A.U.L.A., 1965, 148 pp.
(Colección Volvo, 7.)
    Won the Premio Sésamo.
                                                                  KHC

Muchacha en el exilio. Bilbao: Col. Alrededor de la Mesa, 1959.
    Poetry.
                                                                  CLG

Un tiempo irremediable falso. Madrid: Organización Sala Editorial,
1973, 341 pp.
                                                                  KHC

El último verano en el espejo. Barcelona: Destino, 1967, 265 pp.
(Ancora y delfín, 301.)
    An indictment of the education Spanish girls receive, the novel
portrays the mid-twentieth-century malaise of the protagonist, Marta.
As Marta recalls her childhood and adolescence in a small town, and
the repression, prejudices and frustrations that entailed, she sees
herself reduced to a figment, dominated by the men in her life,
revealed only within the narrow confines of her mirror.
                                                                  CLG

*BARTRE, Llúcia (1881-?).
    Born in Illa, she dedicated herself to the theater.

Primers passos. 1931.

Retalls. 1933.

Rialles. 1942.

Els set pecats capitals. 1948.

KM

*BASSA, Maria Gracia. (1883-1961). Pseud. Gracia B. de Llorens.
A poet, born in Llofriu.

Branca florida. 1933.

Esplais de llunyania. 1919.

KM

BECKER, Angélicka.

Definiciones. Colección Poética Leopoldo Panero, 7. Madrid:
Cultura Hispánica, 1968, 98 pp.
    The major theme of this poetry collection is men and women's
relationship to them, from a feminist point of view. The book is
divided into eight chapters, containing such feminist poems as well
as short poems about island imagery and street types ("el Chulo,"
"Vendedor ambulante," "El señor" and "La portera"). "Ocho
definiciones sobre un mismo tema" is eight poems about men, often
acrid or sarcastic in nature. "Nunca ha sido cantado" purports that
"Nunca ha sido cantado el hombre en la fea desnudez, de su cuerpo
hermosamente pútrido." ("Man has never been sung about in the ugly
nakedness of his beautifully putrid body.")

Figuras y meditaciones. Adonais, 230. Madrid: Rialp, 1965,
ISBN 84-321-1556-8, 82 pp.
    This 34 poem collection won the Mención Honorífica del Premio
Adonais de Poesía for 1964. The four divisions of the book cover
(1) Meditaciones--personal reflections on love and life, (2) Figuras
--portraits of different "types" such as "El viejo amante," "El
político," "Dios biocolor," "El Hedonista" and "El poeta," (3) En
este teatro--a very long poem dedicated to the poet's mother, and
(4) Meditaciones--similar to part I. All poems in this collection
are dedicated to individuals.

MDJ

BELL-LLOCH, Maria de. See MASPONS I LABROS, Maria del Pilar.

*BENETA MAS I PUJOL, Margarida (1649-1700).
(She became Anna Maria del Santíssim Sagrament in the convent.)
    Born in Valldemossa, she wrote an explanation of the Llibre de l'Amic
i de l'Amat by her fellow-Majorcan Ramon Llull. She also wrote poetry
which was not published.

KM

*BENEYTO CUNYAT, Maria (1925-).
She was born in Valencia and spent her infancy in Madrid. She wrote
in Castilian and Catalan. She published short stories in the Spanish
and Venezuelan press as well as literary criticism. Her poetry reflects
a great sensitivity and is rich in symbolism. She obtained the prize
"Premi ciutat de Barcelona" with her poems "Ratlles a l'aire."

CF

Altre veu. Valencia: Torre, Col.lecció L'Espiga 10, 1952, 54 pp.

CF

La dona forta. Valencia: Senent, 1967, 180 pp.
A psychological novel in which the author analyzes and focuses on
the relationship between a mother and her son. The mother, as the
title indicates, is a strong woman, of character, but who is lacking
in sentiments, especially in tenderness toward her son. This lack
has an extraordinary effect on the character of her son, who, in
contrast to her, becomes a weak person. This novel won the Senent
Prize in 1965 and is one of the first novels written in Catalan from
the province of Valencia.

ISS

La gent que viu al món. Valencia: L'estel, Serie Blava, 1966,
114 pp.

CF

Ratlles a l'aire. Barcelona: Torre, Col.lecció L'Espiga, Premi
ciutat de Barcelona, 1956, 51 pp.

CF

Vidre ferit de sang. Gandia: Ajuntament de Gandia, Premi Ciusiàs
March, 1976, ISBN 84-500-1953-2, 38 pp.

CF

*BERTRANA, Aurora (1899-1974).
Born in Gerona, she was the daughter of the famous Catalan writer
Prudenci Bertrana. She travelled all around the world (Europe, North
Africa, Oceanic Islands, South America). She used scenery from these
exotic places in her stories. The fact that she has a deep knowledge of
other countries which largely influenced her fiction does not explain
her great success as a writer. She also possesses a wonderful style.

Ariatea. Barcelona: Alberti, Nova Col.lecció Lletres 59, 1960,
164 pp.

Camins de somni. Barcelona: Alberti, Nova Col.lecció Lletres 13,
1955, 99 pp.

La ciutat dels joves. Barcelona: Pòrtic, Llibre de butxaca 71,
1971, 117 pp.

Entre dos silencis. Barcelona: Aymas, Club dels novel.listes 10,
1958, 265 pp.
The novel is based on a real situation the writer experienced
during the Second World War. Working as a volunteer in a village
completely destroyed, she shares the same endurance of the villagers.

This is a story of friendship between people who suffered the tragedy of the last war.

Fracàs. Andorra: Alfaguara, Novella popular 13, 1966, 100 pp.
   This novel is a direct accusation against a definite part of the society. The upper classes with the mask of respectability and religious pactice only live with ambition and selfishness.

El Marroc sensual i fanàtic. Barcelona: Mediterrànea, 1936, 291 pp.
   The narrator herself said she limited her work to giving her impressions during a trip to Morroco in these short stories. She paints the landscape, the monuments and the different images according to her sentimental and intellectual reactions.

La nimfa d'argila. Barcelona: Alberti, Nova Collecció LLetres 47, 1959, Editor Alberti, 156 pp.
   Analysis of infantile psychology. The author relates the story of the failed infancy of a young child in this novel.

Oviri i sis narracions més. Barcelona: Selecta 375, 1965, 204 pp.
   The protagonist of the first story is a cat called "Oviri." The other stories also have animals as central protagonists. With a sharp sense of observation the author demonstrates the reason why humans feel so close to animals.

Paradisos Oceànics. Badalona: Proa, Biblioteca Rodamon, 1930, 213 pp.

Peikea, princesa caníbal i altres contes oceànics. Barcelona: Butxaca Plentiluni, 1980, ISBN 84-85752-01-5, 192 pp.
   These different stories reflect her trip to the oceanic islands. The author makes us discover a dream world where the landscape favorable to love and tenderness is the main source of human life.

Tres presoners. Barcelona: Alberti, Nova Col.lecció Lletres 26, 1957, 140 pp.
   A novel of great emotion based on a situation occurring during the civil war among three prisoners. The story is simple but intensively human and maybe for this reason, very emotional.

Vent de grop. Andorra: Alfaguara, Ara i Aci 4, 1967, 179 pp.
   In a small fishing village located in the Costa Brava where tourists and fishermen share their lives, a sentimental tragedy occurs: two young people who love each other with an instinctive love arrive at the moment when one gets tired of the other while the other wants to continue the relationship. A novel that does not aim to hurt moral conscience nor to hurt the heart of sentimental people.
                                                                CF

BLANC DE PANERO, Felicidad (birth date unknown).
Born into a well-to-do family, Felicidad Blanc married the poet
Leopoldo Panero and had three sons, all of whom are poets. Blanc published several short stories which were well received, but she abandoned
her literary interests because she was discouraged by her husband's
attitude. He relegated her to the role of wife and mother, and excluded
her from his intellectual life. After Panero's death Blanc made a documentary film called "El desencanto" which describes her frustration and
resentment with family life. She presently resides in Spain.

Espejo de sombras. Taped and edited by Natividad Massanés.
Barcelona: Argos Vergara, S.A., 1977, ISBN 84-7178-339-8, 246 pp.
Espejo de sombras is a book of memoirs which describes the life of
Felicidad Blanc from her childhood and the Spanish Civil War to her
marriage to Leopoldo Panero and his sudden death years later. With
startling frankness and in a poetic and melancholic fashion, she
describes the loneliness of her marriage and her disappointment upon
being relegated to the role of wife and mother. Her powerful account
reveals the rigid infrastructure of Spanish society during the Franco
regime as well as the author's deep sentiments regarding love,
maternity, family ties and literature. Transcription of tape and
prologue are by Nati Massanés. Available in paperback in Spain
(Librería de Mujeres, Madrid). Of general interest on the role of
Spanish women in contemporary society.

SMG

BÖHL DE FABER Y LARREA, Cecilia (1796-1877), Pseud. Fernán Caballero.
Credited with restoring the novel to a place of prominence in Spanish
letters, Fernán Caballero is also known for her short stories,
sketches, and folklore collections. Critics have said she belongs to
Romanticism, Costumbrismo (local color writing) or Realism; but it may
be best to classify her as a transitional writer. Extremely popular in
Spain and abroad in the 1850's and early 1860's, her work had become
unfashionable at the time of her death. This was due to the strongly
felt, traditionally conservative religious and moral convictions
expressed in it.

"Callar en vida y perdonar en muerte," in Obras completas. Prologue
Duque de Rivas. Madrid: Mellado, 1856, 194 pp. (published with La
familia de Alvareda). (In Obras completas, ed. José María Castro y
Calv. Biblioteca de Autores Españoles, vol. 137, Madrid: Atlas,
1961, pp. 237-249).
One of the relaciones whose purpose is to emphasize some moral
point, "Callar en la vida" traces the history of a murder. The
victim, an elderly woman, is killed by her son-in-law. No one
suspects him. Some years later his wife learns of his deed. She
guards the truth to protect her children and only discloses her
knowledge of it to her husband as she lays dying. Although there is
much moralizing in the relación, this is one of Fernán Caballero's
more interesting and better written works.

Clemencia. Madrid: C. Gonzalez, 1852 (ed. Julio Ródriguez Luis,
Madrid: Cátedra, 1982, 382 pp.).
A somewhat romantic novel said to be based in part on the author's
own unhappy first marriage. The story treats the life of a long-
suffering, obedient woman given to tears. The author exalts religion

as a means of solace as well as the beauty of the simple, country
life. The first part of the novel has more action than the second
part. The 1982 edition contains bibliographical references.

Colección de artículos religiosos y morales. Cadiz: Gautier,
1862, 306 pp. (In Obras completas, ed. José María Castro y Calvo,
Biblioteca de Autores Españoles, vol. 140, Madrid: Ediciones, 1961,
pp. 394-361.)
   A few examples of the religious lore incorporated into this
collection find their way into Fernán's novels, in particular, La
familia de Alvareda.

Con mal o con bien a los tuyos te ten. Prologue by Juan Eugenio
Hartzenbusch. In Obras completas. Madrid: Establecimiento
Tipográfico de Mellado, 1856, 192 pp, published with Una en otra.
(In Obras completas, ed. José María Castro y Calvo, Biblioteca de
Autores Españles, vol. 138, Madrid: Atlas, 1961, pp. 297-322.)
   Based on a proverb, this novel begins with a description of
beggars in Cádiz, and then continues to relate how four of them--a
crippled man, a woman, and two children, came to be in such a state.
The woman left her intended (now the cripple) to marry (in a sham
ceremony) a wealthy young man who had befriended her dying father.
Within this frame the author voices her opinions on the bullfight,
British aloofness, members of the nobility who squander their
inheritance, and marriage outside of one's social class.

"Cosa cumplida...sólo en la otra vida," in Otras completas, Madrid:
Mellado, 1862, 248 pp. (published with "Diálogos entre la juventud y
la edad Madura," "La noche de Navidad," "El día de Reyes"). (In
Obras completas, ed. José María Castro y Calvo, Biblioteca de
Autores Españoles, vol. 139, Madrid: Atlas, 1961, pp. 7-76.)
   This is a series of six separate stories or sketches included as
illustration to conversations between the Marquesa de Alora and her
friend the Count of Viana. In all the theme is that God's ways are
best although not always understood at the time by men. The author
glorifies the family, motherhood, children, and the campo. The
stories are entitled: El albañil, El marinero, El sochantre del
lugar, El general, El quinto, and Un tío en America.

Cuentos, oraciones, adivinas, y refranes populares e infantiles.
Madrid: Imprenta de T. Fortenat, 1877, 504 pp. (In Obras completas,
ed. José María Castro y Calvo, Biblioteca de Autores Españoles,
vol. 140, Madrid: Ediciones Atlas, 1961, pp. 195-287.)
   This folklore collection contains examples of religious lore and
local proverbs which the author incorporates into her works.

Cuentos y poesías populares andaluces. Sevilla: La Revista
Mercantil, 189, 435 pp. (In Obras completas, ed. José María Castro
y Calvo, Biblioteca de Autores Españoles, vol. 140, Madrid: Atlas,
1961, pp. 64-191.)
   This folklore collection contains many of the coplas and other
songs the author includes in her novels, short stories, local color
sketches, relaciones.

Deudas pagadas. Prologue by Manuel Canete. Madrid: Tello, 1860,
70 pp. (Published with Cuadros de costumbres populares de la

actualidad.) (In Obras completas, ed. José María Castro y Calvo, Biblioteca de Autores Españles, vol. 139, Madrid: Atlas, 1961, pp. 331-349.)

The story treats the anguish a mother experiences because her sons must fight in North Africa. The title comes from the fact that the adopted son saves the life of his half-brother, thus repaying the family for having raised him. The author glorifies Isabel II and details victory parades. Published with Deudas are short essays in which Fernán gives her impressions of foreign places, and sermons on suffering, heroism, and religious life. These include: "El Eddistone," "Una excursión a Waterloo," "Aquisgrán," "Una madre," "Un naufragio," "El vendedor de Tagarninas."

"El día de Reyes," in Obras completas. Madrid: Establecimiento Tipográfico de don Francisco de P. Mellado, 1857, 371 pp. (published with Elia; o España treinta años ha, "El último consuelo," "La noche de Navidad"). (In Obras completas, ed. José María Castro y Calvo, Biblioteca de Autores Españoles, vol. 139, Madrid: Atlas, 1961, pp. 257-264.)

Classified by Castro y Calvo as a relato breve this seems also an example of local color writing. As a tandem piece to accompany "Noche de Navidad, this concentrates on a tableau and pageant held in the town church as a part of the Epiphany celebration. The father of the child who was abandoned in the previous story returns. In typical Fernán fashion he marries the woman who cared for the child and he is the missing son of the crusty Tía Pavona.

"Dicha y suerte," in Relaciones. Obras completas. Madrid: Establecimiento Tipográfico de F. de P. Mellado, 1862 (published with "El útlimo consuelo," "Simón Verde," "Más honor que honores," "Lucas García," "Obrar bien que Dios es Dios," "El dolor es una agonía sin muerte"). (In Obras completas, ed. José María Castro y Calvo, Biblioteca de Autores Españoles, vol. 139, Madrid: Atlas, 1961, pp. 139-155.)

Beginning with a lengthy description of the town of San Lucar then followed by a list of the wildlife found in the coto de Doñana, this relación contrasts opposites. One of the protagonists, Vicente, finds happiness despite poverty and blindness; the other, Próspero, becomes embittered and yellowed despite his wealth and good fortune. There is also a portrait of the woman who remains faithful to the man she loves.

"El dolor es una agonía sin muerte," in Cuadros de costumbres. Obras completas. Madrid: Establecimiento Tipográfico F. de P. Mellado, 1857, 360 pp. (published with "Simón Verde," "Más vale honor que honores," "Lucas García," "Obrar bien que Dios es Dios.") (In Obras completas, ed. José María Castro y Calvo, Biblioteca de Autores Españoles, vol. 139, Madrid: Atlas, 1961, pp. 237-241.)

In this sketch the author shows the effects the military draft have on a woman: her fears, grief, insomnia, assumptions, illnesses, and then death. Ironically she dies when her son returns from the army. The author also takes on a second cause when she speaks against the Spaniards' cruel treatment of draft animals.

"Los dos amigos," in Relaciones. Obras completas. Madrid: Mellado, 1857 (published with "Justa y Rufina," "Más largo es el tiempo que la fortuna," "No transige la conciencia," "La flor de las ruinas," "El ex-voto," "La hija del sol"). (In Obras completas, ed. José María Castro y Calvo, Biblioteca de Autores Españoles, vol. 137, Madrid: Atlas, 1961, pp. 287-291.)

The two friends of this relación, Ramiro and Félix, are inseparable. As children of close friends they were raised together, they joined the army together, they fight together. When Ramiro has an appointment to see a woman he loves (she is married), Felix offers to exchange duty assignments with him. That evening Félix is killed. A remorseful Ramiro becomes a Capuchin monk. The theme which predominates is that of true friendship, the selfless sacrifice for another.

Las dos Gracias o la expiación. Prologue by Pedro de Madrazo. Madrid: Centro de Administración, 1865, 286 pp. (published with La farisea. (In Obras completas, ed. José María Castro y Calvo, Biblioteca de Autores Españoles, vol. 138, Madrid: Atlas, 1961, pp. 349-392.

This short novel contrasts two women of the same name, born the same day, raised next door to each other, then related by marriage. The one, Gracia López, is beautiful, proud, and treacherous; the other, Gracia Vargas, is plain, caring, and forgiving. Although the "bad" Gracia has made life miserable for the "good" Gracia, the latter through Christian charity helps her to a noble death. The theme of good and bad character is repeated with the males Ramón and Alfonso. The story moves from one set of circumstances to another, good is always rewarded, bad is punished.

Elia; o España treinta años ha. In Obras completas, Madrid: Establecimiento Tipográfico de don Francisco de P. Mellado, 1857, 371 pp. (published with "El último consuelo," "La noche de Navidad," "El día de Reyes"). (Ed. Julio Rodríguez Luis, Madrid: Alianza Editorial, 1968.)
Elia, or Spain Fifty Years Ago. Trans. New York: D. Appleton and Company, 1868.

Set amid the social and political polarization into traditional and liberal camps, the novel shows how a young girl caught up in the conflict of emotion and duty retires to a convent. Predominant themes are 1) a person cannot serve two masters, 2) marriage between social classes is unacceptable, and 3) sacrifice. Much dialogue and characters are types who act impulsively.

"Estar de más," note by Fernando Gabriel de Gabriel y Ruiz Apodaca. Sevilla: Gironés y Orduña, 1878, 37 pp. (published with "Magdalena"). (In Obras completas, ed. José María Castro y Calvo, Biblioteca de Autores Españoles, vol. 137, Madrid: Atlas, 1961, pp. 375-383.)

This relación treats an old folk theme of a woman who believes her husband dead and then marries another. When the first husband returns after a long absence, he hides his identity to protect her happiness. In Fernán's version the first husband joins an order, lives as a hermit, and dies a saintly death.

"El ex-voto," in Relaciones. In Obras completas, Madrid: Mellado, 1857 (published with "Justa y Rufina," "Más largo es el tiempo que la fortuna," "No transige la conciencia," "La flor de las ruinas," "Los dos amigos," "La hija del sol"). (In Obras completas, ed. José María Castro y Calvo, Biblioteca de Autores Españoles, vol. 139, Madrid: Atlas, 1961, pp. 267-282.)

Called a relación by the author but classified as a relato breve by Klibbe and Castro y Calvo, "El ex-voto" repeats anti-British sentiment and contains many examples of local lore. The weak story line has a convict dare an extortionist to kill the first person who crosses his path. When the extortionist is about to strike the death blow, he sees that his victim is wearing a cross and spares him. The metaphor of the cross as protection is repeated in the victim's name, Juan de la Cruz. In a concluding note the author compares her story to a similar, true incident.

La estrella de Vandalia: cuadro de costumbres. Madrid: Imprenta de Antonio Andrés Babi, 1855, 135 pp. (In Obras completas, ed. José María Castro y Calvo, Biblioteca de Autores Españoles, vol. 138, Madrid: Atlas, 1961, pp. 93-141.)

This short novel is built around coincidences. The main characters represent types: the pure Gracia, the poor priest Father Buendía, the insolent Raimundo for whom the author first indicates hope and then shows him to be beyond redemption. There are two love triangles (Raimundo takes his brother's intended; Raimundo kills Gracia's intended) and the usual exaltations of the campo. Other items on which the author speaks are 1) glory vs. esteem, and 2) the lack of equality among individuals.

La familia de Alvareda. Prologue by the Duque de Rivas. In Obras completas. Madrid: Mellado, 1856, 194 pp. (published with "Callar en la vida y perdonar en muerte". (Ed. Julio Rodríguez Luis, Madrid: Castalia, 1979, 272 pp.)
The Castle and the Cottage in Spain. Trans. of La familia de Alvareda by Lady Wallace, London: Saunders, Otley, & Co., 1861.
The Alvareda Family. Trans. Viscount Pollington, London: Newby, 1872.

With the first draft written before Dec. 1828, La familia is one of Fernáns earliest works. It is a novel of customs in which the author sets out to depict the things of the pueblo with pueblo meaning the nation, its people, the town of Dos Hermanas, and its residents. The novel therefore is one of her most ambitious. The themes are faith vs. passion underlined by folkloric references. The 1979 edition of J. Rodríguez Luis has a good introduction, a select bibliography, and variants of the text from El Heraldo, and the handwritten manuscript.

La farisea. Prologue by Pedro de Medrazo. Madrid: Centro de Administración, 1865, 286 pp. (published with Las Dos Gracias o la expiación). (In Obras completas, ed. José María Castro y Calvo, Biblioteca de Autores Españoles, vol. 138, Madrid: Atlas, 1961, pp. 325-346.)

This well-written short novel deserves more attention. Based on the Biblical account of the Pharisee, the story treats a proud woman who marries an elderly general in order to achieve acclaim. Themes which run through the story are: 1) to be a man, one must have a

good man as a model; 2) no one can be happy married to an egotist; 3)
military men have one code and that is honor. Contrasting the pride-
filled woman is her sister who prefers country to city, and the simple
instead of the ostentatious.

"La flor de las ruinas," in Relaciones. Obras completas. Madrid:
Mellado, 1857 (published with "Justa y Rufina," "Más largo es el
tiempo que la fortuna," "No transige la consciencia," "El ex-voto,"
"Los dos amigos," "La hija del sol"). (In Obras completas, ed. José
María Castro y Calvo, Biblioteca de Autores Españoles, vol. 137,
Madrid: Atlas, 1961, pp. 276-283.)
    "La flor de las ruinas" is a "romantic," almost "gothic,"
relación in which a pretty girl is used by her outlaw brothers to
trap their victims. She falls in love with the latest, alerts the
authorities about what is to happen, and dies as a result. The
brothers also die and the young man suffers from brain fever.
Mystery and tragedy prevail.

La gaviota. In Obras completas. Madrid: Mellado, 1856 (ed. Carmen
Bravo Villasante, Madrid: Castalia, 1979, 340 pp.).
The Seagull. Trans. and introduction Joan Maclean, Woodbury, New
York: Barrons, 1965.
    Fernán's first work serialized in El Heraldo, its instant
acceptance gained for her national and international acclaim.
Considered the work which reestablished the novel's prominence in
Spain, La gaviota treats the topic of adultery, the rural-urban
conflict, and the author's thoughts on the novel of her day coupled
with what a good novel should be. The 1979 edition of C. Bravo
Villante contains a good introduction, a select bibliography, notes,
and the juicio crítico of Eugenio de Ochoa which compares Fernán to
Walter Scott.

"La hija del sol," in Relaciones. In Obras Completas. Madrid:
Mellado, 1857 (published with "Justa y Rufina," "Más largo es el
tiempo que la fortuna," "No transige la conciencia," "La flor de las
ruinas," "El ex-voto," "Los dos amigos"). (In Obras completas, ed.
José María Castro y Calvo, Biblioteca de Autores Españoles, vol.
137, Madrid: Atlas, 1961, pp. 295-300.)
    A relación which enters the realm of el más allá, "La hija del
sol" concerns a young woman who has married an old man out of duty.
During her husband's absence and encouraged by her maid, the woman
falls in love with a handsome neighbor. One night as the neighbor
visits her, he is killed by intruders. The woman and the maid must
remove the body. The following day the woman is stunned as the "dead
man" greets her. She confesses her affair to her husband and enters
a convent. The "death" remains unexplained, the story is supposedly
"true."

"Justa y Rufina," in Relaciones. In Obras completas. Madrid:
Mellado, 1857 (published with "Más largo es el tiempo que la
fortuna," "No transige la conciencia," "La flor de las ruinas," "El
ex-voto," "Los dos amigos," "La hija del sol"). (In Obras completas,
ed. José María Castro y Calvo, Biblioteca de Autores Españoles,
vol. 137, Madrid: Atlas, 1961, pp. 305-322.)
    With this relación Fernán expresses the idea that one's
character is genetically transmitted. The good (as Justa) are from

good mothers and will in turn give birth to good children. The same
is true for those of bad character (as Rufina). Nothing but nothing
can change them, not surroundings, nor finances, nor good fortune.
Other favorite themes which appear are 1) the Christian death and 2)
the eventual punishment of those who are evil.

Lady Virginia. In Obras completas. Madrid: Establecimiento
Tipográfico F. de P. Mellado, 1858 (published with Un verano en
Bornos). (In Obras completas, ed. José María Castro y Calvo,
Biblioteca de Autores Españoles, vol. 138, Madrid: Atlas, 1961,
pp. 209-228.)
    Lady Virginia is a short novel which treats an English woman who
becomes involved with an influential man in order to aid her husband's political career. As a result the woman has an illegitimate
son whom she entrusts to a friend. When the son learns of his background, he travels to Spain where he commits suicide. Her husband
dead, Lady Virginia also visits Spain, learns of her son's tragic
end, and converts to Catholicism. The novel attacks political
machinations, British life, and the Protestant religion.

Lágrimas. Corrected edition. Cádiz: Librería Español y
Extrangera de A. de Carlos, 1853, 364 pp. (In Obras completas, ed.
José María Castro y Calvo, Biblioteca de Autores Españoles, vol.
137, Madrid: Atlas, 1961, pp. 103-232.)
    The author bases this novel of customs on the theme that money
wields an undue influence in Spanish society. What was once noble is
replaced by a new order of riches rather than one of honor. Other
social phenomena against which Fernán speaks in this novel are 1)
the manner in which mothers raise their daughters and 2) the low
esteem Spaniards have for their traditions contrasted with their high
praise for things foreign. There are textual references to characters of La gaviota and there is a more faithful rendering of local
speech patterns.

"Lucas García," in Cuadros de costumbres. Obras completas. Madrid:
 Establecimiento Tipográfico F. de P. Mellado, 1857, 360 pp.
(published with "Simón Verde," "Más vale honor que honores," "Obrar
bien que Dios es Dios," "El dolor es una agonía sin muerte").
(In Obras completas, ed. José María Castro y Calvo, Biblioteca de
Autores Españoles, vol. 139, Madrid: Atlas, 1961, pp. 196-226.)
    The author shows how a family is nearly ruined by a "free" woman.
The mother dies of a broken heart, the father takes to drink and must
sell his lands, the daughter becomes the mistress of a colonel. Only
the son Lucas preserves that which is good, right, and true (although
he is quite judgmental and most unforgiving). The descriptions of
houses and people are vague and stereotyped.

"Magdalena," note by Fernando Gabriel de Gabriel y Ruiz Apodaca.
Sevilla: Gironés y Orduña, 1878, 37 pp. (published with "Estar de
más"). (In Obras completas, ed. José María Castro y Calvo,
Biblioteca de Autores Españoles, vol. 137, Madrid: Atlas, 1961,
pp. 375-383.)
    This relación introduces an English lord who meets then seduces
Magdalena. To restore the family's honor, her brother kills the
Englishman and is hanged. In the romantic finale set at midnight
Magdalena's corpse lies stretched out at the foot of the gallows.

The servants in the story resemble the criada and gracioso of Golden Age plays. Another reminder of these plays is the theme of honor.

"Más largo es el tiempo que la fortuna," in Relaciones. In Obras completas. Madrid: Mellado, 1857 (published with "Justa y Rufina," "No transige la conciencia," "La flor de las ruinas," "El ex-voto," "Los dos amigos," "La hija del sol"). (In Obras completas, ed. José María Castro y Calvo, Biblioteca de Autores Españoles, vol. 137, Madrid: Atlas, 1961, pp. 325-345.)

Based on a proverb, this relación shows that 1) crimes are solved with time and 2) justice is met. The crime is the murder of an old man for his money. The criminal flees to the New World where he changes his name and through wealth becomes a respected member of society. Returning to Spain he is recognized and accused of murder. Fleeing again to the New World, he meets his death. The author shows her unfavorable opinion of the New World and condemns the judicial process in Spain. She builds her story around incredible circumstances.

"Más vale honor que honores," in Cuadros de costumbres. Obras completas. Madrid: Establecimiento Tipográfico F. de P. Mellado, 1857, 360 pp. (published with "Simon Verde," "Lucas García," "Obrar bien que Dios es Dios," "El dolor es una agonía sin muerte"). (In Obras completas, ed. José María Castro y Calvo, Biblioteca de Autores Españoles, vol. 139, Madrid: Atlas, 1961, pp. 159-192.)

Another local color sketch which could be classed as a short story or relación, "Más vale ..." shows how attitude and character rather than bloodlines make a person honorable. The story is romantic in that it treats an abandoned baby, recognition by the father 20 years later, and a love triangle in which the young man wins the girl he wants. The local color scenes present the family gathering in the evening. The author speaks out against frivolity and wealth while she exalts the basic values held by the common people.

"No transige la conciencia," in Relaciones. In Obras completas. Madrid: Mellado, 1857 (published with "Justa y Rufina," "Más largo es el tiempo que la fortuna," "La flor de las ruinas," "El ex-voto," "Los dos amigos," "La hia del sol"). (In Obras completas, ed. José María Castro y Calvo, Biblioteca de Autores Españols, vol. 137, Madrid: Atlas, 1961, pp. 253-271.)

With a baby taken from a hospice, a young woman convinces her husband who had been on assignment in Havana the child is his. Before she dies her conscience has her reveal the truth. The husband in turn guards the truth from the boy. When the husband is on his deathbed he intends to tell the child but cannot when he sees how the child has become as close to him as his other two sons. The idea of the Christian death repeats itself; also the themes of woman's treachery. Fernán may attribute this in part to the woman's English parentage.

"La noche de Navidad," in Obras completas. Madrid: Establecimiento Tipográfico de F. de P. Mellado, 1857, 371 pp. (published with Elia; o España treinta años ha, "El último consuelo," "El día de Reyes"). (In Obras completas, ed. José María Castro y Calvo, Biblioteca de Autores Españoles, vol. 139, Madrid: Atlas, 1961, pp. 248-253.)

This <u>relato breve</u> resembles a local color sketch in that it depicts an idyllic celebration of Christmas eve. Children and adults sing or recite appropriate songs or stories. The maid, Tía Pavona, a crusty old woman embittered by the loss of her sons in the war with Napoleon, is better developed than many of Fernán's characters. The thin story line concerns the retrieval of an abandoned child by the hostess of the party.

"Obrar bien...que Dios es Dios," in <u>Cuadros de costumbres. Obras completas</u>. Madrid: Establecimeinto Tipográfico F. de P. Mellado, 1857, 360 pp. (published with "Simón Verde," "Más vale honor que honores," "Lucas García, "El dolor es una agonía sin muerte"). (In <u>Obras completas</u>, ed. José María Castro y Calvo, Biblioteca de Autores Españoles, vol. 139, Madrid: Atlas, 1961, pp. 229-234.)
     A girl on the point of being raped protects herself by repeating three proverbs given her by the parish priest. The priest in turn is threatened by the would-be rapist but the latter has a change of heart. According to the author this is a true account told her by the priest to whom it had occurred.

<u>Obras completas</u>. 19 vols. Madrid: Mellado, 1855-1858. (2nd ed., 16 vols. Madrid: Mellado, 1861-1864) (14 vols. Madrid: Sanez de Jubera, 1865-1893) 17 vols. in Colección de escritores españoles. Madrid: Sucesores de Rivadeneyra, 1893-1914) (17 vols. Madrid: Rubiños, Romero, 1905-1921) (Ed. José María Castro y Calvo. Biblioteca de Autores Españoles, vols. 136-140, Madrid: Atlas, 1961.)
     The different editions follow no specific pattern for the presentation of this author's work. There is even disagreement about the classification of some of the minor works. The first edition is not readily accessible, although some of its volumes are. The most recent edition (1961, Castro y Calvo, BAE) is the most accessible but inadequate. The editor has written a lengthy introduction. The few notes which are included treat vocabulary. An appendix contains Ochoa's comments in which he compares Fernán Caballero to Walter Scott.

<u>Pobre Dolores</u>. In <u>Cuadros de costumbres populares andaluces</u>. Sevilla: Librería Español y Extrangera de J. M. Geofrín, 1852 (also includes <u>La noche de Navidad</u>, <u>Un verano en Bornos</u>, <u>El día de Reyes</u>, El ex-voto). (In <u>Obras completas</u>, ed. José María Castro y Calvo, Biblioteca de Autores Españoles, vol. 137 Madrid: Atlas, 1961, pp. 389-425.)
     Set in a small Andalusian town so favored by the author, this short novel presents Dolores, one of Fernán's ideal women: humble, religious, self-sacrificing, who stoically accepts her fate. The lengthy beginning contains many songs, proverbs, and anecdotes. The plot, when it unfolds, treats the fateful shooting of Dolores' brother by her fiancé who wrongfully suspects the brother to be her lover. There are comments by the author about the injustices of war and those of the military draft.

<u>Un servilón y un liberalito; o tres almas de Dios</u>. Prologue by Antonio Aparisi y Guijarro, Madrid: F. P. de Mellado, 12857, 205 pp. (The newest edition was published in Puerto de Santa María, Spain: Casa de Cultura, 1975, 99 pp.)

Classified as a short novel, Un servilón shows how a young man who expresses liberal views must seek refuge in the castle of Menester where a loyalist family cares for him. In spite of the collisions of opinion regarding the King and the Constitution, or religion and superstitious tradition, a bond of human caring develops. Several years later the young man returns to the castle, befriends the surviving benefactors, and reveals a complete change in his political philosophy. The author seems to say that liberalism, an aberration of youth, will pass with age.

"Simón Verde," in Cuadros de costumbres. Obras completas. Madrid: Establecimiento Tipográfico de F. de P Mellado, 1857, 360 pp. (published with "Más honor que honores," "Lucas García," "Obrar bien que Dios es Dios," and "El dolor es una agonía sin muerte"). (In Obras completas, ed. José María Castro y Calvo, Biblioteca de Autores Españoles, vol. 139, Madrid: Atlas, 1961, pp. 81-115.)
    Called a local color sketch, Simón Verde also could be classified as a relación, or a short story. Its only distinguishing difference is a lengthy and more idyllic description of the campo. The good hearted Simón, who carries out charitable acts at the expense of his family, is contrasted with the mayor, who is out for profit. The first part contains many sayings, anecdotes, songs; the second presents Simón's misfortunes and the pure love between his daughter and the mayor's son.

"El último consuelo," in Obras completas. Madrid: Establecimiento Tipográfico de don Francisco de P. Mellado, 1857, 371 pp. (published with Elia; o España treinta años ha, "La noche de Navidad," "El día de Reyes"). (In Obras completas, ed. José María Castro y Calvo, Biblioteca de Autores Españoles, vol. 139, Madrid: Atlas, 1961, pp. 121-155.)
    A mercifully short sketch which shows how a son who follows wanton ways returns to the Catholic faith as he dies in quicksand, his fingers forming the sign of the cross. His sorrowing mother finds consolation in this.

Una en otra. Prologue by Juan Eugenio Hartzenbusch, Obras completas. Madrid: Establecimiento Tipográfico de Mellado, 1856, 192 pp. (published with Con mal o bien a los tuyos te ten). (In Obras completas, ed. José María Castro y Calvo, Biblioteca de Autores Españoles, vol. 138, Madrid: Atlas, 1961, pp. 239-293.)
    This is a well-structured epistolary novel written under the pretext of providing a young Frenchman a more accurate description of Spain. Rather than presenting descriptions, the letters reveal two stories: the first centers around the love the correspondent, Javier Barrea, has for Castita; the second treats the unfortunate circumstances which befall a family with whom the correspondent's uncle is acquainted. The author would have us believe that these misfortunes result when a daughter goes against her father's wishes and marries a man deigned unsuitable.

Un verano en Bornos. In Cuadro de costumbres populares andaluces. Sevilla: Librería Español y Estrangera de J. M. Geofrín, 1852 (also includes La noche de Navidad, El día de Reyes, Pobre Dolores, El ex-voto). (In Obras completas, ed. José María Castro y Calvo Biblioteca de Autores Españoles, vol. 138, Madrid: Atlas, 1961, pp.

145-205.)
    An epistolary novel in which two sisters vacationing in Bornos
fall in love with men who mirror their character: one is retiring,
the other more social. The young men are friends and one of them is
related to a friend of the sisters. There is a great deal of
description especially of homes and gardens.

Vulgaridad y nobleza. Sevilla: E. do Rojas, 1860, 97 pp. (bound
with Deudas pagadas). (In Obras completas, ed. José María Castro y
Calvo, Biblioteca de Autores Españoles, vol. 138, Madrid: Atlas,
1961, pp. 395-420.)
    Vulgaridad y nobleza repeats favorite themes of Fernán Caballero:
1) the humble and God-fearing are the most noble people, 2) money
drives men to crime, 3) the Spanish court system is ineffectual,
4) evildoers will eventually be punished, 5) those who return to
Spain from the New World are ill-mannered. The narrative begins with
a lengthy description of an Andalusian town, proceeds by contrasting
noble with vile people, and concludes with a rapid series of coincidences.

                                                                MM

BOIXADOS, María Dolores (192?-).
    She was born in Sort (Lérida) in the 1920's. She studied medicine,
worked in a bank, and was a music enthusiast. She married in 1946 and
moved to Venezuela and in 1959 to Oak Ridge, Tennessee. She has helped
her husband with cancer research. Her novel Aguas muertas was a
finalist for the first Nadal Prize (in 1945, won by Carmen Laforet). In
1966 she won the "Premio Don Quijote" in Mexico for her novel Retorno.
Chronologically, she belongs to the "generación de la posguerra," but
her literary career seems to have ceased. A book announced to appear,
Niños abandonados en el mundo, does not show up in any sources.

Aguas muertas. Madrid: Punta Europa, 1970, 203 pp.
    This novel was a finalist for the first Nadal Prize of 1945, which
was awarded to Carmen Laforet for Nada. The book remained unpublished until 1970. In the note to the publisher the author states
that she wrote it when she was 20 years old (which puts her birth
date in the 1920's). Narrated in third person, it is the story of a
young woman from Alicante, Elena Just, who comes to Madrid to study.
The novel takes place in the years after the Civil War in a residence
for women. The protagonist is a shy, withdrawn person who becomes
obsessed with some letters, which she finds in her room, written by a
former student, Juana. The style is somewhat dated and unoriginal.
The use of adjectives is excessive. It would be interesting, however, to compare it with Nada.

Balada de un músico. Colección Orbita de Novela. Madrid:
Quevedo, 1968, 228 pp.
    This novel reflects the musical interest of the author. It is the
story of a pianist, Señor Mases, who plays at a cafe in Barcelona in
the years before the Civil War. The descriptions of the political
times and the characters: the old monarquist, his granddaughter and
the protagonist's dutiful wife are of interest. There is symbolism
between the bloody events which are taking place and the symphony
which Señor Mases is writing. It is the best of Boixadós novels
annotated here.

Retorno. Oaxaca, México: España Errane, 1967, 407 pp.
     This novel won the "Premio Don Quijote" of 1966 in México.
Divided in 24 chapters in traditional form, it contains two different
narrative lines. One takes place in Pueblo, a fictitious town in
Catalonia after the Civil War. The other, narrated in first person
and printed in cursive, is the story of a woman from Spain who lives
in the South of the United States. An unrealistic element is present
in this narrative which contrasts with the sordid life in Spain. The
novel presents an interesting view of life in the United States as
seen by an immigrant.

                                                                    CA

BORBON, María Luisa (1662-1689). Also: **María Luisa de Orleans.**
     Nothing has yet been written on María Luisa de Orleans, niece of
King Louis of France, who was married against her will to Charles II,
the last of the Habsburg kings of Spain. She was the daughter of Philip
d'Orleans and Henriette of England. She was born in Paris on March 27,
1662. Her marriage to Charles II took place on August 31, 1679 in
Fontainebleau and the Veiling ceremony took place at a nuptial mass in
Quintanapalla on November 18 of the same year. Immediately after the
marriage, María Luisa encountered the hostility not only of the Queen
Mother, but of other members of the Habsburg family. Louis XIV had high
hopes for his niece, María Luisa. His secret plan was that immediately
after the marriage he would announce the transfer of the rights to the
Spanish throne to his grandson, Philip, Duke of Anjou, the second son of
the Dauphin. He based his claim through his wife, Maria Theresa, sister
of Charles II of Spain. However, this was contrary to Louis XIV's
marriage contract, which stated no Bourbon should succeed to the throne
of Spain. Based on the memoirs and documents of the first two years in
Spain, she was considered a pleasant and gracious child, but hardly
prepared to play such a difficult role. Her presence on the throne did
not further the designs of the Bourbons. Superficial, frivolous and
coquettish, María Luisa played her part very badly. Rejected,
surrounded by intrigue and the hostility of the military, she quickly
took a dislike to her husband and Spain. María Luisa, although she was
a faithful consort to King Charles and procured for him the few happy
moments of his life, was subjected to tyranny on the part of a jealous
and treacherous entourage. (A. Legrelle, The Death of María Louise,
pp. 276-7.) The Habsburgs, headed by the Queen Mother, wished to get
rid of her and marry Charles II to his first cousin, María Antonia, but
after the Bavarian marriage of 1685 this substitution was no longer
possible, and thereafter the Queen's enemies were not satisfied until
they had destroyed her. The treatment she received was remarkable even
in the history of European dynasties. Her two favorite parrots were
strangled because they spoke French; her French servants were sent away;
letters were forged with the intention of proving that she had been
guilty of a liaison with a guardsman, and, last insult of all, she was
declared the cause of Charles's having no heir. Disillusioned and
isolated at court, she died an unhappy death on February 12, 1689 at "El
Escorial." The defenders of the unfortunate queen brought out an
entirely romanticized version of her death and it is impossible to try
to separate the authentic part from that of their imagination. For
instance, did her enemies poison her? For what purpose? Her contemporaries, the French court and and Saint Simon believed that she was
poisoned by the Habsburgs Austrians, whose designs she thwarted and
hence, incurred their enmity. Legrelle prefers the thesis that the

crime was engineered by a group of Spaniards who blamed the queen for
her sterility and inability to provide a Spanish heir. Powerful drugs
were administered to her for the purpose of producing childbirth, and
these had the effect, whether intentional or accidental is not certain,
of causing her death.

Cartas familiares á Carlos II. 1679. Biblioteca Nacional. Mss. P.
V.4.0.C.1. Núms. 3y5.

EM-L

BRAVO-VILLASANTE ARENAS, Carmen (1918-).
Born in Madrid, her biographies of literary figures include Bettina
Brentano, Juan Valera, Pardo Bazán, La Avellaneda, Galdós, Heinrich
Von Kleist, E.T.A. Hoffmann. On feminine topics she has authored
studies of women disguised as men in Golden Age Comedia; and collections
of women's letters. Interested in children's literature, she has
participated and served as panelist in International Congresses of youth
literature. She is the author of histories and anthologies of children's literature as well as a compilator of children's folklore in a
book of short stories and in a collection of nineteenth century riddles.

Adivina, adivinanza. Folklore infantil. Madrid: Interducschroedel,
1978, ISBN 84-388-:651-1, 80 pp.

El alucinante mundo de E.T.A. Hoffmann. Madrid: Nostromo, 1973,
185 pp.

Antología de la Literatura Infantil Española. Vols. I y II.
Madrid: Doncel, 1963. 2a ed., Madrid: Doncel, 1966, 2 vols.
Madrid: Doncel, 1973, 3 vols.

Antología de la Literatura Infantil Universal. Madrid: Doncel,
1971, 309 pp.

Biografía de don Juan Valera. Barcelona: Aedos, 1959, 366 pp.
Vida de don Juan Valera. 2a ed., Madrid: Magisterio Español, 1974,
Novelas y Cuentos, #142, ISBN 84-265-7145-X, 312 pp.

Biografía y Literatura. Barcelona: Plaza y Janés, 1969, 222 pp.

Cuentos fantásticos. E. Santillana, 1970.

Galdós visto por sí mismo. Madrid: E.M.E.S.A., 1970, 316 pp.
Madrid: Magisterio Español, 1976, ISBN 84-265-70674, 318 pp.

Historia de la Literatura Infantil Española. Madrid: Revista de
Occidente, 1959. Madrid: Doncel, 1963. Madrid: Doncel, 1972.

Historia de la Literatura Infantil Universal. Madrid: Doncel, 1962.
Literatura infantil universal. Madrid: Almena, 1978, ISBN
84-701-40175.

Historia y Antología de la Literatura Infantil Iberoamericana.
Vols. I y II. Madrid: Doncel, 1966.

La mujer vestida de hombre en el teatro español. Siglos XVI y XVII.
Madrid: Revista de Occidente, 1955, 238 pp. 2nd ed. Madrid:
S.G.E.L., 1976, ISBN 84-7143-1068, 191 pp.

Veinticinco mujeres a través de sus cartas. Madrid: Almena, 1975,
ISBN 84-701-41643, 225 pp.

Vida de Bettina Brentano. Barcelona: Aedos, 1957, 314 pp.
   Premio de Biografías Aedos 1956.

Vida de un poeta: Heinrich Von Kleist. Madrid: Prensa Española,
1971, 234 pp. Colección Vislumbres, #24.

Una vida romántica: la Avellaneda. Barcelona: E.D.H.A.S.A., 1967,
251 pp.
Gertrudis Gómez de Avellaneda. Madrid: Fundación Universitaria
Española, 1974, ISBN 84-600-6223-6, 80 pp.

Vida y obra de Emilia Pardo Bazán. Madrid: Revista de Occidente,
1962, 393 pp. Madrid: E.M.E.S.A., 1973, Novelas y Cuentos, 2nd
época, #134, ISBN 84-265-7135-2.

                                                                    PS

BURGOS SEGUI, Carmen (1867-1932). Pseud. **Colombine.**
   A multifaceted figure with a strong social commitment, Carmen de
Burgos was a single parent, a teacher, a reporter and a writer of both
fiction and prose. She was an ardent fighter for women's rights and
published the first public survey on divorce in Spain. She had a daily
newspaper column directed to women. As an active participant in the
struggle for the vote for women, she led many marches and also wrote La
mujer moderna y sus derechos (1927) an important treatise on the status
of women throughout the world which predates De Beauvoir's The Second
Sex. From 1907 she contributed extensively to the many short story
magazines that flourished during this period. Her long-standing
relationship with Ramón Gómez de la Serna was one of love and mutual
intellectual inspiration. Her home was a salon to many of the literary
figures of the moment, such as R. Cansinos Assens, Felipe Trigo, A.
González Blanco. She translated Leopardi, Ruskin and other writers,
wrote biography and essay and founded La Revista Crítica in support of
the Jews in Spain and throughout the world. Her bibliography includes
hundreds of newspaper articles, more than 50 short stories, essays, and
speeches, novels, biographies and many practical books for women. Her
rich, varied and extensive contribution is an important facet of Spain's
history that is quite unknown and demands further study.

Los anticuarios. Madrid: Biblioteca Nueva, sf.
   Novel.

"El artículo 438". Madrid: Prensa Gráfica, 1921. Also in Mis
mejores cuentos. Madrid: Prensa Popular, 1923, pp. 7-42.
   Taking its title from the part of the Spanish Civil Code that
refers to adultery, this short story shows the victimization and
murder of a wife by her unscrupulous husband. He is vindicated by a
jury of his peers for having defended his "honor." The author uses a
fairly typical situation between husbands and wives of the Spanish
middle class to criticize the unequal treatment of women before the

law. She also expresses very advanced ideas on love, motherhood and the role of the Church. Available in hardcover from interlibrary loan.

Cuentos de Colombine. Valencia: Sempere, 1908.
    Collection of 16 short stories.

Ellas y ellos, o ellos y ellas. Madrid: Alrededor del Mundo, 1917.
    Short story collection. Contains: "Ellas y ellos o ellos y ellas," "Lo inesperado," "La travesía," "Una bomba," "El perseguidor."

En la guerra. Valencia: Sempere, 1908, subsequent editions 1912 and 1918.
    Short story collection. Contains: "En la guerra," "La indecisa," "Siempre en tierra," "La justicia del mar," "El veneno del arte," "El honor de la familiar."

Los endemoniados de Jaca. Madrid: Novelas y Cuentos, 1932.
    Novel.

Los espirituados. Madrid: Sucesores de Rivadeneyra, 1923.
    Novel.

La hora del amor. Madrid: V. H. de Sanz Calleja, 1917.
    Short story collection. Contains: "La hora del amor," "Don Manolito," "Villa María," "Sorpresas."

Los inadaptados. Valencia: F. Sempere, 1909, 209 pp.
    A novel of local color and the customs of the isolated region of the Valley of Rodalquilar in Almeria, Spain, the childhood home of the author. It depicts the schism between official Spain and the autonomous local leaders. The abuse of the wife and honor of the headman leads to the death of the visiting landowner. As in Fuente-ovejuna, the villagers close ranks in defense of their own.

La malcasada. Valencia: Sempere, 1923.
    Novel.

Mis mejores cuentos. Madrid: Prensa Popular, 1923.
    Short story collection. Contains: "El artículo 438," "El abogado," "El novenario," "Los huesos del abuelo," "La mujer fría."

Quiero vivir mi vida. Madrid: Biblioteca Nueva, 1931, 249 pp.
    This novel integrates the current ideas on psychology and sexuality, particularly those of Gregorio Marañón, who introduces the book. It is a study of the psychological and physical breakdown of a middle-class woman who cannot come to terms with the restrictions inherent in her role as a wife in bourgeois Spanish society. Unable to break the bonds of a conventional male/female relationship, she kills her husband in the quest for the "soul" of a man. Available in hardcover through interlibrary loan.

La rampa. Madrid: Renacimiento, 1917, 249 pp.
     This novel is dedicated to "all the destitute and disoriented
women" who sought advice from the author on how to proceed in life.
It contains an extensive and detailed description of a lower middle-
class woman who does not have the practical skills to maintain
herself. It shows the cruelty of big city life (Madrid) through the
humiliation and suffering of its main character, while touching on
the difficulties of many other women. It is a cry of rage at the
treatment of these women by Spanish society. Contains list of works
by the author.

El retorno; novela espiritista. Lisboa: Lusitania Ed., 192?.

El tío de todos. Barcelona: Ribas y Ferrer, 1925.
     Novel.

El último contrabandista. Barcelona: Ramón Sopena, sf.
     Novel.

                                                              ES

C

CABALLERO, Fernán. See: Böhl de Faber, Cecilia.

*CABRE DE CALDERO, María.
A poet, born in Reus, she wrote <u>Espurnes</u> in 1978 and <u>Pingellades</u> in 1981, both published in Reus.

KM

*CAIMARI, Margalida (1839-1921).
A poet born in Majorca, she lived for a long while in Bolivia. Her work appeared in collections such as <u>Calendari Català</u> and <u>Lo gay saber</u> in the 1880's. Her story inspired one of the characters in Maria-Antònia Oliver's <u>Crònica de la molt anomenada ciutat de Montcarrà</u>.

KM

CAJAL, Rosa Maria (1920-).
Born in Zaragoza, Cajal felt her literary vocation as a child. She went to work in offices, but during that period wrote many stories and novels "for practice," with no intention of publishing them. She then began publishing stories in various magazines. She won third prize in a Zarzuela libretto contest and was also a finalist for the Premio Gijón for short novels in 1951.

El acecho. Madrid: Bullón, 1963, 289 pp.

Juan Risco. Barcelona: Destino, 1948, 233 pp.
An existentialist novel, in which the protagonist bitterly with-draws from human society. Only the neighbors' young daughter is able to establish contact with him. He helps Susana, a young woman down on her luck, and she falls in love with him, but he insists he is worthless. He cynically arranges for her to meet an editor, who will be her next lover. When the editor's wife Cristina dies, Risco's past is revealed: He had been Cristina's husband, a famous journ-alist, but had faked his own suicide and taken on another identity in order to free Cristina. However, it is evident that the new identity is a lack of identity, an emptiness which cannot be called life.

Un paso más. Barcelona: Garbo, 1956, 235 pp.
This novel tackles a unique topic for the period: the young woman who leaves her village to build a career in business in the city. Despite conflicting emotions on her departure, she seeks independence and, despite self-doubts, proves stronger than the men and other

women against whom she is juxtaposed. As a successful bookstore owner, she gives a job to a male friend and serves as his mother figure but does not return his love. Women friends and relatives are weak, dependent and shallow; but the protagonist takes step after step - in personal life and in business - until she becomes a complete woman.

Primera derecha. Barcelona: L. de Ceralt, 1955, 206 pp.
A finalist for the Premio Ciudad de Barcelona, this novel depicts the life of a matriarch, Mamá Petra, who lives for her children, her husband (in her eyes another child) and her home. Throughout the novel, she is never shown doing anything outside the four walls of her house. After seven children and two miscarriages, motherhood is her very being.

CLG

CALVO DE AGUILAR, Isabel (1916-).
During six years, Isabel Calvo de Aguilar was the President of the "Asociación de escritoras españolas," an association which she founded in the 1950's. Around that time she also edited her important work, Antología biográfica de escritoras españolas, to disprove the allegation that there were no contemporary Spanish women authors of note. As a novelist, the author's aim has been to entertain a wide public. To achieve this, she combines love stories with fantastic adventures, exotic settings, intrigue and crime.

Antología biográfica de escritoras españolas. Madrid: Biblioteca Nueva, 1954, 892 pp.

La danzarina inmóvil. Madrid: Rumbos, 1954, 236 pp.
The story takes place in New York and unfolds in flashbacks as various family members and friends of a murdered ballerina testify in a hearing. It evolves that, just as in Doce sarcófagos de oro, the husband wanted to preserve the dancer's beauty eternally. This novel presents the Pygmalion theme in reverse: the artist changes his wife, the ballet dancer, into a statue in order to immortalize her poise and grace. This novel is a good example of the Gothic elements in Isabel Calvo de Aguilar's novels. Available through interlibrary loan. In its Portuguese translation, the novel went through two editions.

Doce sarcófagos de oro. Madrid: Rumbos, 160 pp.
Like Calvo de Aguilar's other novel with an oriental background (El misterio del palacio chino), this work was broadcast on the radio and in addition it was also made into a movie by a German producer. Though the setting is Granada, Spain, exotic and oriental aspects predominate when the protagonist discovers that his fiancée's uncle is neither deaf nor mute as he pretends to be, but rather a demoniacal madman who kills and embalms the beautiful girl he brings back from his travels to the Far East. Prefaced by excerpts from book reviews praising the novel; copy available only from the author.

La isla de los siete pecados. Madrid: Rumbos, 1951, 175 pp.
2nd ed. Madrid: Rumbos, 1952, 175 pp.
Unhappy love is the catalyst of this novel in which unrequited

love is analyzed from various points of view. There is also a
romantic novel-within-the-novel which exerts considerable influence
on the protagonist, himself a writer. Though set in modern Spain,
the second half of the book moves beyond realism into the realm of
imagination and fantasy with the adventures of a woman reporter and
self-styled detective. Foreword by the author; copy available at the
Biblioteca Nacional in Madrid.

El misterio del palacio chino. Madrid: Reus, 1951, 173 pp.
    Like all of Calvo de Aguilar's novels, this is light reading for
entertainment. As the author points out in her Prologue, her only
wish is to make the reader spend a pleasant hour. El misterio del
palacio chino is a love story in the form of a Chinese legend. The
novel ends tragically because the prophecy that no first-born of the
Lotus Palace could ever be happy in love is fulfilled. In this work
the author makes successful use of local color and in general manages
to capture the oriental flavor. Author's Prologue; copy available at
the Biblioteca del Ateneo in Madrid.

El monje de los Balkanes. Madrid: ed. Rumbos.

El numismático. Madrid: ed. Rumbos.

                                                                A-MA

CAMPO ALANGE, Condesa de. See: LAFITTE PEREZ DEL PULGAR, María de los
Reyes.

*CANALIAS, Anna (1886-1934).
    A poet born in Zaragoza, she wrote books entitled Líriques, Natura,
Sonets erudits and Poesies.

                                                                  KM

CANELO GUTIERREZ, Pureza (1946-).
    Pureza Canelo, a precocious poet (she won the coveted Premio Adonais
when she was 24) writes a kind of poetry which, if stemming from the
vanguardist thrust, is quite unusual in the present day panorama. In
her approach to creation, Canelo ignores tradition, as Gerardo Diego
puts it, she "has invented a grammar and a syntax" which never
correspond to logic but are true albeit mysterious; "everything makes
sense only within the poem" says the poet herself. She deepens our
understanding of the myriad of facets of the poetic word, and makes her
reader dive into the hidden mechanics of language.

El barco de agua. Madrid: Cultura Hispánica, 1974, ISBN
84-7232-227-0, 138 pp.
    This is the third book written by Canelo, and it shows the
coherent line of development of her poetic thrust. The main theme
continues to be, as in her previous creations, the quest within self
and universe by means of the poetic word. Poetry becomes here the
subject of the poet's reflections to the point almost of an obsession. She centers all her energy on the understanding of her own
poetry; paradigmatically she is reflecting on the universal power of
poetry. Rather than experience itself, her words call forth the
readiness for experience in a nascent moment which has not yet been
fixed in orderly words.

Celda verde, Colección Poesía. Madrid: Editora Nacional, 1971,
116 pp.
    This is the first book written by the author. In it poetry
emerges as the result of the encounter between the poet and the
universe; it possesses the freshness of spontaneity and inspiration,
and there is no longing for understanding, only for recognition of
life. This poetry, nonetheless, already shows the new approach that
has singled out Canelo among the younger Spanish poets: there is a
lack of logical order, and the semantic significance is surprisingly
fluctuating. The book includes several poems from her adolescence
which point to the continuous line of development of her particular
kind of creation.

Habitable (Primera Poética). Madrid: Rialp, 1979,
ISBN 84-321-1978-4, 88 pp.
    As its title suggests, this book represents a tenacious search on
the part of the poet for the essence of poetry, using as an instrument for this analysis the poetic word itself. Apparently floating
words, which are not anchored by a logical order, force the poet and
the reader to constant adjustment; the result is complex, often
obscure; it may seem a random gathering of words lacking the order of
syntax and with dubious semantic value. But allowing thought and
association to emerge, it is clear that both lucidity and inspiration
bring forth this new daring poetry.

Lugar Común, Colección Adonais. Madrid: Rialp, 1971, 82 pp.
    The poet wrestles with poetry as a force which engulfs her. She
appears both as an instrument of poetry which overcomes her, and the
creator of this work which expresses her. Canelo discovers life and
discovers herself as part of life, there is no sense of isolation or
solitude but a constant recognition of universe, always by means of
the poetic word as an instrument of analysis and a way of existence.
This work won the Adonais prize for its author in 1971, and caused
a considerable stir due to its unconventional use of language.

                                                            M-EB

*CANYA I MARTI, Llucieta (1898-).
    Born in la Bisbal d'Empordà, she wrote plays and poetry.

L'amor té cops amagats. 1954.
    Drama.

L'estudiant de Girona. 1935.
    Drama.

Caixa de núvia. 1933.
    Poetry.

Mare. 1929.
    Poetry.

                                                            KM

*CANYELLES, Antonina (1942-).
Majorcan poet.

Quadern de conseqüències. Palma de Mallorca; ACC, 1980. With
illustrations by Esperança Mestre.
    Very personal poetry, at times looking back at childhood, at times
a poetry of protest. It includes an occasional glimpse of her
Majorcan predecessors Maria-Antònia Salvà and Cèlia Vinyes.

KM

*CAPMANY FARNES, Maria Aurèlia (1918-).
    Born in Barcelona, of a family where all members shared an interest
in intellectual pursuits, she studied in the Institut Escola, the most
liberal and advanced school in pre-war Spain. She graduated from the
Univerity of Barcelona in the post-war era and after teaching for some
years at the University and other schools, decided to devote her time to
writing and the theater. With R. Salvat, she founded the School of
Dramatic Art Adrià Gual, where she acted and directed. She has also
worked for radio and TV and is currently Cultural Counselor for the City
of Barcelona. She has written novels, essays, plays, and has collaborated in newspapers and literary magazines. She has studied, in all
her works, the social condition of women.

MM

L'alt rei en Jaume. Barcelona: Aymà, Quaderns de teatre 31, 1977,
ISBN 84-209-6051-9, 124 pp.
    This play was written as the script for a TV miniseries. As a TV
production, it was provided with excellent medieval atmosphere, with
music composed by Romà Escala. As a regular theater play, it is a
brilliant dramatization of a glorious period of Catalan history: the
life of King James the Conqueror. The work is extremely accurate in
its historical references and in the attitudes and beliefs reflected
in the characters' words. The language is modern, but adapted to the
era represented. Paperback.

MM

L'altra ciutat. Barcelona: Selecta, Bibl. Selecta 181, 1955,
235 pp.
    The "other city" of the title is the city of the past, which lives
again in the mind of Rosa, the main character, when she returns to
the city of her youth, -Tarragona-, the real city, with a group of
her students. Without breaking the narrative of the visit, the past
comes into the present, sometimes brought in by a thought, sometimes
by a simple word, often by the smell or presence of the sea, always
there. The author evokes past and present, bitterness and longing,
and the sadness of realizing that the past is lost forever and that
nothing will ever be the same again. Paperback.

MM

Betùlia. Barcelona: Selecta, Bibl. Selecta 218-219, 1956, 336 pp.
    A city, Betúlia, is the main character in the narrative. There
are, however, no descriptions of streets and parks in the book.
Referring in reality to the city of Badalona, what the author
portrays here is the life and thoughts that accumulate behind the
walls of the city and the faces of its inhabitants. In fact, instead

of conveying the real life of the city or what its men and women
really are, the novel presents what they would like to be and what
they appear to be, and the bitter realization of the impossibility of
their wishes. Paperback.

MM

Ca, barret! (In collaboration with Jaume Vidal Alcover.) Palma de
Mallorca: Francesc de B. Moll, Raixa 136, 1984,
ISBN 84-273-0452-8, 236 pp.
    This is a collection of four "cabaret" plays, in which the
characters, through monologues and songs, criticize contemporary
politics and society. The plays were written twelve years before
their publication, that is to say, during the dictatorship. The
satire, therefore, is often obscurely expressed, but it is always
forceful and amusing. The plays require very simple staging, but are
extremely lively and a good evidence of the constant efforts to
preserve Catalan culture and traditions. There is an introduction by
Capmany, pp. 5-6, and a Preliminary Note by Vidal Alcover, pp. 7-15.
Paperback.

MM

Carta abierta al macho ibérico. Madrid: Ediciones 99, 1973,
114 pp.
    The author's name is given as Campmany for this work. Written in
Castilian, it is part of a series of open letters by various authors
to various Spanish groups or institutions. The series also includes
Carta abierta a TVE by "Campmany." The author poses and attempts to
answer such questions as whether the Iberian male exists or is
extinct; is he exclusively Iberian or does he exist in other indus-
trialized societies; should he be done away with so that women can
live peacefully?

CLG

Cartes impertinents. Palma de Mallorca: Francesc de B. Moll,
Raixa, 1971, 177 pp.
    The book consists of 27 letters written by women from all levels
of society. Through these letters Capmany deals with her main
subject of interest: women and their social standing. The women
that write the letters are of all ages and tendencies; every letter
is a story on its own, either presenting a case for study, or
attacking hypocrisy, or denouncing what old regulations, beliefs and
traditions have meant for women at home and in the world. The sharp
style and ironic criticism are a delight for the reader, while the
content makes the work essential for all students of sociology and
researchers on the status of women. Paperback.

MM

Lo color més blau. Barcelona: Planeta, Ramon Llull, Sèrie
Novel.la, 1982, ISBN 84-320-3507-6, 246 pp.
    An epistolary novel, on the first level, it deals with the lives
of two women; on a deeper level, with the destruction brought by war
and the pain of defeat. The two women, still in their school years,
are separated in 1939: one of them, from a Communist, militant
family, goes to exile; the other, member of a middle-class, conventional family, remains in the city. Through their letters the reader
knows their lives, and the indecisions, weaknesses, and strengths of

husbands, sons, and friends. The circumstances of post-war in the
city and the descriptions of events in the exile should be of
interest to students of Sociology and Political Science. Paperback.
MM

Com una mà. Palma de Mallorca: Francesc de B. Moll, Raixa, 1952,
ISBN 84-273-0096-4, 120 pp.
  A volume of short stories with a variety of styles. In some of
the stories there is a mixture of surrealism and stream of
consciousness, in others a sharp irony, almost a parody of a horror
story. Among the subjects of the stories the reader will find: the
devastating division produced in a family by the Spanish Civil War; a
parody of a scientific lecture, delivered by a mentally ill man; the
life of a woman, disclosed by her interior monologue from the moment
of her birth; a portrait of a man seen by his widow as a saint and as
a devil by the community, etc. Paperback.
MM

Coses i noses. Barcelona: La Magrana. Les ales esteses 2, 1980,
ISBN 84-740-060-7, 213 pp.
  Most of Capmany's short stories are put together in this volume,
representing many years of good work. Most of the main characters in
these stories are women. The stories were written from 1952 to 1980
and one of them, the first in the book, "Uns ulls miren de lluny"
(1975), is remarkable on its own and because it was intended as the
second chapter of a collective novel. Paperback.
MM

El desert dels dies. Barcelona: Occitània, El barret de Danton, 6,
1966, 48 pp. Theater. Out of print.
MM

Dietari de prudéncies. Barcelona: Hogar del Libro, Nova Terra 20,
1982, ISBN 84-7279-123-8, 232 pp.
  Written in the form of monthly entries, or as a monthly "diary,"
about some relevant fact or event of that month (literary, social,
political, familiar or even in the theater or in movies), the book
really deals with ten years of life in Catalonia, from 1970 to 1980.
Through her words, every month is transformed into short narratives,
almost sketches of plays, where all characters are real and some well
known to the reader. Any researcher in contemporary Catalan history
will find here a first-hand source of knowledge. The book has a
prologue-explanation-presentation by the author, pp. 9-11.
Paperback.
MM

Dona, doneta, donota. (In collaboration with Avel.lí Artís-
Gener as illustrator.) Barcelona: EDHASA, El be negre, 1979, ISBN
84-350-0243-8, 166 pp.
  The book is concerned with the fight that women have always had to
undertake to achieve their right place in society. The ideas are
given through the excellent combination of Artís-Gener drawings and
the incisive and ironical wording provided by Capmany. The author
repeats here her idea that the injustice in our society is everywhere
and has chosen irony, and mockery to fight against it. Both the
drawings and the text expose the false premises that society has used

against women, and advises them to fight back using laughter as their weapon, since "laughter is the only weapon for all oppressed peoples." Paperback.

MM

Feliçment, jo sóc una dona. Barcelona: Nova Terra, Actituds 18. 1st. ed. 1969. 2nd ed. 1970. 3rd ed. 1977. ISBN 84-280-0433-1, 276 pp.

This novel is written partly as the autobiography of Carola, the central figure, and partly in third person to emphasize critical points in the development of the narrative. The life of the woman, born in December 31, 1899, is used by Capmany to show, through a woman's eyes, half a century of living through political unrest, strikes, Civil War, and post-war dictatorship. The life of that woman is developed on many different levels, allowing Capmany to describe the situation of women in all levels of society. As often happens in her books, Capmany fights here against hypocrisy, injustice and ignorance. Paperback.

MM

El gust de la pols. Barcelona: Destino, El Doff, 1962, ISBN 84-233-0372-1, 252 pp.

Through flashbacks interwoven in the narrative of contemporary events, diverse characters and their private lives and thoughts appear in a complicated mosaic of facts, ideas, and reflections. The novel is concerned with the difficulty of knowing the real being behind anyone's outside appearance, together with a hard criticism of the false values of the bourgeois society in Catalonia. Interesting for sociologists and for those interested in the evolution of the status of working people and of family customs. Hard cover.

MM

El jaqué de la democràcia. Barcelona: Nova Terra, J.M. 6, 1972, ISBN 84-280-0017-4, 290 pp.

A novel that might be classified as political fiction, its main subject is the fight of the so-called "strong men" against progressive groups. The fight takes place in a fictitious city and country, both, easy to recognize. In the end, the fight wipes out a whole generation and the bullets destroy the democracy's "tuxedo" of the title. The author has used an interesting technique: first we are given some disordered fragments of the novel; then, these fragments are put in order and extended; finally, and as requested by the "author" of the fragments, Capmany writes the novel, collecting all fragments in a harmonious whole and appearing as the transmitter of the facts. Both the originality of the development and the study of characters are remarkable. Paperback.

MM

Un lloc entre els morts. Barcelona: Nova Terra, Actituds 14, 1969, ISBN 84-280-0199-5, 184 pp. Barcelona: Laia, Les Eines 55, 1979, ISBN 84-7222-923-8, 192 pp. Sant Jordi Prize, 1968.

Written as a biography of a fictitious young poet, the novel presents the reader with so much documentation and historical research that the poet seems completely real. There is a strong, hard and forceful criticism in this book of the "bourgeois" society and the men and women that live in it. There is also a powerful

attack directed to two kinds of women often criticized in Capmany's
books: the shallow and vain woman, who uses her sex and her femi-
ninity to achieve her goals; and the apparently honest, sincere, and
religious woman, who is in fact hypocritical in all her acts. The
hardest criticism is directed against the saintly hypocrite, as the
embodiment of the kind of society denounced in the book. Paperback.

MM

El malefici de la reina d'Hongria. With a subtitle "o les aventures
dels tres patrons de nau." Vocabulary of difficult words by
Montserrat Camps i Mundó. Illustrated by Ismael Balanyà.
Barcelona: Barcanova. Lit. Juvenil, Centaure, 1982, ISBN
84-7533-004-5, 125 pp.
   The author places the action of the novel at the end of the
XVIIIth century, when Barcelona tries to recover from destruction and
poverty. The world powers, meanwhile, are fighting for supremacy in
the Mediterranean: the novel, therefore, could very well refer to
the present day. In the narrative, three brothers live through
exciting adventures; one of them, Maciàs, achieves victory without
violence, since he is a peace-loving young man. Based on an old
legend, the novel is realistic, with accurate historical references.
Paperback.

MM

Necessitem morir. Barcelona: Aymà, A tot vent 177, 1977.
2nd ed., ISBN 84-209-4591-9 (paperback), 84-209-4592-7 (hard cover).
   The book begins with a fragment of a poem by Salvat-Papasseit,
from which the title of the novel is derived. Prologue by Joan
Triadú (pp. 7-9) to the first edition and a comment by the author to
the second. The novel, whose publication was not allowed for years
in Franco's time, is developed around Georgina, the mystery of her
birth paralleled in the nebulous possibility of her death at the end
of the book. The central point of the novel is Georgina's need to
escape from all that surrounds her, an escape that is tried by her in
many ways, and always fails. The book portraits an insecure and
fearful woman, destroyed by the cultural, religious and family
traditions that overwhelm her during all her life.

MM

L'ombra de l'escorpí. València: Gorg, Els quaderns 4, 1974,
ISBN 84-8505-013-4, 64 pp. Theater. Out of print.

MM

La pluja als vidres. Barcelona: Club Editor, Club dels Novel.listes
27, 1963, 232 pp.
   Originally the title was El cel no és transparent. It was
awarded the Joanot Martorell Prize, but its publication was forbidden for many years. A well-planned novel, full of interest and
clarity, with good sense for dramatic narrative; an inner tragedy is
presented with sober and clear language. The poignant reality of the
characters is explained by the author in a short prologue: "I knew
all these characters, and I knew them very well." A fragment of real
life is brought to us with painful intensity, but also with hope.
Hard cover.

MM

Preguntes i respostes sobre la vida i la mort de Francesc Layret,
advocat dels obrers de Catalunya. (In collaboration with Xavier
Romeu, in charge of research.) Barcelona: Magrana, La Magrana 4,
1976, ISBN 84-7410-004-6, 94 pp. First edition by Edicions Catalanes
de Paris in 1971, forbidden in Spain at the time, 103 pp.
    A play written to honor the memory of Layret, murdered in 1920,
the "questions" in the title or n.20, 1982, ISBN 84-7279-123-8, 232
pp. Written in the form of monthly entries, or as a monthly "diary,"
about some relevant fact or event of that month (literary, social,
political, familiar or even in the theater or in movies), the book
really deals with ten years of life in Catalonia, from 1970 to 1980.
Through her words, every month is transformed into short narratives,
almost sketches of plays, where all charain "a man and a world." It
is a very realistic play that climaxes in the last scenes, with
Layret's burial and the desolation left by his death. In pp. 87-94
there are biographies of historical figures of the time. Paperback.
                                                                  MM

Quim/Quima. Barcelona: Estela, 1st edition 1971. Ed. Laia, El Nus
13. 2nd ed., 1977, ISBN 84-7222-661-1, 240 pp.
    A prologue by the author in the form of a letter to Virginia Woolf
(pp.5-8) says that she has imitated the idea of Woolf's Orlando. The
change of sex in the hero is here, and also a span of life of hundreds of years, but the similarity ends here. Quim/Quima takes its
hero from the year 1000 to the Spanish Civil War, and in his adventure the history of Catalonia comes alive. Quim/man becomes Quima/
woman and goes back to being a man when injustice, in one form or
another, is too overwhelming to be endured. All through the book a
thought keeps appearing: the only world we have is wonderful, and
should be made fit for living. At the end of the book a chronological tale lists the main events of the hero's life and the contemporary events in Catalonia and the rest of the world. Paperback.
                                                                  MM

Tana o la felicitat. Palma de Mallorca: Francesc B. Moll, Raixa,
1956, ISBN 84-273-0086-7, 112 pp.
    Although the novel is of less extension than the others, the skill
of the author and the interest of the story are not diminished. The
book is centered around Tana's wedding, and both the wedding and the
years before it are seen through the eyes of the family members:
every chapter is thus a deep analysis of each of them, from the
selfish father and the unbelievable submissive mother to the different personalities of brothers and sisters. Tana herself is the
embodiment of strength of will: she knows what she wants and she
goes for it. The bridegroom is never important: the event is Tana's
wedding as a result of Tana's will. An excellent study of a young
woman's strong character. Paperback.
                                                                  MM

Vent de garbí i una mica de por. Dones, flors i pitança. Dos
quarts de cinc. Breu record de Tirant lo Blanc. Palma de Mallorca:
Francesc de B. Moll, Raixa 73, 1968, ISBN 84-273-0161-8, 190 pp.
    Vent de garbí i una mica de por, the first play, is presented as
a comedy. However, the play soon turns to a bitter acknowledgment of
the human nature of the characters, and results in a sharp portrait

of a social class--the Catalan bourgeoisie--that is found lacking in
the moment of need. The play has a prologue by Espriu, pp. 9-11, and
a comment by R. Salvat, pp. 87-94. Dones, flors i pitança is a
satire, denouncing evil both in the knightly medieval times and in
the present day. There is an introduction to the author's theater
work by Jaume Vidal Alcover. The last two plays are very short; one
of them is a dialogue of a couple full of remembrances and
reproaches, the other remembers the hero of the first European novel.
Paperback.

MM

Tu i l'hipòcrita. Palma de Mallorca: Francesc de B. Moll, Raixa
47, 1960, ISBN 84-273-0169-3, 110 pp.
   The play, with a prologue by Gonçal Lloveres, is called "a comedy"
by the author; however, a strong feeling of dramatism is easily
perceived. The main theme of the play is the idea that time, in its
course, binds the individual to his own decisions, made in previous
years. The main character, believing that his present and his future
are the result of his past, does not dare to build for the future,
and even fears the freedom to act. Obviously, there is a reference
to the political atmosphere in which the play was written and a very
ironic treatment of contemporary society. Paperback.

MM

Vés-te'n, ianqui! o, si voleu, traduit de l'americà. Barcelona:
Laia, Les Eines, 1st ed. 1959; 2nd ed. 1980; ISBN 84-7222-929-7,
150 pp.
   As often happens in Capmany's books, two levels can be discerned
in this novel: one, at first reading, shows a mystery/adventure
novel. A young American has disappeared and a special agent is sent
to Albania to follow his tracks. The young man is found, but has
decided to forsake his father's fortune and remain there, to build
his own life. At a deeper level, Capmany describes a small country's
problems and difficulties, one of them being its geographical
situation between two powerful and big nations. The allusion is
unmistakeable, and very artistically developed; the interest is
maintained throughout the book. Paperback.

MM

Vitrines d'Amsterdam. Barcelona: Club Editor, Club dels
Novel.listes, LX, 1970, 176 pp.
   A novel in which mystery and poetic descriptions are combined, the
introduction of "chapter bis," or parallel chapters, is a new device
showing the thoughts of the main character in different moments of
his life. The novel deals with the shock suffered by two brothers,
representative of upper middle class, bourgeois well-to-do Catalonia,
when confronted with the darker side of life in the Amsterdam red-
light district and its inhabitants. The disappearance of one of the
brothers is at the same time the mystery of the novel and the point
of departure of the narrative. Excellent study of personalities, in
both surroundings. Hard cover.

MM

*CARDONA, Fina.
Poet. She published <u>Plouen pigues</u>, Valencia: 3&4, 1978, and
<u>Pessigolla de palmera</u>, St. Boi de Llobregat: May, 1981.

KM

CARO MALLEN DE SOTO, Ana (1569?-after 1645).
A Golden Age Spanish playwright and poet who lived in Sevilla and
Madrid, she was best known during the seventeenth century for her plays.
We preserve two of them: <u>El conde de Partinuplés</u> and <u>Valor, agravio y</u>
<u>mujer</u>. Ana Caro wrote a number of accounts in verse of important events
and celebrations that took place during her lifetime. Although she was
praised by many of her contemporaries, including Vélez de Guevara and
Matos Fragoso, she is virtually unknown today. Not much is known about
her life and only a few scholarly articles have been devoted to her
works.

<u>El conde de Partinuplés</u> in <u>Laurel de comedias de diferentes autores.</u>
<u>Quarta parte.</u> Dirigidas a Don Bernardino Blancalana. Madrid:
Imprenta Real, 1653. Modern edition included in the <u>Biblioteca de</u>
<u>Autores Españoles</u>, Vol. 49. <u>Dramáticos posteriores a Lope de Vega</u>,
ed., Ramón Mesonero Romanos, Madrid: Sucesores de Hernando, 1924,
pp. 125-38.
This virtually forgotten <u>comedia</u> was popular in seventeenth
century Spain. It is based on a romance of chivalry of the same
title. It is also one of many Golden Age plays that utilize a plot
labeled as the Invisible Mistress. In works dealing with this plot,
a man, although moved by a woman's angelic voice or soft touch, is
not allowed to see her. In this play, Princess Rosaura is the
Invisible Mistress. She has been called a <u>mujer esquiva</u> since she
refuses to marry. Her disdain of men is not based on vanity or
pride, but on a prophecy. The atmosphere of romance pervades this
delightful <u>comedia</u> where the magician Aldora is able to bring about a
happy conclusion.

<u>Contexto de las reales fiestas que se hizieron en el Palacio del Buen</u>
<u>Retiro a la coronación de Rey de Romanos, y entrada en Madrid de la</u>
<u>Señora Princesa de Cariñán en tres discursos.</u> Madrid: Imprenta
del Reino, 1637, 39 folios. There is a modern facsimile edition by
Antonio Pérez y Gómez, Valencia: Talleres de Tipografía Moderna,
1951.
These works, of interest primarily to scholars, consist of three
poems describing celebrations at the Buen Retiro to commemorate the
naming of Ferdinand III as Holy Roman Emperor and the arrival of the
Princess of Cariñán in Madrid. As the sister of the Count of
Soissons, this lady was of importance to Spanish politics since her
brother had fought against Cardinal Richelieu. Laudatory commonplaces abound in these poems, including references to Philip IV as
the Sun King and to his minister Olivares as a new Atlas.

<u>Grandiosa vitoria que alcanço de los Moros de Tetuán Iorge de</u>
<u>Mendoça y Piçaña, General de Ceuta, quitándoles gran suma de</u>
<u>ganados cerca de las mesmas puertas de Tetuán.</u> Sevilla: Simón
Faxardo, 1633.
This work has not been reprinted since the seventeenth century and
is of primary interest to scholars. It is described in Manuel
Serrano y Sanz, <u>Apuntes para una biblioteca de escritoras españolas</u>

desde el año 1401 al 1833. Madrid: Atlas, 1975, pp. 213-14.
Loa sacramental, que se representó en el Carro de Antonio de Prado,
en las fiestas del Corpus de Seuilla, este Año de 1639. Sevilla:
Juan Gómez de Blas, n.d.
   This work has not been reprinted since the seventeenth century and
is of primary interest to scholars. It is described in Manuel
Serrano y Sanz, Apuntes para una biblioteca de escritoras españolas
desde el año 1401 al 1833. Madrid: Atlas, 1975, pp. 212-13.

Relación de la grandiosa fiesta, y octava, que en la Iglesia
parroquial de el glorioso san Miguel de la Ciudad de Seuilla, hizo
don García Sarmiento de Sotomayor, Conde de Saluatierra, Marqués de
Sobroso, Gentilombre de la Camara del Rey nuestro señor, y del
Sereníssimo Infante, Cauallero de la Orden de Santiago, Assistente,
y Maese de Campo General de la gente de guerra de Seuilla, y su
partido, por su Magestad. Sevilla: Andrés Grande, 1635.
   This work has not been reprinted since the seventeenth century and
is of primary interest to scholars. It is described in Manuel
Serrano y Sanz, Apuntes para una biblioteca de escritoras españolas
desde el año 1401 al 1833. Madrid: Atlas, 1975, p. 214.

Relación, en qve se da cventa de las grandiosas fiestas, que en el
conuento de N. P. S. Francisco de la Ciudad de Seuilla se an hecho a
los Santos Mártires del Iapón. Sevilla: Pedro Gómez, 1628.
   This work has not been reprinted since the seventeenth century and
is of primary interest to scholars. It is described in Manuel
Serrano y Sanz, Apuntes para una biblioteca de escritoras españolas
desde el año 1401 al 1833. Madrid: Atlas, 1975, pp. 214-15.

Valor, agravio y mujer in Manuel Serrano y Sanz, Apuntes para una
biblioteca de escritoras españolas desde el año 1401 al 1833,
Vol. 1. Madrid: Sucesores de Rivadeneyra, 1903. The Apuntes,
including the play, is reprinted in the Biblioteca de Autores
Españoles, Vol. 268, Madrid: Atlas, 1975, pp. 179-212.
   This cape and sword play incorporates many of the more astonishing
situations utilized by Golden Age playwrights. The plot centers on a
typical motif found in the dramas of the epoch, the dishonored woman
who, dressed as a man, searches for her treacherous and fickle lover.
The audience is regaled with duels in the night and intricate scenes
of mistaken identities and led to a happy conclusion where the man
acknowledges his mistakes and marries the adventurous and valiant
heroine.

                                                              FADA

CARRE SANCHEZ, María del Pilar (1921-).
   María del Pilar Carré Sánchez was born in La Coruña. She is a
teacher and the author of numerous novels of the Novela Rosa genre. She
has a sister or cousin, María de la Purificación Carré Sánchez
(pseudonym May Carré) who is also the author of a great number of books
of the same genre. Many of these authors' works have been translated
into Portuguese and Italian and have had numerous editions.

                                                              EF-D

CARTAGENA, Sor Teresa de (born 1420 or 1935-?).
     She was a Franciscan nun, granddaughter of the Talmudic scholar, Don
Selomó ha-Leví, converted to Christianity and assuming the name of
Pablo de Santa María de Cartagena, Catholic Bishop of Burgos and
Chancellor of Castile. Sometime after 1450 Sor Teresa decided to write
the account of her spiritual pilgrimage, addressing herself to Doña
Juana de Mendoza, wife of Gómez Manrique. In so doing she became the
first woman writer in Spanish literature.

     Arboleda de los enfermos y Admiración Operum Dey Hutton, Lewis
     Joseph, estudio preliminar y edición. Anejo XVI de Anejos del
     Boletín de la Real Academia Española. Madrid: Imprenta Aguirre,
     1967, 153 pp.
          Arboleda de los enfermos. Deafness, afflicting her in her youth,
     caused the writer both physical torment and emotional bitterness.
     She could not enjoy the society of normal people and was shunned by
     them. After 20 years of suffering, she wrote to express the conso-
     lation she had found. Conceiving her situation to be that of a
     barren island, she saw it converted into a beautiful grove of peace
     and refreshment by means of wholesome books. First among these books
     were the Scriptures and the Church Fathers.
          Admiración Operum Dey. This second treatise was written in
     answer to the criticism of the first that no woman was capable of
     writing so well and therefore had to have been plagiarized. The
     author defended her right to receive inspiration from God and to
     express it in writing. She advised men to praise God that both men
     and women could be inspired instead of condemning a woman selected by
     God to receive a special gift. In publishing this work, Sor Teresa
     became the first woman in Spanish history to write in defense of the
     rights of women to be authors.

                                                                      LJH

*CARTANA DOMENGE DE S. DE OCANA, Elvira.
     Elvira Cartañá Domenge de S. de Ocaña is a poet. She wrote Terra
blava, Barcelona: 1981, and Clarianes, Barcelona: Torrell de Reus,
1980.

                                                                      KM

CARVAJAL Y SAAVEDRA, Mariana (born 1615?-1664?-).
     She is a little known novelist of the seventeenth century who lived
in Granada and had connections in the nobility and high bureaucracy of
that city. At an early age she became a widow with three boys and six
girls to raise. With this in mind she wrote eight moral, didactic
novels, which were published three times from 1663 to 1728. Under the
general heading of Navidades de Madrid y noches entretenidas we find
titles such as "Quien bien obra siempre acierta," "Celos vengan
desprecios" and "Amar sin saber a quien." The last edition added two
more novelettes to the collection and in its prologue the author
mentions 12 comedies, of which nothing further is known.

     Navidades de Madrid y noches entretenidas. Madrid: 1663-1728.
     It is a series of ten short novels centered on the people living in
     the house of Lucrecia de Haro, a high-born widow reduced to taking in
     paying guests. All her dwellers combine their resources and talents
     to support and entertain each other. They dance, talk, play music
     and exchange ideas and educational concepts. In the later novels, a

few of the relationships turn into marriages. The novels, written in
a simple and straightforward style, are treasure troves of details
and daily concerns and responsibilities, especially on girls'
education, among the upper-class society of seventeenth-century
Spain. Feminine ideals and domestic virtues are heavily portrayed.

                                                                    AR

CASANOVA DE LUTOSLAWSKI, Sofía (1862-1958).
     Born Sofía Pérez Casanova in Almeiras (Coruña), Casanova married a
Polish nobleman-philosopher in 1887 and thereafter lived mainly outside
Spain. She collaborated assiduously in the Spanish press, making frequent visits to Spain, and published numerous volumes on Poland and
Russia. Best known as a poet and short story writer, Casanova published
travelogues, histories, novels and wrote as well in Polish. She was
active in the turn-of-the-century women's movement, writing on the
Spanish woman abroad and working to improve hygiene and combat tuberculosis. She received the Cross of Alfonso XII and was made a member of
the Real Academia Gallega.

     El cancionero de la dicha. Madrid: Imprenta de Regino Velasco,
     1911, xvii + 184 pp. 2nd ed., Madrid: Imprenta de Regino Velasco,
     1912, xvv + 184 pp.
     Introduced by an "Ofrenda de poetas" containing eight poems
dedicated to Casanova's volume, the Cancionero reproduces in the
first two sections, "Versos de lejanos días" and "Ausencia," many of
the poems from Fugaces without some dedications. The most topical
poems are omitted and a few new poems are added in these sections.
The "Cancionero de la dicha" contains poems of frustrated, impossible
love and life as anguished searching. The last section, "Los días
de hoy," brings the volume to 1911, with incidental poems from visits
to Spain. Meditations on life and love prevail throughout in a
romantic quest for meaning.

     Las catacumbas de Rusia roja. Madrid: Espasa-Calpe, 1933, 224 pp.
     Divided into three sections, "Espías," "Prisiones de Rusia," and
"La urbe roja," the novel treats the confrontation between   revolutionary and counterrevolutionary forces in the aftermath of the
Bolshevik revolution, pitting Russian refugees in Poland against
Konsomol youth. The idealistic struggle to restore the old order to
the homeland leaves no place for love, as Alix, the widowed Russian
princess of Como en la vida, discovers as she follows her lover and
adopts his mission. The hero Zarief finds the peasant attachment to
the nobility inevitable, but his commitment to Russia leads to
solitude, imprisonment, disguise and a mysterious death, following
the wasting away of Alix. Bolshevik free love contrasts with
traditional marriage and Zarief's solitary mission.

     Como en la vida; novela. Madrid: Manuel Aguilar, 1930, 212 pp.
     2nd ed., Novelas y Cuentos, Madrid: Imprenta Diana, 1947, 30 pp.
     Written in Poznañ-Ynowroclaw, this novel contrasts the values of
life in a rural Galician pazo with the rootless life of the wealthy
international set, especially Eastern European exiles. On his
father's death Fernando, a diplomat, abandons his childhood sweetheart for a lover, a widowed Russian princess whom he follows across
Europe. Her unfaithfulness finally kills his passion and he falls
ill. Returning to Spain, he confronts the reality of war with

Morocco and volunteers his service. Romantic still, he seeks salvation in a patriotism which may restore traditional virtues and
strength to him and to his country.

De Rusia. Amores y confidencias. In Obras completas, IV, Madrid:
Librería y Editorial Madrid, 1927, 279 pp.
    A collection of essays and stories from earlier volumes, including
Sobre el Volga helado, El pecado, Exóticas and En la corte de los
zares, the volume bears a dedication to her brother, the poet Vicente
Casanova, similar to that in Exóticas. Subtitled "Rusia. Ayer y
hoy," in acknowledgement that time has made some of her geographical
and historical observations obsolete, Casanova divides the volume
into two sections, "Como eran" and "Como son." Along with Russia,
social issues, such as divorce and censorship, predominate,
complemented by stories of human drama from El pecado.

El doctor Wolski. Páginas de Polonia y Rusia. Madrid: F.
Marqués, 194, 321 pp. 2nd ed., Obras completas, II, Madrid:
Madrid, 1925, 253 pp.
    Written in Kazán, Russia, and dedicated from London to Ramón de
Campoamor, Casanova's first novel traces the friendship between the
idealistic, Russian-educated Polish doctor and his sceptical,
hedonistic Russian friend. Wolski's theory for improving the human
race leads him to reject his Russian fiancée, tubercular from
excessive studying, and to marry a Polish woman of healthy stock who
nevertheless provides him no heirs. The ironic hand of fate destroys
all his ideals; his friend commits suicide to avoid unjust imprisonment. Spirit, the tubercular woman, triumphs over matter; faith over
science.

Lo eterno; narración española. Madrid: Librería de Escritores y
Artistas y Fernando Fe, 1907, 119 pp. 2nd ed., Lo eterno; novela.
La novla Corta, 5, No. 218, 1920.
    Warning in the prologue that the editor found this a work which
will scandalize the Spanish reader, Casanova queries her own possible
"foreignness." A headstrong priest, influenced by his Andalusian
blood and tainted by his freethinker father, struggles between his
duty and his attraction to a young woman abandoned by her seducer.
Protestantism also surfaces as a tempting resolution in this romantic
novel. Although the temptation and salvation scenes are melodramatic, Casanova attempts a psychological study before invoking the
martyrdom typical of the genre.

Exóticas. Madrid: Sucesores de Hernando, 1912, 181 pp.
    A collection of short pieces, this volume combines essays with
sketches, family scenes and social commentary. Social issues,
women's issues and literary subjects predominate. The author also
relates her own experiences with Russian censorship regarding the
ownership and publication of books. Written in Spain and Poland, the
pieces embrace the years 1908 through 1912.

Fugaces. Biblioteca Gallega, Vol. 47, La Coruña: A. Martínez,
1898, vii + 161 pp.
    Spanning two decades and written from across Europe, this volume
contains the poems of "Juventud" (1882-1886), some of which appeared
in Poesías, and "Ausencia" (1887-1897). Incidental in nature,

nostalgic and often prosaic in tone, the poems bear dedications to female friends and to family. The themes of absent country, the sea, travel, nostalgia, life as anguish and impossible love prevail. Religion offers no solace, only the certainty of suffering and nothingness. The poems belong to the romantic, sentimental tradition.

Idilio epistolar. Madrid: Aguilera, 1931, 248 pp.

La madeja. Comedia frívola en tres actos y en prosa. Madrid: Imprenta de Regino Velasco, 1913, 83 pp. 2nd ed., illus. F. Mota, Los Contemporáneos, Nos. 241, 1913, 21 pp.
    A comedy of manners set in a French spa, the play self-consciously weaves the web of emotions involving a young Spanish bride and an emancipated Yankee woman. The presentation of the themes of love and marriage is three-tiered: the separated American and a Spanish bachelor, the married couple, and a newly-engaged pair. The trials of a wife, the unfaithfulness of the spouse, the idealism of young love, and the bitter solitude of the separated woman all come into play. Light crisp dialogue expresses traditional sentiments in a weakly-structured play performed in the Teatro Español on March 11, 1913.

Más que amor; cartas. Madrid: Librería de Escritores y Artistas y Fernando Fe, 1909, 268 pp.
    Epistolary in format, the novel presents the letters between an exiled Spanish widow living with her children in Poland and a Madrid politician known as a philanderer. The developing relationship, built on two encounters in the previous 12 years, follows the traditional Romantic pattern from silence, to spiritual compenetration, to a meeting in Aranjuez. The widow attempts to restore idealism and morality to her correspondent, while she blossoms into renewed life. Although the regeneration fails to take root, the two remain committed to a permanent epistolary relationship. The language and events reflect a first-hand knowledge of correspondence and isolation and demonstrate a pervasive pessimism about human relationships.

El pecado. Intro. Prudencio Canitrot. Biblioteca de Escritores Gallegos, 10. Madrid: Sucesores de Hernando, 1911, 151 pp. 2nd ed., Obras Completas, III, Madrid: Madrid, 1926, 226 pp. "El pecado," Novelas y Cuentos, Madrid: Dédalo, 1942, 16 pp.
    A collection of 11 stories set mostly in Galicia, this is the first volume in the collection by a woman. The fundamental incompatibility of man and woman in love and marriage and sympathy for life's victims are the main themes. Several are psychological studies of guilt and responsibility, especially from the female point of view; several are written in dialogue form. The title story also appears in Novelas y Cuentos.

Poesías. Intro. R. Blanco Asenjo. Madrid: Imprenta de A. J. Alaría, 1885, xvi, 106 pp.
    The early poems of Casanova are Romantic in tone and subject, reflecting as well an awareness of the social conditions of such Galician groups as miners and sailors. Casanova devotes poems to shipwrecks and mine disasters, from the human perspective. Themes include melancholy, impossible love, a search for absolutes and the enigma of life after death prevail.

Princesa rusa. Illus. Echea. Madrid: Publicaciones Prensa Gráfica, II, No. 55, 1922, 64 pp.
   Set among the frivolous international society on the Riviera and in Saint Petersburg, the novel treats the theme of divorce in the relationship between a married femme fatale, a Russian princess, and an Italian-Spanish Marquis who renounces his military career for love during the war. Abundant dialogue reflects the cynicism and super-ficiality of the wealthy in the midst of social and economic crisis. The character of the hedonistic, unfaithful Slav clashes with that of the proud, jealous Mediterranean. Duty and honor triumph over the Princess's perversity and degradation of her lover. The Marquis dies in battle, while the Princess continues her escape from reality. The obliviousness of the Russian nobility to changing circumstances is underscored.

Sobre el Volga helado; narración de viajes. Madrid: Librería de Fernando Fe, 1903, 107 pp. 2nd ed., La Novela Corta, 4, No. 196, 1919.
   The narrative of a trip taken by Victor (Casanova?) and the author from her home in Poland, the Manor of Drozdowo, to Kazan and back, the volume opens in the fall and closes the following spring. The siblings travel by sleigh, train and troika via Warsaw, Saint Peters-burgh, Nizny Nowgorod to Kazan. Casanova offers reflections on Polish and Russian history, social and economic conditions, descrip-tions of landscapes and reported conversations. Casanova adopts the Polish patriot's view of Russia and the Spanish patriot's attachment to Poland, a land "civilized and watered with Spanish blood for four centuries."

Viajes y aventuras de una muñeca española en Rusia. Illus. Gutiérrez Larraya. Burgos: Hijos de Santiago Rodríguez, 1920, 112 pp. IV láminas.
   A didactic story for children told in the first person by a Spanish doll who accompanies her owner during six years of travel, the work moves from Madrid to Galicia, Paris, Germany, Poland and Russia. After three years in Russia during the war, the family returns home to Poland where Krysia begins to favor her studies over her doll. Conversational in tone, the story is told from the doll's point of view with some moralizing observations about children and reported adult conversations about behavior. Political events and social conditions in Poland and Russia are mentioned.

MB

CASTRO, Rosalía de (1837-1885).
   Though largely ignored at the time, she was an important figure in the revival of Galician literature. She was also a significant influence on modernist poets at the end of the century. Born in Galicia, she went to Madrid at 19 and married a fellow Galician--an art critic and historian--at 21. Despite a difficult marriage, the birth of six children and a life of frequent travelling, she wrote three novels and three collections of verse before 1871, when she returned to Galicia. She published two more collections of verse before dying of cancer at 48. Her themes ranged from the poverty and exploitation of Galicia to the profound conflicts of the romantic sensibility.

A mi madre. Vigo: J. Compañel, 1863. In Obras Completas, Madrid: Aguilar, 1966, pp. 243-255.

A mi madre is an elegiac poem of 60 strophes of varied meters divided into nine parts, dedicated to the poet's recently deceased mother. The poet dreams of the lost parent and presents a vision, not of tender love but of alienation and fear of death's alterations. Even if the ghostly presence of the mother lingers on and is of some consolation to the poet, her life has nonetheless become a living death. Uncannily, she feels what can only be felt by those who have died.

El Caballero de las botas azules (Cuento extraño). Lugo: Soto Freire, 1867. In Obras Completas, Madrid: Aguilar, 1966, pp. 1157-1404.

This mixture of fantasy and social satire develops from the proposition that frivolous, fickle mid-nineteenth-century people are irresistibly drawn to novelty. The protagonist, of mysterious origin (often suggesting Lermontov's Pechorin) with his blue boots, eagle in place of a cravat, and baton with a bell at the tip, incarnates novelty. He uses his power to attract people to him so that he can then castigate them. Two groups come in for major criticism: those who write or promote bad literature; and women who use men for perverted purposes. Principal themes: the disgraceful pandering to bad taste; the wasted lives of women of all social classes; the distortions of the romantic sensibility. Of interest to scholars and available in hardback.

Cantares gallegos. Vigo: Imp. de D. Juan Compañel, 1863, 186 pp. In Obras Completas, Madrid: Aguilar, 1966, pp. 256-381.

This collection of poems in Galician was dedicated to Fernán Caballero in gratitude for her novelistic treatment of Galicians and was preceded by a prologue stating that the principal reason for publishing the Cantares was to dispel erroneous ideas about Galicia. Many of the poems evoke the beauty of Galicia or serve to illustrate the concerns, preoccupations, joys and sorrows of ordinary people. Several poems cast blame on Castile for its treatment of Galicia. Castro's major contributions have lain in her successful tapping of folk poetry and in her sympathetic rendering of the sensibility of common people. These aspects of her work influenced later poets such as Machado and García Lorca.

En las orillas del Sar. Madrid: Imprenta de Ricardo Fe, 1884, 159 pp. In Obras Completas, Madrid: Aguilar, 1966, pp. 555-656.

One of the principal themes of his collection focuses on Galicia. The poet describes the hopeless poverty which forces emigration, the exploitation of the land by outsiders, and her deep love of the homeland. Other poems express disillusion with human nature: the failure of love, the presence of envy, greed, lust. The poet often relates nature to her state of mind. Finally, there are poems expressing her doubt in a life hereafter as well as some verses suggesting sudden promptings of faith. This volume made a meaningful contribution to continued discussion concerning the development of neglected regions such as Galicia. Of general interest and available in hardcover.

Flavio, ensayo de novela. Madrid: Impr. de "La Crónica de ambos munos," 1861. In Obras Completas, Madrid: Aguilar, 196, pp. 836-1080.

This psychological novel, devoid of references to the contemporary world, focuses on the struggle for dominance between a young man raised in isolation and a girl reared in society who balks at living a secluded life with her jealous and tyrannical suitor. Woman's powerlessness is a principal theme: she cannot obtain justice or avenge herself for injuries. She is not allowed privacy nor is she considered an adult human being, but rather, at best, a toy for the amusement of men, at worst, a sack of corruption. From the male protagonist's point of view, woman is an obstacle to the pursuit of liberty. Flavio's eventual liberation rests on the debasement of women. Available and of interest to scholars.

La flor (Poesías). Madrid: M. Gonzalez, 1857. In Obras Completas, Madrid: Aguilar, 1966, pp. 213-242.

This collection consists of six allegorical narratives and two lyrical meditations. Two poems are cast in varied meters. Love and the loss of faith and illusions provide the themes. The poet apostrophizes the rare love of two doves who move in a purified atmosphere. Unrequited or imperfect love leads to death. Meditations on doubt make use of desolate and threatening nature images. Doubt brings a powerful presentiment of death. The poet's suffering persona clearly emerges from verses which are otherwise largely derivative of earliest Romantic poetry: "I was alone with my profound grief in the abyss of an imbecile world."

La Hija del Mar. Vigo: Imprenta de J. Compañel, 1859. In Obras Completas, Madrid: Aguilar, 1966, pp. 660-833.

The vulnerability of females abandoned in infancy is the theme: the complicated plot allows all the characters to experience or inflict a variety of indignities, sorrows, and criminal acts. The archvillain is an atheistic exploiter of defenseless women. From the protagonist's appearance as an abandoned infant in a rock off the Galician coast to the novel's conclusion in which the heroine throws herself into the sea, the author insists on a mysterious bond between nature and the lives of the characters. The heroine's suicide is a return to an eternal reality. Her miserable life (eight years of it passed in madness) was lived almost as a dream. There are passages of local customs. The author's preface is a plea for tolerance of women who step outside of traditional roles. Available and of interest to students of women's history.

Follas Novas. Versos en gallego, precedidos de un prólogo de Emilio Castelar. 1st ed., Madrid: Biblioteca de la Propaganda Literaria, 1880. In Obras Completas, Madrid: Aguilar, 1966, pp. 392-552.

The two principal subjects of Follas Novas are Galicia and the author's deep-rooted melancholy. In her preface, Castro indicated a preference for her more personal poems but granted that they were often colored by her perception of her Galician surroundings. Galicia's landscape, its monuments, its poor, its relegation to a position of scant importance - all furnished matter for reflection. Castro's melancholy stemmed from disillusion in love and friendship, from religious doubt, from constant awareness of time passing, from a painful recognition of our forgetfulness of the dead. This collec-

tion confirmed her position as a major poet in Galician. Available
and of general interest.

El primer loco (Cuento extraño). Madrid: Maya y Plaza, 1881, 160
pp. In Obras Completas, Madrid: Aguilar, 1966, pp. 1407-1494.
    Three principal themes are developed in the narration of the
protagonist, Luis: his impious, idolotrous, obstinate love for a
woman whom he recognizes as being as fallible and earth-bound as he
himself is; his conviction that nature is animate and, specifically,
that the spirits of the departed return to their earthly haunts; his
realization that the two preceding preoccupations have prevented his
participating in the regeneration of Galicia. This portrayal of
obsessive passion à la Poe does reveal an attempt, in the introduction of the idea of regeneration, to link Luis' personal plight to
the situation of contemporary Galicia. Available in hardcover and of
interest to scholars.

Ruinas (desdichas de tres vidas ejemplares). Madrid: El Museo
Universal, 1866. In Obras Completas, Madrid: Aguilar, 1966, pp.
1093-1156.
    The "Ruinas" of the title are three individuals--a formerly
wealthy merchant now reduced to penury because of his lavish,
unbounded largesse, an elderly aristocratic woman also living in
poverty, and a young aristocrat who has been deprived of his
inheritance by unscrupulous relatives. The themes explored by the
author evolve around the characters' reactions to adversity. The
dignity, forbearance and trust in an ultimately just God are not
proof--in the case of the young aristocrat--against the pain of
unrequited love. The scorn of the socially-inferior woman he loves
leads to his madness and death. The story lays bare the un-Christian
behavior and attitudes which make the three suffer, but not the
injustices and absurdities of the social and economic system of mid-
nineteenth century Spain.

                                                                    DJO

CASTROVIEJO BLANCO-CICERON, Concha. Also: **Concha Castroviejo** (1915-).
    Born in Santiago de Compostela, she attended the University there and
in Bordeaux. From 1930 to 1950 she lived in Mexico and taught at the
University of Campeche. A graduate of the Escuela de Periodismo de
Madrid, she has lived in Madrid since the 1950's and has been active in
journalism and as the author of short stories and detective novels. She
has also written children's books, including El jardín de las siete
puertas (1962), which won the Premio Doncel, and Los días de Lina
(1971), which some critics consider a work that can also be appreciated
by adults.

Los que se fueron. Barcelona: Planeta, 1957.
    The result of the author's experience in exile, the novel follows
a group of post-Civil War Spanish exiles to Paris and then to Mexico.
Tiche, a widow with a young son, refuses to sit around in cafes
bemoaning the loss of her patria or to marry a wealthy Mexican.
She develops a successful career, gives up hope of return to Spain
and realizes that her son's future lies in Mexico.

Víspera del odio. Barcelona: Garbo Editorial, 1959. Second ed., Madrid: Círculo de Amigos de la Historia, 1976, 253 pp.
    This psychological novel, which received the Premio Elisenda de Montcada, explores the development of a woman's hatred for her husband; but the Civil War provides the impetus for the narrative structure. Teresa is married off to a miserly older man who despises the civil disorder of the Republic and fears the loss of his money. After suffering shortages, bombings and hunger at the outbreak of war, Teresa follows her lover José through war-torn areas. Fore-going plans to escape with their child to France, she nurses José when he is wounded. Her husband has his personal and political revenge by causing José's arrest as a "red, atheist, immoral revolutionary."

                                                                    CLG

CATALA, Víctor. See: ALBERT I PARADIS, Caterina.

*CHORDA I REQUESENS, Mari (1942-).
    A poet, born in Amposta, she studied education and fine arts at Sant Jordi in Barcelona. In 1967 she had a daughter. For ten years she earned her living by painting and teaching art. She taught film at the University of Barcelona and wrote and directed two short and one medium-length films. Finally, in 1975, she opted for writing as the easiest means of communicating with the public, since paper and pencil are the only technical equipment necessary. Chordà formed part of the col-lective which opened the first women's bar in Barcelona, and then part of the collective which created laSal, the only feminist publishing house in the country, where she still works.

    ...i moltes altres coses. Barcelona: laSal, 1975, 52 pp.
        The author's first book of poems, it includes her own drawings. The prologue of the first edition speaks of words, suppressed for many years, which are finally pronounced with rage. The reality shown in the poems is not based on a play between oppositions - night-day, man-woman, black-white, tenderness-harshness - since that is not relevant, but poetry itself, as the title of the prologue says. These first verses gather together the cry of women to reclaim as their own the streets, the city, and all other spaces.

    Locomotora infidel del passat. Barcelona: in press, 1985.
        The book is a collection of 40 poems and a screenplay for a six-minute film. It is a love story, which waxes and wanes, like all love stories. The transcription, or poetic form of these sentiments, take the following geometric form: ◇

    Quadern del cos i l'aigua. Barcelona: laSal, 1978, 68 pp.
        In this book, the poetry by Chordà and the drawings by Montse Clavé are equally important. In the prologue, the authors reclaim the body for things other than putting the laundry into the washing machine and bathing the children. In these poems, a broader sexu-ality than the strictly genital is proclaimed and the work as a whole is a song and the discovery of one's own body.

                                                                    ISS

*CISTARE, Lali.

   La burra espatllada. Barcelona: Selecta, 1980.
     In this volume of 15 short stories, two are dialogues. The others
are all written from the first person point of view, and the protagonist is a female. Many of the stories describe the problematic of
the couple, with frustration and dissatisfaction.

KM

CIVERA, Beatriu. See: MARTINEZ I CIVERA, Empar Beatriu.

CONDE ABELLAN, Carmen. Pseud. Florentina del Mar (1907-).
   Carmen Conde, born in Cartagena, Murcia, lived there from 1907-1936
except for the years 1914-1920 when her family lived in Morocco
(Melilla). In 1939 she moved to Madrid. Having studied and taught
literature, she also began writing poetry. She has written over 20
books of poetry, eight novels, many stories and plays for children,
various books of critical essays and biographical studies of authors.
In 1978 she was elected the first woman member of the Real Academia de
la Lengua Española. She has also won numerous prizes for her prose and
poetry. Conde has stated that she is a writer "sin generación" because
she has little in common with the Generation of 1927, though she admires
them, and less in common with those of 1936. If she and her husband,
poet Antonio Oliver Belmás, had died early or gone into exile, she
states, they may have been included in the later generation. She is
best known as a poet.

   A este lado de la eternidad. Madrid: Biblioteca Nueva, 1970.
     Poetry.

   A la estrella por la cometa. Madrid: Doncel, 1961, 110 pp.
     This collection of three plays for children won the Premio Doncel
de Teatro in 1961. The first play, El lago y la corza (music by
Matilde Salvador), is similar to a fairy tale, containing enchant-
resses, a metamorphosis, and mythological characters. A spell is
broken only by loving another. The work is written entirely in
octosyllabic verse. El conde Sol was republished in 1979 (Madrid:
Escuela Española). This two-act play (songs by Rafael Rodríguez-
Albert) takes place in the Middle Ages and includes historical and
stock figures. A typically Byzantine story with mysterious disap-
pearances and a final recognition scene. Lastly, El monje y el
pajarillo is a didactic religious play written in free verse. God's
perception of time and the importance of Christian faith are treated.
Written with A. Oliver Belmás. Available only through interlibrary
loan services.

   Ansia de la gracia. Madrid: Adonais, 1925.
     Poetry.

   Brocal. Madrid: Ed. La Lectura, 1929.
     Prose poems.

   Cita con la vida. Madrid: Biblioteca Nueva, 1976.
     Poetry.

Cobre, Colección El Grifón, Vol. IV. Madrid: El Grifón, 1953,
237 pp.
    Two short novels appear under the title Cobre: Destino hallado
and Solamente un viaje. The first (pp. 7-121) is a first-person
account of the social and psychological development of a young woman
painter. A secondary theme is how the Spanish Civil War affects
individuals. The second novel (pp. 123-237) describes in third
person a young woman's increasing indifference toward a husband she
once loved, because of the boring repetition of household routines.
When she travels to Italy, she finally confronts her reality, while
the student she accompanies travels toward love. Two examples of
works with feminist themes. Almost inaccessible.

Corrosión. Madrid: Biblioteca Nueva, 1971.
    Poetry.

Creció espesa la yerba. . .. Barcelona: Planeta, 1979,
ISBN 84-320-7123-4, 181 pp.
    The title and theme of this novel are taken from Alexander
Solzehnitsyn's Gulag Archipelago: "The grass grew thick on the tomb
of my youth." Years after a trauma in her family, a woman returns
to her home to confront her past and rediscover the person she once
was. The work is important as a psychological study of the suppres-
sion of the memory of an incestuous relationship and of the painful
process of remembering. Available in both hardback and paperback.

Derraman su sangre las sombras, 1983, 68 pp.
    This collection contains poems with themes such as hope,
disillusionment, quiet desolation and "the cry of a woman wounded by
the loss of her only daughter."

Derribado arcángel. Madrid: Revista de Occidente, 1960.
    Poetry.

Días por la tierra. Madrid: Nacional, 1977.
    Poetry anthology.

Doña Centenito, Gata Salvaje: Libro de su vida. Madrid: Alhambra,
1943. 2nd ed., Milán, Italy: Fratelli Fabbri Editori, 1954, trans.
Cala Brunetti. 3rd ed., Barcelona: Editorial 29, 1979, illustrated
by Carlos Torres, ISBN 84-7175-166-6, 48 pp.
    Of particular interest in this children's story are the amusing
anthropomorphic actions of the animals, understated lessons, and
commentaries about humans. Children are taught the importance of
obeying one's parents and of tolerance in an unobtrusive way. A
lesson on protecting the environment is ahead of its time, since the
work was first published in 1943. Available in colorfully
illustrated paperback.

Empezando la vida. Tetuán, Morocco: Revista Al-Motamid, 1955.
    Prose poems. Subtitled "Memorias de una infancia en Marruecos."

En la tierra de nadie. Murcia: El Luarel de Murcia, 1960.
    Poetry.

En manos del silencio, Colección Los Escritores de Hoy. Barcelona:
José Janés, 1950, 192 pp. Barcelona: Plaza y Janés, 1979,
ISBN 84-01-43606-0, 256 pp.
   Conde finished this novel, one of her better ones, in 1945 but did
not publish it until 1950. The themes of love, passion, marriage,
and incest are explored. A man in his late 40's has an affair with
both his friend's wife and the friend's daughter, leaving both
pregnant. The various walls which prevent communication (as well as
new ways to communicate) between the friend, husband, wife, and
daughter are examined. Because all share the blame, all end
tragically either in death or in total isolation. Outstanding
features are 1) commentaries on the atmosphere in Spain after the
Civil War and at the beginning of World War II, and 2) the presentation of each chapter from a different perspective, e.g., that of
the mother or the daughter. Out of print.

En un mundo de fugitivos. Buenos Aires: Losada, 1960.
   Poetry.

Iluminada Tierra. Madrid: Published by the author, 1951.
   Poetry.

Jaguar puro inmarchito. Madrid: Published by the author, 1963.
   Poetry.

Júbilos. Murcia: ed. Sudeste, 1934.
   Prose poems. Prologue by Gabriela Mistral. Illustrations by
Norah Borges.

Mi fin en el viento. Madrid: Adonais, 1957.
   Poetry.

Mientras los hombres mueren. Milan, Italy: Instituto Editorial
Disalpino, 1953.
   Prose poems. Preface by Juana Granados de Gagnasco.

Los monólogos de la hija. Madrid: published by the author, 1959.
   Poetry.

Mujer sin Edén. Madrid: Ed. Jura, 1947.
   Poetry. Poems from this collection have been translated into
English, French, German, Italian, Hindi, Russian and Japanese.

La noche oscura del cuerpo. Madrid: Biblioteca Nueva, 1980.
   Poetry.

Obra poética (1929-1966). Madrid: Biblioteca Nueva, 1967

Las oscuras raíces. Barcelona: Garbo, 1953, 224 pp. Libro Amigo,
Barcelona: Bruguera, 1968, 331 pp.
   This work won the Elisenda de Montcada Prize for novels in 1953.
The themes of destiny and all-consuming love are treated through the
histories of four couples who have lived in or visited the same house
by the sea. The house appears to have a spell or curse on it so that
married happiness is always ruined by a third party. The fourth
couple attempt to overcome these "deep roots" of Destiny. Interest

is maintained by the gradual unraveling of several mysteries surrounding the house and its inhabitants. Out of print. This novel is
available only through interlibrary services.

Poemas del mar menor. Murcia: Cátedra Fajardo de la Universidad de
Murcia, 1962.

La rambla. Madrid: Magisterio Español, 1978, ISBN 84-265-7211-1,
149 pp.
    This short novel includes several interpolated stories. Two
themes presented are conscience and disillusionment. When a woman
discovers that her husband killed a man 20 years earlier, all the
trust and communication on which the marriage was founded disappear.
The extensive treatment of the poverty of miners near Cartagena makes
the work the closest to a social novel of any of Conde's writing. It
presents poverty but does not examine the causes of it nor is blame
placed on another social class. Prologue by Milagros Sánchez
Arnosi, pp. 9-24. Available in hardback.

Sea la luz. Madrid: Ed. Mensaje, 1947.
    Poetry.

Soplo que va y no vuelve, Colección Europa, 2. Madrid: Alhambra,
1944.
    Published under pseud. **Florentina del Mar.**

Soy la madre. Barcelona: Planeta, 1980, ISBN 84-320-553-1X, 306 pp.
    Winner of the Premio Ateneo de Sevilla in 1980, this novel
explores the themes of caciquism, maternal love, and rape. The
trauma of facing one's sexuality even years after being raped is well
presented here. The treatment of obsessive and completely self-
sacrificing love of a mother for her son is somewhat overdone, but
usually believable in the limited and limiting social context of the
novel. The work is best when it presents a psychological portrait of
one woman. Available in hardback.

Su voz le doy a la noche. Madrid: published by the author, 1962.
    Poetry.

El tiempo es un río tentísimo de fuego. Barcelona: Ediciones 29,
1978.
    Poetry.

Vidas contra su espejo, Colección Europa, 1. Madrid: Alhambra,
1944, 289 pp. Pseud. **Florentina del Mar.**
    Although this novel was published in 1944, it was written in 1935
and resembles the novels of the generation of 1927. As Conde
describes it in a short preface, it is "una novela pasiva ... (like
the novels of its epoch) libros ... meditabundos o abstraídos ("a
passive novel ... meditative and abstract"). All action is intellectual in the novel. The theme of intellectual versus instinctual
love is examined. The style is poetic and at times is similar to
Unamuno's essays within a novel. Of interest mainly to scholars, the
work is only available from a few libraries through interlibrary
loan.

Vivientes de los siglos. Madrid: published by the author, 1954.
    Poetry. Winner of the Premio Internacional de Poesía Simon
Bolívar.

Zoquetín y Martina, illustrated by Carlos Torres. Barcelona:
Ediciones 29, 1979, ISBN 84-7175-171-2, 56 pp.
    The better sections of this children's story contrast the world of
children to that of adults in a humorous way, introduce fantasy, and
include episodes from Conde's own childhood experiences in Morocco.
Available in colorfully illustrated paperback.

                                                                    EDM

CORONADO, Carolina (1823-1911).
    Coronado became famous at 16 when Espronceda wrote a poem praising
her talent. The false report of her death in 1844 provoked expressions
of sorrow from public figures in Madrid. When she moved there from
Badajoz, she was crowned in the Liceo. Her marriage to a wealthy
American diplomat enabled her to establish a fashionable salon. While
she did not pursue literary fame during the period of her marriage, she
did cultivate the literati. Her cordial relations with the Queen helped
her to win pardons for political dissidents, including Castelar. Her
position on issues of the time such as materialism and socialism was
traditional, but her stance on the unfavorable position of women and on
the baleful effects of religious fanaticism was generally progressive.

Antología. Prólogo y Selección de Fernando Gutierrez. Barcelona:
Montaner y Simon, 1946, 229 pp.

Jarilla. Páginas de un diario. Adoración. Madrid: Biblioteca
Univeral, 1951, 40 pp.
Jarilla. Madrid: Imp. y fundición de M. Tello, 1875, 287 pp.
Jarilla. Madrid: Imp. y fundición de M. Tello, 1878.
Jarilla. Madrid: Prensa Popular, 1920, 20 pp.
Jarilla. Barcelona: Montaner y Simón, 1943, 345 pp.
    Jarilla is a brief historical romance set in the late fifteenth
century. The extraordinary adventures of a young favorite of Juan II
provide the tale's framework. Themes include the urgency of innocent
first love, the subordination of personal happiness to political
purposes, the attraction exerted by a parent's religion on a child
raised in a different religion, and death as a solution to conflicts
of religion. The protagonist's renunciation of his own and Jarilla's
happiness because of religious principle is clearly viewed as admi-
rable by the author. Available through interlibrary loan and of
interest to scholars.
    Páginas de un diario. Adoración, like Jarilla, which Coronado
described as a novela, is really a short story. A view of Madrid
aristocracy and its sexual mores, its principal theme is the vulnerability of women in a society that condones male philandering but
reacts cynically to the misfortunes of those women who lose in a
complicated and dangerous game. The condemnation of suicide (said in
the story to be prevalent among the youth of Madrid) is another concern of the author. Of interest to scholars and available through
interlibrary loan.

Poesías. Madrid: Imprenta de Alegría y Charlain, 1843, 123 pp.
Poesías. Mexico: Imprenta de J. R. Navarro, 1851, 72 pp. (No
additions to the 1843 edition.)
Poesías de la señorita Doña Carolina Coronado. Madrid: 1852,
139 pp.
Poesías, the majority of these poems are lyrical meditations on
nature--flowers, birds, trees, solitary places. Commonly-observed
characteristics of natural objects are described or the objects are
made to symbolize human emotions and states of mind. Recurrent
themes include the anticipation of inevitable grief and the pangs of
love. Exceptionally, "The Husband Executioner" is a graphic
description and condemnation of wife-beating. The playwright Juan
Eugenio Hartzenbusch wrote an introduction containing reflections on
masculine and feminine poetry. Of interest to scholars. Available
through interlibrary loan.
    Coronado's poems from the 1843 collection are included in
(Poesías de la señorita Doña Carolina Coronado). Themes of
subsequent poems range beyond regret for lost childhood and the love
of nature and Christ to include poems on the limitations imposed on
women, the horrors of civil war, wonderment at the advances of
science together with a sense that the desire for knowledge is over-
stepping the bounds imposed by religious piety. Several poems on the
events of 1848 concentrate on personal suffering rather than on
social or political issues. Poems dedicated to monarchs, poets and
conquistadores are followed by entries from albums. A biographical
sketch by Angel Fernández de los Ríos is followed by a truncated
version of the prologue Hartzenbusch wrote for the 1843 Poesías.
Available and of interest to scholars.

Poesías. Madrid: M. Tello, 1872, ? pp.
Poesías completas, precedidas de un prólogo por Emilio Castelar.
México: Librería Hispano-Mexicana, 1883. 1st ed., 412 pp.
3rd ed., 1884, 412 pp.
Poesías. Madrid: Imprenta de Alegría y Charlain, 1943, 123 pp.
Poesías. Proemio de Julio Cienfuegos Linares. Badajoz: Biblioteca
de Autores Extremeños, 1953, 178 pp.
Poesías. Badajoz: Arqueros, 1953. 2nd ed., 178 pp.

La Rueda de la Desgracia. Manuscrito de un conde. Madrid:
M. Tello, 1873.
    Contact with non-Spanish materialistic philosophies and modes of
life leads to moral decline on a personal and national level.
Coronado's work is a thesis novel illustrating the dangers of the
contemporary lack of national integrity and patriotism. Issues such
as feminism, socialism and the penetration of foreign capital into
Spain are raised and dealt with from a conservative, traditionalist
point of view. The revolution of 1868 is condemned; traditional
Basque customs and traditions are praised. This sombre, partial and
melodramatic view of post-revolutionary Spain is available through
interlibrary loan and is of interest to social historians.

La Sigea. Madrid: Anselmo Santa Coloma, 1854, 2 vols., 369 pp.
     This historical novel set in sixteenth-century Portugal deals with
two principal problems, both of compelling interest to contemporaries: first, the envy and calumny which often undermine the
careers of talented, distinguished people, especially women; and the
nature of the Inquisition. The author counsels conformity until
conditions for women improve. The Inquisition she saw as an
institution supported primarily by the masses whose barbarity and
blood-lust together with a vague spirit of the times forced otherwise
good people to act against their true natures. La Sigea is the
Spanish Latinist and poet, Luisa Sigea. Other characters include
Luis de Camoens and Juan de Austria. Of interest to scholars and
available through interlibrary loan.

DJO

*CORNET I PLANELLS, Montserrat (1934-).
A writer of limited production, she was born in Barcelona.

Entre dos estius. Barcelona: Pòrtic, 1984.

KM

**CORRAL, Clara (1847-1904).
     Born in Orense, her only book is A Herminia (Pontevedra, 1981), a
collection of poems dealing with love and the Galician homeland, very
much in the mood of Rosalía de Castro's writings.

CNC & AM

CRUSAT, Paulína (1900-).
     Born in Barcelona, of an upper-middle-class family, her surroundings
during her young years inclined her towards the literary world and
writing. Her first poem, "El buen D. Luis de Milanos," written at age
12, was awarded the "Flor natural" at "Juegos florales de a Câ
l'herbolari," Viladrau, 1912. She married and moved to Sevilla, where
she pursued a double career as literary critic and novelist. She has
not published any fiction since 1965.

     Historia de un viaje. Aprendiz de persona. Barcelona: Destino,
     1956, 255 pp.
        The first volume of a series of two novels, the book is divided in
     two parts. The author describes the childhood and youth of a female
     character. It concentrates on the development and the changes that
     the persons experience. During her adolescence, Monsi has to follow
     the rules imposed by society. At the end of the novel we see a
     little description of what happened to her after marriage. She
     finally discovers freedom and becomes an individual. Out of print.
     Available only in hardback.

     Mundo pequeño y fingido. Barcelona: José Janés, 1953, 522 pp.
        This novel is out of print and impossible to locate.

     Las ocas blancas. Barcelona: Destino, 1959, 326 pp.
        This novel is the continuation of Historia de un viaje and deals
     with the adult life of the characters of the first novel. Out of
     print.

Relaciones solitarias. Barcelona: Plaza y Janés, 1965, 264 pp.
    This epistolary novel is divided according to the different
seasons: spring, summer, fall and winter. The only reference
is one found in an anthology. Out of print.

CH

CHACEL, Rosa (1898-).
   A member of the Generation of 1927, Chacel collaborated on Revista de Occidente, Hora de España, Ultra, and other magazines of the period. She and her husband, painter Timoteo Pérez Rubio, lived in Italy (1921-1930), where she wrote her first novel. During and after the Spanish Civil War she lived in Europe until moving to Río de Janeiro in 1940. She and her son divided their time between Brazil and Buenos Aires, while her husband remained in Brazil. After Pérez Rubio's death in 1977, Chacel returned to Spain to live. She continues to write novels, essays, poetry, and short stories, as she has done since 1930. She has also published her memoirs and an autobiography. Chacel's novels are intellectual while maintaining contact with emotions.

   Acrópolis. Biblioteca Breve, 642. Barcelona: Seix Barral, 1984, ISBN 84-322-0491-9, 368 pp.
   This second novel in a trilogy continues the story of Chacel's generation's introduction to and experiences in the world of literature and art. The two young girls of Barrio de Maravillas are now older adolescents who live their historical moment (1914-1931, approximately) through their own early artistic works, their excursions with mentors to see modernist paintings, and their personal and academic experiences. Chacel's prose, which has become increasingly dense with each novel since La sinrazón, has reached its zenith in Acrópolis. The combination of interior monologue, omniscient narrative, Platonic dialogue, and the narrator's philosophical and esthetic discussion, makes this work both challenging and rewarding.

   Barrio de Maravillas. Biblioteca Breve, 386. Barcelona: Seix Barral, 1976, ISBN 84-3220-2924, 282 pp. Colección Libro Amigo. Barcelona: Bruguera, 1980, ISBN 84-02-07109-0, 281 pp.
   This is the first novel in a trilogy which Chacel describes as a history of her generation of writers (Generation of 1927). Through two adolescent girls, their teacher and families, Chacel shows her generation's introduction to the arts (literature, painting, sculpture, music, and cinema) during the years preceding 1914. Thus it is important as a personal and artistic view of the period prior to World War I. The work is also a biography of female adolescence. Available in both hardcover and paperback.

Estación, ida y vuelta. Madrid: Ulises, 1930. Madrid: CVS
Ediciones, 1974, ISBN 84-354-0014-X, 199 pp. Libro Amigo, Barcelona:
Bruguera, 1980, ISBN 84-02-07610-6, 151 pp.
　　The first novel by Chacel is a Bildüngsroman or, more accurately,
a Küntslerroman, which deals with the formation and development of a
young novelist. Influenced most directly by A Portrait of the Artist
as a Young Man, the book also shows important influences by Unamuno
and Proust. Chacel has stated that this novel was the seed which
later produced another, more profound, novel La sinrazón. Available
in hardcover and paperback.

Icada, Nevda, Diada. Biblioteca Breve Relatos, 325. Barcelona: Seix
Barral, 1971, 271 pp. 2nd ed., Barcelona: Seix Barral, 1982, ISBN
84-322-0223-1, 271 pp.
　　In this collection of short stories, Chacel includes all the
stories in two previous collections (Sobre el piélago and Ofrenda a
una virgen loca, q.v.) plus some stories published in journals and
some unpublished works. The title is based on three variations on
the word nada and refers to the concept of nothingness. Subjects and
themes include double suicide, the exercise of will to overcome
situations, self- created realities, a child's view of the world, and
the artist's Weltanschaung. Best new additions are "En la carretera"
with an O'Henry-style ending, and "Ví lapidar a una mujer," in which
one part of a dialogue is written and the other half surmised. The
collection is significant in that ideas and impressions take
precedence over plot. Available in paper and hardcover.

Memorias de Leticia Valle, Colección Hórreo. Buenos Aires:
Emecé, 1945, 189 pp. Palabra Seis, v. 7, Barcelona: Lumen, 1971,
174 pp. Libro amigo, Barcelona: Bruguera, 1980, ISBN 84-02-07051-5,
174 pp.
　　Eleven-year-old Leticia seeks to remember and understand what has
happend to her by writing a kind of diary, or memorias. Through it,
one sees the coming-of-age of a precocious adolescent, trapped
between childhood and adulthood. Themes of jealousy, artistic
education, and possible child molestation are also treated in this
novel. The ambiguity of who seduces whom (the professor or Leticia)
and the feelings of confusion and self-hate capture well the psyche
of a troubled young girl. A book ahead of its time in its treatment
of sexual abuse (published in 1945). Available in paperback and
bound editions.

Novelas antes de tiempo. Barcelona: Bruguera, 1981, ISBN
84-02-07701-3, 254 pp.
　　This collection of four unfinished novels and two brief outlines
is prefaced by Chacel (pp. 9-19). She states her wish to publish the
works because she will probably not have time to finish them all:
she was 82 years old when the first edition appeared. After each of
the fragmentary novels (previously published in literary magazines),
Chacel discusses at length the process of creating a fictional work
and outlines the problems present and the plans for the remainder of
each work. In Suma and La fundación de Eudoxia, an intellectual
searches for perfection in nature and society respectively while the
protagonist in El pastor seeks his origins. Margarita (zurcidora) is
an excellent portrayal of free association in the thoughts of an
aging woman who lives alone. Available in paperback.

Ofrenda a una virgen loca.   Xalapa: Universidad Veracruzana, 1961.
See: Icada, Nevda, Diada.

La sinrazón, Colección Novelistas de nuestra época. Buenos Aires:
Losada, 1960, 416 pp. Biblioteca Valira, 3, Barcelona: Andorra La
Vella, 1970, 554 pp. Bilbao: Albia, 1977, ISBN 84-7436-004-8,
432 pp.
   The entire text of this novel is a confessional diary of the male
protagonist as he seeks to discover how he lost his psychological and
spiritual innocence. Although the historical years 1918-1941 are
covered, the action is limited to the psyche of one character in his
quest for understanding himself, his reason for being, and the
possible existence of God - a search which leads him beyond reason to
la sinrazón. This most ambitious and successful of Chacel's novels
won the Premio de la Crítica in 1977. Available in hardcover and
paperback.

Sobre el piélago. Buenos Aires: Imán, 1952. See: Icada, Nevda,
Diada.

Teresa. Buenos Aires: Nuevo romance, 1941, 257 pp. Colección
Literaria: Novelistas, dramaturgos, ensayistas, poetas, Madrid:
Aguilar, 1963, 380 pp. Libro Amigo, Barcelona: Bruguera, 1980,
ISBN 84-02-06883-9, 345 pp.
   Chacel's second novel explores the themes of political exile (both
outside and inside Spain) and the ostracism and alienation experienced by a woman who dares to defy nineteenth-century mores. This
fictional biography of Teresa Mancha, Espronceda's companion, cap-
tures the joy and the tragedy of a passion worthy of the Romantic
movement. Available in both hardback and paperback.

Versos prohibidos, Colección Pentesilea, 2. Madrid: Caballo Griego
para la Poesía, 1978, ISBN 84-85417-02-X, 111 pp.
   After almost 40 years, Chacel returns to poetry with this
collection of sonnets, odes, and a variety of other verse forms,
including "moral epistles" inspired by Fernández de Andrada's moral
epistle to Fabio. In her preface, Chacel clarifies the meaning of
the title: the publication of the verses was prohibited by her.
Although most had been written in the 1930's and 1940's, she reacted
against her own facility for writing classical, rigid poems. The
most recent poem is "Oda a la alegría," written after the death of
her husband. She has explained that only in the depths of sorrow was
she able to write clearly about happiness.
                                                            EDM

CHAMPOURCIN Y MORAN DE LOREDO, Ernestina de (1905-).
Perhaps the best-known woman poet of the Generation of '27 and the widow of Juan José Domenchina (1898-1959), Champourcin's works can be divided into three distinct periods: (1) Human love (1926-36), (2) Divine love (1952-1974), and (3) Retrospective (1978-present). The second period reflects her years in exile with her husband in Mexico, where she translated extensively. She has also written a novel, an anthology, literary criticism, and most recently (1981) her memoirs of Juan Ramón Jiménez. Born in Vitoria (Alava), she now resides in Madrid.

Ahora. Madrid: Librería León Sánchez Cuesta, 1928, 60 pp.
Fervently Generation of '27 with echoes of Lorca, Juan Ramón, Darío, and Machado, Ahora's free-verse, occasionally assonantally rhymed, poems combine early surrealism, extended personal metaphors, and indulgent nature imagery with Modernist tendencies to lush exoticism and color bursts, some Generation of '98 Castilianism, and an innocent desire to unite soul with the infinite through contemplation of nature. Available in U. of Illinois-Urbana and U. of Miami-Coral Coral Gables libraries.

Cántico inútil. Madrid: Aguilar, 1936, 166 pp.
Prefaced by "Cinco glosas excéntricas" by Juan José Domenchina, whom Champourcin married in the year of its publication, Cántico inútil stands out in all of her production: it is her longest, most intricate, and most structurally varied volume; it both epitomizes and closes the "human love" period, and is her last book before exile from Spain, signaling a lapse in poetry publication that will continue to 1952. Many of the earlier Modernist and Generation of '98 tendencies are abandoned, with emphasis turning to exalted and exuberant surrealist and mystic flights and fantasies in search of polysemious unions: platonic, sexual, cosmic, temporal, personal, collective, and above all, love and deital ones, precursing an orientation to God that will in later works overshadow all other themes. Available at Arizona State-Tempe and Vanderbilt-George Peabody libraries.

Cárcel de los sentidos. Mexico: Ecuador 0° 0'0"--Finisterre, 1964, 55 pp.
Covering the period 1953-63, Cárcel de los sentidos sustains the religious themes of the Divine love cycle. Its mixed structures--décimas, free verses, and predilection for assonantal rhyme in 7- or 14-syllable lines--are among the author's most characteristic. Thematically, the poet desires to escape the "prison of senses" of darkness, dust, thirst, and silence and dedicate self to the Light, Truth and Eternity epitomized by God. Located in U. of Texas-Austin and U. of California-Irvine libraries.

Cartas cerradas. Mexico: Ecuador 0° 0'0"--Finisterre, 1968, 48 pp.
The philosophical premise of Cartas cerradas is that the nature of poetry, far from being social or message-laden, is to dialogue with God; thus, these "closed letters" are directed to him or to others (a sickly stranger, Thomas Merton, San Juan de la Cruz) about him. Written in a "running pen" fashion with uneven syllabification and no rhyme, the first ten "letters" are lengthier than other poems of the Divine love period and biographically telling through personal

remembrances ("19 March"); one, directed to her dead husband, renews the Castilian theme of her earliest poetry. Remaining sections repeat structures and themes typical of the Divine love period. Available from U. of Texas-Austin and West Virginia U.-Morgantown libraries and from the author.

La casa de enfrente. Madrid: Signo, 1936, 278 pp.
    After publishing this diary-format novel of a girl's childhood and adolescent memories and first love affair, Champourcin abandoned the genre, preferring poetry, and, following exile to Mexico, translated literary works and served as interpreter at international conventions for more than a decade. Available from Library of Congress and Cleveland public Library.

En Silencio. Madrid: Espasa Calpe, 1926.
    Published when she was 21, Champourcin's first book of poetry--initiating her self-labeled "amor humano" period--is not available in the U.S. nor from the author.

Hai-Kais espirituales. Mexico: Ecuador 0° 0'0"--Finisterre, 1967, 70 pp.
    Technically not hai-kus, for they do not follow the Japanese format, but thematically spiritual, Hai-Kais espirituales contains 62 two- or three-line prose miniorations to God (also Christ and Mary), arising from everyday encounters and experiences of foreign landscapes, which reiterate concepts of light, eternity and grace. Available from author or in U. of Texas-Austin and Arizona U.-Tucson libraries.

El nombre que me diste, 1st ed., Mexico: Ecuador 0$^{o}_{o}$0'0"--Finisterre, 1960, 25 pp. 2nd ed., Mexico: Ecuador 0° 0'0"--Finisterre, 1966.
    The 21 poems of El nombre que me diste typify, both structurally and thematically, Champourcin's "Divine love" period. Although pages are unnumbered and most are untitled, the poems' rhyme schemes divide them, all having 7-syllable lines and assonantal rhyme--usually in even-numbered lines. The "tú" form of address is consistently used, with the poet as seeker-worshipper desirous of clarity and redefinition of self in God's (or Christ's) presence. Biblical oppositions and imagery, personages and referents, and passages--one incorrectly quoted as Psalm 90 (91)--appear throughout this series of standard religious poems, available from Princeton, N.J. library or from the author.

La pared transparente. Los libros de Fausto, Anaquel de poesía/12. Madrid: Los libros de Fausto, 1984, ISBN 84-85978-13-7, 64 pp.
    This, Champourcin's most recent book, signals a change in her philosophic perception of the world. Partly retrospective, the "Luz en la memoria" section reminisces using Mexican settings and familiar themes. However, the titular imagery of "walls" opens a fourth period: one of earthy alienation and annihilation. Walls in all forms imprison and separate the poet whose soliloquies fall on dehumanized urban deserts where desperation, lack of communication, and loneliness wrench hope and human comfort away. No longer is religion an easy answer for spiritual longings, nor do earthly relationships reciprocate or satisfy; clarity and truth can be

realized only through the absolutes of poetry and cosmic enternity. Available from the author or editorial house.

Poemas del Ser y del Estar. Colección Agora. Madrid: Alfaguara, 1974, 68 pp.
In the period from 1968-74, Champourcin edited an anthology, Dios en la poesía actual, which had three editions--a fourth is expected --and which kept her in contact with her preferred religious theme. This six-year lapse in imaginative production is broken by Poemas del Ser y del Estar, which continues the themes and structures charac-teristic of the "Divine love" period. A few touches reminiscent of her earliest poetry such as nature depictions and mystic flights appear in this, her first published poetry after returning to Spain from exile in Mexico. Available from U. of California-Irvine library.

Presencia a oscuras. Adonais Collection # 87. Madrid: Rialp, 1952, 84 pp.
After a 16-year silence, Presencia a oscuras is Champourcin's first published poetry following her exile, with poems from 1948-50. Although dedicated to her husband, "J.J.", it literally and figura-tively remains faithful to the poet's credo that "God is in all poetry," initiating the period which she calls "amor divino." No longer surrealistic or worldly in any sense, the focus is defini-tively religious, though lacking the mystic quality of Cántico inútil. Except for ten décimas, the prose-like structures have longer lines and uneven syllabification, are not rhymed, and often follow religious forms with invocations, prayers, litanies, and magnificats directed to God, the Holy Spirit, Jesus (in 12 Via Crucis poems) and Mary, with inspiration from cited Biblical passages or allusions and standard Biblical imagery of light, water, fire, etc. Available at U. of California-Berkeley, Michigan State and Knox, Ill. libraries.

Primer Exilio. Adonais Collection # 355. Madrid: Rialp, 1978, ISBN 84-321-1958-x, 87 pp.
Primer Exilio brings some abrupt, almost astounding changes into Champourcin's poetry. Shorter, choppier verses without assonantal rhyme appear for the first time in what can only be called a "Retrospective period" incorporating qualities of both earlier periods with a more worldly and philosophic vision. The best of these image-laden poems observe the negative, impending silences and urgencies of the outside world: war, anxieties, and other human gropings. In a series of water and sea images, journeys away from such a world are achieved by liquifying the yo into cosmic unity through art, nature-identification and time distortion. Standard deital themes and biographically signifiant verses about her travels, exile and old friends are included in a promising book which is available from the publisher.

La voz en el viento. Madrid: Compañía General de Artes Gráficas,
1931, 138 pp.
    Covering the years 1929-31, the poems in La voz en el viento
reflect Champourcin's "human love" period and a continued attempt to
unite with the infinite through nature. Much of Juan Ramón
Jiménez' influence--including rose imagery--is present, along with
his hand-written introduction to the volume. Available in North
Carolina-Chapel Hill library.

                                                                    JBL

D

**DATO MURUAIS, Filomena (?-1926).
Born in Orense, she collaborated in the literary movement taking place in Orense in the second half of the nineteenth century. A good friend of Lamas Carvajal, she published articles and contributions in El Heraldo Gallego.

Follatos. Poesías gallegas. Orense: A. Otero, 1891.
The book, which starts with a poem on women's rights that was awarded a prize at a literary contest in Orense, "Defensa das mulleres," is rhymed prose rather than poetry.

CNC & AM

*DENIS DE RUSINOL, Lluisa (1867-1946).
A writer of comedies and poetry, she was born in Barcelona.

KM

DIAZ DE SAEZ, Francisca.
Poet.

Cumbre de lirios. Barcelona: Díaz de Sáez, 1974.
Poetry.

Tres palomas blancas. Reus, Artes Gráficas Diana, 1963.
Poems.

CLG

DIOSDADO, Ana (1938-).
The foremost woman dramatist of contemporary Spain, she has been actively involved in the theatrical world since early childhood in Argentina. Multifaceted, she is a novelist as well as an actress, director, and playwright. Her credits include stage plays, television and movie scripts, translations, and adaptations. Her original plays criticize the consumer society and deplore the lack of communication and human understanding that leads to social conflict and civil war.

Campanas que aturden. Barcelona: Planeta, 1969.
Novel. Finalist, Premio Planeta.

Casa de muñecas. Adaptation of the play by Henrik Ibsen. Madrid:
Ediciones MK, "Colección Escena," no. 36, 1983, ISBN 84-7389-032-9,
99 pp.
  This is the most controversial of Diosdado's several translations
and adaptations of foreign plays. Rather than ending Ibsen's drama
with Nora's slamming of the door, Diosdado added a concluding scene
between Tor and his little daughter that underscored his noncompre-
hending machismo. In order to maintain her overtly feminist conclusion in production, the playwright had to file a complaint with
the Sociedad General de Autores.

Los comuneros. Madrid: Ediciones MK, "Colección Escena," no. 4,
1974, ISBN 84-400-7401-8, 101 pp.
  An episodic, expressionist approach to a particular moment in
Spanish history, the play failed in its initial production because of
an excessively realistic staging. Through oneiric characters representing two life stages of King Carlos I, Diosdado presents once
again her plea for greater tolerance and an end to civil war. Of
particular interest is her portrayal of two women, Juana la loca and
María de Padilla, the wife of one of the rebel leaders whose
execution frames the action.

En cualquier lugar, no importa cuándo. Barcelona: Planeta, 1965,
336 pp.
  An immature first novel, set in the American West during the
nineteenth century, it traces the experiences of a Spanish girl who
seeks a home with her American cousins. It follows the family and
their friends over a period of years. There is an excessive number
of characters primarily based on stereotypes. Out of print. Copy
available in the Biblioteca Nacional in Madrid.

El okapi. Madrid: Escelicer, "Colección Teatro," no. 742, 1972, 73
pp. In Teatro español, 1972-73, ed. F. C. Sainz de Robles, Madrid:
Aguilar, 1974, ISBN 84-03-11091-X.
  This allegorical play whose deeper meaning was missed by critics
and spectators at the time of its original staging, perhaps because
of an excess of realism in the production itself, is set in a middle-
class nursing home. The play features the problems of the elderly
but simultaneously calls for freedom. The sheltered home, with its
provision of creature comforts and isolationism, represents an aging
Francoist Spain.

Olvida los tambores. Madrid: Escelicer, "Colección Teatro," no.
667, 1972, 82 pp. In Teatro español, 1970-71, ed. F. C. Sainz de
Robles, Madrid: Aguilar, 1972.
  A prize-winning first play from 1970, this is still the author's
most successful work. It has been televised in Spain and staged in
Argentina, Peru, and Germany. Featuring the careful construction of
the well-made play, its first act is a model of stage crafting. It
juxtaposes two young couples--one ostensibly representing liberal
views and the other the conservative status quo. The lack of understanding between them leads to tragedy. It explores sex-role
stereotypes and the consumer society as well as social hypocrisy.

Usted también podrá disfrutar de ella. Madrid: Ediciones MK,
"Colección Escena," no. 7, 1975, ISBN 84-7389-007-8, 97 pp. In
Teatro español, 1973-74, ed. F. C. Sainz de Robles, Madrid:
Aguilar, 1975, ISBN 84-03-11093-6.
    The second of Diosdado's major successes, this play features a
carefully constructed and innovative flow in time and space. A non-
representational stage setting facilitated the spectators' immersion
into the nonchronological action. A criticism of the consumer
society, with its exploitation of the female body, the play ends in
suicide but suggests that the solution is activism not despair.

                                                                    PZ

*DOMENECH I ESCATE DE CANELLAS, Maria (1877-1952).
Pseud. **Josep Miralles.**
    Born in Alcover, she moved to Barcelona, where she participated in
the movement for the women of educational character. She founded a
trade-union for working women called "Federació sindical d'obreres."
Her literary work is characterized by the European tradition of the
1930's; that is, a general tendency to escape from the historical
reality and a great emphasis on analyzing the spiritual crisis of the
individual.

    Al rodar del temps. Barcelona: Editor N.A.G.S.A., 1946, 79 pp.

    Confidències. Barcelona: Editor N.A.G.S.A., 1946, 99 pp.
        Nine short stories about nine different women, written as
    monologues or dialogues. These women make us discover their most
    intimate feelings.

    Contrallum. Barcelona: La novela nova, 25, Editor Publicació
    Catalana, 1917, 24 pp.
        A psychological novel about a young man who suffers from the
    conventions of his own family and his social class. Obligated by his
    parents to stay in his native village and work in his father's
    business, the protagonist sees all his ambitions unsatisfied. Being
    married to a girl he does not like, he commits suicide.

    Els gripaus d'or. Valencia: Novela d'ara, Fidel Giro, 1919, 146 pp.

    Herències. Barcelona: Societat catalana d'edicions 110, 1925,
    204 pp.

    Neus. Barcelona: Biblioteca Joventut, 1914, 236 pp.

                                                                    CF

DONA JIMENEZ, Juana (1919-).
    Juana Doña worked for the Group of Anti-Fascist Women during the
Spanish Civil War. Of humble origins, she married a Communist activist
who was assassinated when the war ended in 1939. Doña was jailed for
her Communist sympathies at the end of the war and was sentenced to
death, later commuted to 30 years, though she was released after 20
years. Since her release, she has written, in addition to her memoirs,
Desde la noche y la niebla, a book entitled La mujer, on the topic of
Spanish feminism (Madrid: Editorial Escolar, 1977).

Desde la noche y la niebla (mujeres en las cárceles franquistas).
Novela-testimonio. Madrid: Ediciones de la Torre, 1978,
ISBN 84-85277-41-4, 294 pp.
   A book of memoirs which the author presents in the form of a historical novel, Desde la noche . . . is a unique testimony by a female
activist from the Spanish Civil War who spent 20 years of her life as a
political prisoner in Franco's jails. Doña's is a poignant, shattering
story of the degradation and suffering that the protagonist, Leonor, and
her comrades experienced during those years. The book is of interest to
students of contemporary Spanish history, women's studies or psychology.
Topics include torture, rape, maternity, hunger, solidarity in prison,
repression and the psychological effects of the death sentence, all from
the viewpoint of women who spent their youths in prison. The prologue
is by Alfonso Sastre. Available in paperback, but difficult to find
(see Librería de Mujeres, Madrid).

                                                                    SMG

DRACS, Ofèlia.
   A collective of writers including a few women but with a great
majority of men.

                                                                    KM

E

ECHEGARAY EIZAGUIRRE (DE GONZALEZ), Pastora. Pseud. Jorge Lacosta.
   Writing plays and poetry seems to have run in the Echegaray family.
Pastora's brothers were José, the Nobel prize-winning dramatist, and
Miguel, a festive journalist and popular playwright, both of whom
encouraged her to develop her talents. She was known as a modest poet
in her own right, publishing her poems under various pseudonyms. In
1882 she was declared a "socio (sic) de mérito" for her prize-winning
entry Morir dos veces in the Sociedad Julián Romea's literary contest
in Barcelona. When the play was published in 1890, acerbic critic
Manuel Cañete spoke very highly of it in the Ilustración Española y
Americana (p. 126).

   Morir dos veces, drama en tres actos y en verso. Madrid: J.
   Rodríguez, 1890, 92 pp.
                                                                   NJM

ECHEVARRIA, María Jesús.

   Las medias palabras. Barcelona: Garbo, 1960, 269 pp.
      This novel, which won the Premio de Novela Elisenda de Montcada of
   1959, focuses on La Niña, a 30-year-old Madrid spinster who still
   hopes that the right man will come along. Scenes on the streets, in
   bars and restaurants present a lively picture of Madrid daily life.
   Available Florida International Univ. library.

   Poemas de la ciudad. Madrid: Trilce, 1961.
                                                                   CLG

(H)ENRIQUEZ, Cristobalina (c. 17th century).

   "Las claras ondas del Tajo," a poem in Juan Pérez de Guzmán, "Bajo
   los Austrias," Series: La España Moderna, Dir. José Lázaro,
   Madrid (Establecimiento Tipográfico de Idamor Moreno), 1898, no.
   117, pp. 79-80.
      In this Moorish ballad, the only known poem written by
   Cristobalina (H)enríquez, the beautiful Jazmelina, who has hopes of
   being Queen, is in the tower of the royal palace in Toledo. Day is
   dawning as she gazes down on 30 Moorish knights in elegant dress
   showing off and skirmishing on horseback in the sandy area below.
   The soldiers are watching her eagerly, much to the jealousy of the
   Moorish women. This poem evokes the colorful, exotic romanticism of
   Moorish Spain in the Middle Ages.
                                                                   LAS

ENRIQUEZ DE GUZMAN, Feliciana (b. last third 16th century-?).
    One of few women dramatists in Siglo de Oro Spain, she is also the
author of poems and a short critique of the comedia as a dramatic form.

    Tragicomedia los Iardines y Campos Sabeos. Primera y segunda parte,
    con diez coros y quatro Entreactos. Coimbra: Iacome Carvallo, 1624.
    Primera Parte reprinted in Apuntes para una biblioteca de autoras
    españolas, ed. M. Serrano y Sanz, Madrid: Biblioteca de Autores
    Españoles, 1975, Tomo 269, pp. 358-387.
        A dramatic retelling of the story of Maya, daughter of King
    Atlantis, and Clarisel, King of Sparta, in form and content it is a
    typical comedia of the day, replete with love triangle and convoluted
    plot. The prologue suggests that it may be partly autobiographical
    in nature. It is accompanied by four comic interludes which ridicule
    classical mythology. The Second Part is not readily available and
    the First Part is most accessible in Serrano y Sanz. There is also a
    "carta executoria" ridiculing the dramatic conventions of the day.
                                                                        DD

*ENSENYAT, Franxesca (1952-).
    A poet, she was born in Pollensa on the island of Majorca.

    Amagatall de guipur.

    Ciutat d'horabaixa. Palma: Cors, 1969.
                                                                        KM

*ESCOBEDO, Joana (1942-).
    Born in Barcelona, she is the author of several erudite works. As a
librarian, she has worked with special collections at the Biblioteca de
Catalunya. She teaches Catalan to foreigners, and has collaborated on
texts for this purpose. In her imaginative work, she prefers the novel
to short stories, needing the time and space to elaborate her themes.

    Amic, amat. Barcelona: Edicions 62, "El Balancí," 1980,
    ISBN 84-297-1640-8, 180 pp.
        In a search for identity within a difficult relationship, the
    protagonist, Magda, struggles with herself and her dependence on love
    while questioning conventionality and defending herself from pain,
    both psychic and physical. Daily life in Barcelona is the back-
    ground, with a contrapuntal visit/vision/memory of New York. Time is
    fractured, and dialogue alternates with interior monologue.

    Silenci endins. Barcelona: Edicions 62, "El Balancí," 1979,
    ISBN 84-297-1475-8, 145 pp. 2nd ed., 1980.
        The work is a non-linear story of passions, intuitions, frustrated
    desires, powerlessness and insecurity. Through a long night of
    sleeplessness, moving from conscious to unconscious, half dreaming
    and then recognizing reality, the protagonist shows the imprint of
    years of repression, a rigid, formal education, to an awakening to
    existential thought and a realization of nothingness.
                                                                        KM

ESPINA, Concepción (1869-1955). Also: Concha Espina.
   Concha Espina is the first Spanish woman writer to earn her living
exclusively from her writings. Essentially independent of the major
literary movements of her time, she was influenced by both Realism and
the sentimental novel of late Romanticism. Although she cultivated all
genres, she is primarily known as a novelist. Focussing mainly on
female protagonists, Espina portrays women as victims of their own
sentimentality and of the conflict between their expectations and the
reality of male-female relations. Ideologically moderate to conservative, Espina at times espouses a feminist outlook and occasionally
experiments with new literary forms. She was a prolific writer with
several very fine novels and one prize-winning play among a number of
conventional works.

   Agua de nieve. 1911.
   The Woman and the Sea, trans. Terrell Louise Tatum. New York: R. D.
   Henkle, 1934, 279 pp.
      The novel studies the evolution of Regina de Alcántara from
   egotism to self-denial. Espina portrays Regina as the embodiment of
   the dangers of rationalist and voluntarist philosophies. Divided
   into two parts, the first half of the novel portrays Regina's travels
   in search of a meaningful existence. Loosely structured, it reflects
   her aimlessness. The second part takes place in a small town in
   northern Spain and relates Regina's marriage, the death of her
   husband, and her eventual shedding of rationalism in favor of
   altruism and sentiment. This is the first of Espina's novels to
   study Spanish women in the context of the contemporary world. Available in Obras Completas and in a now out-of-print translation.

   Alas invencibles. Madrid: Afrodisio Aguado, 1938.
      This novel is a reworking of a previously published short story.
   Here the crippled female protagonist is rescued by a Falangist
   aviator and flown to a new life in Nationalist Spain. The novel
   represents a shift from Falangist rhetoric to a defense of Franco and
   of the military aggression of his forces. Available only in a now
   out-of-print hardbound edition.

   Altar mayor. Madrid: Espasa-Calpe, 1954, 217 pp. 2nd ed. 1972.
      Awarded the National Prize for Literature, this novel is no longer
   considered one of Espina's better works. The main value of the work
   lies in the superb descriptions of the Covadonga region, the Asturian
   mountains from which the Reconquest originated. The plot relies
   heavily on melodramatic effects and the characters are excessively
   one-dimensional. Imbued with the nationalistic fervor of the conservative factions during the period preceding the Spanish Civil War,
   Altar Mayor is a novel of national exaltation.

   Aurora de España. Madrid: Biblioteca Nueva, 1955, 306 pp.
   See: La virgen Prudente.

   El caliz rojo. 1923.
      This novel contrasts the moral and spiritual bankruptcy of
   post-World War I Germany with the unshakable idealism of Soledad
   Fontenebro, the protagonist of an earlier novel, La rosa de los
   vientos. In the exaltation of sentiment and the presentation of the
   ideal as unattainable, the novel follows the Romantic vision evident

in many of Espina's works. It differs, however, in the lack of plot,
the elimination of all but the two major characters, and the mini-
mization of conflict. It represents Espina's continued search for
new novelistic forms appropriate to the depiction of sentimental
idealism. Available in Obras completas.

Despertar para morir. 1910.
    This novel studies the conflict between good and evil in the
corrupt Spanish aristocracy of the turn of the century. The action
revolves around two couples, the pure and sentimental Pilar, the
materialistic and cynical Eva, the idealistic young poet Diego, and
the ambitious and deceitful Gracián. Typical of Espina's novels,
the sentimentally vulnerable are paired with insensitive marriage
partners but through their pain, the morally superior come to realize
that suffering is the only true path to a full comprehension as well
as appreciation of life. Overly sentimental in parts, the novel
provides an effective satire of aristocratic decadence and an
interesting study of the evolution of Eva from moral decadence to
self-knowledge and virtue. Available only in Espina's Obras
completas.

Dulce nombre. 1921.
The Red Beacon, trans. Frances Douglas, New York: Appleton, 1924,
286 pp.
    This novel combines a description of mountaineer poverty with the
study of the female protagonist's search for self-realization. It
traces the story of Dulce Nombre and her changing view of life and
her fellow characters as she moves through marriage, widowhood,
rivalry with her daughter, and finally, loss of the only man that she
ever really loved. The novel's attempt to capture the unpredictable,
illogical aspects of human character is only partly successful but
will be more fruitfully developed in later works. Available in Obras
completas and a now out-of-print translation.

La esfinge maragata. 1914. Madrid: Espasa-Calpe, 1954, 1972.
Mariflor, trans. Frances Douglas, New York: Macmillan, 1924, 425 pp.
    One of Espina's best novels, this study of life in the Leonese
district of Maragateria combines the regionalistic vision of
nineteenth-century Realism with the regenerationist interest of the
Generation of 1898. The action revolves around Mariflor, a young
girl of Maragatan descent who is transplanted to the region in late
adolescence. Her gradual adaptation to an unknown culture takes the
reader deeper and deeper into the stark, impoverished world of
Maragateria. The novel is the story of a people's adaptation to
their environment as exemplified by Mariflor and her relatives. The
emphasis is largely on the women characters and on the submission of
their individual needs to the demands of the group. Available in
paperback and a now out-of-print translation.

Flor de ayer. 1934.
    This novel is the first in a series of politicized works written
during the Republic, Spanish Civil War, and the early post-war years.
It combines a melodramatic, highly complex plot with Falangist
rhetoric. The protagonist is a young woman of high moral principles
who triumphs over illegitimacy, poverty, and cruel and immoral

caretakers to emigrate to South America, in a journey of recovery of the old Spanish values. Available in Obras completas.

El fraile menor. 1942.
   A collection of short stories written between 1920 and 1942, El fraile menor reflects the various changes that Espina and her art have undergone in this critical period of Spanish history. The earliest stories reflect her belief that life, in particular the amorous experience, leads to disillusionment. The second section contains more social commentary and suggests the need for social reform. The four war stories reveal Espina's Nationalist sympathies, but the tone is more moderate. Available in Obras completas.

El jayón. 1918.
   One of Espina's only incursions into the world of theater, this play is one of her best works and won a prestigious national prize. The five major characters include a husband and wife, their hunchbacked son, the husband's former fiancée, and her healthy but illegitimate son, who is abandoned by his mother and adopted by Marcela, the legitimate wife. Further complication arises when Marcela switches the two children, so that the recognized legitimate heir will be the healthy child. The play presents Marcela's inner torment as she wrestles with her own guilt and her doubts as to her husband's love for her. Available in Obras completas.

Llama de cera. 1925.
   A collection of two stories and a short novel, all of which depict the conflict between traditional values and the materialism and frivolity of the Post-World War I era. Written in a succinct, journalistc style the narratives reflect a more objective Espina, who balances the positive and negative aspects of the past with those of the present. Increasingly sensitive to feminist issues, several of the stories attempt to break down sexual and national stereotypes.

El más fuerte. Madrid: Aguilar, 1947, 302 pp.
   This novel is the first of Espina's works to focus on a male protagonist and to narrate in full detail the dissolution of an amorous relationship. It relates the story of Adrián Montaves and the multiple social contacts that influence him. After 18 years of happy marriage, the Montaves are now faced with the test of parenting their three children through adolescence. In the process, Adrián grows to know himself and his children while his wife, whose identity is bound to her children's success, remains trapped in a hopeless effort to recover the past. Modern in theme and in execution, this novel is one of Espina's best. Available in Obras compeltas.

El metal de los muertos. 1920. Madrid: Afrodisio Aguado, 1941, 253 pp.
   This ambitious novel of social protest is based on life in the Rio Tinto copper mines in Andalucía. Through an epic cast of characters, Espina studies the period of British exploitation, concentrating on a miners' strike which she places between 1910 and 1920. Espina here advocates a more active resistance to human suffering. Without proposing any specific political solution, she presents the injustices of the miners' situation and the complicity of the Spanish government, the Catholic Church, and Spanish and British capitalists.

Frequently cited as one of Espina's best novels, it is available in
paperback but not in translation.

Moneda blanca. 1942.
   This play is a melodrama with a moral lesson. The action is
complicated by multiple interconnections among the characters and
hints at an occult tragedy that is not revealed until the final act.
The central character is a young girl who discovers on the eve of her
marriage that her father had killed her mother in a jealous rage
after discovering that his wife had been unfaithful. In keeping with
the radically Catholic character of Franco Spain, the tragedy is
resolved with the daughter's entry in the convent, where she will
expiate her parents' guilt. Available in the original edition.

La niña de Luzmela. 1909. Madrid: Espasa-Calpe, 1953, 1971,
149 pp.
   Espina's first novel combines several popular novel forms of the
nineteenth century: the serialized, melodramatic novel known as the
folletín, the sentimental novel, and the moralistic novel. From the
folletín it takes the element of suspense, the frequent use of
coincidence, and the subordination of character to the construction
of a complex plot. From the moralistic and sentimental novel it
borrows the simplistic division of characters into virtue and evil
and the resolution of the action in the reunion of the hero and
heroine. Available in paperback.

Una novela de amor. 1953.
   The last of Espina's novels, this work is based on Marcelino
Menéndez y Pelayo's youthful romance with Conchita Pintado. It is a
simple story of a relationship that fails to sustain itself. This
aspect of the novel is well developed and interestingly presented but
the work is flawed by excessive historical documentation and the
glorification of Menéndez y Pelayo as standard bearer of the Spanish
right. Available in Obras completas.

Obras completas. Madrid: Edición FAX, 1972, Vol. I-II, 2242 pp.

La Otra. 1942.
   This play represents a step toward the presentation of limited
conflict in the literary production of post-war Spain. The action
contrasts two couples, each with one member from the aristocracy and
the other from the lower classes. The play attempts to vindicate
Espina's contention that Spanish society has always respected individual merit over social origins. The young wife from the lower
class proves to her aristocratic father-in-law that her moral
character and her values are closer to his own than those of his
daughter. Available only in the original edition.

Retaguardia, 3rd ed. Córdoba: Nueva España, 1937. First
published in Nationalist-held Burgos.
   Written during the Spanish Civil War, this novel describes the
fall of Santander to the Republican forces. The characters are
divided into two groups: the newly wealthy who are interested only
in increasing their material power, and those of long-established
wealth who are dedicated to the nation's welfare. The plot is a

pretext to describe Republican atrocities and defend the Nationalist cause. Available in Obras completas.

La rosa de los vientos. 1916. Madrid: Espasa-Calpe, 1953, 1972.
    The novel relates the sentimental autobiography of Soledad Fontenebro during her teenage years. The most autobiographical of Espina's fictional works, it describes the emotional maturation of the heroine up to the moment of her marriage. Soledad's gradual elaboration of an extraordinary sensitivity and an exalted, almost mystical view of romantic love is presented with the much-repeated fear that personal happiness will elude her. The novel ends without resolving the issue and suffers from a general lack of precision in the description of the protagonist and her relation with other characters. Available in paperback and in a now out-of-print translation.

La tiniebla encendida. 1940.
    This play is one of Espina's first post-war productions and represents the tendency of the period to sidestep conflict. The action is based on a blind writer's love for two women, his wife and his ex-fiancée. Unlike other works, there is no antagonist, for in the end the materialistic, vain wife reforms and recaptures her husband's love. Social commentary is reduced to the minimum and all tragic overtones are avoided. The ex-fiancée is the only trace of suffering, but will occupy an exalted position as the spiritual inspiration for the writer and for his wife. Available in Obras completas.

Un valle en el mar. 1950.
    This novel attempts to depict the social ideals, the human types, and the physical characteristics of Espina's native Cantabria. Heavily influenced by the nineteenth-century Regionalist writer, José María de Pereda, the main focus of the novel falls on the more contemporary theme of rape and its consequences in a rural, socially stratified society. Although a number of the minor characters suffer from a one-dimensional characterization derived from the melodramatic novels of the previous century, the two central characters of Un valle en el mar, Antonio and Salvadora, are extremely well drawn. Available in Obras completas.

Victoria en América. 1944.
    This novel is the promised continuation of Flor de ayer. With Victoria, Espina constructs a contemporary version of Spanish woman-hood, adapting the qualities of many previous heroines to the histor-ical moment. The novel is more, however, than a panegyric of the superior moral character of Spanish women. Victoria is an adven-turous, spirited young woman who in many respects contradicts the values which Espina the novelist imposes on her. The novel repre-sents a transitional moment, in which Espina moves away from Nationalist rhetoric toward the creation of independent, multi-dimensional characters. Available in Obras completas.

La virgen prudente. 1929.
Espina's only true "feminist" novel, this work is a study of the contradictory tendencies, cultural pressures, and prejudices that condition women's attitudes. The protagonist, symbolically named Aurora de España, is an idealistic young lawyer who struggles with family, suitors, and friends who resist her unorthodoxy. Although Aurora is temporarily lulled into conventional female passivity, in the end she insists on pursuing an independent course. One of the most optimistic of Espina's novels, it reveals her faith in the talents and power of women. Available in Obras completas. A hardback edition was published with the title Aurora de España.

MLB

F

*FABREGAT I ARMENGOL, Rosa.

El cabdell de les bruixes. Barcelona: Huguet Pascal, 1980.
Poetry.

Estelles. Barcelona: laSal, 1979.
Poetry.

Laberints de seda. Barcelona: Pòrtic, 1981.
Novel in which the author identifies quite strongly with the
protagonist.

El turó de les Forques. Barcelona: Pòrtic, 1983.
A novel which combines personal diary, fiction and dreams, divided
into two parts -- fiction and reality, differentiated by theme,
literary form and typography. The author changes everyday happenings
into fantastic and mysterious events. Through the course of the
novel, one sees the development of the feminist movement in its
effects on female protagonists of succeeding generations.

KM

FAGUNDO, Ana María (1938-).
Born in Tenerife, Canary Islands, she studied business, but due to
literary interest came to the USA at age 20. She received a B.A. in
English, University of Redlands, CA; Ph.D. in Comparative Literature,
1967, University of Washington, Seattle. Her book on the life and works
of Emily Dickinson was published in 1972. Since 1967, she has been
Professor of Spanish and Comparative Literature at University of
California, Riverside. Publications include six poetry books, many
articles, short stories, various other poems. She is the editor of
"ALALUZ," a literary review.

Brotes. Santa Cruz de Tenerife, 1965, 61 pp.
Brotes is the author's first book of poetry. She is very
conscious of this, her first published efforts, but her lines are
musical and rhythmic. She delves into the themes of life, solitude,
love and poetry itself. Sensitive and extraordinarily rich vocabulary. Prologue by E. Gutiérrez Albelo, who accurately states that
the reader with high expectations will not be deceived. A paperbound
volume is out of print but accessible in libraries.

Configurado tiempo. Madrid: Oriens, 1974, 103 pp.
     This, the author's fourth book of poems, prompted the publisher to
state that Fagundo is probably one of the most spiritual poets of
contemporary Spanish literature. This volume states undeniably that
life and poetry are inseparable and so it is obviously autobiographical. The familiar themes of life and love emerge again but are
expressed now in terms of a new and fresh beginning, using her
beloved island as a solid base and source of inspiration. Paperback.
Available in libraries.

Desde Chanatel, el canto. Sevilla: Coleccíon Angaro, 1982, 91 pp.
     Chanatel is the author's sixth and latest book of poetry and was a
finalist in the annual Angaro literary prize competition in 1981.
"Chanatel" is a symbolic place which serves as the point of
departure. This volume emerges as a synthesis of the previous
collections. The author reaffirms her origins, remembers her past
and looks with hope to the future. The themes are universal. Poetry
is the essence of life and life begins on the island. Paperback.
500 copies printed in first edition. Available in Spanish
bookstores.

Diario de una muerte. Madrid: Alfaguara, 1970, 85 pp.
     This volume follows Isla adentro, published the previous year.
The prevalent theme is death. An elegy to her father, her poetry is
an eloquent, anguished and gripping lament about this most universal
theme. The language is elegant, precise; the emotion is controlled
while the use of metaphor is rich and abundant. This collection is
characterized by shorter poems with a generous intercalation of a
variation of the classic Spanish sonnet. Out of print but accessible
in libraries.

Invencíon de la luz. Barcelona: Vosgos, 1978, 112 pp.
     This is the author's fifth volume of verse. It won the "Carabela
de oro" prize for poetry in Spain, 1977. A joyful song to poetry,
which is equivalent to light, is expressed in a vivid and boundless
torrent of metaphors and colorful images. Poetry and love are portrayed as being inseparable, while life, a result of this eternal
love, weaves all the sensations into verse and light and hope for
renewal. Paperback. Accessible in libraries.

Isla adentro. Santa Cruz de Tenerife: Gaceta Semanal de Las Artes,
1969, 154 pp.
     The poet's second book of verse, contains a preface by Hugo
Rodríguz-Alcalá, who expresses his high acclaim by referring to her
"poetic mysticism." The dominating theme is the relationship between
the poet and poetry expressed in mystical terms as San Juan de la
Cruz did with the preparation of the soul in order to be worthy of
the union with God. Original, musical poetry which reveals sensitivity, maturity and the definite control and self-assurance of the
poet. Paperback. Accessible in libraries.

                                                                 HPM

FALCON O'NEILL, Lidia (1935-).
   Lidia Falcón, born in Madrid, has been the guiding intellectual and activist force in Spanish feminism for over 20 years. She is the founder of the first Feminist Party in Spain (1979) and the founder of Spain's first feminist magazine, Vindicación Feminista (1976-1979). She is a nationally-known journalist and has published 14 books of fiction, as well as socio-political treatises on women and society. As a product of the Spanish Civil War, a child of the defeated Republicans, her autobiographical books and articles document this silenced and anguished chapter in Spanish history. Falcón has experienced torture and interior exile for her staunch support of women's rights and human freedom.

   El alboroto español. Barcelona: Fontanella, 1984, ISBN 84-244-0531-5, 261 pp.

   Cartas a una idiota española. Barcelona: Dirosa, 1974, 365 pp. 2nd ed., 1975; 3rd ed., 1976. Edición de Bolsillo. Barcelona: Plaza y Janés, 1980.
   Lettres à une idiote Espagnole, Paris: Editions des Femmes, 1975.
      Cartas a una idiota española is a series of accounts of women's fate in Spain using the literary device of letters from a female lawyer (Falcón) to her friend. It is an irreverent and humorous criticism of male exploitation of women. The importance of the book is its broad view of women in Spanish society seen from a militant and political feminist point of view. Falcón includes university students, single women, textile workers, seamstresses, typists and secretaries, peasants and housewives. Their funny, but sad stories include the frustrated ambitions of a diplomat's wife, the amorous disasters of a hippie, a Catholic nun's alienation, a prostitute's exploitation and a housewife's laments. Originally a series of journalistic pieces in a Spanish daily newspaper, Cartas is sold in both Spain and Latin America. Danish translation is also available.

   Los derechos civiles de la mujer. Barcelona: Nereo, 1963, 600 pp.

   Los derechos laborales de la mujer. Madrid: Montecorvo, 1965, 507 pp.

   En el infierno. (Ser mujer en las cárceles de España.) Ediciones de Feminismo, 1977, ISBN 84-4003279-X.
      This is a novelized account of the situation of women in Spanish jails, reformatories, psychiatric and prison hospitals. The book's infernal world centers on the prison hospital where Falcón lived for some time and includes the horror of a hunger strike, an epidemic of venereal disease, repression against lesbians, and the rape and pregnancy of a retarded woman in the prison hospital. Falcón describes the underworld of detention and torture in the basement of Police Security in Madrid and life in a prison where 20 women and 40 children were crowded together in a few square feet. The book is written in a poetic voice and the literary style is as important as the theme. The author wrote it while in jail, and it was smuggled out of prison to her children. It was finally published after Franco's death, and it remains her most dramatic and shocking work, evoking intense reactions in its readers. It is in its second edition in Spanish and is also available in French (Enfers des Femmes, 1979).

Es largo esperar callado. Barcelona: Pomaire, 1975. 2nd ed., 1976,
    ISBN 84-286-0478-9. 3rd ed., Editorial Vindicación Feminista-
Hacer, 1984, ISBN 84-85348-55-9, 338 pp.
    The backdrop of this novel is Spain's Communist Party and the
political machinations that shape its participants. The novel
centers around the conflict between outspoken Athenea, the first one
to criticize the Party leadership because of its authoritarianism and
revisionism, and her ex-compañero Rubén, who always plays it safe
and thus maintains the Party's favor. Although they both leave the
Party and join a splinter group, Athenea is still not allowed to
transcend her position of marginality as a defined, political woman.
The novel's importance lies in its realistic portrayal of over 20
years of clandestine struggle in Spain, fictionally recreating key
historical figures such as Santiago Carrillo, Dolores Ibarruri and
Enrique Lister. It is also significant for its portrayal of the
lives of Spanish exiles in France and in the socialist countries, for
its picture of the difficulties women have had to endure in Spanish
society at large, as well as in the supposedly progressive circles of
leftist politics.

Los hijos de los vencidos. Barcelona: Pomaire, 1979, ISBN
84-296-0376-6, 255 pp.
    Los hijos de los vencidos is an autobiographical work which
documents post-Civil War Spain and Falcón's own first 14 years as a
child of the defeated Republicans. Falcón's Spain is sordid,
depicting ubiquitous poverty, smuggling, prostitution, fraudulent
business deals, and police persecution against union and political
leaders. Her family is an anomaly, four generations of women alone:
her father has abandoned them; her Republican uncle has been executed; her aunt has been imprisoned. The book is written from the
double perspective of a child, as Falcón remembers herself, and it
also incorporates her sharp socio-political observations and analyses
of the importance of World War II, Nazism, Franco's complicity with
Hitler and the Allied Forces' victory. The book's importance lies in
painting a faithful picture of Spanish society, focusing particularly
on the lower classes: the workers, the maids; and the petty bour-
geosie too, the shopkeepers, the school teachers. The book is a link
that describes the depressing post-war climate and augurs the darkness of the next 25 years of fascist rule.

El juego de la piel. Barcelona: Argos-Vergara, 1983, ISBN
84-7178-717-2, 197 pp.
    The novel describes the hippie atmosphere of the 1970's in Europe.
The protagonist, Elisenda, flees her middle-class Barcelona home to
join a commune in London, then a gang of juvenile delinquents in
Paris and eventually to become a heroin addict in Barcelona, where
she almost dies. The leitmotif of the novel is its feminist message,
the final hope for Elisenda. The traditional religious training at
an all-girls Catholic school, the small town atmosphere she comes
from, the political struggles, incipient feminism, drugs and juvenile
delinquency form the framework of the novel. It has been considered
a forerunner of many other novels on the subject of delinquency and
drugs, but the only one with a vision of the world through the female
experience.

Mujer y sociedad (Análisis de un fenómeno reaccionario).
Barcelona: Fontanella, 1969. 2nd ed., 1974. 3rd ed., 1984.
ISBN 82-244-0333-9, 390 pp.

The militant tone, as well as the content of Falcón's book caused
it to be detained by the Spanish censors for over two years. In 1967
when it was written it constituted a ground breaking study in women's
history, sociology, anthropology and politics. It includes analyses
of the oppressive situation of women in Spain, the Arab countries,
Hitler's Germany, Mussolini's Italy, Latin America and the U.S.
through an examination of religious texts, customs, and legal institutions. It looks at prostitution and witchcraft and concludes with
an analysis of the most significant events in the twentieth century
and their effects on women. It contains a bibliography and is distributed in both Spain and Latin America.

La razón feminista (La mujer como clase social y económica. El
modo de producción doméstica) Tomo I. Barcelona: Fontanella,
1981, ISBN 84-244-0501-3, 637 pp.

In this volume Falcón analyzes deeply the material causes of the
exploitation of women throughout history and in all types of commun-
ities. It is one of the first times that feminism is made the
subject matter of a scientific investigation. Not only a historical
and anthropological treatise, it also uncovers the laws which govern
reproduction and turns the existing schemes upside down by affirming
that reproduction determines production. The relationship between
the domestic mode of production and the capitalist mode of production
is also scrutinized. Finally, production relationships between men
and women, class consciousness and the myth of the bourgeois woman
close this first volume. Extensive bibliography.

La razón feminista (La reproducción humana) Tomo II. Barcelona:
Fontanella, 1982, ISBN 84-244-0508-0, 717 pp.

In this work Falcón demythifies the taboos, falsities and legends
accumulated by the ruling ideology during the last century which
attempt to convince women of the positiveness of motherhood. She
discusses genetic experiments and in vitro fertilization and
concludes that only by maternity in vitro will women liberate
themselves from their physiological and ancestral destiny and thus
from thir current servitude, to become the protagonists of the
future. Extensive bibliography.

Sustituciones y fideicomisos. Barcelona: Nereo, 1962, 500 pp.

Viernes y trece en la Calle del Correo. Barcelona: Planeta, 1981,
ISBN 84-320-3583-1, 342 pp.

This is an autobiographical account in novel form of the judicial
process against various political activists and intellectuals accused
of collaborating with the Basque terrorist organization, the ETA, in
September, 1974. The author was arrested, along with her companion,
journalist Eliseo Bayo, and children and 20 other people and remained
imprisoned in Yeserías, the women's penitentiary in Madrid, for nine
months. It is a chronological narrative in journalistic style that
describes and analyzes the events she experienced, within the framework of her intimate knowledge and perspective on the history of the

Franco regime and its abuses. Dramatist Antonio Buero Vallejo has
called this mystery, detective and political novel "the last word on
the subject of terrorism."

GFW

**FARIÑA E COBIAN, Herminia (1904-1966).
Born in Santiago, she was very active as a writer in Galician in the
1920's. Two plays written by her were produced at the time: Margarita
a malfadada and O soldado de froita.

Seara. Poesías gallegas. Illustrated by Luis Pintos Fonseca.
Pontevedra: Celestino Peón, 1924.
These 34 poems in the modernista vein deal with the Galician
homeland and the rural landscape. In colloquial language, it is very
sentimental, sad poetry.

CNC & AM

FERNANDEZ CUBAS, Cristina (1945-).
Born in Arenys de Mar, Barcelona, she studied law and journalism and
is a journalist at present. She lived two years in Latin America and
studied Arabic in Cairo. She belongs to the group of 12 new women
writers who started to publish after 1970 included in Doce relatos de
mujeres, edited by Ymelda Navajo, Madrid: Alianza, 1982. Very relevant
to women's studies because she brings her own subjective view.

Los altillos de Brumal. Cuadernos ínfimos, 112. Barcelona:
Tusquets, 1983, ISBN 84-7223-612-9, 126 pp.

Mi hermana Elba. Cuadernos Infimos, 92. 1st ed., Barcelona:
Tusquets, 1980. 2nd ed., Barcelona: Tusquets, 1981. ISBN
84-7223-592-0, 127 pp.
The author's first book, it contains four narrations: "Mi hermana
Elba," "La ventana del jardín," "Lúnula y Violeta" and "Provocador
de imágenes." The story which titles the book is about the remem-
brances of an adolescent told in first person by an adult narrator.
The cruelty and selfishness of youth is poignant. "Lúnula y
Violeta" has a magical quality in the contrast of the two women who
possibly are only one. The book has a fresh and innovative feeling.
The reader plays an important role, given the ambiguity of the
situations.

El vendedor de sombras. Illus. by Montserrat Clavé. Barcelona:
Vergara, 1982, ISBN 84-7178-479-3.
El venedor d'ombres. Trans. by María Eulalia Cistaré. Barcelona:
Argos Vergara, 1982, ISBN 84-7178-480-7.
El venedor d'ombres. Trans. by Basilio Losada. Barcelona: Argos
Vergara, 1982, ISBN 84-7178-481-5.
Itzal Saltzailea idazkera. Illus. by Montserrat Clavé. Barcelona:
Argos Vergara, 1982, ISBN 84-7178-482-3.

CA

*FERRAN I MORA, Eulàlia.
A poet, she is the author of Pensament endins, Barcelona: Claret,
1976, and Dos pobles, un cor, L'Hospitalet de Llobregat: Romargil,
1979.

KM

FIGUERA AYMERICH, Angela (1902-).
Though not publishing her poetry until late in life, she is
remembered for a unique expression in debt to Antonio Machado, León
Felipe, and Pablo Neruda. Born in the Basque Region, she cultivated the
down-to-earth attitude for which Northern poets are noted. By taking a
feminine viewpoint on social and ethical issues, she developed protest
themes popular in the 1950's, when she began participating in Madrid
literary life. In this sense, she is historically grouped with Blas de
Oteo, Gabriel Celaya, and José Hierro. Her poetry, as did theirs, met
delays before censorship by the Franco Regime.

Angela Figuera Aymerich. México: Universidad Nacional
Autónoma. Dirección General de Difusión Cultural, Departamento
de Humanidades, 1979, 36 pp.
    A selection of 29 representative poems from the poet's major
works, this anthology is a popular edition of Figuera Aymerich's
poetry directed to Mexican readers. Edition and Introduction by
Carmen Alardín.

Antología. Monterrey, N.L.: Sierra Madre, 1969, 36 pp.
    This selection of Figuera's poetry emphasizes poems from Mujer de
barro and Toco la tierra. It publishes "Romance de puebloespaña"
for the first time as well as the following material: A greeting
from the poet dated 26 March 1968; selected aphorisms from her
correspondence, a biobibliographic note. Edition and Introduction by
Alfredo Gracia Vicente.

Antología total, 1948-1969. Madrid: Videosistemas, 1973,
ISBN 84-300-5946-6, 139 pp. Madrid: Videosistemas, 1975,
ISBN 84-354-0036-0, 139 pp.
    In addition to poems from all her works to 1969, this anthology
publishes three other poems for the first time. Of general scholarly
interest as an introduction to Figuera's poetry, it includes a bibliography of her works, a list of anthologies that include her poems,
and a list of critical mentions of her work. Edition, Prologue, and
Notes by Julián Marcos. With phonodisc in pocket.

Belleza cruel. México: Compañía General de Ediciones, 1958,
134 pp. Barcelona: Lumen, 1978, ISBN 84-264-272-8, 67 pp.
    Nineteen poems, separated into three sections, explore social
topics such as the poet's duty to protest human suffering and
injustice as well as the need for peace and freedom. Because of
censorship, the first edition was published abroad. This work,
Figuera's best known, is of general interest to scholars of the
period. With Introduction by León Felipe and, in the second
edition, a Prologue by Carlos Alvarez also. Available in paperback.

De la nueva poesía española, Angela Figuera. Monterrey, México:
Poesía en el Mundo, No. 14, 1959, pp. 309-327.
    The program of a poetry reading held 28 March 1959 in Monterrey,
Mexico, this publication reprints the ten poems by Figuera that were
read. It also includes brief biographies of the poet and of Alfredo
Gracia Vicente, in charge of reading, and reproduces the well-known
letter from León Felipe to Figuera.

Los días duros. Vencida por el angel. Víspera de la vida. El
grito inútil. Madrid: A. Aguado, 1953, 192 pp.
    This volume contains the second edition of the last three works
listed in the title and the first edition of "Los días duros." The
11 poems divided into two sections--"Los días duros" and "Clamor"--
deal with existentialist themes: the purpose of human existence, the
poet's duty to protest injustice and to face the future without
despair. The candidly feminine speaker renounces passivity, speaking
with authority and sensitivity about difficult times and issues.

El grito inútil. Alicante: Colección Ifach, 1952, 61 pp.
    In the first poem, the speaker asks what one protesting woman can
accomplish. The next 17 poems are tentative answers to that
question; their themes: laborers, the struggles of women, and the
poet as superfluous in society. The final poem, dedicated to Blas de
Otero, affirms the need to protest and seek solutions. Of scholarly
interest for a feminist view of postwar social issues. Available
through interlibrary loan.

Mujer de barro: Poemas. Madrid: S.A.E.T.A., 1948, 71 pp.
    The clearly feminine speaker in this work recreates a primary
universe, peopled by the self, the lover-husband, and the son. The
85 poems are divided into three sections. In the first, the speaker
celebrates moments of total identification between self and,
variously, sister-earth, lover, and child. The second part, "Poemas
de mi hijo y yo," consists of light verse on anecdotal topics. The
final section, "El fruto redondo," includes introspective poems, many
commenting upon the creation and purpose of poetry. Of scholarly
interest for feminist themes.

Mujer de barro. Madrid: Afrodisio Aguado, 1951, 151 pp.
    This is the second edition of the work; it includes the second
edition of Soria pura as well. Available in the Biblioteca Nacional
(Madrid).

Primera antología. Caracas, Venezuela: Lírica Hispana, No. 215,
March 1961, 80 pp.
    Thirty-two poems selected from her major works make up this
collection. They are preceded by a Prologue written by Conie Lobell
and Jean Aristeguieta, editors of Lírica Hispana, and followed by
biographical and bibliographical notes about Figuera, as well as by
other notes concerning Venezuelan literary life. With a dedicated
photo of the author.

Soria pura. Madrid: Jura, 1949, 73 pp.
    Among the 48 poems, divided into six sections, is one in homage to
Antonio Machado, who greatly influenced this work. The major theme
is the amorous surrender of the speaker to nature. With sketches by
Rafael Figuera.

Toco la tierra: Letanías. Madrid: Rialp, 1962, 54 pp.
    Twenty-three poems on social themes continue the passionate style
of Belleza cruel. With pledges of humanitarian commitment in the
dedicatory poem, among others, the speaker calls for brotherly love
toward the less fortunate. Some poems are patriotic, others protest
various injustices. "Tierra" symbolizes, in different poems, Spain,

mankind, source of harvest, and the true reality. Of scholarly
interest for its social themes.

Vencida por el ángel. Alicante: "Verbo," 1950.
    This brief collection consists of five poems that are important
within Figuera's development as statements about her motives for
writing. "Egoismo" evokes the attitude of a "pure" poet; the title
poem, that of an existentialist poet. The remaining poems express
commitment and protest. The second edition (in Los días duros) is
available through interlibrary loan.

Víspera de la vida. Madrid: Colección Neblí, 1953, 34 pp.
    This collection's emblems, taken from a verse by Rilke, are two
moments of supreme struggle, those of birth and death. They mark the
metaphysical limits for poems that skeptically speculate on the
nature of human life within a Christian context. The 12 poems,
divided among five sections, tend toward introspection and elegy.
With eight drawings and cover design by Nuñez-Castelo.

                                                                    EW

FIGUEROA GAMBOA, Natalia (1939-).
    Born in San Sebastián, she has written since childhood and published
her first book at the age of 18. She knows several languages and frequently writes articles and feature stories for major newspapers and
magazines (ABC and Sábado gráfico). She worked on series for Televisión Española and won the Premio Nacional de Televisión Española
and won the Premio Nacional de Televisión in 1969 and the Antena de Oro
in 1973. She also created programs for Radio Madrid/Radio España and
has had her own shows on R.T.V. El caballo desavanecido, her translation and adaptation of Françoise Sagan's 1966 play Le Cheval évanoui
was staged in Madrid in 1967.

    El caballo desavanecido. Colección teatro, no. 576. Madrid:
    Alfil, 1968, 67 pp.

    Decía el viento. . . Madrid: Espejo, 1957, 178 pp.
        The author's first book published when she was 18, this collection
    of prose poems shows the influence of J. R. Jiménez. Figueroa
    converts her experiences into a literary diary. A solitary observer,
    she transcribes what she sees, often unfortunate people, sometimes
    celebrations, as well as what she feels and the love she hopes for.
    Prologue by Gonzalo Torrente Ballester. Difficult to find.

    Palabras nuevas. Madrid: Círculo, 1960, 102 pp.
        Figueroa's second book of poetic prose reveals a greater emphasis
    on the provincial scenes, people and unfortunate, infirm children of
    Sigüenza. The title reflects a maturing attitude in the treatment of
    love; words, voice, even silence play a significant role in the
    author's search for expression. Available in few U.S. libraries.

    Los puntos sobre las fes. Madrid: Prensa Española, 1975,
    ISBN 84-287-0362-0, 230 pp.
        A collection of 35 short articles dated 1970 to 1974, mostly from
    Madrid with a few from London and Russia. The subject matter varies
    as the author focuses on the present conditions of the family, the
    media, arts and letters, everyday attitudes and language as well as
    other societal procedures and behavior. Often she criticizes the

thoughtless devaluation of custom in the push toward modernization.
Paperback.

Tipos de ahora mismo. Madrid: Myr, 1970, ISBN 84-400-0674-8,
248 pp.
    The author's prologue attributes her inspiration to a nineteenth-
century book on diverse personages of that epoch. Figueroa's work is
a collection of prose sketches on 51 Spanish "types" of today. The
lighthearted book includes the tour guide, the stewardess, the
go-go girl and several types of movie people. Illustrations by
Mingote. Paperback.

GM

FOREST, Eva (1928-). Pseud. Julen Agirre.
    Forest's family roots are in Catalonia. She studied medicine in
Madrid and then worked in the psychiatric clinic of José López Ibor.
Today she writes on conditions in the Basque provinces, where she lives
with her husband, the dramatist Alfonso Sastre. Her commitments have
involved her in various solidarity movements; though often claimed as a
feminist writer (she is one of ten interviewed in Feminismo ante el
franquismo, ed. Linda Gould Levine and Gloria Feiman Waldman, Miami,
Fla.: Ediciones Universal, 1979), she usually sets the woman's question
in the context of social justice. Her personal narratives blend
autobiographical writing with philosophical inquiry.

Diario y cartas desde la cárcel-Journal et lettres de prison,
bilingual ed. (French and Spanish). Paris: Editions des Femmes,
1975, 538 pp.
Journal et lettres de prison, traduit de l'espagnol par le collectif
de traduction des Editions des femmes. Paris: Editions des femmes,
1975, ISBN 2-7210-0036-5, 251 pp.
Diario y cartas desde la cárcel. Donostia: Hórdago, 1978,
ISBN 84-7099-041-1, 189 pp.
From a Spanish Jail. Translated from the French by Rosemary Sheed;
translated from the French of a work originally published in Spanish
under the title, Diario y cartas desde la cárcel. Harmondsworth:
Penguin, 1975, ISBN 0-14-052320-0, 191 pp.
From A Spanish Prison, originally published as Diario y cartas desde
la cárcel. Berkeley, Calif.: Moon Books; New York: distributed by
Random House, 1975, ISBN 0-394-40769-5, 191 pp.
    This book has two almost equal parts: A journal written for her
children between September 29 and October 5, 1974, the time when she
was in solitary confinement and just after spending nine days at the
Dirección General de Seguridad where she was tortured; and letters
written to her children from the women's prison, Yeserías, in
Madrid, and the prison hospital (Oct. 26, 1974 to Feb. 28, 1975).
Though filled with practical matters and family concerns, they reveal
how she transmuted the torture and suffering she underwent.

Operación Ogro: cómo y por qué ejecutamos a Carrero Blanco.
Hendaye: Mugalde, 1974, 192 pp.
Operation Ogro: comment et pourquoi nous avons exécuté Carrero
Blanco, premier ministre espagnol, traduit de l'espagnol par Victoria
Pueblos. Paris: Seuil, 1974, 220 pp.

Operacion Ogro, diez años después; edición popular en la que se
revela que "Julen Agirre" fue el seudónomo de Eva Forest. (Punto y
Hora, número extraordinario el 20 de diciembre de 1983.) 94 pp.
Operation Ogro: the execution of Admiral Luis Carrero Blanco, trans.
frm the Spanish, adapted and with an introduction by Barbara Probst
Solomon. New York: Quadrangle/New York Times Book Co., 1975,
ISBN 0-8129-0552-0, 196 pp.
    This pseudonymous work tells the story of the Basque commandos
responsible for assassinating Admiral Luis Carrero Blanco in Madrid,
December 20, 1973. Its authorship was one of the charges brought
against Forest in her imprisonment from September 16, 1974 to the end
of May, 1977. Of historical value, its testimony, given in question
and answer form, provides an interesting example of responses to a
disguised female voice. Appended are ETA manifestos and police
documents which provide background and dramatize the conflicting
points of view.

Testimonios de lucha y resistencia, Yeserías 75-77. Hendaye:
Mugalde, 1977, 256 pp.
Témoignagne de lutte et de résistance. Paris: Editions des
Femmes, 1978, ISBN 2-7210-0119-1.
Testimonios de lucha y resistencia: Yeserías 75-77, con palabras
sobre la tortura de A. Sastre. Donostia: Hórdago, 1979, ISBN
84-7099-081-0, 293 pp.
    The theme of institutionalized torture in a modern bourgeois state
occupies Sastre in a long preliminary essay in the 1979 edition.
Forest then introduces her own story and the often verbatim testimony
of 31 other prisoners, all women but one. She then supplies the
context for the stories of these Basque political prisoners and
theorizes about such subjects as marginal existence and the psycho-
social difficulties of seeking expression. Her book poses questions
for Spaniard and non-Spaniard, for lay reader and specialist in
literature, politics, sociology and psychology.

NV

FORMICA CORSI, Mercedes (1918-).
    Brought up in several Andalusian cities, notably Sevilla, as a member
of the elitist bourgeoisie, Fórmica moved temporarily to Madrid during
the years of the Republic. While studying law there she became aware of
the Institución Libre de Enseñanza, and also met the founders of
Falange Española, which she joined. Engaged in the difficult but lucid
synthesis of many cultural tendencies, this writer stands as a tolerant
intellectual during the post-war years. Her novels are linked to her
life experience, and show a projection of her future development as a
lawyer striving for women's rights, as a historian, and as a writer of
her memoirs.

A instancia de parte. Madrid: Cid, 1954, 244 pp. 2nd ed., 1955.
    The third and latest novel of Fórmica, it follows the documentary
line of the previous ones. This book deals with two cases which
intertwine in the course of the narration. One of them, the most
artistically achieved, presents the situation of a woman trapped by
her husband, deprived of her son, held incommunicado, and eventually
deported to her native Philippines, through a judiciary monstrosity
which denounced the defenselessness of married women. The second
story, less convincing, shows a man as a victim of a machista

society. From this novel the future endeavor of Fórmica as a lawyer is readily perceptible.

La ciudad perdida. Barcelona: Luis de Caralt, 1951, 192 pp.
    This novel deals with life in Madrid ten years after the end of the Civil War, and is rigorously contemporary to the problem it presents: the encounter and subsequent conflict between an intellectual socialite and a fugitive maquis who has made an unfortunate incursion into the city, and is holding her hostage for several hours. The novelist shows great capacity for the creation of dramatic tension through the use of techniques which were quite new in fiction writing in Spain at the time. Both because of the subject matter and the way it is treated, this novel stands as an important contribution to the genre.

Escucho el silencio. Pequeña historia de ayer II. Barcelona: Planeta, 1984, ISBN 84-320-4323-0, 191 pp.
    In this volume of her recollections Fórmica approaches an obscure period with such autobiographical sincerity as to make her book required reading for access to a substantial part of the intellectual background of war and post-war years. War-time Sevilla, then Madrid are shown as worlds not yet fixed, where the reminiscences of the old culture struggle to survive in a new order eager to forget. Alberti, Guillén, Machado, Lorca, Hernández appear with José-Antonio, La Pasionaria, Azaña as experiences, while for emergent generations these were to be only shadows. This book shows cultural survival at its best.

La hija de don Juan de Austria. Ana de Jesús en el proceso al pastelero de Madrigal. Madrid: Revista de Occidente, 1973, ISBN 84-292-9304-3, 402 pp. There are four editions in all, the last one in 1975; the book is currently out of print.
    This work received the Fastenrath prize awarded by the Royal Academy of the Language; in it Fórmica enters with the historian's rigor into a legendary topic. The book reveals the legal usages of sixteenth-century Spain, as it shows the pressures to which women were subjected. The whole Madrigal trial is treated, and the scholarship clarifies the hazy reputation of the Abbess of the Monastery of Las Huelgas in Burgos, who, if eventually vindicated, was a key to a scandal that shook the court of Philip II. There are transcriptions of documents discovered by Fórmica; the book also has a prologue by Julio Caro Baroja.

María de Mendoza (Solución a un enigma amoroso). Madrid: Caro Raggio, 1979, ISBN 84-7035-056-0, 379 pp.
    Rather than a biography of D. Juan de Austria's secret lover, this work is an exploration of the status of women during sixteenth-century Spain; it also concerns itself with the integration of converted Jews into the nobility. The interrelation of old and new Christians, their secret genealogies, are laboriously traced, exposing a fascinating hunt for the identity of María de Mendoza, sifting through all possibilities to eventually discover the true woman. Fórmica incorporates this information in her interpretation of modern Sevilla in a new, yet unpublished novel. Four appendixes complete the work.

Monte de Sancha. Barcelona: Luis de Caralt, 1950, 200 pp.
     The novel focuses on the tragedy of upper class Málaga families
of foreign extraction during the outbreak of the Civil War. The
heroine dies, as do all her relatives, in revengeful executions
perpetrated by the working class. Constructed as a retrospection on
several chronological levels, this novel shows literary culture and
artistry, and it is the first one to deal with the war as a direct
theme where the motives of both sides are considered. As a link in
the evolution of the Spanish novel, Monte de Sancha deserves more
critical attention that it has so far received.

Visto y vivido, 1931-1937. Pequeña historia de ayer. Barcelona:
Planeta, 1982, ISBN 84-320-3641-2, 261 pp. 2nd ed., 1983.
     This is the first volume of Fórmica's memoirs, comprising her
childhood and up to the outbreak of the Civil War. A school girl in
Córdoba and Sevilla, an adolescent in Sevilla and Cádiz, and later
a young woman in Málaga, Fórmica reconstructs the pre-war atmosphere of the Andalusian bourgeoisie. Her parents' divorce forced her
to move to a socially more modest but intellectually more rewarding
Madrid, where she attended the university, got a glimpse of the
"residencias" which remained for her "paraísos inalcanzables," and
joined Falange. The book ends with an account of the war in Málaga
which is a reminder of her first novel.

M-EB

FORRELLAD, Luisa (1925-).
     In 1953 Luisa Forrellad received the coveted and prestigious literary
prize, Premio Nadal, for her first novel, Siempre en capilla. This book
has proved highly popular and has gone through ten editions. In a brief
biographical note to the last edition, it is mentioned that the author
was born in Sabadell and has worked for the theatre as a writer and an
actress. Apparently she has not published anything besides her prize-
winning novel.

     Siempre en capilla. Barcelona: Destino, 1954, 282 pp.
9th ed., Barcelona: Destino, 1970, 282 pp. 10th ed., Barcelona:
Círculo de Lectores, 1983, ISBN 84-226-1442-6, 304 pp.
     The novel is a first-person narration of a young English doctor
who, along with his two friends and colleagues, works in a poor
neighborhood of London at the time of a severe diphtheria epidemic.
The ravages of the epidemic and the doctors' efforts to save its
victims are described with a great deal of realistic details. A note
of melodrama is introduced, however, with the figure of an escaped
convict and killer whom the doctors hide from the police in order to
use him as an experimental guinea pig.

A-MA

FRANCO, Dolores (1912-1977).
     Franco received a baccalaureate degree from the University of
Madrid, field of specialization: Modern Philology. She studied under
Ortega y Gasset, Zubiri, Américo Castro, Navarro Tomás, Dámaso Alonso
and Salinas. Married to Julián Marías, she was Professor of
Literature and Philosophy at several Spanish institutions such as Aula
Nueva and Hispanic Studies courses in Soria. She also taught for
American university programs in Madrid: San Francisco State, Tulane

University and Bowling Green University. Her writings trace the concern for Spain in major Spanish writers through the centuries.

La preocupación de España en su literatura. Madrid: Adán, 1944, 420 pp.
España como preocupación. 2nd ed., Madrid: Guadarrama, 1960, 576 pp. (Expanded and revised edition of La preocupación de España en su literatura.)
España como preocupación. 3rd ed., Barcelona: Vergara, S.A., 1980, 445 pp. (Expanded and revised edition.)
     Commencing with Cervantes, Dolores Franco proceeds chronologically to select passages from Spanish authors which reflect their concern for the enigmatic reality which is Spain. She includes a concise and lucid analysis of each period and author, ending with the Generation of '98, one of whose members, Azorín, prologues her book. The second edition bears the title she had chosen initially, but was rejected by the censors: España como preocupación. The major change here is the inclusion of a long section on Ortega y Gasset. The third and posthumous edition of 1980 contains a sensitive epilogue by Julián Marías (her husband of 36 years) evaluating the work. There is also an appendix containing three of her unpublished essays. First two editions are out of print, but third is readily available.

EFC

FUENTES BLANCO, María de los Reyes (1927-).
     Born in Sevilla, Fuentes still lives there and has been active in its cultural life, in addition to serving as Jefe del Negociado de Asistencia Social for the city. She has received the following prizes: Poesía castellana Ciudad de Barcelona, 1965; Literatura Ciudad de Sevilla, 1966; "Marina" de Orense, 1963; Amigos de la Poesía de Valencia, 1975. (She is listed under Reyes Fuentes, María de los in the National Union Catalog.)

Acrópolis del testimonio. Sevilla: Ayuntamiento de Sevilla, 1966.
     Poems.

Aire de amor. Madrid: Ed. Rialp, 1977, 92 pp.
     A collection of 51 poems which, according to the author's preface, fits within the cycle which goes from Sonetos del corazón to Elegías Tartessias. In the poems love is portrayed as agony and a chimera. Passionate love is described as an eruption, a storm, a cascade, a conflagration. Love is astonishing; it rushes headlong, leaping, galloping. Occasionally love is nostalgic and melancholy, but more often words like "tortura," "sangre" and "herida" attest to its violence. Available University of Texas at Austin; limited edition of 50 copies was published.

Concierto para la Sierra de Ronda. Málaga, Librería Antecuaria El Guadalhorce, 1966, 23 pp.
     Poesía.

Elegías del Uad-el-Kebir. Sevilla, 1961.

Elegías Tartessias. Orense: Comercial, 1964.

Oración de la verdad. Jerez: Grupo Atalaya de Poesía, 1965,
59 pp.

Poetas jóvenes sevillanos. Caracas, Lírica Hispana, 1956.

Pozo de Jacob. Sevilla: Ayuntamiento de Sevilla, 1967, 96 pp.

Romances de la miel en los labios. Sevilla: La Muestra, 1962.

Sonetos del corazón adelante. Arcas de la Frontera, 1960.

CLG

FUERTES, Gloria (1918-).

Born in Madrid, Gloria Fuertes was a teenager in the Spanish Civil
War, marked forever by hunger, misery, orphanhood and a longing for a
peaceful Spain. Her life's message is love and peace. Her poems evoke
lost love, solitude, melancholy and death. Her children's poems,
innocent and naughtily playful, include religious and social motifs too.
Hers is testimonial poetry, at once personal and accessible, combining a
strong lyrical personality with colloquial language and popular themes.
For Fuertes, poetry is the most direct way to reach another's sensibil-
ities, imagination and social conscience. She belongs to the Generation
of 1950, nonconformist and socially motivated, and looks toward the
varied life and language of Madrid as her main source of inspiration.
Her sensitivity to the poor, and to women's plight, in love and daily
life, is especially noteworthy.

Aconsejo beber hilo. Madrid: Arquero, 1954.
    This volume contains quintessential Fuertes themes and techniques
as well as some departures. There is a series of surrealistic poems,
unique for their departure from her more realistic style: "dreams of
being sane," of flying, of "robbing souls from crowded buses." One
of her favorite stylistic devices is the enumeration of objects,
experiences or emotions to create surprise and delight in the reader.
There are also a number of poems with a feminist theme, for example
"They don't allow writing" which expressively comments on the
unacceptability of women writing, and "I confess," where she laments
the difficulty of always having to be a strong woman alone. The
volume is filled with wonderfully alive images, such as, "I believe
that the moon is a rose that smells of the sea in the afternoon."

Antología poética. 1950-1969. Barcelona: Plaza y Janés,
1970, 269 pp. Prologue and selection by Francisco Ynduráin. 2nd
ed., 1972.

Antología y Poemas del suburbio. Caracas: Lírica Hispana # 134,
1954.
    Fuertes reveals a clear and defined poetic voice in this early
volume of poetry whose theme is that God is in the city along with
love, loss and inspiration. Her work is strongly autobiographical as
she weaves her past (the Spanish Civil War and the death of loved
ones), with her solitary present, defined by her primordial need to
write poetry. She reinforces her popular roots in her poem "The
leavetaking of the man" and when she laughingly asserts, "What? I'm
not a mystic because I sing the city?"

Canciones para niños. Madrid: Escuela Española, 1952.

Cómo atar los bigotes del tigre. Barcelona: El Bardo, 1969.
     This book provides a range of poems that reveal Fuertes' unique
voice: her poetic wish "to be a huge aspirin for the world's ills,
whoever tries me, gets cured;" a scolding tête-a-tête with Poetry,
whom she admonishes "Don't hide, let's speak like we always do--or
else I'll just have to send you on your way;" her particular credo,
"Now I only believe in Christ, in me, and in something in your
voice;" and the poignant confession, "My best poems are only meant
for one reader, they are letters I have wept." One of her most
feminist poems is included here: "I am only a Woman," at first
glance a litany of reasons why she couldn't be what she wanted to,
and then finally, the affirmation, "I am only a woman, complete and
upright, I am only a woman, and that's enough."

Isla ignorada. Madrid: Colección Musa Nueva, 1950.
     Some of Fuertes' most moving poems on love reciprocated and love
unrealized are included in this volume. So too is her treatment of
death, which reveals Fuertes' totally personal relationship with
death, essentially very Spanish; familiar and not fearful. Once
again, she proves herself to be the poet of the people, of our
universal feelings and everyday objects. She has the gift to
transform a simple sentiment, "I am sad and alone and I don't know
why," into poetry, and achieve drama and intensity through her
technical choices.

Ni tiro, ni veneno, ni navaja. Barcelona: El Bardo, 1966, 47 pp.
     The tone of this volume of poetry is evident in Fuertes' cautious
New Year's resolution, not to suffer too much--unless it's for a good
reason. The title poem reinforces the theme of hope, in the face of
hopelessness. Her language is direct, affecting and full of images
that never fail to surprise: for example, "in the afternoon, my
beard grows with sadness" or "I suddenly assassinated anguish." She
defines her ars poetique "I write urgent telegrams; more than
singing, I tell about things."

Piruli. Versos para párvulos. Madrid: Escuela Española, 1955.
     This book of children's verse filled with seemingly effortless
rhyme and alliteration, also makes adults laugh. Fuertes treats
familiar children's themes such as religion, nature and the animal
kingdom, with fresh eyes, as in "Celestial Sport" where she describes
angels on bicycles in heaven, or the more mysterious "Storm" where
she minutely recounts the effect of a storm on every variety of
insects and animals.

Poeta de guardia. Barcelona: El Bardo, 1968.
     This is one of Fuertes' most expressive volumes of poetry. One of
its major themes is the poet's calling: its all consuming nature,
how life goes on for the rest of the world, but she the poet must be
as a sentry, ever on the alert to communicate the range of life's
experiences. Here she also develops some of her favorite themes:
life as a raffle, the temptation and constant battle against suicide;
the existential sadness of life and the difficult condition of being
alone, the dangers of love, and too, moving tributes to the loved
one, as well as a series of uniquely intimate and playful

Gloria-to-God poems, where, for example, she invites God the plumber, to repair her broken faucet of tears ... .

. . .Que estás en la tierra. . . Barcelona: Colección Colliure, 1962, 105 pp.

Sola en la sala. Zaragoza: Javalambre, 1973, ISBN 84-400-5999-4, 196 pp.
    This is a painful collection of poems about solitude and sadness, not originally destined to be published, but rather written as a personal expression of the author's anguish during a particularly difficult time in her life. These short, telegraphic poems are quite different from her usual, more developed style. There is a surface humor, certain irony, that barely covers the hurt just below it. Fuertes expresses her disappointment with love and with people, but nevertheless continues to write, as she clarifies in her opening poem.

Todo asusta. Caracas: Lírica Hispana, #182, 1958.
    It is significant that Fuertes would choose as the book's title the poem "Todo asusta," which reflects her belief that fear permeates life, whether they be rational fears or not. The importance of Fuertes' poetry is that it gives the reader permission to own his/her own special images, pictures, dreams, fears and feelings. In this volume she lyrically defines the poet's mission, to document life, and also includes her special mixture of poems on death, memories, family hope and love.

GFW

G

GALINDO, Beatriz (1475?-1534). Also: "La Latina".

Humanist and humanitarian, she was born in Salamanca and had a wide knowledge of the classics. She became the Latin teacher of Queen Isabella and all her children. Beatriz also became her confidante in state affairs and married the secretary of King Ferdinand. The Madrid hospital where she died, popularly known today as La Latina, is the reminder of her entrepreneurial and humanitarian spirit. She is believed to have written a commentary on Aristotle, several Latin poems and annotations to the classics, although her authorship has been contested.

AR

GALVARRIATO, Eulalia (1905-).

Born in Madrid, she was married to Dámaso Alonso. A novelist and short story writer, she published a novel, Cinco sombras (1947), finalist in the Nadal Prize of 1946. Her best known short story, "Raíces bajo el agua," published in Clavileño (June, 1953), was awarded a prize as a film script. Other short stories: "Tres ventanas," "Los hijos," "Final de jornada," "Solo un día cualquiera." Her work depicts a poetic and nostalgic world, seen through the eyes of a pessimistic sensibility, in sharp contrast with the harsh tone of the testimonial literature of her contemporaries. She also collaborated with Dámaso Alonso on the publication of Góngora's related documents and in the editing of San Juan de la Cruz's poems.

Cinco sombras. Ancora y Delfín, No. 36. Barcelona: Destino, 1947, 243 pp. 2nd ed., Barcelona: Destino, 1951. 3rd ed., Barcelona: Destino, 1963. 4th ed., Barcelona: Destino, 1967.

A retrospective narrative on the life of five sisters who live a secluded life within the family walls restrained by a domineering father who was unable to forget the death of his wife nor forgive the survival of his offspring. The author presents a nostalgic view of the past through the sentimental lives of the five sisters congregated around their sewing table. The passing of time in the monotonous but gentle world seems to have been captured in the insistent but distant aroma that exudes behind the doors of the closed room. Pessimistic, with less poignancy than in her contemporaries Laforet and Matute, there is a search for human understanding and happiness although the quest is in vain. Only available in hardback.

PS

GALVEZ DE CABRERA, María Rosa de (1768-1806).
   María Rosa de Gálvez is considered a minor transitional figure
between Neoclassic and Romantic drama. She was the first woman to have
a number of her plays published and performed, partly due to her
personal friendship with Godoy. She tried her hand at both comedy and
tragedy, with better luck at the former, being an imitator to a certain
degree of Leandro Fernández de Moratín. It should be said, however,
in her defense, that she tried, like many others in the eighteenth
century, to develop a national tragedy working, against the tide of
translations of French tragedies and the popular dislike for this genre.

   Ali-Bek; tragedia original en cinco actos. In El nuevo teatro
español. Madrid, etc., 1787-1935, v. 52, pp. 117-192. Madrid:
B. García, 1801.

   Bión. Opera lírica en un acto, traducida del idioma francés. In
Obras poéticas, vol. 1. Madrid: Imprenta Real, 1804, pp. 57-109.

   Catalina, o la bella labradora; comedia en tres actos traducida del
francés. Madrid: Benito García, 1801, 120 pp. Louisville, Ky.:
Falls City Microcards, 1964, 2 cards.
   Of this work the Memorial Literario said at the time that it "had
been translated from the French but not precisely into Spanish," an
allusion to the frequent gallicisms throughout the text. This comedy
of intrigue is set in a rural district of France where Catalina, a
beautiful, virtuous tenant farmer lives under a false name and disguised identity. She abhors the company of men because of an
unfortunate previous marriage. After several love entanglements
involving members of the local landed gentry, we learn of the true,
high background of Catalina in a final recognition scene with the
traditional multiple wedding and the peasant dance. Available to
scholars in microform.

   El Egoista. Comedia original en tres actos. In Obras poéticas,
vol. 1. Madrid: Imprenta Real, 1804, pp. 111-236.

   Los figurones literarios. Comedia original en tres actos. In Obras
poéticas, vol. 1. Madrid: Imprenta Real, 1804, pp. 237-367.

   Un loco hace ciento; comedia en un acto en prosa para servir de fin
de fiesta. In El nuevo teatro español. Madrid, etc. 1787-1935,
v. 62, pp. 359-408. Madrid: Quiroga, 1801. Madrid: Benito García
y Compañía, 1801.
   This one-act play, in the tradition of Moratín's El sí de las
niñas, is a defense of young women in the late eighteenth century,
whose parents try to overlook their preferences regarding who is
likely to be the best husband for them. In this case, the father's
candidate is a ridiculous Marquis, afrancesado in the worst sense of
the word, who admires anything French simply because it is not
Spanish. Through an ingenious device, the man whom the daughter prefers, and who is indeed engaged to her, manages to bring the father
back to his senses. In the preface, the author explains that her
purpose in writing the play is to show that the light comedy of manners that was being imported so often could also be done successfully
by national playwrights. Available to scholars in microcard.

<u>Obras poéticas</u>. Madrid: Imprenta Real, 1804, 3 vols.

<u>Saúl; escena trágica unipersonal con intermedios de música</u>.
Valencia: Imprenta de Estevan, 1813, 8 pp.
    This one-character, one-scene Biblical tragedy is built around the
expected soliloquy of King Saul, whose army has been defeated by the
Philistines before the curtain rises. He complains to the God of
Israel for having favored David--his successor--over him. At the
close he commits suicide, choosing to die rather than to live without
honor. Saul is presented as a passionate type, in the tradition of
the Romantic hero. Written in hendecasyllabic lines, the play is
highly declamatory. Thus the musical intervals provide a rest for
the actor. Of interest primarily to scholars and available on
microcard.

                                                                    FLC

GARCIA BALMASEDA (DE GONZALEZ), Joaquina (1837-1893).
Pseud. J.G.B., Ketty, Lady, Baronesa de Olivares, Aurora Pérez, Aurora
Pérez Mirón, Adela Samb, Zahara.
    A Madrid native, Joaquina García Balmaseda attended the Conservatory
and acted for four years with Joaquín Arjona's theater company before
embarking on a literary career. She was editor-in-chief of <u>El Correo de
la Moda</u> for ten years, penned several books on domestic crafts and
responsibilities, translated numerous French novels and collaborated on
other periodicals, often using her pen names. Nevertheless, her
comedies remain her most significant contribution to literature.

<u>A grandes males</u>.... Madrid, 18--.
    This play was not available for review. However, it is mentioned
by the <u>Enciclopedia Universal Ilustrada</u>, v. 25, p. 772.

<u>Adolescencia</u>.

<u>Album de señoritas</u>.

<u>El ángel del hogar</u>. Madrid, 18--.
    This play was not available for review. However, it is mentioned
by the <u>Enciclopedia Universal Ilustrada</u>, v. 25, p. 772.

<u>Diálogos instructivos</u>.

<u>Donde las dan</u>, proverbio en un acto y en verso. Madrid: E. Cuesta,
1868, 31 pp.
    Since a judicial dispute has pitted the dashing Luis' and young
widow Victoria's families against one another, the obvious solution
appears to be a marriage of convenience. This comedy of manners
revolves around the couple's first meeting, in which the widow tests
her suitor's resolve by pretending to be an old woman. However, with
the maid's complicity the tables are turned several times (hence the
proverb "Donde las dan, las toman") before all ends well.

<u>La educación pintoresca</u>.

Entre el cielo y la tierra, poesías. Madrid: Imprenta de M.
Campo-Redondo, 1868, 160 pp.
    In this book of some 32 poems of varying meters, the themes are
diverse, touching on nature (especially flowers), death, the Virgin,
her alegrías, and even the abolition of slavery. In her poem to
Calderón de la Barca she acknowledges his influence on her work.
The book also includes a lengthy leyenda, titled El Cristo de
Villarejo, which easily could have become a verse drama. Discerning
literary critic Manuel Cañete wrote the prologue.

Genio y figura, proverbio en un acto. Madrid: Imprenta de José
Rodríguez, 1861, 29 pp. 2nd ed., Madrid: Imprenta de José
Rodríguez, 1879.
    This was García Balmaseda's first play. It is dedicated to
famous actress Teodora Lamadrid who starred in it when it debuted at
the Teatro del Príncipe on April 6, 1861. A comedy of manners, it
concerns two betrothed first cousins who have not seen each other
since childhood. Both believe they have outgrown their faults but,
as the proverb indicates, "genio y figura hasta la sepultura;" their
personalities have not changed. After much ado, the couple makes up,
much to their families' relief.

Historia de una muñeca contada por ella misma. Barcelona:
Bastinos, 1889.

Lo que no compra el dinero. Comedia inédita.

La madre de familia.

La mujer laboriosa.

La mujer sensata.

Un pájaro en el garlito, comedia en un acto y en prosa. Madrid: J.
Rodríguez, 1871, 22 pp.
    Easily her best play, Un pájaro en el garlito was first performed
at the Teatro de Variedades in Madrid in 1871. It is a situation
comedy in which a newly widowed woman and her brother's best friend
find themselves stranded in Avila, fighting over the only available
room at the inn. The repartee is quick as she defends her right to
travel alone without a "Lazarillo." But, when the innkeeper slyly
implies that the two have spent the night together, the play ends
ironically (or perhaps too patly) with the widow throwing away her
freedom and promising to enslave herself to her new husband, the
brother's best friend of course.

Reo y juez. Comedia inédita.

                                                              NJM

GARCIA BELLVER, Carmen. No biographical information available.

Huyendo del Pasado. Valladolid: Diputación Provincial, 1954.
    Novel.

Princesas modernas. Valencia: Altana, 1959.
    Novel for children. Available U. Illinois library.

Romance de cielo y agua. Almería: Ayuntamiento de Almería, 1973.
  Composed for the literary competition in honor of the "Semana
Naval del Mar de Alborán."

La sangre inútil. Alicante: Pub. de la Caja de Ahorros del Sureste
de España, 1966.
  A novel which was a finalist for the Premio Planeta.

El silencio acosado. Alcoy: La Victoria, 1964.
  Poems.

CLG

GARCIA DIEGO, Begoña (1926-).
  García Diego's reputation began with the winning of the prestigious
"Café Gijón" prize in 1957 for the novel Bodas de Plata. Her
production after that novel belongs to the creative journalism genre.
She wrote a column for women in the well known conservative magazine
Blanco y Negro, and also in the daily newspaper ABC, during the late
1950's and the 1960's. Her work, witty, colorful, and rigorously
perceptive, gives an invaluable account of the stance, crisis, and
change coming upon middle-class women during the central years of
Franco's Spain.

Los años locos. Madrid: Prensa Española, 1972, 200 pp.
  The book is a collection of articles, some of them written as
short stories, which represent the reaction of a sensitive, intelligent and educated woman to everyday routine during the early 1960's.
The writer's interlocutors are women in different situations, and by
way of the narration, one can reconstruct the quiet but relentless
crisis that was changing the mentality of middle-class Spanish women,
and which prepared the way for the transformation in the 1970's.
Independence of judgment about work, man-woman relationships, and
family is stressed in García Diego's delightful writing.

Bodas de plata. Madrid: Afrodisio Aguado, 1958, 110 pp.
  Bodas de plata is a short novel, winner of the 1957 Café Gijón
prize. Built around the death of a young woman, its greatest merit
is the convincing play with several levels of time, including the
past and a hypothetical future which arises from the night of the
main character's wake. At the same time the aging and corruption of
the woman develops, only to vanish in the last pages of the novel,
when her husband wakes from his imagined future life with his wife.
This is one of several novels to appear during the 1950's in Spain
showing the influence of Faulkner's As I Lay Dying.

Chicas solas. Madrid: Prensa Española, 1962, 293 pp.
  This book consists of a compilation of García Diego's columns in
Blanco y Negro during the late 1950's. The narration sometimes
adopts the form of short stories which reveal their author as a humorous, perceptive observer of precise details. Throughout the work
a very important aspect of Spanish, of Madrid, bourgeois society is
portrayed: the "niña de Serrano" attitude is questioned from within; this decadent and cold prototype will give way to an independent,
hard-working, and optimistic woman if the readers follow the incita-
tions of the writer. There is a prologue by novelist Manuel Halcón.

M-EB

GARCIA RATA, Felisa (1921-).
   Felisa García, a native of Madrid, explains that she is forced to
work ("my economic obligation") and thus cannot devote herself to
writing ("my vocation") as she would like to. She wrote her only novel,
Se busca a un hombre, in the hopes of receiving the important literary
prize of the Premio Nadal, but the editors did not publish her manuscript. When the publishing house of Aguilar solicited unpublished
first novels, she submitted her work again and this time it was
published.

   Se busca a un hombre. Nova Novis, vol. III, Madrid: Aguilar, 1956,
   170 pp.
      As the author points out in a Prologue, she based her story on a
   small newspaper ad which had as its headline "Se busca a un hombre."
   Her novel was inspired by the true story of a man who had been bitten
   by a dog which, unbeknown to the victim, had rabies. In basically
   realistic and straightforward prose, the author relates the ten days
   in the life of her imagined protagonist which elapse between the time
   of the accident and the day he discovers the truth. Copy available
   at the Biblioteca del Ateneo, Madrid.

                                                                  A-MA

GARCIA DE LA TORRE, Ana. Pseud. Ana García del Espinar.
   Very little is known about this novelist whose works are contemporary
with those of the great Spanish realists of the 1870's and 1880's. Her
novels, all of which are "costumbrista" in nature, touch upon the
crucial social topics of the day--including the plight of women and the
urban proletariat--but deal with these issues in an idealistic and
moralistic manner. For the most part, however, she writes compelling
fiction, and her work deserves critical attention. The Harvard
University Library posseses most of her novels.

   Amor y vanidad. Novela de costumbres. Manila: Establecimiento
   tigográfico "La Industria," 1887, 309 pp.

   La asociación. Barcelona: P. Casanovas, 1878, 254 pp.
      This is the second part of the novel Los esclavos del trabajo. It
   is a Utopian social novel that condemns the First International
   which, according to the author, had failed to provide the jobs and
   job security that it had promised. In this novel, a proletarian,
   rather than lose hope altogether, devises a Utopian plan for the
   workers of Barcelona by which they each contribute one peseta a week
   and collectively form a corporation which would then build factories
   and which they, as shareholders, would own and operate. The plan is
   successful. This novel is of interest to anyone studying the
   syndicalist movements or Utopian socialism in nineteenth-century
   Spain.

   Cosas del mundo. Novela de costumbres. Barcelona: P. Casanovas,
   1877, 267 pp.
      This is García de la Torre's first novel, and it contains many of
   the themes of her later work. A major concern here is the value of
   marriage, for some of the characters find themselves shackled in an
   unfortunate relationship while others find happiness in the institution. Ultimately, it is the moral character of the individual that

determines one's happiness in marriage, as the contrast between the
two friends Ramiro and Jorge proves. The former is egocentric and
opportunistic while the latter is selfless. Another theme is the
need in modern society to put up appearances. As an ironic twist,
Ramiro, who warns Jorge of this vice, is himself a victim of a
woman's deceitfuless.

Los esclavos del trabajo. Novela de costumbres. Barcelona: P.
Casanovas, 1878.

Por una lágrima. Novela de costumbres. Barcelona: P. Casanovas,
1878.
    The novel narrates the life of a virtuous working girl of
Barcelona in the 1870's. Of interest is the number of different
male-female relationships depicted, ranging from savage concubinage
to happy marriages. One woman, Quima, feels trapped as a mistress
and marries an older man for his money, only to discover even greater
retrictions in a marital relationship. Malvina, a woman of high
society, says at one point, "al hablar de dichas y de felicidad, en
mi opinión, deben ir unidas ... a la libertad, pues sin esta unión,
son aquéllas un imposible" ("to speak of happiness, in my opinion,
it ought to go along with ... liberty, because without this union,
the former is impossible"). But despite these statements of independence, the women in the novel who emerge happy and victorious are
those who lead traditional roles as selfless wives.
                                                                    RR

GATELL, Angelina (1926-).
    Gatell was born in Barcelona. Her poetry is largely testimonial; it
is a lyric protest against any kind of injustice. The horror of the
Spanish Civil War, of any war, and the lack of political freedom are the
main themes of the three books of poems published so far by this author.
 Her poetry belongs to what has been called "social poetry" in Spain.
Her contribution as a poet lies in the lyrical quality of her realistic
verse and in the solidarity that Gatell shows for humanity's sufferings.

Las claudicaciones. Biblioteca Nueva, Madrid, 1969, 74 pp.
    The theme of the lack of freedom and social justice for those who
were defeated during the Spanish Civil War acquires, in this book of
poems, an even more urgent and dramatic expression than in the first
two books of this poet. The title, The Claudications, points at a
leitmotif in the book: the many times that the poet--that many
people--had to give up their hopes and their rights in silence. Yet,
the book also expresses a desire for a better future where justice
and freedom prevail. Of interest to any reader of poetry. Available
in paperback.

Esa oscura palabra. Santander: La Isla de los Ratones, 1963, 70 pp.
    In this book Gatell denounces, in a veiled way, the circumstances
of oppression, injustice and lack of freedom that were characteristic
in this historical period in Spain. The book, nonetheless, is perme-
ated by a very strong feeling and hope that a change is close and
that the future will bring better times for the people and the

country. Gatell expresses herself in a direct, yet poetical language; she is altogether away from surrealistic modes of expression
or even from a more or less intellectualized language. Her poetry is
highly communicative. In this way, then, Gatell belongs very much to
her generation, to the poetry that was being written during the late
1950's and 1960's in Spain. The book is dedicated to the mother of
the poetess. It has a quote from Rafael Alberti.

El hombre del acordeón. Madrid: Espasa Calpe, 1984,
ISBN 84-239-2736-9, 143 pp.
    This is a book of short stories for children ten years old and up.
It relates, through the narrator, an accordion player, the adventures
of life in the circus; the acrobats playing with death, the clowns,
the horses, etc. There are stories of a realistic nature but also
stories in which fantasy is all important. It is a book for children
and youngsters but also for adults who have not lost the playfulness
of youth.

El poema del soldado. Valencia: Diputación de Valencia, 1954,
55 p.
    This book received the poetry prize of the "Diputación Provincial
de Valencia." The memory of Miguel Hernández, the Spanish poet who
died in a Franco jail in the 1940's, permeates Gatell's soliloquy.
She denounces the violence and injustice of war, of any war, with a
direct and powerfully poetic expression. Her language is always
passionate and compassionate. She seems to feel the ravishment of
war in her own maternity.

AMF

*GAY, Simona (1898-1969).
    A poet born in Illa, she wrote Aigües vives (1932), Lluita amb
l'angel (1938), and La guerra al sol (1965).

KM

GEFAELL DE VIVANCO, María Luisa (19?-). Also: **María Luisa Gefaell.**
The majority of her work is for children.

Antón Retaco. Barcelona: Noguer, 1983, 119 pp. Colección Mundo
Mágico, # 38.
    Puppets and puppet plays; fiction.

Antón Retaco 2: La función. Madrid: Narcea, 1975, 22 pp.
Illustrations by Pilarín Bayes. Reference found to what seems to be
another edition: Dibujos de Carlos Lara; no date, no editor or
place, 24 pp.

Antón Retaco 3: Por los caminos. Madrid: Narcea, 1972, 24 pp.
Illustrations by Pilarín Bayes.

Antón Retaco 5: Los niños tristes. Madrid: Narcea, 1973, 24 pp.
Illustrations by Pilarín Bayes.

Antón Retaco 6: el ancho mundo. Madrid: Narcea, 1973, 24 pp.
Illustrations by Pilarín Bayes.

El Cid. Barcelona: Noguer, 1965, 134 pp. Colored illustrations.
La gesta del Cid. Italian translation by Carlo Montella. Milano:
Mendadori, 1965, 134 pp.
El Cid, Soldier and Hero. London: Hamlyn, 1968. Also New York:
Golden Press, 1966.

Las hadas de Villaviciosa de Odón. Madrid: Alfaguara, 1979,
131 pp. Illustrations by Benjamín Palencia.
    Juvenile fiction; fairies, folklore.

Orlando paladino di Francia. Translated to Italian by I. L. Gal.
Milan: Mendadon, 1968, 133 pp.
    Juvenile fiction.

Siegfried, the Mighty Warrior. New York: Golden Press, 1968.
English translation of original Spanish.
I Nibelunghi. Milano: Mondadori, 1966, 136 pp. Italian translation
by Carlo Montella.
    Juvenile fiction.

                                                                    JP

*GILI I GUELL, Antònia (1856-1909).
    Poet from Vilafranca del Penedès, she wrote Poesies, Lo miracler de
Barcelona (1899) and Maria (1911).
                                                                    KM

GIMENO DE FLAQUER, Concepción (1860-1919).
    Born in Alcañiz (Teruel); Gimeno traveled widely with her writer
husband, living for some years in Mexico. She edited a number of
women's magazines in both countries, starting with La Ilustración de la
Mujer in Madrid in 1872, and wrote over a dozen volumes on women in the
present and in history. In numerous conferences and essays she upheld
the right to education and a more public life for women but always
within marriage and without the vote. One of the most influential and
well-seasoned conservative, Catholic feminists of her day, Gimeno wrote
four heavily romantic novels.

    ¿Culpa o expiación? Novela original con retrato y biografía de la
autora. Mexico: Secretaría de Fomento, 1890, 282 pp. 2nd, 3rd,
4th eds., Mexico, 1890, 283 pp.
    First published as Suplicio de una coqueta, the new novel adds a
Post Scriptum (pp. 279-81) which situates the debate over the interpretation of the protagonist's life among a lawyer, a doctor and the
author. They argue her responsibility, her destructive power, her
expiation through death and her possible redemption through repen-
tance. The author confronts the reader with the decision whether to
judge the protagonist harshly or benevolently. A biography of Gimeno
by Eduardo de Valle prefaces the volume (pp. 7-23).

    El doctor alemán; novela original. Zaragoza: C. Ariño, 1880,
267 pp.
    Set in Cabañal, Valencia, among the country homes of the monied
middle class, the novel is romantic in structure, plot, themes and
language. The opposition of art and science, freethinking and faith,
love and solitude resolves in harmony when the doctor discovers God

through the study of nature and the life of a simple fisherman, and
the lovers marry. The plot is convoluted, depending on disguise and
intercalated life histories; the language is heavily adjectival and
florid. The woman's role of love and abnegation receives attention.

Suplicio de una coqueta; novela original. Mexico: F. Díaz de
León, 1885, 315 pp.
    Set in Madrid and Mexico in the 1870's, the novel centers on a
young woman surrounded by admirers from different cultures whose
responses to her flirtation range from suicide to adoration. Women's
responsibility for their impact on men, marriage for wealth versus
love, and love outside marriage are treated. An attempt is made to
explain the protagonist's early death in scientific terms. This is
essentially a romantic plot with moral overtones which raises
troubling social questions about the role of women.

Victorina, o heroísmo del corazón; novela original. La Epoca.
1873. 2nd ed., 2 vols., intro. Ramón Ortega y Frías, Madrid:
Imprenta de la Asociación del Arte de Imprimir, 1873, 245 and
218 pp. 5th ed., Madrid: Imprenta de la Sociedad Tipográfica,
1879, 245 pp.

                                                                    MB

*GINESTA, Marina.
    A novelist from Catalonia, she lives in exile in the Caribbean.

Els antípodes. Barcelona: Dopesa, ISBN 84-7235-272-2, 1976,
329 pp.
    A love story that takes place on a Caribbean island between two
exiles from Catalonia, between the defeat of the Republic and the
beginning of the Second World War. The pain of exile, always with
some hope of return, is lessened by mutual comprehension. The
background is of Caribbean politics, with domination by North America
and a tradition of Hispanic civilization and colonization.

                                                                    KM

GOMEZ OJEA, Carmen (1945-).
    Born in Gijón, she received her licenciatura in Romance Philology
from the University of Oviedo. She is married and has five children.
Aside from her two published novels, she has eight novels, 50 stories
and a book of poetry that have not been published. She develops the
perspective of her female protagonists in her two published novels in a
rich and complex style that combines stream of consciousness with a kind
of fantasy and humor often associated with Galician writers such as
Valle-Inclán, Torrente Ballester and Cunqueiro.

Cantiga de agüero. Colección Ancora y Delfín, vol. 561. Barcelona:
Destino, 1982, ISBN 84-233-1177-5, 213 pp.
    This novel, winner of the 1981 Nadal Prize, is a family saga in
the tradition of Gabriel García Márquez's Cien años de soledad.
It incorporates an insistent cadence of language, events endowed with
magical overtones and allusions to the history and destiny of Spain,
but the message is more feminist than political. The feminist
perspective is revealed in an unusual narrative technique in which
the narrative voice shifts mid-way through the novel to reveal the

Heroine's true nature and insinuates a re-reading of Spanish history from a feminist viewpoint. Paperback.

Otras mujeres y Fabia. Colección En Cuarto Mayor. Barcelona: Argos Vergara, S.A., 1982, ISBN 84-7178-412-2, 109 pp.
  Winner of the 1981 "Tigre Juan" Prize (Oviedo), this novel narrates the daily lives of the women of a modest neighborhood from the perspective of Fabia, a school teacher. Interspersed with the sights, sounds and smells of her neighbor's mundane chores are Fabia's evocations of famous women in history, her own female ancestors and conversations with her cousin, Señora Efe, whose upper-middle-class surroundings contrast with Fabia's. The banal events that occupy Fabia's attention assume epic proportions through the incantational rhythm of the prose and the numerous literary allusions. Paperback.

RJ

GONZALEZ, Assumpta. No biographical information available.

El Passadís de la mort. Barcelona: Millà, 1978.

El crit del cel. Barcelona: Millà, 1973.

Especialitat en homes. Barcelona: Millà, 1979.

La Pepeta no és morta. Barcelona: Millà, 1980.

El polític supersticiós. Barcelona: Millà, 1981.
    Drama.

Quan aparegui l'Estrella o El somni del Rabadà. Barcelona: Millà, 1976.

KM

GRASSI DE CUENCA, Angela (1826-1883).
  Born in Italy and raised in Barcelona, she began her writing career in 1842 with a play and an historical romance, and although she dabbled in poetry and the short story, she is remembered as a novelist of some 18 works of a sentimental and moralistic bent. Her style may seem maudlin today, but it may well represent an effort to foster a poetic style in Spain during an age of Realism. She aligned herself with the incipient women's movement, collaborating with C. Coronado in El Pensamiento and later directing a review of her own, El Correo de la Moda, where many of her works first appeared in serial form. Although her novels were widely recognized (even by the Real Academia), Fernán Caballero found them "sentimental y pedante." In addition to the works cited below, the following works are listed in the bibliographies of Cejador y Frauca, Criado y Domínguez, or Palau, but their existence cannot be verifed.
    Amor y orgullo. (Genre not given.)
    Un episodio de la guerra de siete años. Barcelona, 1849. Drama.
    Espigas y amapolas. Novela original.
    El hijo. Novela. Madrid, 1865.
    León o los dos rivales. Comedia.
    La paloma del diluvio. Novela original.

El príncipe de Bretaña. Drama.
Rafael o los efectos de una revolución. (Genre not given.)
El último rey de Armenia. Novela histórica.
Los últimos días de un reinado. Comedia.

El bálsamo de las penas. Novela de costumbres. 4th ed., Madrid: G
Estrada, 1878. Palau cites the first edition as Madrid, 1864. There
is another edition in Valencia: Imprenta Católica de Piles, 1874.
    The struggling middle class of Madrid during the 1860's forms the
background of this novel--one of Grassi's most socially conscious
works. Claudio, a scribe to a lawyer, loses his job, but through the
generosity of a friend manages to secure another post as secretary to
a wealthy lady. Claudio finds in her a kindred spirit, and they fall
in love and marry. They dedicate their lives to helping others, and
this, more than their material wealth, brings them happiness.

El camino de la dicha. Novela original. Madrid: Imprenta El
Cascabel, 1866.

El capital de la virtud. Novela de costumbres. Valencia: Imprenta
Católica, 1877, 498 pp.
    While most of Grassi's novels show how virtue is always rewarded,
this one adds a new capitalist dimension--economy and hard work are
also virtues that can bring happiness and self-satisfaction. As she
says at the end: "no olvides que no hay nada que restituya al hombre
su dignidad, su independencia, su ventura, como el capital, y que no
hay ningún capital más sólido que el honroso capital de la
virtud." ("Don't forget that there is nothing that restores to a man
his dignity, his independence, his good fortune, like capital, and
there is no capital more solid than the capital of virtue.")

El copo de nieve. Novela de costumbres. Madrid: G. Estrada, 1876.

Cuentos pintorescos. 2nd ed. Barcelona: Bastinos, 1886.
Unable to locate the 1st edition.
    A collection of stories--mostly parables--intended for a young
audience. They are not original but rather versions of well-known
stories from the Bible (Ruth and Naomi), history (Ramón Berenguer),
and traditional folk tales.

La dicha de la tierra. Novela histórica. In Diario de Barcelona,
1868.

El favorito de Carlos III. Novela histórica. In El Correo de la
Moda, 1884-1887.

La gota de agua. Madrid: G. Estrada, 1875, 128 pp.
2nd ed., Coatepec: Antonio Rebolledo, 1876.
    A touching novel about the tribulations of a brother and sister
who are blind and must beg for a living. The girl is exploited by a
group of people who need her to claim an inheritance, and her brother
deperately looks for her and finally finds her. An odd note in the
novel is that the brother and sister actually get married and have a
blind child named Jesús, who, after his parents' death, founds a
home for orphans like himself. How was a blind orphan able to

accomplish such a mission, one might ask. Grassi implies that faith
and determination can accomplish miracles. The novel was awarded the
Rodríguez Cao prize.

El heroísmo de la amistad o los Condes de Rocaberti. 2 vols.
Barcelona: Mayol y Cía., 1842, 225 and 236 pp.

Los jucios del mundo. Novela de costumbres. In El Correo de la
Moda, 1882-84.

Lealtad de un juramiento o Crimen y expiación. Drama. Barcelona:
D. M. Saurí, 1842. 2nd ed., Madrid: Vda. de Rozola, 1842.

Los que no siembran, no cogen. Madrid: M. Galiano, 1868.
    An ambitious young man who comes from humble but distinguished
origins is unsatisfied with his station in life and seeks fame and
wealth. Taking what little money he has, he puts up a front in
Madrid socety as a rich dandy, and at the same time he tries to make
a name for himself as a poet. He fails spectacularly, but he
continues to lead a life of deception and depravity until true love
permits him to see his errors. Typical of other Grassi novels, it
has an intricate plot and is written in a tender, poetic style.

El lujo. Novela de costumbres. Madrid: Academia Tipográfica,
1865, 244 pp. It was published again in El Correo de la Moda, 1881.
    A novel of greed and ambition that follows the lives of a brother
and sister who, following in the footsteps of their envious and
status-conscious mother, sell their comfortable home in the country
and set out to make their fortune in Madrid. There they attempt to
move in the proper social set, but they are made fun of as provin-
cials. They eventually deplete their money and seek an illusory
inheritance and titles of nobility. Their lives end in poverty and
frustration. The clear moral is that if you make material things
your main goal in life you will never achieve happiness. It is one
of Grassi's more successful novels because of the many costumbrista
scenes of Madrid life.

Marina. Narración histórica. Madrid: G. Estrada, 1877, 366 pp.
2nd ed., Manila: Ramírez y Giraudier, 1878.

Palmas y laureles. Lecturas instructivas. Barcelona: Bastinos,
1884, xvi-384 pp.
    A book of short instructional readings for children. Grassi was
interested in education, as we may discern by the number of articles
on that topic that she published in El Correo de la Moda. The book
is divided into two parts ("Noches de invierno" and "Cartas de una
madre a sus hijos"), but there is no difference between the two. In
both parts one finds short readings on various topics like Shakespeare, painting, the history of paper and printing, birds, moral
duties, etc.

Poesías. Madrid: M. Campo-Redondo, 1871, 279 pp.
    This volume contains all of the poems of the 1851 edition plus her
subsequent production. Most of these poems appeared earlier in El
Correo de la Moda. The inspirational-religious tone of the earlier

collection continues, but there are new themes. "La despedida" is a poem about unrequited love (perhaps autobiographical), and "España en el siglo XVI," in which she condemns Spain's martial traditions, is historical. Of special interest is a long elegy to Jaime Balmes.

Poesías de la señorita doña Angela Grassi. Madrid: J. Trujillo, 1851, 89 pp.
    Most of the poems in this collection have a religious or inspirational tone, such as "Himno al creador," "La inmortalidad," "A la virgen María," and "Confianza en Dios." There are also a number of longer narrative poems, but in the same vein as the religious poems. "Recuerdos de la patria" are reminiscences of Italy where she was born and where she would like to return. There is also an elegy to Pablo Piferrer. She employs a variety of traditional meters.

El primer año de matrimonio. Cartas a Julia. In Biblioteca Ilustrada de las familias, 1877.

Las riquezas del alma. Novela de costumbres. 2 vols. Madrid: Imprenta El Cascabel, 1866, 272 pp. and 229 pp. After apearing in El Correo de la Moda between 1881 and 1882, it had a 2nd ed.: Madrid; G. Estrada, 1886.
    A novel with a complex and dramatic plot about a virtuous orphan girl who comes to Madrid seeking to make an honest living and encounters many obstacles. Despite the novel's marked social background, it is really a love story, for the orphan Bruna falls in love with the noble Felipe who is unhappily married. As things work out, Bruna is finally able to marry Felipe. The vast social and educational barriers that divide them are easily bridged, for, as Grassi suggests, they have certain moral values in common, and these should be the basis for equality among men. The novel is rich in scenes of Madrid life, and like other of Grassi's novels, it attacks the materialism of the nineteenth century. It was awarded a prize by the Real Academia de la Lengua.

                                                                    RR

*GUASCH, Maria Carme.
    From Figueres, she studied Romance Philology and teaches Catalan at the University of Barcelona. She also collaborates on magazines and local radio programs. She won prizes for her poetry in 1969 and 1970. She has also written a novel.

Trena de Cendra. Barcelona: Pòrtic, 1984.
    A long meditation on the death of a loved one in the form of a novel. As in an elegy, the loved person is idealized. The narrator-protagonist-author overdoes the autocriticism and the praise of the other.

Vint-i-cinc sonets i u dia. 1978.
    Poetry.

                                                                    KM

*GUILLO FONTANILLES, Magdalena.

En un vall florida al peu de les espasses. Barcelona: Destino,
1978.
  Novel.

KM

GUTIERREZ TORRERO, Concepción (1909-). Pseud. Concha Lagos.
  Heeding a poetic vocation rather late in life, Concha Lagos has
maintained a steady rhythm of publication until the present. In the
mid-1950's she became active in Madrid literary circles--associated with
Gerardo Diego, José García Nieto, José Hierro and Jorge Campos--and
founded Cuadernos de Agora (1956-64) and the "Colección Agora." Born
in Córdoba, she writes in the Andalusian tradition of personal poetry,
cultivating classical and popular meters as well as free verse in the
expression of traditional themes. Continually striving for a more
evolved expression, she has achieved a philosophical manner based on
increasingly hermetic images.

  Agua de Dios. Málaga: Meridiano, 1958, 31 pp.
      Thirteen somber poems comprise this collection based on the theme
  of children. As if from a frustrated maternal impulse, the speaker
  expresses herself with awe, nostalgia and occasional bitterness.
  Includes four drawings by Julio Maruri. First book of trilogy
  including Arroyo Claro and Canciones desde la Barca. Available in
  the Biblioteca Nacional (Madrid).

  Al sur del recuerdo. Madrid: Agora, 1955, 131 pp. Philadelphia:
  Center for Curriculum Development, 1972, 112 pp.
      This short novel of 29 unnumbered fragments is based on childhood
  memories of Andalusian life. The fragments--some, colorful sketches
  of villagers; others, dealing with an aged dog, companion to the
  young main character--create a child-like view of reality. First
  edition with Prologue by Rafael Morales and drawings by Alvarez
  Ortega. Second edition with Introduction, Notes and Glossary by
  Rafael Millán. Both editions available through interlibrary loan;
  the second is of interest for teaching purposes.

  Los anales. Madrid; Palma de Mallorca: Ediciones de Papeles de Son
  Armadans, 1966, 153 pp.
      Divided into six parts, the 55 poems of this mature collection are
  of scholarly interest. In reading order, the poems deal with the
  mystery of Christian faith, the tormented despair of those forsaken
  by God, the relation of reality to poetry, reality seen from the
  perspective of hope, the difficult path of faith, and--in the final
  poem--writing as compensation for human mortality. With Prologue by
  José Hierro. Available through interlibrary loan.

  Antología 1954-1976 / Concha Lagos. Esplugas de Llobregat: Plaza y
  Janés, 1976, ISBN 84-01809-47-9, 367 pp.
      Includes representative selections from all works through Gótico
  florido. Of scholarly interest as an introduction to Lagos' poetry.
  With Prologue by Emilio Miró. Available through interlibrary loan.

Arroyo claro. Madrid: Agora, 1958, 94 pp.
    Composed of 51 poems of varying lengths, this collection is part
of the trilogy including Agua de Dios and Canciones desde la barca.
In the first part, images centering on water--the sea, streams,
rivers--symbolize potential transformation; in the second, the topic
is the Spanish landscape. The third part contains lullabies. The
fourth, influenced by "Cante Jondo," evokes loneliness. The last
part is dominated by concern for temporality. Available in the
Biblioteca Nacional (Madrid).

La aventura. Madrid: Alfaguara, 1973, ISBN 84-204-9999-4, 96 pp.
    Second part of trilogy. The title poem proposes a view of life
based on semi-mystical notions of time and space by which individual
lives consist of transformations. Themes developed in other poems
are on the defects of human nature, life as the past "dressed in the
present and future," and praise for life. Of scholarly interest.
Available through interlibrary loan.

Balcón. Madrid: Gráficas Bachende, 1954, 75 pp.
    Her first published work, Balcón, contains 59 poems, mostly brief
lyrics on topics of love, nature and being. With six sketches by
Mingote. Available in the Biblioteca Nacional (Madrid).

Campo abierto. Madrid: Gráficas Orbe, 1959.
    Variously considered a brief collection of ten poems or a single
poem divided into ten parts, this work, dedicated to 11 poets of the
Generation of the Fifties, is at once dialogue and instruction
concerning the nature of poetry. Of scholarly interest for comments
on poetry. Also published as the third section of Para empezar.
Available in the Biblioteca Nacional (Madrid).

Canciones desde la barca. Madrid: Editora Nacional, 1962, 175 pp.
    These brief, musical poems are primarily in ballad meter. The
theme of sailing is the motive for reflections, in the manner of folk
songs, on life's experiences. With eight sketches by Gregorio
Prieto. Available through interlibrary loan.

El corazón cansado. Madrid: Agora, 1957, 64 pp.
    Written in a deliberately unpretentious style, the poems in this
collection undercut nostalgia with a subsequent mood of indifference.
Some poems comment directly upon the role of women; the collection as
a whole is from a distinctly feminine perspective. Available through
interlibrary loan.

El cerco. Madrid: Alfaguara, 1971, 86 pp.
    The 22 poems, including two composed of several sections, are
divided into three parts with a logical progression. The first deals
with the poet as creator of transcendental prophesies, windows on the
infinite; the second portrays human defects that justify the poet's
prophesying and ends with a call to plumb memory for a paradise to be
recreated; the last carries out the order. Being the first of a
trilogy including La aventura and Fragmentos en espiral desde el
pozo, this work is of scholarly interest. Available through
interlibrary loan.

Diario de un hombre. Caracas: Arbol de Fuego, 1970, 31 pp.
Composed of 23 poems, this collection is dedicated to the theme of
mankind. From a perspective of serene melancholy, the speaker
reflects upon man's loneliness, questions God's existence, and
ponders human defects. Available through interlibrary loan.

Elegías para un álbum. Madrid: Gráficas Orbe, 1982,
ISBN 84-300-3543-5, 61 pp.
Twenty central poems, framed by two others, "Album" and "Broche,"
form this nostalgic collection in which the poet creates a world
where planes of time intersect as shadowy figures in a family album
come to life again. Available in the Biblioteca Nacional (Madrid).

Fragmentos en espiral desde el pozo / Concha Lagos. Sevilla:
Aldebarán, 1974, 49 pp.
Third part of trilogy. Impersonal poems forming a metaphysical-
religious search are divided into three sections: The first explores
the nature of "Pozo," a variously characterized source or origin; the
second--14 sonnets--relates attempted ascents from the source; the
third presents an encounter with the mysterious eternal. Of
scholarly interest. Available through interlibrary loan.

Golpeando el silencio. Caracas, Venezuela: Lírica Hispana, No. 20,
1961, 64 pp.
Twenty-seven poems, including a series of seven elegies, one poem
dedicated to Gabriel Celaya, another to a group of exiled poets,
compose this collection. Diverse themes, explored in earlier works,
reappear here without significant transformations. With a brief
introduction to the poet and this work, and a general essay on her
poetry by Manuel Mantero. Includes the poet's portrait on inner
cover. Available through interlibrary loan.

Gótico florido. Sevilla: Católica Española, 1976,
ISBN 84-85057-79-1, 92 pp. Madrid: Gráficos Orbe, 1977,
ISBN 84-400-2022-8, 90 pp.
In the introductory poem and those of the first two sections, each
architectural feature referred to--not all strictly Gothic--evokes
historical associations with other ages and a metaphysical
reflection. Poems of the remaining three sections--"letters,"
elegies, "wandering" poems--return to existential themes. Available
through interlibrary loan.

Luna de enero. Arcos de la Frontera: Alcaraván, 1960, 56 pp.
In the 19 poems of this work, whose theme is a passionate but
renounced love, the speaker traces her intensified sentiment through
questions and conjectures addressed to the object of her love. With
a Prologue by José Hierro and a sketch of the author by Zamorano.
Available through interlibrary loan.

Los obstáculos. Madrid: Agora, 1955, 44 pp.
Primarily expressing sorrowful disillusion with existence, the 24
poems of this collection are brief lyrics with rhythmic images of the
natural world and daily life. With a sketch of the poet by Antonio
Povedano. Available in the Biblioteca Nacional (Madrid).

La paloma. Alicante: Sinhaya Colección de Poesía, 1982,
ISBN 84-300-7409-0, 65 pp.
   The poet's third collection of songs, following Arroyo claro and
Canciones desde la barca, is divided into five thematic sections.
The first glosses lines from Rafael Alberti concerning a dove. The
second finds in a bell and silence the reason for being of a tower.
The third celebrates a sower who names each seed cast; the fourth, a
turning mill. The final section contains aphoristic songs to the
elements and to the South of Spain. Available in the Biblioteca
Nacional (Madrid).

El pantano (del diario de una mujer). Madrid: Gráficas Bachende,
1954, 126 pp.
   Consisting of some 49 unnumbered fragments, this fictionalized
diary is narrated in the first person by a woman from Andalusia
forced to live on the northern boggy coast of Spain. With simple,
lyrical prose, the narrator recounts the effect nature, other people,
literature and short journeys have on her sensibility. With Prologue
by Rafael Millán. Available through interlibrary loan.

Para empezar. Madrid: Editora Nacional, 1963, 74 pp.
   This miscellaneous collection blends poems on traditional themes
and reprints Campo abierto in its entirety. Available through
interlibrary loan.

Por las ramas. Barcelona: V. Pozanco, 1980, ISBN 84-74571-00-6,
96 pp.
   Divided among six thematically unified sections, the poems
synthesize metaphysical motifs--spiritual search, illusion and
disillusion, nature of destiny--and contain some critical social
commentary. Available through interlibrary loan.

La soledad de siempre. Torrelavega, Santander: Colección
Cantalapiedra, 1958, 60 pp.
   Based on existential and religious themes--mortality, loss,
consolation, hope--this work is divided into two sections of 13 and
14 poems respectively and is prefaced by the title poem. Available
through interlibrary loan.

Tema fundamental. Madrid: Agora, 1961, 114 pp.
   The 69 poems of this work, divided among five sections, develop
religious themes of spiritual growth and plenitude, using highly
musical imagery of remarkable sensorial beauty. With three plates.
Available through interlibrary loan.

Teoría de la inseguridad. Madrid: Gráficas Orbe, 1980,
ISBN 84-300-3544-3, 107 pp.
   Fifty-one poems among seven parts compose this collection, which
develops the vision continued in Por las ramas. With an extended
metaphor of life as a voyage guided by faith over a sea of mysterious
harmonies, these poems answer eternal questions concerning destiny,
death, and God's silence by proposing a vision of the universe based
on harmonious love. The fifth section, in which the speaker declares
Woman to be an unheeded prophet, is of particular note. Available in
the Biblioteca Nacional (Madrid).

La vida y otros sueños: Cuentos. Madrid: Nacional, 1969, 121 pp.
    Sixteen sketch-like narrations make up this collection written in
a simple, realistic style. Topics are the events of everyday life,
principally among villagers and young people. Tending to description
and dialogue, these selections have a static tranquility despite
events recounted. With Prologue by Medardo Fraile. Available
through interlibrary loan.

                                                                    EW

GUZMAN Y DE LA CERDA (Y DE SOUSA), María Isidra Quintina de (Marquesa
de Guadalcázar) (1768-1803).
    Despite subsequent derision of her accomplishments, nothing can alter
the fact that María Isidra, a child prodigy who basked in Carlos III's
enlightened protection, was the first woman elected to the Real Academia
Española (1784), earned a doctorate (and chair) at the University of
Alcalá (1785) and was admitted to the Real Sociedad Matritense (and
Vascongada) de los Amigos del País (1786). Even after her marriage
(1789) to Rafael Alonso de Sousa and the birth of three children, she
continued her intellectual pursuits. Sadly, "la doctora de Alcalá"
died at age 35 from a life-long tubercular condition before all her
talents were completely realized. Some manuscripts of poetry (according
to one source "of strong neoclassical influence") are said to survive.
All her other works, including her papers on the Aristotelian system,
are believed lost.

    Oración de ingreso. 1785.

    Oración eucarística. 1786.

    Oración del género eucarístico que hizo a la Real Academia
    Española (1785). According to one source: Published in the
    Memorial Literario (de la Sociedad Económica), v. 5.

    Oración del género eucarístico que hizo a la Real Sociedad de
    Amigos del País de esta corte la Excelentísima Señora Doña.
    Doctora en Filosofía y Letras humanas, Consiliaria perpetua,
    Examinadora de cursantes en Filosofía, y Cathedrática honoraria de
    Filosofía moderna en la Real Universidad de Alcalá, Socia de la
    Real Academia Española, y Honoraria y Literarata, de la Real
    Sociedad Bascongada de los Amigos del País. En el día 25 de
    febrero del año de 1786, Madrid: Antonio de Sancha, 1786, 12 pp.
    An extract appeared in the Memorial Literario (de la Sociedad
Económica), marzo de 1786, pp. 357-361.

                                                                   NJM

**HEINE, Ursula.
  Of German birth, she is married to Ramón Lorenzo, a Professor of
Galician at Santiago.

  Remuiños en coiro. Vigo: Xerais, 1984.
    A collection of short stories.

  O soño perdido de Elvira M.. Vigo: Xerais, 1982.
    In this novel about the lives of two women and their relationship
  with several male characters, she creates several narrators and
  points of view.
                                                        CNC & AM

(H)ENRIQUEZ, Cristobalina. See: **ENRIQUEZ, Cristobalina.**

HERNAN, Josita (1919-).
  From Mahón (Baleares), she has been an actress in a great number of
movies and stage plays, a Spanish instructor at the National
Conservatory of Dramatic Art of Paris, a painter and translator of
André Maurois, Georges Barbain and others. Recipient of important
awards and prizes, she wrote several volumes of poetry, a book on health
and beauty, and articles for the press in Spain and abroad.

  Antar. 1944.

  Una muchacha bajo las estrellas. Barcelona: Tartessos, 1942.
    Novela cinematográfica.

  El pescador de estrellas. Madrid: Editores Librería Sousa y
  Pereda, 1935, Ed. Alhambra, 1939.
    Poetry; prologue by Eduardo Marquina.

  Sirenita, yo. Madrid: Gran Capitán, 1941, Ed. Alhambra.
    Poetry; illustrations by the author.

  Tan-Ya. Barcelona: Tartessos, (n.d.).
                                                        GM

**HERRERA GARRIDO, Francisca (1869-1950).
She was born and died in La Coruña, but lived for almost 30 years in Madrid. A member of La Coruña's upper class, she met Rosalía de Castro and became a friend of Murguía after Rosalía's death. Conservative, anti-feminist, Rosalía was her literary model. She wrote in Galician and Castilian and was one of the first women to publish narrative in Galician. She was a member of the Galician Royal Academy.

A ialma de Mingos. Ferrol: 1922.
    Short story.

Almas de muller . . . Volallas na luz! La Coruña: 1915.
    Poetry.

Familia de lobos. Madrid: 1928.
    Novel.

Flores do noso paxareco. La Coruña: 1919.
    Poetry.

Néveda. La Coruña: 1920. 2nd ed., Vigo: Xerais, 1981.
    Narrative.

Martes de antroido. La Coruña: 1925.
    Narrative.

Pepiña. Madrid: 1922.
    Novel.

Réproba. Madrid: 1926.
    Novel.

Sorrisas e bágoas. Madrid: 1913.
    Poetry.

                                                              CNC & AM

*HERREROS I SORA, Manuela de los (1845-1911).
A poet and prose writer born in Ciutat de Mallorca, she was the daughter of a professor at the State Grammar School of Palma. She studied languages and was devoted to the art of drawing and painting. She married Enric Bonet and had 14 children. She was devoted to studying popular genres. Her compositions in the Majorcan dialect are easy and entertaining. Her literary production embraces the period between 1863 and 1902, and her poems range from impressions of the landscape to familiar anecdotes. Her work created literary value for popular verse. She was the first woman to be awarded "filla ilustre de la Ciutat de Palma."

Obra literaria dispersa. Colection Sa Nostra Terra. Volume I.
Palma de Mallorca, 1978, ISBN 84-300-02510, 264 pp.

See: Sanchis Guarner, M.: Els Poetes Romántics de Mallorca.
    The book includes two of Herreros' poems: "Lo so d'un infant," which is about the feelings of love a mother has for her child, and "Ses matances," where she narrates the popular tradition of pig killing.

See: Sanchis Guarner, M.: Els Poetes Romàntics de Mallorca. Palma
de Mallorca: 1950, Moll Publishing House, Mossen Alcover Printing
House, 286 pp.

Obra literaria dispersa.
This edition is a compilation of all her literary work, which was
scattered in different magazines and newspapers, from the Bertomeu
March Servera Library of Palma de Mallorca. The research has been
done by Llorenç Pérez and the introduction is by Guillem Cabrer.
The poems refer to the customs of that period. Herreros ridicules
the different social classes and emphasizes the importance of the
Mother Country. Some of her poems are written in Castilian.

VC-E

HIPOLITA DE JESUS, Sor. See: ROCABERTI, María de.

HORE Y LEY (de Fleming), María Gertrudis de (1742-1801).
Pseud. H.D.S. (Hija del Sol).
María Gertrudis de Hore y Ley, born of Irish parents, was called "la
hija del Sol" in her native Cádiz for her beauty and intelligence. She
married Esteban Fleming, spent time in Madrid high society and had an
affair which ended in tragedy. According to "Fernán Caballero," after
unknown assailants murdered her lover in her garden, she sought--and
received--her husband's permission to enter the convent in 1778. She
composed most of her poetry prior to her religious life, approximately
1760 to 1780. Some of these poems she later burned; most were saved by
her Bishop. Her manuscripts are now located at the Biblioteca Nacional.

"Poesías," in Apuntes para una biblioteca de escritoras españolas
desde el año 1401 al 1833, by Manuel Serrano y Sanz. Madrid:
Biblioteca de Autores Españoles, 1903-05, v. 1:2, pp. 523-532.
Serrano y Sanz reproduces portions of Hore's poems, many of which
were originally published in El Diario de Madrid; others he copies
from Cueto's Poesía lírica del siglo XVIII. He also includes her
certificates of baptism, marriage, religious profession and death.

"Poesías," in Poesía lírica del siglo XVIII, v. 67, edited by
Leopoldo Augusto de Cueto. Madrid: Biblioteca de Autores
Españoles, 1875, pp. 555-559.
Editor Cueto wrote in the introduction (pp. 553-555) to Hore's
poetry, "sólo publicamos escasa parte, como muestra del estilo de la
escritora." ("We publish only a small portion, as an example of the
writer's style.") In these few pages of sonnets, endechas,
endecasílabas and anacreónticas, she describes life in Madrid,
nature, the death of her son from smallpox and her decision to enter
religious life. In placing her historically, Eustaquio Fernández de
Navarrete declared that eighteenth-century luminaries "D. Nicolás
Fernández de Moratín y el gaditano D. José Cadalso ... apenas
escribían cuando ésta era ya conocida ... y en el tiempo de que
tratamos aún escribía (Meléndez) con mano tan insegura que pudiera
acaso recibir lecciones de nuestra gaditana." ("D. Nicolás
Fernández de Moratín and 'el gaditano' D. José Cadalso ... had
scarcely begun to write when she was already well known. And in the
period we are dealing with, even (Meléndez) wrote with such an
unsure hand that he could have taken lessons from our 'gaditana.'"
(p. 554).

NJM

HUIDOBRO, María Teresa de (1922-).
   Little is known about María Teresa de Huidobro, aside from her date and place of birth, Santander, Spain. It seems that she did not publish anything more after Por caminos del aire, almost 40 years ago. Nevertheless, Martín Alonso, the author of Ciencia del lenguaje y arte del estilo (Madrid: Aguilar, 1967), thought her important enough to be included in his section of Spanish and Hispanic poets ("Antología de cien poetas contemporáneos") where she is represented by two of her poems (pp. 942-3).

   Por caminos del aire. Santander: Fosca, 1948, 95 pp.
      This slender volume of short, lyric poems is divided into three sections: "Canciones en la mano," "Poemas del corazón" and "Ansia de luz." All 60 poems included in the book (of which 19 are sonnets) deal with love, loneliness, nature and God. The majority of the poems, particularly the love poems, are imbued with a sense of longing, dreaming and hoping. In many cases there is some ambiguity as to whether the speaker is addressing her beloved or God. In the final poem, "Mi muerte," the poet clearly offers herself to God. Foreword by Nicolás González Ruiz; copy available at the Biblioteca del Ateneo, Madrid.

A-MA

I

IBAÑEZ NOVO, Mercedes (1946-).
A poet born in Santander, she spent a great part of her infancy in Penilla, a town of the valley of Toranzo, the landscape she refers to continuously in her poetry. Her first poems were published by Poesía española and other journals and periodicals. She is married to the painter Vaquero Turcios and resides in Madrid.

Luz de orilla. Madrid: Biblioteca Nueva, 1971, ISBN 84-7030-183-7, 57 pp.
Ibáñez Novo's poetry does not emulate or show influence of the great male poets according, to the prologue by Carlos Martínez Rivas. The strangely calm and wonderful poems shift in visual focus yet embrace life, death, solitude, encounter, countryside and children's games. The title represents the basic image of the poet's expression. It is her first book and is dedicated to her dead brother.

Un soplo apenas cálido. Salamanca: Autores-Editores de Obras Propias, 1978, ISBN 84-400-5473-4, 64 pp.
Ibáñez Novo's second book of verse was published as part of the Colección Alamo, under the auspices of the Delegación Nacional de Cultura in Salamanca. Very difficult to locate.

GM

IBARRURI, Dolores (1895-). "La Pasionaria".
One of the leaders of the Spanish Communist Party and a key figure in the Republican faction of the Spanish Civil War, she is most important as a skilled orator and fervent defender of the Spanish proletariat. Her famous "No pasarán!" speech became the rallying cry for the Republican forces. Author of numerous political and historical essays, largely concerning the Spanish Civil War and the Spanish Communist Party, she was in exile in the Soviet Union from 1939-1977.

En la lucha. Palabras y hechos. 1936-1939. Moscow: Progreso, 1968, 365 pp.
A series of articles and written speeches, largely of an exhortative character, which reflect the writer's oratory skill, and to this extent they may be considered "creative." Most are anti-fascist in nature and are intended as a rallying cry for the Republicans.

Many reveal the author's steadfast adherence to the orthodox Communist ideology of the Soviet Union. Of interest to any student of the Spanish Civil War.

El único camino. Barcelona: Bruguera, 1979.
    This is the author's autobiography, tracing her development from a young girl in poverty-stricken northern Asturias to her role as a major political figure during the Spanish Civil War. It is largely a narration of her ideological growth, with emphasis on pre-war and war years. There is very little of a truly personal nature, but as a statement of personal political development, it is of relevance to any student of the Spanish Civil War.

DD

*IBARS IBARS, Maria (1892-1965).
    Poet from Denia.

A l'ombra del Montgó. Valencia: 1949.
    Poetry.

KM

ICAZA, Carmen de (1899-).
    A native of Madrid, she is the daughter of the respected Mexican diplomat, Francisco A. de Icaza. She has traveled extensively throughout Europe and the Americas. For her commitment to the needy she has received various awards and titles. For example, she was an active member of the Red Cross' supreme assembly, was given the title Baroness of Claret, and was the recipient of the Gran Cruz de Beneficiencia.

RK

La boda del Duque Kurt. Barcelona: Juventud, 1935, 112 pp.
Madrid: Afrodisio Aguado, 1942, 205 pp.
Talia; la boda del Duque Kurt. 5th ed., Madrid: 1951, 269 pp.

RK

La casa de enfrente. Madrid: 1960, 329 pp.

RK

Cristina de Guzmán, professora de idiomas. Barcelona: Juventud, 1936, 160 pp. 3rd ed., Valladolid: Afrodisio Aguado, 1939, 264 pp. 4th ed., Madrid: Afrodisio Aguado, 1942, 264 pp. Buenos Aires: Juventud, 1942. Madrid: Imprenta Diana, 1949. Madrid: 1951, 271 pp. Madrid: Cámara, 1968.
Cristina, professora moderna, trans. Alsacia Fontes Machado. Lisboa: Portugalia Editora, 1952, 299 pp.
Cristina; libro de lectura y conversación, adapted for class use by Isabel Snyder. New Orleans: Loyola University, 1958, 80 pp.

RK

La fuente enterrada. Madrid: Clemares, 1947, 347 pp.
5th ed., Madrid: Clemares, 1949, 347 pp.
Irene, trans. Hilde Lackenbucher, Berline: Deutche Buchgemeinschaft, 1953, 322 pp.

RK

Las horas contadas. Madrid: 1953, 386 pp.

Obras selectas. Barcelona: AHR, 1957, 1385 pp. Contents: <u>Cristina
Guzmán, Vestida de tul, La fuente enterrado, Yo, La reina, Las horas
contadas</u>.

RK

Obras selectas. Barcelona: AHR, 1971, 995 pp. Contents: <u>Cristina
Guzmán, La fuente enterrada, Las horas contadas</u>.

RK

!Quién sabe!. Madrid: Afrodisio Aguado, 1939, 398 pp.
Madrid: Afrodisio Aguado, 1940, 351 pp. Madrid: Afrodisio Aguado,
1941, 351 pp. Madrid: Afrodisio Aguado, 1943, 351 pp. Madrid:
Afrodisio Aguado, 1951, 351 pp.

RK

Soñar la vida. Madrid: Afrodisio Aguado, 1941, 318 pp.
Madrid: Afrodisio Aguado, 1942, 319 pp. Madrid: Afrodisio Aguado,
1943, 317 pp. Buenos Aires: Juventud, 1944, 162 pp. Madrid:
Afrodisio Aguado, 1945, 319 pp. Madrid: Imprenta Diana, 1950,
35 pp. Buenos Aires: Juventud, 1943, 162 pp.

RK

Talia. Madrid: Cid, 1960, 144 pp.

RK

El tiempo vuelve. Madrid: Afrodisio Aguado, 1945, 414 pp.
Aguado, 1945, 414 pp. 5th ed., Madrid: 1945, 302 pp.
8th ed., Madrid: 1945, 302 pp.

RK

Vestida de tul. Madrid: Afrodisio Aguado, 1942, 346 pp.
Madrid: Afrodisio Aguado, 1943, 346 pp. Madrid: Afrodisio Aguado,
1951, 344 pp.

RK

Yo, la reina. Madrid: Clemares, 1950, 338 pp. Buenos Aires:
Espasa-Calpa, 1954, 273 pp. 2nd ed., Buenos Aires: Espasa-Calpa,
1955, 273 pp. 8th ed., Madrid: Clemares, 1958, 314 pp.

RK

    The Polish heroine of this novel travels throughout Europe on the
eve of World War II, and lives in New York after the war. Having
suffered once because of love, she is empty and feels incapable of
loving again. Very much on her own, dependent upon her own talents,
she only once admits how difficult this situation is for a woman,
referring to "the fatality of having been born a woman."

CLG

*JACQUETTI I ISANT, Palmira (1895-1963). Pseud. P. de Castellvell.
From Barcelona, she lived for a time in the Vall d'Aran. A poet, in
addition to her two published books, she wrote some poetry which has not
been published. Roser Matheu did a bibliography on her, and she appears
in Quatre dones catalanes (Fundació Vives).

Elegies. 1955.
    Poetry.

L'estel dins la llar. 1938.
    Poetry.

KM

JANES, Clara (1940-).
Born in Barcelona, Janés is a novelist, poet, translator, essayist
and biographer. She received her degree in history and also studies
comparative literature at the Sorbonne. Her biography "La vida callada
de Federico Mompou" won the Premio de Ensayo Ciudad de Barcelona in
1975.

CLG

Antología personal. (1959-1979). Madrid: 1979.

AR

Antología poética. Madrid: 1984.

AR

Cartas a Adriana. Madrid: 1976.

AR

Desintegración. Madrid: Eds. Júcar, 1969.
    Novel.

CLG

En busca de Cordelia and Poemas rumanos. Salamanca: Alamo, 1975.
    Poetry.

CLG

Eros. Madrid: 1981.

AR

Las estrellas vencidas. Madrid: Agora, 1964.
    Poetry.

CLG

Libro de alienaciones. Madrid: 1980.

AR

Límite humano. Madrid: Arbolé, 1973.
    Poetry.

CLG

La noche de Abel Micheli. Madrid: Alfaguara, 1965.
    Novel.

AR

Obra poética. Madrid: 1981.

AR

Pureza Canelo. Madrid: 1981.

AR

Sendas de Rumanía. Barcelona: Plaza y Janés, 1981,
ISBN 840144263-X, 156 pp.
    This is a book of feelings and perceptions while visiting Rumania
in the summer of 1973 at the invitation of the Rumanian Ministry of
Culture. Accompanied by an interpreter, she visits the capital and
makes a circuit tour of the country going through Moldavia,
Transylvania and Wallachia. We become acquainted with churchmen,
politicians, men of letters and their surroundings through her eyes
and comments. The meeting of President Cauceuscu and the Spanish
Pasionaria, back in the capital, mark the highlight of her tour,
ending at the Black Sea to visit Ovid's tomb. The book, alternating
prose and poetry, is nominally apolitical, but slightly tinted
political observations are everywhere.

AR

La vida callada de Federico Monpou. Barcelona: 1975.

AR

Vivir. Madrid: Hyperion, 1983, ISBN 8475170889, 76 pp.
    Illustrations and songs. This book of 63 poems has fully
transcended the stage in which the existential feeling once targeted
creation around temporality and the existence of human beings. Man
appears here as a rebel afraid of the protean world in which he
meanders. The complexity of the work gives place to all elements
that allow the poet to make a strong affirmation of life: love and
friendship are not the only findings; animals, landscapes and objects
are also treated. Toward its end, the search for new ways of communication undertaken by Clara Janés propels her to create a poem
known as the planctus or plaint, a form of expression vinculated to
the origins of lyricism.

AR

JIMENEZ FARO, Luz María (1937-).
    A poet in Madrid, she has several volumes of poetry in preparation.

Por un cálido sendero. In collaboration with Antonio Porpetta.
Ed. Sala, 1978.

NLB

*JULIO, Montserrat (1929-).
   From Mataró, she lived in exile in Chile, where she became known for her work in the theater. She continues her work in the theater in Madrid, and also writes novels.

   Memòries d'un futur bàrbar. Barcelona: 62, 1975.
      An apocalyptic science fiction novel, it is well written and well constructed. A doctor from Sarrià is profoundly preoccupied with the dictum of Tagore, which appears before the novel begins: "Mentre neixi un infant, és que Déu espera alguna cosa dels homes." ("As long as a child is born, God expects something from mankind.")
                                                                        KM

K

*KARR I ALFONSETTI, Carme (1865-1943). Pseud. L. Escardot.
  Niece of the French novelist Alphonse Karr, the Barcelona writer
Carme Karr first published Catalan songs under her pseudonym. Her
collaboration in literary magazines led to the publication of
collections of short fiction. Part of the Modernisme movement, Karr
added a female voice and perspective to much of her fiction. From 1907
to 1918 she edited the monthly magazine Feminal and became a leading
figure in Catalan feminism. Dedicated to furthering education for
women, Karr spoke and wrote on women's social and literary issues and
founded La Llar, a residential college for women teachers and students
which she directed.

  Bolves, quadrets. Biblioteca Popular de "L'Avenç," No. 52.
  Barcelona Llibreria "L'Avenç," 1906, 123 pp.
    Published under the pseudonym L. Escardot and with a prologue by
  Lluís Via, this collection of seven short narratives contains two
  sections, country vignettes and city sketches. Heavy with descriptions of nature, the first group focuses on the margination of
  children and a childless woman. The second group opposes ironically
  the life of rich and poor in Barcelona. Structured on the dichotomy
  of dream and reality, the sketches demonstrate strong sympathy for
  children, a sense of the unnaturalness of social priorities, and the
  incongruity of human actions.

  Caritat. Barcelona, 1918.
    A play.

  Clixfes, estudis en prosa. Barcelona: Publicació "Joventut,"
  1906, 268 pp.
    Signed with the pseudonym L. Escardot, this second collection of
  narratives, some published previously, is structured on the visual
  metaphor of photography: snapshots, backlighting, interiors, sea-
  scapes, flash, etc. The volume closes with a brief afterward to the
  "Dear Reader" which continues the photographic metaphor. The pieces
  depict women trapped in unresponsive relationships, the contrast
  between the spontaneity of the poor and the artifice of the rich, and
  scenes of human unfulfillment. Situational irony occurs widely.

Cuentos a mis nietos. Illus. Rosario de Velasco. Burgos: Hijos de Santiago Rodríguez, 1932, 97 pp.
   These nine stories are told by a grandmother to her grandchildren. Simple in style and language, the stories are variations of well-known myths and tales, sometimes identified as such. The principles of goodness, self-sacrifice and hard work prevail.

Garba de Contes. Gerona: Dalmau Carles Plá, 1935, 109 pp.

Els idols, comedia en un acte i en prosa. Biblioteca "De tots colors". Barcelona: B. Baxarias, 1911, 34 pp. 2nd ed., Barcelona: Ráfols, 1917, 16 pp.
   Performed at the Teatre Romea on May 10, 1911, the play is a contemporary drama set among the Catalan bourgeoisie. The characters are female, a mother and daughter, who deal with the problem of marital infidelity. The daughter learns society's double standard and the patient wife's resignation, tolerance and life-long solicitude. Men are the idols with feet of clay, children who never grow up. The theme is treated with some irony.

El libro de Puli. Illus. Mariana Lluch. Barcelona: Ars, 1942, 60 pp. 2nd ed., 1958.
   Written for Paulina, nicknamed Puli, this collection of fables and exempla is prefaced by the desire to see the book in the family libraries and schools of the new Francoist Spain.

Raig de sol.
   A play.

La vida d'en Joan Franch. L'esquitx. Barcelona: Ilustració Catalana, 1912, 32 pp.
   A short novel, La vida d'en Joan Franch received the silver cup at the 1912 Jocs Florals in Barcelona. L'esquitx appeared previously in the collection Bolves (1906).

                                                                    MB

KENT, Victoria (1897-).
   Victoria Kent was the first woman lawyer in Spain and a member of the Radical Socialist Party in the government of the Second Spanish Republic. She was appointed Director General of Spanish prisons in 1931 and began radical reforms to humanize the prison system. She fled to Paris after the Spanish Civil War and Franco attempted to extradite her in 1940. Living under the name Madame Duval, Kent wrote her memoirs Cuatro años en París (1940-1944). She later established herself in New York, working on prison reform for the United Nations. In 1954, she founded the anti-Franco magazine Ibérica which she published until 1975. She presently resides in New York.

Cuatro años en París (1940-1944). Buenos Aires: Sur, 1947, 189 pp.
   This autobiographical document was written, according to Kent, in order not to forget the bitter years of exile and persecution by the Franco regime within Nazi-occupied Paris. Narrated, curiously, in the first and third person, the protagonist of these memoirs is a man, Plácido, though the author later clarifies that Plácido is her literary alter-ego. Cuatro años en París is a reflective and

philosophical monologue which describes her obsession with freedom caused by bewilderment and the isolation of persecution, and the radical disillusionment war and destruction produced in her. She also comments on the plight of the Jews in Paris under Nazi occupation and provides an analysis of Nazism in Europe. Out of print. Available through interlibrary loan.

SMG

**KRUCKENBERG SANJURJO, María del Carmen (1926-).
Born in Vigo, where she lives now, she was a member of the Alameda "tertulia" between 1945 and 1949. She lived in Italy and Buenos Aires until 1953 and now works as a saleswoman for a chemical products company. She has published four volumes of poetry in Galician and nine in Castilian.

A sombra ergueita. Vigo: Author's edition, 1976.

Cantares de mi silencio. Vigo: Acebo, 1980.

Cantigas a vento. Vigo: Author's edition, 1956.

Cantigas de amigo a Ramón González Sierra do Pampillón. Vigo: Author's edition, 1972.

Carnaval de Ouro. ?: Salnés, 1962.

Farol de aire. Vigo: Author's edition, 1958.

Memoria de mi sueño. Vigo: Author's edition, 1964.

Las palabras olvidadas. Vigo: Author's edition, 1956.

Los parajes inmóviles. Prólogo de Celso Emilio Ferreiro. Vigo: Author's edition, 1956.

Poemas inevitables. Vigo: Author's edition, 1960.

Poemas y canciones de aquí y de allá. Bilbao: Alrededor de la mesa, 1962.

Rumor de tiempo. Vigo: Author's edition, 1957.

Tauromaquia en línea y verso. Vigo: Author's edition, 1964.

CNC & AM

KURTZ, Carmen. See: **RAFAEL MARES KURZ, Carmen de.**

LABORDA MEDIR, Clemencia (1908-1980). Also: **Clemencia Laborda.**
  Born in Lérida of a Cuban mother, she spent her childhood in Avila, then moved to Madrid. An avid reader of Jiménez and Lorca, she took no university degree. Her poetry, praised by such as Machado and Alonso, varies in theme and includes religion, family love and even salutes the first man on the moon. She was also a playwright and contributor to Cuadernos de Poesía Contemporánea and Alma.

  Caudal.
    Poetry.

  Aniversario de bodas.
    Play.

  Ciudad de soledades. Madrid: 1948.
    Poetry.

  Don Juan en la niebla.
    Play.

  En busca de los recuerdos perdidos.
    Poetry, reported unpublished at the time of her death.

  En media hora de sueño.
    Play, in collaboration with Concha Suárez de Otero.

  Fachada a la calle.
    Play.

  Una familia ideal.
    Play, inspired by Jane Austen's Pride and Prejudice.

  Historia de una niña.
    Novel.

  Jardines bajo la lluvia. Madrid: Talls. Afrodisio Aguado, 1943, 116 pp.
    Laborda's first book of poetry received good critical notice. She preferred the classic forms (décimas, romances, tercetos, sonetos,

octavas reales) in which she developed diverse themes. Each of the
following sections contains several short poems: Rogativa, Glosa,
Versos bobos, Homenaje a los dulces nombres, Poesías dedicadas,
Primer amor, Canto espiritual. Not easily found.

Laura y el ángel.
    Play.

Niños y jardines.
    Poetry.

Poesías religiosas.

Retorno a la provincia. Caracas: Lírica Hispana, 1961, 64 pp.
    A tiny, informative book with anecdotal and interpretive intro-
ductions by editors Conie Lobell and Jean Aristeguieta, a biographical note, a bibliography (incomplete) and a photo of the poet. At
the editors' request, Laborda sent 26 poems to Venezuela. They are
loosely grouped by the themes of distant places and nostalgia. The
poet's preference for classical forms is still evident.

La sacristía; comedia dramática en tres actos. Madrid: Escelicer,
1957, ISBN 84-238-0455-0, 88 pp.
    The author's first play, staged in Madrid in 1953, is intended to
give vitality to Catholicism in theatre. It presents the drama of
all that surrounds a crime of passion which finds its purification in
the symbolic sacristy of a Franciscan monastery. This self-conscious
and literary comedia is one of the few available pieces by Laborda.

El sobrino.
    Novel.

Tiempo del hombre, tiempo de Dios. 1972.
    Poetry.

Vacaciones bajo los árboles.
    Poetry reported unpublished at the time of her death.

                                                                    GM

LACACI, María Elvira (19??-).
    Born in El Ferrol, Galicia, in 1952 she took up residence in Madrid.
At that time, she began writing and publishing poetry. Influenced by
the taste for realism, which reigned in Spanish poetry during the
1950's, she was considered a social poet. Nevertheless, her poetry is
fundamentally religious, in search of God as witness to events of daily
life.

Al este de la ciudad. Barcelona: Juan Flors, 1963, 200 pp.
    The speaker, devoutly Christian, introspective, transfixed by the
sorrow of life, advocates a poetics of realism by deliberately
avoiding expressive brilliance in favor of simple directness. The 82
poems, divided into four heterogeneous parts, are primarily of two
types: religious meditations on moments of transcendental illumi-
nation; descriptions of society's unfortunate and their shabby
surroundings. With nine thematically related photographs by Nicolás
Muller. Available through interlibrary loan.

Humana voz. Madrid: Rialp, 1957, 109 pp.
   Her first published collection, this work consists of 38 poems in
which an introverted speaker explores traditional themes--death,
pain, tenderness, patience--in their everyday manifestations.
Against a metaphysical background presided over by a paternal,
protective God, the speaker finds motives for remembrance and
reflection in such ordinary topics as buses, streetcars, movie
houses, city streets. Also includes a poem of homage to Rosalía de
Castro. Available through interlibrary loan.

Sonido de Dios. Madrid: Rialp, 1962, 88 pp.
   Consisting of a title poem and 39 other poems divided into three
parts, this work deals with a search for and encounters with a
humanized deity having attributes of both Christ and God the Father.
Each part of the work emphasizes different aspects of the speaker's
passionate relationship with the deity: The first, her anguished
search and struggle; the second, her stirred emotions during
encounters; the third, her accounts of illuminating moments based on
scriptures and personal experiences, all related in a personal
manner. Available through interlibrary loan.

EW

LACASA, Cristina (1929-).
   Born in Tarrasa, Lacasa's extensive literary work is composed of
poetry and two books of short stories. Lacasa is a highly lyrical voice
in contemporary Spanish literature; a very personal poetic voice who
works mostly isolated from groups or generations of poets, but a voice
among the most important in the poetry of contemporary Spain for its
purity of vision, its humanness, its testimonial quality, its authenticity and its beauty of expression. Her poetic language has the
freshness and clarity of a limpid brook. The joys and sorrows of the
human condition are the main theme of Lacasa's poetry.

Los brazos en estela. Lérida: Estudios Gráficos Artis,
1958, ISBN 51-1958, 58 pp.
   Memories of childhood, dreams, pains and joys, are the elements
that give birth to the lyrical poems of this second book of poems by
Lacasa. The poet reflects on the past, the present and hopes for the
future, seeing in everything lived an occasion for positive evalu-
ation and even rejoicing. Her attitude is filled with great
expectancies. Her poetry, thus, is song, and also leans towards a
future of fulfillment. Available in paperback. Preface by the poet
Jaime Ferrán. Illustrations of Ernesto Ibáñez.

Los caballos sin bridas. Lérida: Dilagro, 1981,
ISBN 84-7234-054-6, 158 pp.
   A collection of short stories dated from 1955 to 1981 in which,
with the lyrical quality that characterizes the creative work of
Cristina Lacasa, the author narrates realistic stories full of
tenderness, hope, joy and misery and, also, stories of a somewhat
esoteric nature. In the latter, new dimensions of reality are hinted
at. In this way, this book is more varied and richer, perhaps, than
her first book of short stories. The natural language and direct
style give to the reader a feeling of life. Available in paperback.
Contains a biographical note about the author.

Con el sudor alzado. Madrid: Colección Agora, 1964, ISBN 918-1964, 78 pp.
   This book of poems is a lyrical x-ray of the poet's own life, her dreams, her ambitions and her failures. It is a book that leaves in the open the soul of the author, but, it is also a book in which Lacasa, through a serene inward journey, explains herself as a human being, as a poet, as the profoundly lyrical poet that she is. This book obtained the second poetry prize "Agora." Available in paperback. Contains a biographical account of the poet.

En un plural designio. Carboneras, Cuenca: El Toro de Barro, 1983, ISBN 84-5339-37-1, 43 pp.
   A book of poems about the defenseless position of children and their rights. All the deeply felt idealism of Lacasa reaches its highest point in this book inspired by childhood and its vulnerable position in the hard, and many times insensible, world of adults. Lacasa explains poetically the significance of children and the responsibility that adults should have in providing a better world for them. Some of the aspects of child rearing that Lacasa addresses so lyrically, reveal that the poet is a woman poet. Available in paperback. Contains a biographical note about the poet and quotes from the Declaration of the Rights of Children and of authors such as Sontag, Otto Rank and Millichamp.

Encender los olivos como lámparas. Madrid: Colección Agora, 1969, ISBN 10558-1969, 82 pp.
   In this book of poems, Lacasa turns her attention to a universal concern of many other contemporary writers: violence, war. To the devastation and brutality of war, Lacasa opposes her lyrical song in favor of love and beauty. The theme is treated with such an urgency that the poems become as communicative and important as her more personal or biographical poems. Lacasa has, as a poet, the rare quality of making anything that she touches highly personal and really authentic. Thus, her poetry is powerfully testimonial and human. This book received the second poetry prize "Agora".

Ha llegado la hora. Caracas: Arbol de fuego, 1971, 22 pp.
   This short book composed of 17 poems appeared in the poetry journal Arbol de Fuego, number 44. Through these poems dealing with various parts of the human body and ending with a poem to the soul, Lacasa affirms that love, understanding and beauty are the vehicles to defeat pain, discouragement, sadness and anguish.

Jinetes sin caballo. Barcelona: Ambito Literario, 1979, ISBN 84-7457-032-8, 183 pp.
   In this book of short stories dated from 1955 to 1977, Lacasa treats the theme of frustration and margination suffered by a number of characters of lower social class. The stories are very direct in style and plot, giving the feeling of something lived rather than invented by the narrator. Some of the stories, for example the one entitled "The mute," are dramatic reflections of the effects of the Civil War in Spain. Man in all his facets, the inner and the outer man, is the main lyrical concern of Lacasa's poetry and prose. In short, humankind is her main theme. Available in paperback.

Opalos del instante. Madrid: Rialp, S. A. (Adonais), 1982,
ISBN 84-321-2190-8, 88 pp.
   In this book of poems Lacasa returns to her past (childhood and
adolescence) and to her present, attempting to penetrate, through her
personal experiences, into the enigma of the human condition.   The
book goes from the optimism and vitality of the childhood poems to
the somber mood and somewhat disillusioned tone of the poems of
maturity.   Nonetheless, Lacasa returns, in the third part of the
book, to a serene acceptance of existence as it is and not as we
would like it to be.   The book ends with a note of hope.   Available
in paperback.   Contains a biographical note about the poet.

Poemas de la muerte y de la vida. Lérida: Diputación Provincial
de Lérida, 1966, Registration number 5-66, 77 p.
   Through an inward journey into the self Lacasa reflects upon the
recurrent themes of her poetry: love, life, death.   Her tone is
lucid and serene and from this journey the poet emerges with renewed
hope in life and in her poetic gift.   Her lyrical quest reaches
heights of perfection.   Her command of poetic language, feeling and
tone is in this book the best so far in her poetic career.   This book
was awarded the poetic prize "Ciudad de Barcelona" for 1964.
Available in paperback.   Contains a quote from Euripides, and a
biographical note and photograph of the poet.

Ramas de la esperanza (Poemas ecológicos. Lérida: Dilagro
Ediciones, 1984, ISBN 84-7234-70-8, 127 pp.
   Nature occupies a central part in all the poetry of Cristina
Lacasa; thus, it is not surprising that her most recent book of
poems, subtitled "Ecological Poems," deals with the danger that
besieges the planet Earth because of man's ravishment.   The poet
denounces very strongly, passionately, yet lyrically, the risks that
the landscape, the sea, the historical sites and the atmosphere are
suffering because of the unlimited ambition of man.   The book is
illustrated with photographs and drawings of landscapes of various
kinds.   Most of the poems are dedicated to contemporary Spanish
poets.   The book contains a biographical note and photograph of the
poet.   Of interest to any reader of poetry and, certainly to
ecologists.

Un resplandor que no perdonó la noche. Barcelona: Atzavara, 1961,
ISBN 6026-61, 45 pp.
   In this book of poems Lacasa talks of the joy and pain of life
with a language that is traditional but fresh and suggestive.   The
profound lyrical quality of her verse puts her among the best lyrical
voices in her generation.   She proclaims that life is worth living
through love, beauty and understanding.   Her message is a hopeful and
optimistic one.   The poet's humanity is powerfully perceived through
the poems, yet her presence in the poems is never sentimental but
beautifully alive, delicately woven in the mesh of the verse.   Her
poems are a fine lace of emotion, thought and sensation.   This book
was a finalist in the poetry prize "Ciudad de Barcelona."   Available
in paperback.   Contains a biographical note about the poet.

La voz oculta. Lérida: Editora Leridana, 1953, 74 pp.
   In this first book of poems, Lacasa concerns herself with themes
of poetry and love. The poetry shows a young poet in search of her
expression. She is closer to Bécquer than to the Generation of '27.
The work has the mark of a very first book; it is biographical and
romantic but it already points to some aspects that will later be so
characteristic of the poetry of Lacasa, such as her lyricism and her
basically positive rendition of humanity's experience in this
mysterious universe. Available in paperback. Preface by Miguel
Lladó. Illustrations by Nuri Serra.

                                                                AMF

**LAFITTE Y PEREZ DEL PULGAR, María de los Reyes - Condesa de Campo
Alange** (1902-).
   The Condesa de Campo Alange, a woman of great culture and talent, has
distinguished herself as a historian and sociologist of Spanish women; a
novelist, critic of art and literature. She was born in Sevilla, where
she lied until her marriage in 1922 to José Salamanca y Ramírez de
Haro, Conde de Campo de Alange, Grandee of Spain. She and her husband
lived in Madrid until 1931 and then they went to Paris where they stayed
for three years. While in Paris she studied drawing, painting and the
history of art. In 1934 she and the Count returned to Spain to live.
In 1944 she wrote her first book, a critical biography of María
Blanchard and she participated as a member of several Academies of Art
and Literature. She belongs to the Real Academia Sevillana de Buenas
Letras, Real Academia Gallega and The Hispanic Society of America. Her
works on Concepción Arenal merited her the "Cruz distinguida de primera
clase de San Raimundo de Peñafort." She has been very active as a
lecturer and has conducted several workshops about the social condition
of women and also about Teilhard's thought.

   Concepción Arenal 1820-1893. Madrid: Ediciones de la Revista de
Occidente, 1973.
   This fine study of Concepción Arenal by the Condesa de Campo
Alange was much needed in the study of Spanish letters. The author
offers a perspective of Arenal's times, years of political and social
difficulties and civil wars which never ceased except briefly in
appearance and time. The author treats in great detail the participation of Arenal together with Fernando de Castro, Giner de los
Ríos, and Gumersindo de Azcárate in the cultural revolution that
was taking place. This was a difficult task at a time when a woman
had to cross so many barriers in order to develop herself. The
Countess then proceeds to provide an objective study of Concepción
Arenal--her infancy, youth and mature life. She refers to the
periods of austerity, public life, and specifically to her work
towards achieving the reform of the penitentiary system. The book
ends with Arenal's activities as a novelist, writer and educator.

De Altamira a Hollywood. Madrid: Revista de Occidente, 1953.

La flecha y la esponja. Madrid: Arion, 1959.
   This book is a series of seven short stories dealing with a new
and complex world, where the relationship of the sexes is presented
by certain sexual and emotional elements which eventually become
symbols. The title, La flecha y la esponja, refers to certain
masculine and feminine characters typical of our time. The author

has attuned herself to the conflicts, presenting them with great
imagination and intellectual curiosity. Her style is very personal
and she tends to view art as something in itself. She presents
unexpected conflicts of atavistic and psychopathic nature. Some of
her narrations, Electroamor, Pajarito remind the reader of Huxley's
short stories. Her sensitive interpretation of a woman's mind and
heart is a distinctive contribution to the Spanish short story. The
Condesa, also as a creator of moods, irony and dramatic effects, has
brought new beauty to the Spanish literature of this period.

Metamorphosis del arte. Madrid: Revista de Occidente, 1953.

Mi atardecer entre dos mundos: Memorias y cavilaciones.
Barcelona-8: Planeta, S.A., 1983.
   The author presents in this book memoirs, anecdotes, and personal
and public experiences of her life. She outlines the development of
her intellectual life, from her youth up to the year 1975, the year
in which she ended her memoirs. The first part of the book is
devoted to her youth in Sevilla, her marriage, her move to Madrid,
her trips to Paris and Biarritz and her return to Spain after the
Spanish Civil War. The second part of the book is an ample and
panoramic view of the intellectual life of the period, in which she
enthusiastically participated. She was an active member of the
Academia Breve de Crítica de Arte, and she was vice-president of the
Ateneo. She organized several cultural functions and published
various books. She succeeds in expressing incisive appraisals of the
intellectual circles of Madrid and emits accurate judgments about
prominent personalities of the time. The final chapters are devoted
to her reflections about her literary and scientific preoccupations
and about the basis of her thought and intellectual development. The
book is an accurate and incisive view of Spanish intellectual life
and its most prominent personalities seen through the author's experiences. She was a witness to her time and therefore feels obli-
gated in a certain way to collect remains of happenings that were so
small they would be destined to be eliminated from recorded history.

Mi niñez y su mundo (1906-1917). Madrid: Revista de Occidente,
1956.

La mujer en España, cien años de su historia 1860-1960. Madrid:
Aguilar, 1963-1964.
   The author studies the Spanish woman not only as a historical
character but as a literary one as well. She says in her "Intention"
that the literary character is more humane than the historical
character although the first one is an entellechy and the second a
reality. The historical character--badly known in its inwardness--is
deformed by hostile feelings or sympathetic currents and we have to
choose among different versions that are offered to us simultaneously. In the literary character there is only one version--the one
created by its author. Besides, thanks to his or her absolute
irresponsibility, the character is shown without false or true
virtues. We could say that we have the curriculum vitae of the
historical character and the psychoanalysis of the literary one. The
author utilizes articles, interviews, letters, together with written
memoirs, unpublished memoirs and oral tradition. Sometimes she uses

polls and statistics. With these materials the Countess has
attempted to reconstruct the social and cultural evolution of the
Spanish woman. She does not pretend to exhaust the theme. Therefore
she does not give the reader a parade of all the famous Spanish women
of the period. She acknowledges that she has based her study on many
representative examples and in concrete episodes, but she seems to
prefer the collective attitudes rather than the personal ones--the
woman as a problem vs. the woman as an individual. She has divided
the book in three parts. The first part encompasses the years
1860-1899; the second begins in 1900 and ends in 1936; the third
covers the years 1939 to 1960. It is, according to the author, an
arbitrary division but it is the only one possible to avoid confusion
and repetition that would distract the reader. The Spanish woman of
1963, says the Countess, enjoys freedom very similar to the women of
the rest of Europe. The Spanish woman has lost her traditional
modesty and has revealed the mystery of her body that she kept
jealously secret for centuries. Now she exhibits it with or without
malice to the lusty or casual look of men. Sweethearts, husbands,
fathers and brothers do not seem to realize the evolution or they
look at it with indifference. Social norms are tolerant toward the
Spanish woman. She goes in and out of the house as she pleases. The
single Spanish woman lets herself be invited out by whomever she
likes. She goes with the man of her choice on an excursion in the
country, either by car or motorcycle. She is kissed at parties, at
the movies or in the public garden without the worry of being seen.
The Spanish woman attends the universities, hospitals, laboratories,
factories, offices, cafeterias, etc. However, we can ask together
with the Countess "Is the Spanish woman equal to the Spanish man?"
Certainly not, but she has advanced and this is what the Condesa
describes in her book.

La mujer como mito y como ser humano. Madrid: Taurus, 1961.

La poética ingenuidad de Papi Sánchez. Madrid: Ateneo, 1959.

La secreta guerra de los sexos. Madrid: Revista de Occidente, 1958.
                                                              EML

*LAFONTANA I PRUNERA, Maite.

   Indrets d'argila. Barcelona: Paraula Viva, 1980.
       P etry.

                                                              KM

LAFORET, Carmen (1921-).
   She was the first woman novelist to achieve wide acclaim after the
Spanish Civil War, making literary history when she received the
first Nadal Prize for her novel Nada in 1944. After spending her
childhood and adolescent years in the Canary Islands, she studied law
at the Universities of Barcelona and Madrid. She married Manuel
Cerezales in 1946 and has five children. In 1951 she underwent a
religious experience that profoundly influenced her fiction for
several years. Her first-hand observations of the difficulties of
Spanish life in the 1940's and 1950's provide the raw material for
many of her novels and stories; some of her fiction could be
considered feminist.

La insolación. Barcelona: Planeta, 1963, 383 pp. Barcelona: Planeta, 1972, 5th ed., Col. Popular Planeta. Barcelona: Planeta, 1980, 2nd ed. ISBN 84-320-21342.

Intended as the first volume in a trilogy to be entitled Tres pasos fuera del tiempo, this novel deals with adolescents growing up in post-Civil War Spain. It is the only one of Laforet's long novels narrated from a masculine point of view. Martín, the protagonist, after three carefree summers (1940, 1941, 1942) on the Mediterranean coast, confronts the harsh realities of the adult world in the form of a Civil War refugee and his father's violent rejection of him for suspected homosexuality. A prologue by the author explains her intent in formulating the trilogy. Out of print.

La isla y los demonios. Col. Ancora y Delfín, Barcelona: Destino, 1952, 304 pp. Col. Ancora y Delfín, Barcelona: Destino, 1964, 4th ed., ISBN 84-233-0423-X. Col. Destinolibro, Barcelona: Destino, 1977, ISBN 84-233-0681.

Laforet's second novel is about a young girl, Marta, who achieves a kind of maturity during a year in her adolescent life when some mainland relatives take refuge with her family on the Canary Islands during the Spanish Civil War. She loses her childish illusions about becoming a writer and decides to accompany her relatives to the Peninsula after the war. Narrated in the third person, the novel does not achieve the complex perspective on a young woman's life that Nada does, but it is in some ways technically superior to the first novel and contains masterful evocations of the Canary Islands ambience. Hardback and paperback.

La llamada. Col. Ancora y Delfín, Barcelona: Destino, 1954, 243 pp. Col. Ancora y Delfín, Barcelona: Destino, 1980, 5th ed., ISBN 84-233-0399-3. Col. Destinolibro, Barcelona: Destino, 1975, ISBN 84-233-08774. Col. Destinolibro, Barcelona: Destino, 1980, 2nd ed., ISBN 84-233-077-4.

This collection of short novels contains works written in 1952 and 1953 when Laforet was writing her long novel La mujer nueva. Many of these novelettes include references to the ambience of Spanish life (especially for women) in the 1950's. "La llamada" centers on a woman who attempts to leave her husband and children for a stage career; "Un noviazgo" reveals the psychology of an embittered spinster; the protagonist of "El piano" balances personal independence and the demands of social responsibility. Others contain specific references to the Civil War or reflect Laforet's religious experience. Hardback and paperback.

Un matrimonio. Col. Pandora, 4. Madrid: Mon, 1956, 63 pp.

La muerta. Madrid: Rumbos, 1952, 115 pp.

This collection of short stories contains pieces written from 1942-1952, some published previously in journals. Several are of a decidedly feminist orientation: "Rosamunda" is a bizarre older woman seen the day after her failed stage debut, and in "El veraneo" a sister's career is sacrificed for a ne'er-do-well brother. Others of these stories reflect the theme of Christian charity that begins to appear in Laforet's work after a religious experience in 1951: "La fotografía," "La muerta," "El aguinaldo," and "Un matrimonio." The

remaining stories deal with motherhood, childhood and hunger in
post-Civil War Spain. Out of print.

La mujer nueva. Col. Ancora y Delfín, Barcelona: Destino, 1955,
291 pp. Col. Ancora y Delfín, Barcelona: Destino, 1975, 9th ed.,
ISBN 84-233-0176-1. Madrid: Círculo de Amigos de la Historia,
1974, ISBN 84-225-0540-1.
    This is a complexly structured novel centering on the mystical
experience of the protagonist, Paulina, and the moral choices she
faces because of it. The novel follows Paulina's life (through
flashback) from her university days during the Spanish Republic
(early 1930's) until the mid-1950's. Thus, after a youth of freedom,
living with her boyfriend, civil marriage, etc., Paulina confronts
the limitations placed on women's lives by the government, Church and
society during the first ten years of the Franco regime. La mujer
nueva received the "Premio Menorca." Hardback.

Nada. Col. Ancora y Delfín, Barcelona: Destino, 1945, 304 pp.
Col. Ancora y Delfín, Barcelona: Destino, 1979, 25th ed., ISBN
84-233-0787-5, Col. Destinolibro. Barcelona: Destino, 1979, Col.
Destinolibro. Barcelona: Destino, 1981, 3rd ed., ISBN 84-233-0989,
eds. Mulvihill, Edward R. and Roberto G. Sánchez. Oxford: Oxford
University Press, 1958, ISBN 0-19-500942-8, 269 pp.
Trans., Inez Muñoz. London: Weidenfeld and Nicolson, 1958, 254 pp.
Andrea, trans. of Nada by Charles F. Payne. New York: Vantage
Press, 1964.
    A first-person narration in which the protagonist, Andrea,
reflects on the year she spent in Barcelona with relatives at age 18
immediately after the Spanish Civil War, the novel is a kind of
Bildüngsroman in which the protagonist matures through observing
people's lives shattered by the war. Nada won the first Nadal Prize
for the novel in 1944 and has had lasting success and impact on
fiction by both men and women in Spain, particularly in its use of
the family as a microcosm of the Civil War and Franco regime and in
its oblique manner of treating recent Spanish history. Hardback and
paperback.

La niña y otros relatos. Col. Novelas y cuentos, Madrid:
Magisterio Español, 1970, 249 pp.
    A collection of short stories and novelettes that had previously
appeared in other collections. Contains "La niña," "El viaje
divertido," "Los emplazados," "Rosamunda," "El veraneo," "La
fotografía," "En la edad del pato," "Al colegio," "Ultima noche,"
"El regreso," "Un matrimonio," "El aguinaldo," "La muerta." A prologue by the author explains the circumstances in which she wrote
these pieces, especially "La niña," which deals with a very
religious woman who marries her brother-in-law in order to care for
her dead sister's children. Paperback.

Novelas, I. Col. "Clásicos Contemporáneos." Barcelona: Planeta,
157, 1347 pp. Col. "Clásicos Contemporáneos." Barcelona:
Planeta, 1977, 12th ed.
    A luxury edition "complete works" containing all of Laforet's
previousy published work, including "La niña," a novelette never
before published in collection but excluding La insolación, her last
long novel. Includes the novels Nada, La isla y los demonios and La

mujer nueva and the following stories and novelettes: "La muerta,"
"El veraneo," "La fotografía," "En la edad del pato," "Ultima
noche," "Rosamunda," "Al colegio," "El regreso," "Un matrimonio," "El
aguinaldo," "La llamada," "El último verano," "Un noviazgo," "El
piano," "La niña," "Los emplazados," "El viaje divertido." A
prologue by the author contains biographical information.

Un noviazgo. Ed. Carolyn L. Galerstein. New York: Bobbs-Merrill,
1973, ISBN 0-672-63131-8, 90 pp.

                                                                    RJ

LAGOS, Concha. See: **GUTIERREZ TORRERO, Concepción**.

**LEDO ANDION, Margarita (1951-).
Born in Castro do Rei (Lugo), she is a professional journalist. She
lived in Portugal for a few years, where she worked as a Professor of
Galician in Porto. Politically involved, she was a member of the
Central Committee of Unión do Pobo Galego.

O corvo érguese cedo. Monforte: 1973.

Mama-Fé. Vigo: Xerais, 1983.
Five short stories of a complex structure. Some of them are
reduced to a collection of apparently unconnected sentences including
many words in different languages.

Parolar cun eu, cun intre, cun inseuto. Monforte: 1970.

                                                              CNC & AM

LEJARRAGA, María de la O (1874-1974). Full name: **María de la O
Lejárraga García de Martínez Sierra**.
Born in San Millán de la Cogolla on Dec. 28, the eldest of a large,
middle-class family of scientists and intellectuals, she was reared in
Madrid from 1880. After graduation from high school, she attended the
Normal School in Madrid to become a language teacher. In 1897, she
began writing works composed jointly with her future husband, Gregorio
Martínez Sierra, six and a half years her junior. They married in
1900, when he was 19 and she was 25, and authored numerous stories and
novels (1898-1910). After the success of their first play in 1907, they
concentrated progressively more on theater, with many successes.
Although they separated in 1922, María continued to write plays
published under her husband's name (his letters to her show that most,
if not all of the work is hers). A commercial attaché of the Republic
in 1936, she spent most of the War in exile in France, moving to New
York in 1950. After living in Arizona and Mexico, she settled in Buenos
Aires, where she wrote several books, numerous articles and stories, as
well as further feminist essays.

Abril melancólico. Madrid: Renacimiento, 1916.
Play. Signed by G.M.S. (Gregorio Martínez Sierra).

La adúltera penitente. Madrid: Renacimiento, 1917.
Play. Signed by G.M.S.

El agua dormida. Madrid: 1907.
Novel. Signed by G.M.S.

Aldea ilusoria. Paris: Garnier, 1907.
    Play. Signed by G.M.S.

Almas ausentes. Madrid: Biblioteca Mignón, 1900.
    Novel. Signed by G.M.S.

El ama de la casa. Madrid: Sucesores de Hernando, 1910.
    Play. Signed by G.M.S.

Amanecer. Madrid: Velasco, 1915.
    Play. Signed by G.M.S.

El amor brujo. Madrid: Velasco, 1914.
    Play. Signed by G.M.S.

El amor catedrático. Barcelona: Domenech, 1910.
    Novel. Signed by G.M.S.

Aventura. Madrid: Blas y Cia., 1907.
    Short novel. Signed by G.M.S.

Aventura and Beata primavera. Madrid: Renacimiento, 1908.
    Short novels. Signed by G.M.S.

Beata primavera. Madrid: 1907.
    Novelette. Signed by G.M.S.

Cada uno y su vida. Madrid: Prensa Gráfica, 1924.
    Play. Signed by G.M.S. Stage version of novel of same title.

Canción de cuna. Madrid: R. Velasco, 1911.
    Play. Signed by G.M.S.

Cada uno y su vida. Madrid: Estrella, 1919.
    Novel. Signed by G.M.S.

Calendario espiritual. Madrid: Estrella, 1918.
    Play. Signed by G.M.S.

Cartas a las mujeres de América. Buenos Aires: Renacimiento, 1941.
    Feminist essays. Signed by María Martínez Sierra.

Cuentos breves. Madrid: Imprenta de Enrique Rojas, 1899.
    Short stories. Signed by María Martínez Sierra.

Cartas a las mujeres de España. Madrid: Clásica Española, 1916.
    Feminist essays. Signed by María and Gregorio Martínez Sierra.

El corazón ciego. Madrid: Estrella, 1919.
    Play. Signed by G.M.S.

Cristo niño. Madrid: Estrella, 1918.
    Play. Signed by G.M.S.

El diablo se ríe. Madrid: Renacimiento, 1916.
    Play. Signed by G.M.S.

Don Juan de España. Madrid: Estrella, 1921.
    Play. Signed by G.M.S.

El enamorado. Madrid: Renacimiento, 1913.
    Play. Signed by G.M.S.

Esperanza nuestra. Madrid: Renacimiento, 1917.
    Play. Signed by G.M.S.

Eva curiosa. Madrid: Pence, 1930.
    Play. Signed by G.M.S.

Feminismo, feminidad, españolismo. Madrid: Renacimiento, 1917.
    Feminist essays. Signed by María and Gregorio Martínez Sierra.

Fiesta en el Olimpo. Buenos Aires: Aguilar, 1960.
    Fiction.

Fuente serena. Madrid: Estrella, 1919.
    Play. Signed by G.M.S.

Las golondrinas. Madrid: Juan Pueyo, 1914.
    Play. Signed by G.M.S.

Granada. Madrid: Estrella, 1920.
    Play. Signed by G.M.S.

Gregorio y yo. Mexico: Biografías Gandesa, 1953.
    Memoir-biography. Signed by María Martínez Sierra.

Hechizo de amor. Madrid: Prieto, 1908.
    Play. Signed by G.M.S.

Horas de sol. Madrid: Ambrosio Pérez y Cía, 1901.
    Novella. Signed by G.M.S.

La hora del diablo. Madrid: Estrella, 1930.
    Play. Signed by G.M.S.

La humilde verdad. Madrid: Heinrich y Cía, 1905.
    Novel. Signed by G.M.S.

El ideal. Madrid: Estrella, 1921.
    Play. Signed by G.M.S.

Juventud, divino tesoro. Madrid: Renacimiento, 1908.
    Play. Signed by G.M.S.

Kodak Romántico. Madrid: Estrella, 1921.
    Play. Signed by G.M.S.

Lirio entre espinas. Madrid: Velasco, 1911.
    Play. Signed by G.M.S.

Madam Pepita. Madrid: Renacimiento, 1912.
    Play. Signed by G.M.S.

Madrigal. Madrid: Renacimiento, 1913.
   Play. Signed by G.M.S.

Mamá. Madrid: Renacimiento, 1913.
   Play. Signed by G.M.S.

Margot. Madrid: Renacimiento, 1914.
   Play. Signed by G.M.S.

Motivos. Paris: Garnier, 1905.
   Fiction. Signed by G.M.S.

Mujer. Madrid: Estrella, 1925.
   Play. Signed by G.M.S.

La mujer del héroe. Madrid: Velasco, 1914.
   Play. Signed by G.M.S.

La mujer española ante la república. Madrid: Ediciones de
Esfinge, 1931.
   Feminist-Socialist essay. Signed by María Martínez Sierra.

La mujer moderna. Madrid: Estrella, 1920.
   Play. Signed by G.M.S.

Una mujer por los caminos de España. Buenos Aires: Losada, 1952.
   Memoir. Signed by G.M.S.

Navidad. Madrid: Renacimiento, 1916.
   Play. Signed by G.M.S.

Nuevas cartas a las mujeres. Madrid: Ibero Americana de
Publicaciones, 1932.
   Feminist essays. Signed by María and Gregorio Martínez Sierra.

El palacio triste. Madrid: Renacimiento, 1911.
   Play. Signed by G.M.S.

Pascua florida. Barcelona: Salvat y Cía., 1903.
   Novel. Signed by G.M.S.

La pasión. Madrid: Renacimiento, 1914.
   Play. Signed by G.M.S.

Los pastores. Madrid: Velasco, 1913.
   Play. Signed by G.M.S.

El peregrino ilusionado. Madrid: 1908.
   Novel. Signed by G.M.S.

El pobrecito Juan. Madrid: Prieto y Cía., 1912.
   Play. Signed by G.M.S.

Primavera en otoño. Madrid: Prieto y Cía., 1911.
   Play. Signed by G.M.S.

El reino de Dios. Madrid: Pueyo, 1916.
    Play.   Signed by G.M.S.

Rosas mustias. Madrid: Prensa Gráfica, 1926.
    Play.   Signed by G.M.S.

Rosina es frágil. Madrid: Estrella, 1918.
    Play.   Signed by G.M.S.

Seamos felices. Madrid: Estrella, 1929.
    Play.   Signed by G.M.S.

La selva muda. Madrid: Blas y Cia., 1909.
    Novel.   Signed by G.M.S.

Sol de la tarde. Madrid: Tipografía de la Revista de Archivos,
1904.
    Novel.   Signed by G.M.S.

Sólo para mujeres. Madrid: R. Velasco, 1913.
    Play.   Signed by G.M.S.

La sombra del padre. Madrid: Revista de Archivos, 1909.
    Play.   Signed by G.M.S.

La suerte de Isabelita. Madrid: Velasco, 1911.
    Play.   Signed by G.M.S.

Sueño de una noche de agosto. Madrid: Renacimiento, 1918.
    Play.   Signed by G.M.S.

Teatro de ensueño. Madrid: Imprenta de Samarám y Cia., 1905.
    Collection of experimental and Modernist theater.   Signed by
G.M.S.   Includes: Saltimbanquis, Por el sendero florido, Pastoral,
Cuento de labios en flor.

La tirana. Madrid: Renacimiento, 1913.
    Play.   Signed by G.M.S.

Todo es uno y lo mismo. Madrid: Revista de Archivos, 1910.
    Novel.   Signed by G.M.S.

La torre de marfil. Madrid: El Cuento Semanal, 1908.
    Short novel.   Signed by G.M.S.   Later dramatized (Madrid:
Estrella, 1924) under same title.

Triángulo. Madrid: Estrella, 1930.
    Play.   Signed by G.M.S.

Tú eres la paz. Madrid: Montaner y Simón, 1906.
    Novel.   Signed by G.M.S.

Viajes de una gota de agua. Buenos Aires: Librería Hachette, S.A.,
1954.
    Stories.   Signed by María Martínez Sierra.

La vida inquieta. Madrid: Renacimiento, 1913.
    Play. Signed by G.M.S.

Vida y dulzura. Madrid: Renacimiento, 1920.
    Play. Signed by G.M.S.

JP

LEON, María Teresa (1904-).
    León was born in Logroño, the daughter of an army colonel, of noble
ancestry, by blood deeply rooted in the bourgeoisie. She is a journalist, novelist, essayist and translator whose sensitivity to feminism
is vinculated to the tradition of Concepción Arenal and Emilia Pardo
Bazán. Her prose reflects the vanguardist style of the 1920's.
Cultivated and of great sensibility, her Memorias de la melancolía is a
testimonial of her rejected childhood. While still very young she contributed to journalism under the pen-name of Isabel Inghirami in Diario
de Burgos. Married to the poet Rafael Alberti, she collaborated on
vanguardist publications from 1930-36 and came openly in defense of the
poor and of workers. Her wide travels include Russia and China. During
the Civil War, jointly with Alberti, she participated in rescue efforts
on behalf of the Republic through the Junta for the Protection of
National Artistic Treasures. She also cooperated with Antonio Machado
in the National Council of the Theatre. With Franco's triumph, she
joined Alberti in exile in France and Argentina. In 1963 they settled
in Rome, close to the homeland to which they returned after the dis-
mantling of the Franco regime. She now resides in Spain.

La bella del mal amor. Burgos: Hijos de S. Rodríguez, 1930,
159 pp.
    A collection of six short stories of rural themes, void of social
and political zeal, they contain some tinge of the traditional
ballads. The first and last tales of the collection explicitly bear
an epigraph from a romance. Contents: "La bella del mal amor,"
"Pinariega," "Manfredo y Malvina," "El tizón de los trigos," "El
mayoralde Bezares," "La amada del diablo." Contains drawings by
Rosariode Velasco.

Cervantes, el soldado que nos enseñó a hablar. Madrid: Altalena,
1978, ISBN 84-7475-003-2, 193 pp.
    Historic and literary fiction. Juvenile literature.
Illustrations by Carlos Alonso and Oscar Mara.

Contra viento y marea. Buenos Aires: Espasa-Calpe, 1941, 329 pp.
    A novel, its leitmotiv is: "Life is a struggle against all odds";
its underlying principle, solidarity with those who suffer. It
strives to be a testimonial of experiences the author witnessed
during the Civil War. The narrative first takes place un Cuba,
depicting sufferings of the poor and dispossessed after 1898. Action
progresses to the 1930's with some unrest and political activism of
the workers. When news of the Spanish Civil War arrives in Havana,
some volunteers sail to join the forces of the Republic in their
struggle against Franco. The second part takes place in Spain, up to
the siege and fall of Madrid. Only briefly we encounter the volunteers who came from Havana. No character particularly developed, it
is mostly a series of vignettes.

Crónica general de la Guerra Civil. Recopilado por María Teresa
León con la ayuda de F. Miñana. Madrid: Ediciones de la Alianza
de Intelectuales Antifascistas, 1939-?

Cuentos de la España actual. Mexico: Dialéctica, 1973?
   This collection of short stories represents social realism,
dealing with oppression in society, class hatred, violence, and
hunger, ideologically reflecting a social consciousness in accord
with the Communist Party doctrine. Some autobiographical aspects are
seen in "Sistema pedagógico" and "Infancia quemada." Although the
propagandistic nature reduces the value of the literary work, there
is an element of sensibility and poetic expression that renders the
stories of literary value. Because of her compassion for the weak,
mainly women and children, León is an advocate of feminine causes.

Cuentos para soñar. Prólogo de María Goyri de Menéndez Pidal.
Illus. Rosario de Velasco. Burgos: Hijos de Santiago Rodríguez,
192-, 111 pp.
   A collection of children's short stories, written by a mother for
her child, the fairy tales are an imaginary journey that incorporates
some characters of traditional juvenile literature. Not entirely
removed from reality, the fable blends in the childlike vision of
some artifacts of the adult world fashionable at the time: pianolas,
radios, gramophones.

Doña Jimena Díaz de Vivar, gran señora de todos los deberes.
Bilioteca Contemporánea, 288. Buenos Aires: Losada, 1960, 176 pp.
Madrid: Biblioteca Nueva, 1968, 212 pp. Russian text. Moscú:
Literatura Artística del Estado, 1971, 174 pp.
   Historic and literary fiction.

Una estrella roja. Prólogo de Joaquín Marco. Selecciones Austral.
Madrid: Espasa-Calpe, 1979, ISBN 84-239-2053-4, 192 pp.
   Selection of short stories from Cuentos de la España actual
(1937?), Morirás lejos (1942) and "Fábulas del tiempo amargo"
(1962). Edition particularly of interest because of valuable
prologue by Joaquín Marco as well as a selection of "Fábulas del
tiempo amargo". Of difficult access, having been originally
published in Revista de Poesía Universal Ecuador 0º 0'0".

"Fábulas del tiempo amargo." Revista de Poesía Universal Ecuador
0º 0'0". 1962.
   This collection of short stories was first published in Revista de
Poesía Universal Ecuador 0º 0'0" under the direction of Alejandro
Finisterre. A selection is included in Una estrella roja, of easier
access. The stories here collected represent a step forward in the
narrative art of the author. Aesthetically a very poetic prose, rich
in metaphors of a belated surrealism. Thematic richness: less
emphasis on the surrounding reality, branching off to American myths
and the world of dreams, with a universal approach. Still there is
nostalgia, with memories of the past while in exile. Although her
style is poetic, her denunciation of injustice and violence pervades
in very subtle form. Some noteworthy stories: "Las estatuas,"
"Comed, comed, que ya estoy invitada."

El gran amor de Gustavo Adolfo Bécquer. (Una vida pobre y
apasionada) Con las rimas del poeta, un poema y un epílogo de Rafael
Alberti. Buenos Aires: Losada, 1946-ᶜ1945, 271 pp. 2nd ed., Buenos
Aires: Losada, 1951-ᶜ1946, 230 pp.
   Historic and fictional biography.

La historia tiene la palabra. Noticia sobre el salvamento del tesoro
artístico de España. Buenos Aires: Patronato Hispano-Argentino de
Cultura, 1944-ᶜ1943, 71 pp. 2nd ed., Madrid: Hispamerca, 1977, ISBN
84-400-2769-9, 122 pp.
   Report on art and the Spanish Civil War. Second edition contains
documented appendix and a bibliography.

Juego limpio. Buenos Aires: Goyanarte, 1959, 264 pp.
   The novel is the memoirs of Camilo, a friar who temporarily leaves
the convent due to the Civil War. Wounded at the front, he later
joins the Guerrillas del Teatro, a group that brings the classics and
popular entertainment to soldiers at the front and in hospitals. The
novel includes testimony of the war: the siege of Madrid, desolation
en route Madrid-Cuenca-Valencia, hunger, affliction among dispersed
persons, and departure of the International Brigades. Although the
characers are fictitious, León also incorporates brief actuali-
zations of real people: the author herself and her involvement in
the Guerrillas del Teatro, Rafael Alberti, León Felipe, Pablo
Neruda. The novel shows a deep love for the Spanish people, compassion for their sufferings, and a fine sensitivity in her prose
when dealing with nature.

Memoria de la melancolía. Buenos Aires: Losada, 1970, 331 pp.
2nd ed., Barcelona: Laia, 1977, 356 pp. Barcelona: Círculo de
Lectores, 1979, ISBN 84-226-1046-9, 334 pp. Barcelona: Bruguera,
1979, ISBN 84-02-06655-0, 383 pp. Barcelona: Bruguera, 1982, ISBN
84-02-08841-4, 382 pp.
   This testimonial of the Spanish exile after the Civil War is
written in the form of memoirs.

Menesteos, marinero de abril. México: Alacena-Era, 1965, 122 pp.
Biblioteca Breve de Bolsillo, Libros de Enlace, 117. Barcelona:
Seix y Barral, 1972, 130 pp.
   A mythical narrative dealing with the origins of Cádiz. The name
of the hero, of Greek origin, is mentioned in the Iliad as a
courageous warrior; also by Strabo as one of the wandering sailors
after the fall of Troy and later as the geographic name of Menesteos,
the seaport and harbour of present Cádiz. León's narrative deals
with the wanderings of Menesteos and his final arrival at the coast
of today's Cádiz. He lands there in quest of a love lost on some
remote beach. In memory of his beloved he builds a house, a sanctu-
ary between sunrise and sunset. There dies this sailor who, navi-
gating in the spring of his life, had lost his true love in the sand.

Morirás lejos. Buenos Aires: Americalee, 1942, 219 pp.
   Collection of short stories. The Civil War as well as exile are
among the themes; also includes Mexican myths. More elaborate in
technique than Cuentos de la España actual, there is some development of psychological dimension in the characters, presence of a
certain sensuality in the situations, and an enrichment in stylistics

with a certain Baroque element. Some of the outstanding stories are "El perfume de mi madre era el heliotropo," "La hora del caballo."

Las peregrinaciones de Teresa. Buenos Aires: Botella al Mar, 1950, 123 pp.
   A series of nine short stories with Teresa as a symbolic character. The narratives are profound explorations of feminine psychology: its passions and resignation, its submission to fatality. The stories depict women under their quotidian burdens. Excellent example of feminine prose about feminine psychology within a universal projection. Contents: "Cabeza de ajo," "Primera peregrinación de Teresa," "El diluvio de Teresa," "Los otros cuarenta años," "La tía Teresa," "Esplendor de Teresa."

Rodrigo Días de Vivar, el Cid Campeador. Ilus. de Jane Wise. Buenos Aires: Peuser, 1954, 211 pp.
El Cid Campeador. Leyenda. Trad. autorizada del español de Nina Tiñanoba. Introd. F. Kelijin. Moscú: Editorial Estatal de Literatura Infantil-Ministerio de Educación, 1958. Russian text.
El Cid Campeador. Buenos Aires: Fabril Editora, 1962, 166 pp.
2nd ed., Buenos Aires: Fabril Editora, 1968.
3rd ed., Buenos Aires: Fabril Editora, 1971.
   Historic and literary fiction. Juvenile literature.

Rosa-Fría, patinadora de la luna. Cuentos. Dibujos de Rafael Alberti. Madrid: Espasa-Calpe, 1934, 113 pp. Madrid: Espasa-Calpe, 1935, 106 pp. Moby Dick, Biblioteca de Bolsillo Junior, 29. Barcelona: La Gaya Ciencia, 1973, ISBN 84-7080-529-0, 116 pp. Madrid: Espasa-Calpe, 1975, ISBN 84-239-1596-4, 138 pp.
   Collection of short stories. For its beauty in the narrative and its novel fantasy, the book transcends the interest of juvenile literature. It is vinculated to the poetics of the Generation of 1927. Contents: "Rosa-Fría, patinadora de la luna," "La Tortuga 427," "El Lobito de Sierra Morena," "El Oso poeta," "El Gallo Perico," "Flor del Norte," "Juan Bobo," "El ladrón de islas," "El pescador sin dinero."

Sonríe China. Por María Teresa León y Rafael Alberti. Ilus. en colore de Rafael Alberti. Buenos Aires: J. Muchnik, 1958, 229 pp.
                                                                    PS

*LEVERONI, Rosa (1910-).
   A poet, born in Barcelona, her father was of Italian origin. She studied at the Escola de Bibliotecàries, where Carles Riba, Antoni Rubió, and Pere Bohigas were among her professors. She graduated in 1933 and worked as a librarian at the Universitat Autónoma until 1939. Carles Riba and Salvador Espriu encouraged her, and both celebrated her as an excellent poet in introductions to her books. She has not produced creative works since 1952. Leveroni is also known for her research on Ausiàs March, her contributions to the journals Ariel and Poesia, and her translations of T. S. Eliot. She published a short story, "L'estranger," in Ariel.

Epigrames i cançons. Carta-pròleg de Carles Riba. Barcelona:
Gili, 1938, 80 pp.; rep. in Presència i record. Barcelona: Ossa
Menor, 1952, pp. 7-25; rep. in Poesia. Barcelona: Edicions 62,
1981, pp. 13-27.
 Leveroni's first book is a small collection of short poems
expressing the excitement, pain, and joy of love in a thoughtful and
circumspect tone. Influenced by Noucentisme, she strives for the
formal perfection of classicism. Her inner self is often compared to
elements of Nature: the sea, the night, the stars. Concise
rendering of subtle emotions. An introductory letter by Carles Riba
praises her as a skilled and transparent poet.

Poesia. Pròleg de Maria Aurèlia Capmany. Cara i creu, 32.
Barcelona: Edicions 62, 1981, ISBN 84-297-1752-8, 197 pp.
 The volume consists of Leveroni's two former books (Epigrames and
Presència) plus a third part of previously uncollected poems
entitled "Altres poemes." It can be considered the most complete
collection of Leveroni's poetry so far. The "Cinc poemes desolats"
won an award in the 1956 Jocs Florals at Cambridge, England. An
especially useful edition, since her former books have long been out
of print and difficult to find.

Presència i record. Pròleg de Salvador Espriu. Precedit de
Epigrames i cançons. Barcelona: Ossa Menor, 1952, 165 pp.; rep. in
Poesia. Barcelona: Edicions 62, 1981, pp. 31-170.
 The publication of Epigrames i cançons in this volume made it a
complete collection of Leveroni's poems up to 1952. Presència is
introduced by Salvador Espriu, whose prologue is more mindful of
Leveroni's uniqueness than Riba's prologue to Epigrames was.
Presència develops the characteristics already apparent in
Epigrames. Again concentrating upon her own intimacy, she describes
her feelings and experiences using classic imagery. There is in this
book a conscious homage to several members of the Catalan poetic
tradition (March, Maragall, Riba, etc.), but Leveroni's own voice
stands firm and recognizable throughout.

                                                              TMV-S

LINARES, Luisa María (1915-).
 Principally a novelist, Linares was born in Madrid. She published
her first novel immediately following the Civil War, and since the
1940's she has authored some 50 popular romances. She has enjoyed wide
popularity among the public, and many of her works have been translated
into French, German, Italian, Portuguese, Swedish, Dutch, Finnish, etc.
Frequently featuring a taming-of-the-shrew plot, her works show ener-
getic and aggressive women eventually submitting to attractive, witty,
dominant men. Her settings are exotic, her action rapid, and her
dialogue clever. Several works have been made into movies or plays, or
adapted for Spanish, French and Argentine television. She has also
contributed to many important journals throughout Europe.

                                                           RK & PWO

Apasionadamente infiel. Barcelona: Juventud, 1955, 208 pp.
Barcelona: Juventud, 1969, 224 pp.
Passionnement infidele. Trans. Marie-Berthe Lacombe. Paris:
J. Tallandier, 1974, 249 pp.

Una aventura de película. Barcelona: Juventud, 1942, 141 pp.
Barcelona: Juventud Argentina, 1944, 149 pp. Contents: Una
aventura de películas, Ojos azules, Una noche en la gran ciudad,
Amor a boro. Barcelona: Juventud, 1951, 159 pp. Barcelona:
Juventud, 1961, 158 pp.

Cada día tiene su secreto. Barcelona: Juventud, 1951, 288 pp.
Barcelona: Juventud, 1960, 288 pp.

Casi siempre te adoro. Barcelona: Juventud, 1960, 192 pp.
Barcelona: Juventud, 1968, 192 pp.
Adoro-te; mas nem sempre. Trans. Joao Amaral. Porto: Livraria
Civilizacao 1958, 174 pp.
Je t'aime presque toujours. Trans. Marie-Berthe Lacombe. Paris:
J. Tallandier, 1968, 253 pp.

La calle desconocida. Barcelona: Juventud, 1945, 192 pp.

Cómo casarse con un primer ministro y otras narraciones. Barcelona:
Juventud, 1961, 200 pp. Barcelona: Emege, 1962, 280 pp. Barcelona:
Juventud, 1966, 200 pp. Barcelona: Juventud, 1974, 200 pp.

De noche soy indiscreta. Barcelona: Juventud, 1965, 188 pp.
La nuit, je suis indiscrete. Trans. Marie-Berthe Lacombe. Paris:
J. Tallandier, 1969, 249 pp.

Doce lunas de miel. Barcelona: Juventud, 1941, 160 pp.
Madrid: Juventud, 1943. Barcelona: Juventud, 1944, 190 pp.
Barcelona: Juventud, 1975, 1v.

La calle desconocida; Regalo de Navidad; Lina es una aventurera.
Barcelona: Juventud, 1950, 191 pp.

En poder de Barba Azul. Barcelona: Juventud, 1940, 96 pp.
Barcelona: Juventud, 1941, 208 pp. Barcelona: Juventud, 1943,
190 pp. Barcelona: Juventud, 1961, 184 pp. Barcelona: Juventud,
1971, 192 pp.
En poder de Barba Azul, comedy consisting of a prologue and three
acts, Madrid, 1941.
En poder de Barba Azul, movie script, Buenos Aires: Juventud
Argentina, 1944, 173 pp.

Esconde la llave de esa puerta. Barcelona: Juventud, 1974, 223 pp.
Pas un mot au president. Trans. Marie-Berthe Lacombe. Paris:
Trevise, 1974, 268 pp.

¡Escuela para nuevos ricos! Barcelona: Juventud, 1939, 88 pp.
Barcelona: Juventud, 1943, 189 pp. Buenos Aires: Juventud, 1940,
197 pp. Barcelona: Juventud, 1957, 206 pp. Barcelona: Juventud,
1974, 208 pp.

Esta noche volveré tarde. Barcelona: Juventud, 1958, 208 pp.
Barcelona: Juventud, 1977, 208 pp.

Esta semana me llamo Cleopatra. Barcelona: Juventud, 1949, 239 pp.
Barcelona: Juventud, 1954, 239 pp. Barcelona: Juventud, 1962, 239
pp. Barcelona: Juventud, 1972, 239 pp.
Anita la jolie; ou, Cette semaine on m'appelle Cleopatre. Trans.
Marie-Berthe Lacombe. Paris: J. Tallandier, 1971, 381 pp.

Hay otros hombres; siete novelas cortas. Barcelona: Juventud, 1953,
191 pp.

Juan a las ocho, Pablo a las diez. Barcelona: Juventud, 1964,
208 pp. Barcelona: Juventud, 1977, 208 pp.

Imposible para una solterona. Barcelona: Juventud, 1959, 175 pp.
Barcelona: Juventud, 1971, 175 pp.

Lusitania express y otras narraciones. Barcelona: Juventud, 1955,
207 pp. Contents: Lusitania express, Vacaciones al sol, Bajo el
signo del miedo, Cómo casarse con un primer ministro.

Un marido a precio fijo. Barcelona: Juventud, 1940, 191 pp.
Barcelona: Juventud, 1941, 191 pp. Barcelona: Juventud, 1955,
224 pp. Barcelona: Juventud, 1961, 208 pp.
Un mari a prix fixe. Trans. Marie-Berthe Lacombe. Paris:
J. Tallandier, 1969, 255 pp.

Mi enemigo y yo. Madrid: Española, 1940, 208 pp. Barcelona:
Juventud, 1942, 73 pp. Barcelona: Juventud, 1947, 160 pp.
Barcelona: Juventud, 1962, 176 pp. Barcelona: Juventud, 1971,
176 pp. Film based on the novel in 1944, Barcelona.

Mi hombre en Ginebra. Barcelona: Juventud, 1977, 238 pp.

Mi novio el emperador. Barcelona: Juventud, 1943, 256 p.
Barcelona: Juventud, 1945, 178 pp. Barcelona: Juventud, 1953,
191 pp. Barcelona: Juventud, 1976, 240 p.

Mis cien últimos amores. Barcelona: Juventud, 1963, 235 pp.
2nd ed., Barcelona: Juventud, 1967, 238 pp.

Napoleón llega en el "Clipper". Barcelona: Juventud, 1945, 190 pp.
Barcelona: Juventud, 1964, 206 pp.

No digas lo que hice ayer. Barcelona: Juventud, 1969, 224 pp.
Barcelona: Juventud, 1972, 224 pp. Barcelona: Juventud, 1977,
224 pp.
Ne dis pas ce que j'ai fait hier. Trans. Marie-Berthe Lacombe.
Paris: J. Tallandier, 1971, 384 pp.

Prueba suerte otra vez; Absolutamente libre; El séptimo cielo.
Barcelona: Juventud, 1979, 222 pp.

Salomé la magnífica. Barcelona: Juventud, 1946, 239 pp.
Barcelona: Juventud, 1957, 240 pp. Barcelona: Juventud, 1966,
223 pp.
Und wieder beginnt ein Morgen. Trans. unknown. Munchen: W. Heyne,
1963, 187 pp.

Socios para la aventura. Barcelona: Juventud, 1950, 271 pp.
Barcelona: Juventud, 1952, 271 pp. Barcelona: Juventud, 1962,
263 pp. Barcelona: Juventud, 1973, 263 pp.

Solo volaré contigo. Barcelona: Juventud, 1952, 191 pp.
Barcelona: Juventud, 1956, 191 pp. Barcelona: Juventud, 1972, 1 v.

Soy la otra mujer. Barcelona: Juventud, 1954, 270 pp. Barcelona:
Juventud, 1959, 270 pp. Barcelona: Juventud, 1974, 270 pp.

Tuvo la culpa Adán. Barcelona: Juventud, 1942, 182 pp. Barcelona:
Juventud, 1944, 192 pp. Barcelona: Juventud, 1954, 158 pp.
C'est la faute d'Adam. Trans. Marie-Berthe Lacombe. Paris:
J. Tallandier, 1971, 252 pp.

La vida empieza a medianoche. Barcelona: Juventud, 1943, 240 pp.
Barcelona: Juventud, 1953, 171 pp. Mexico: Albatros, 1954, 158 pp.
Barcelona: Juventud, 1961, 174 pp. Barcelona: Juventud, 1972,
175 pp. Barcelona: Juventud, 1978, 175 pp.
La vita cominica a mezzanotti. Trans. Gioietta Ciani. Milan:
A. Mondadori, 1958, 189 pp.

Das Leben beginnt um Mitternacht. Trans. unknown. Munchen: Wilhelm
Heyne, 1965, 171 pp. La vie commence a minuit. Paris: n.p., n.d.
                                                              RK

LLORENS, Gràcia B. de. See: BASSA, Maria Gràcia.

*LLORENS I CARRERAS, Sara (1881-1954).
   A folklorist, she spent most of her life in Buenos Aires but wrote in
Catalan.

   Petit aplech d'exemples morals. 1906.

   El cançoner de Pineda. 1931.

   El llibre del cor. 1954.
      A diary.

   El rondallari de Pineda. Unpublished.

                                                              KM

LOPEZ DE CORDOVA, Leonor. Late 14th century.
   Of aristocratic lineage, Doña Leonor was the daughter of a favorite
of King D. Pedro I the Cruel (1350-69) and a descendent of the writer D.
Juan Manuel (1282-1348). On her mother's side she was related to King
D. Alonso XI (1312-1350), father of King Pedro. She married Ruy
Gutiérrez de Finestrosa, son of an important aide to King D. Pedro, who
inherited considerable property, jewelry and Moorish servants. They
lived in a turbulent era as King Pedro encountered the hostility of the
nobility while trying to impose royal authority by force.

   Testamento or Relación que deja escrita para sus descendientes. On
microfilm by Microcard Editions. Series: Colección de documentos
inéditos para la historia de España. Madrid: Imprenta de la Viuda

de Calero, 1842-1895. Vol. 81 of 112 vols., pp. 34-44. Original manuscript in Archivo del Real Convento de San Pablo, Córdoba, Spain.

As supporters of King D. Pedro, Doña Leonor and her husband encountered hardship and persecution as the King's brother, Enrique de Trastámara, claimed the throne with the support of much of the nobility. The author recounts these historical events with emphasis on the physical, emotional and material suffering she and her family endured. This included imprisonment and the loss of all property with no apparent legal recourse. Through the course of the narrative she is revealed as one who loved children and also felt some sympathy for her servants.

LAS

LOPEZ FERNANDEZ ARMAN, Esther (Esther Armán).
No biographical information available.

Mujeres sin pasaporte. Madrid: Quevedo, 1968, 264 pp.
Novel.

BDM

LOPEZ SAINZ, Celia (1927-). Pseud. Sainz de la Maza, María, Sabio Merlin.
Celia López Sainz is a versatile author who, in addition to novels, has also written numerous stories for children, essays and biographies. The author has also done various translations (usually from Italian versions) of fairy-tales, religious articles and novels. Though born in Sonora, Mexico, she has lived almost all her life in Bilbao. Undoubtedly one of her most important works is the Cien vascos de proyección universal (in three volumes) which contains biographies of important historic and contemporary Basque personalities.

Bajo el brillar de las estrellas. Oñate: Franciscana de Aránzazu, 1958, 102 pp.
Since this novel was first published in serial form in a magazine, the author was asked to make each chapter self-contained. In order to achieve this and still preserve a sense of unity, López Sainz chose to write the story of a family. One of the sons is a doctor who at the end decides to become a priest; the second son is an amateur soccer player who accepts a bribe in order to save a friend from destitution; the third son becomes involved in shady dealings but is redeemed through the death of his crippled sister. Available from the Biblioteca Nacional in Madrid.

La canción del desierto. Bilbao: Barquín, 1947, 162 pp.
In this novel López Sainz uses Africa as a picturesque backdrop for the vicissitudes of the two star-crossed lovers. There are numerous coincidences, misunderstandings and obstacles, but, as befits this genre of romantic fantasy, everything is resolved and concludes with a happy ending. The style, as in several of the other novels, is florid since it relies heavily on qualifiers and most works, especially the early ones, share some elements of fairy-tales for grown-ups. Copy available only from the author.

Cien vascos de proyección universal. 1st parte, La Gran
Enciclopedia Vasca, 1978. 2nd parte, Bilbao: La Gran Enciclopedia
Vasca, 1980.
3rd parte, Bilbao: La Gran Enciclopedia Vasca, 1982.

La cortesía en la vida moderna. Ensayo. Madrid: Ripollés, 1955,
327 pp. 2nd revised ed., Madrid: Ripollés, 1965. 3rd revised ed.,
Madrid: Editex, 1975, ISBN 84-7131-001-5, 330 pp.

Crucero de lujo. Madrid: Ripollés, 1954.

Drama en el aire. Bilbao: Paulinas, 1953, 236 pp.
   Though published fourth, this is López Sainz's first novel and it
reveals many of the characteristics of her subsequent works: the
theme of an impossible love (this time two sisters love the same
man), of self-sacrifice and abnegation, of surprise reunions between
long-lost family members and the murderous revenge of an abandoned
wife. The novel is one of fantasy and adventure which depicts the
success story of a young Spanish girl who emigrates to New York and
becomes a famous aviatrix. Copy available only from the author.

Edith Stein. Biografía. Bilbao: Paulinas, 1965, 301 pp.

Encontraron el camino de Cristo. Biografía. Bilbao: Paulinas,
1959, 314 pp. 4th ed., Bilbao: Paulinas, 1965, 278 pp.

El fantasma del castillo. Cuentos. Bilbao: Paulinas, 1954.

El gigante de bronce. Cuentos. Bilbao: Paulinas, 1954.

La historia de los animales domésticos. Bilbao: Paulainas, 1965,
120 pp.

La historia de la casa. Bilbao: Paulinas, 1965, 106 pp.

La historia de las legumbres. Bilbao: Paulinas, 1965, 114 pp.

La historia del reloj. Bilbao: Paulinas, 1965, 95 pp.

La historia del vino. Bilbao: Paulinas, 1965, 113 pp.

Luz de ocaso. Bilbao: María Sainz de la Maza, 1968, 172 pp.
   The author published this novel of romance and espionage under a
pseudonym and at her own expense. The main theme is a conflict
between love and duty since the Russian Cossack officer who is sent
on a spy mission to England falls in love with the girl from whom he
was supposed to recover some incriminating documents. As in many of
López Sainz's novels, this complication, as well as the endeavors of
a wicked woman to thwart the lovers, are overcome in the end. Copy
available only from the author.

Una luz en el camino. Oñate: Franciscana de Aránzazu, 1960,
114 pp.
   In her foreword, the author explains that this is her first
"realistic" novel. In comparison with her earlier works, one could
certainly classify this work as basically realistic. For one thing,

the novel is set in Spain, presumably around 1950, though there are
not many specifications as to time and place. There are few characters and the protagonist, a doctor, is somewhat idealized. As
López Sainz points out, she wanted to depict people who contradict
the general assertion that the younger generation is worthless.
Thus, in some ways, her novel constitutes an apology for goodness in
today's world. Author's foreword; copy available at the Biblioteca
Nacional in Madrid.

El mayor pecado. Oñate: Franciscana de Aránzazu, 1961, 190 pp.
    In what is the author's most realistic novel, there is a depiction
of the working classes and their daily struggle for survival. At
times the novel takes on Dickensian overtones in the description of
poverty, misery and suffering. The lives of several families who, as
the author remarks, represent contemporary Spanish society, are
described. One of the later chapters has traits of a social tract
when two characters engage in a debate over the existing economic
system and one of them makes a stong indictment of capitalism.
Available from the Biblioteca Nacional in Madrid.

¿Por qué no el divorcio? Bilbao: Paulinas, 1966, 210 pp.

Primer Quién es quien en Vizcaya. Diccionario de vizcainos
naturales o adoptivos de destacada proyección pública en las
distintas actividades y profesiones. Bilbao: La Gran Enciclopedia
Vasca, 1975, 406 pp.

¿Quién soy yo? Pseud. Celia López. Colección Pueyo de Novelas
Selectas, 234. Madrid: Pueyo, 1948, 168 pp.
    The title refers to the protagonist's search for his identity
after a war wound causes him to suffer total amnesia. The central
theme, though, of this popular romance is the forced separation of
two lovers who, after many incidents and accidents, are reunited. As
is often the case with Spanish novels of that epoch, the setting is
not Spain but a stylized exotic background. In this instance the
action takes place in an India replete with oriental splendor. Copy
available only from the author.

San Antón de Padua: Vida del santo paduano en viñetas. Oñate:
Franciscana de Aránzazu, 1965, 157 pp.

El secreto que guardó la nieve. Colección Pueyo de Novelas
Selectas, 265. Madrid: Pueyo, 1948, 176 pp.
    One of the characters in this novel gives a good description of it
when she says that the plot is like a feuilleton or serial story
since it relates how a baby, abandoned on the doorsteps of a castle,
without known parents, discovers at the end that she is the granddaughter of the castle's inhabitant. Like ¿Quién soy yo?, the novel
takes place in India and is concerned with revealing the protagonist's true identity. As in several other novels, López Sainz
depicts the turbulent course of love before the lovers are happily
reunited at the end. Copy available only from the author.

La verdad sobre Teresa Neumann. Biografía. Bilbao: Paulinas,
1960, 284 pp.

                                                          AMA

LUJAN, Micaela de (1570 or 1575-1612 or 1613). Pseud. **Camila Lucinda.**
Camila Lucinda is the poetic pseudonym (and near anagram) of Micaela de Luján, lover for a decade (1598-1607) of Lope de Vega and mother of five of his children, including Marcela and Lope Félix. Mention of her as among the most famous living actresses in Suárez de Figueroa's Plaza Universal is important contemporary corroboration of her profession and status. The passion between them was, however, common knowledge, satirized by some, but celebrated in Lope's verse. Other tokens of their relation are Lope's own pseudonym (Lucinda-Belardo) and the initial M before his signature on autograph manuscripts of that decade. The poems attributed to Camila Lucinda, who was probably illiterate, were undoubtedly by Lope, who sometimes prefaced his own works with self-eulogistic verses attributed to others, either real or imaginary.

Rimas de Lope de Vega Carpio. A don Fernando Coutinho ... Lisbon: Pedro Crasbeeck, 1605.
Rimas de Lope de Vega Carpio. Aora de nuevo añadidas con el nuevo arte de hazer comedias deste tiempo. Madrid: Alonso Martín, 1609. Reproduced by the Hispanic Society (New York: De Vinne Press, 1903).
Rimas de Lope de Vega, in Obras Sueltas de Lope de Vega, IV. Madrid: Antonio de Sancha, 1776, 188 pp.

Rimas de Lope de Vega, ed. Gerardo Diego. Madrid: Taurus Ediciones, 1963. 2nd ed., 1981, ISBN 84-306-4104-1, 47 pp.
Twenty-one of the approximately 200 Rimas, primarily sonnets, dating from Lope's passion for Micaela were addressed to her, and many more probably were inspired by her. The sonnet attributed to Camila Lucinda is the author's (i.e., Lope's) profession of love as well as a self-panegyric. A common Renaissance mythological allusion is employed. In this instance an extended metaphor describing Micaela as Eurydice and her lover as "Orfeo español" spans the two quartets, and the tercets reiterate the intensity and eternity of their love. The entire sonnet shows the mastery of form and fluidity and grace typical of Lope, who has infused a traditional classical topos with sincerity and sensuality.

La Hermosura de Angélica, con otras diversas rimas de Lope de Vega Carpio. A don Juan de Arguijo ... Madrid: Pedro Madrigal, 1602.
La Hermosura de Angélica con otras diversas rimas de Lope de Vega Carpio (La Dragontea). A don Juan de Arguijo. Madrid: Juan de la Cuesta, 1605.
La Hermosura de Angélica, in Obras Sueltas de Lope de Vega, II. Madrid: Antonio de Sancha, 1776, xxi.
La Hermosura de Angélica, in Obras Escogidas de Lope de Vega, ed. F. Saiz de Robles, II. Madrid: Aguilar, 1953, 493-612.
A simple, charming redondilla (among the introductory verses of La Hermosura de Angélica), undoubtedly by Lope, who once again creates literature of autobiographical experiences. It is cast in the form of Lucinda's plaint of love and jealousy of Angélica. In these verses, along with the flowing response ("Lope de Vega a Lucinda"), the comparison is to another famous pair of lovers, Angélica and Medoro.

El Peregrino en su patria. De Lope de Vega Carpio. Dedicado a don Pedro Fernández de Córdoua, Marqués de Priego. Sevilla: Clemente Hidalgo, 1604.
El Peregrino en su patria, in Obras Sueltas de Lope de Vega, V. Madrid: Antonio de Sancha, 1776, xiv.
El Peregrino en su patria, ed. Juan Bautista Avalle-Arce. Madrid: Castalia, 1973, p. 53, ISBN 84-7039-161-6.

A prefatory sonnet--an epithalamium to the novel's heroine, Nise, and her beloved, the peregrino, Pánfilo de Luján--stands before El Peregrino en su patria (1604), which contains many allusions to the Lope-Micaela liaison. The polished verses betray the authorship of Lope, who combines the theme of love with a concluding self-encomium.

Relación de las fiestas que la imperial ciudad de Toledo hizo al nacimento del Príncipe N. S. Felipe IIII deste nombre. Madrid: Luis Sánchez, 1605.
Joanquín de Entrambasaguas, Lope de Vega en las justas poéticas toledanas de 1605 y 1608. Madrid: 1969, pp. 78-79 and 129-33.
"Soneto de Lucinda Serrana. No escribe al precio porque no sabe el lenguaje de la corte" by Lucinda Serrana.

This is a poetic pseudonym, according to Entrambasaguas. The author, who says she does not aspire to compete for a prize as she is not familiar with courtly language, is undoubtedly Lope, who entered, pseudonymously, not only his mistress but also his children and himself (Tomé de Burguillos) in poetic contests. The sonnet is a complicated exercise in conceptismo, expressed in unrefined country language, to celebrate "de burlas" the birth of Prince Philip (April 8, 1605) in the Justas Poéticas of Toledo in May 1605.
"Romance a San Juan Baptista" by Clarinda Lisarda, Serrana del Jordán.

Another poetic pseudonym, according to Entrambasaguas. The poem was undoubtedly authored by Lope and was also written for the Justas Poéticas of Toledo of 1605. It shows similar characteristics to the preceding poem: jocose, burlesque, non-sensical verses, in rustic language, all strung together with great facility.

RL

LL

LLORCA, Carmen (1921-).

Carmen Llorca was born in Alcoy (Alicante). She has a doctorate in Philosophy and Letters from the University of Madrid. She was the recipient of the Excellence Extraordinary Award for her doctoral dissertation. She is a Professor of World Contemporary History in The Official Journalism School of Madrid. She has also presided for several years over the Ateneo in Madrid. She has also been a collaborator of Spanish National Radio in Madrid, and is the author of political and historical works, as well as biographies of historical figures.

El Sistema. Madrid: Colección Novelas y Cuentos, Magisterio Español, S.A., 1970, 201 pp.

This is the only novel by the author. It is a complex work. The "sistema" is a concept so inclusive in the novel that its definition becomes as elusive as life itself. The setting, the Italian city of Milano, is described through the omniscient narrator's sharp artistic eye, frequently in poetic ways. This book is mostly a novel of ideas. The meaning of life, death, love, power, money, communism, capitalism, fascism, are cleverly introduced and discussed through the members of the Stoppa family, the founders of a capitalistic complex or "sistema" called Panetolandia. A preface by Manuel Cerezales, director of Editorial Magisterio, precedes the book. This novel is available in very specialized peninsular bookstores.

MCJ

M

MADERA, Asunción (1901-). "Chona Madera".
   Madera, a poet, was born in Las Palmas de Gran Canaria and has published in Canary Islands newspapers and magazines. She has published seven volumes of poetry.

   Continuada señal. Málaga: 1970.

   Los contados instantes. Las Palmas de Gran Canaria: 1967.
      Received the "Tomás Morales" prize and was reprinted in Málaga in 1970.

   Las estancias vacías. Las Palmas de Gran Canaria, 1961.

   Mi otra palabra. Málaga: Librería Anticuaria El Guadalhorce, 1977, 47 pp.
      Divided into three parts: I "Mi otra palabra," containing four poems; II "Aspectos Diversos," with eight poems; III "Dos Elegías y Canciones últimas," five poems. Edition by Angel Caffarena. Some poems speak of her love of language and poetry.

   Mi presencia más clara. Madrid: 1956.

   El volcano silencio. Las Palmas de Gran Canaria: 1944. Madrid: 1947.

   La voz que me desvela. Las Palmas de Gran Canaria: 1965.

                                                                        JSC

MAEZTU (WHITNEY), María de (1882-?).
   Born to a wealthy family, of a Basque father and English mother, Maeztu was raised in an atmosphere of discipline and hard work, but where there was much emphasis on culture. Reversals in the family fortunes at the turn of the century lowered the standard of living, but she received a broad, humanistic education. Most of her work is in the essay and history of ideas, and tends to provide interpretations favoring or advancing a conservative ideology.

   Antología, siglo XX: prosistas españoles, semblanzas y comentarios. Buenos Aires: Espasa Calpe, 1943, 279 pp. Several editions.
      Anthology of prose writers, with commentary.

Historia de la cultura europea: la edad moderna; grandeza y servidumbre; intento de ligar la historia pretérita a las circunstancias del mundo presente para hallar una explicación a los conflictos de la hora actual. Buenos Aires and Barcelona: Juventud, 194, 299 pp. with bibliography, pp. 291-95.
   Essay.

Historia de la pedagogía. Madrid: La Lectura, 1918.
   Translation of English original by Paul Monroe.

El problema de la ética, la enseñanza de la moral. Buenos Aires: Imprenta L. Gotell, 1938, 278 pp. with bibliography.
   Essay.

                                                                    JP

*MALUQUER I GONZALEZ, Concepció (1918-).
   Born in Salas (Pyrenees), she lived in Barcelona and wrote fiction and poetry. In 1957, she won the prize "Premi ciutat de Barcelona" with her long poem La creu dels vents. In 1960 she published another one La ciutat i les hores and was a finalist for the same prize. Later books are novels which depict characters of the upper classes bored by the monotony of their life, notably Parentesi and Que s'ha fet de Pere Cots. Her long novels contain rich observations of contemporary phenomena that affect the life of Catalans: tourism and immigration.

Aigua térbola. Barcelona: Novela popular, Alfaguara, 1967, 227 pp.
   This novel is a social denunciation of the behavior of the upper classes during the post-war period. Their mentality, strongly influenced by a religion wrongly understood, inspired the moral patterns of these years and contributed to a general social nearsightedness.

La ciutat y les hores. Barcelona: 1960, 109 pp.
   Twenty-four hours of the day personified by 24 feminine characters constitute the original theme of this poem, which was a finalist for the Premi Ciutat de Barcelona. The flowing of the hours maintains a perfect rhythm, fluent as our own rotation. The poem resolves the difficulty of the diversification by using a core of short poems with five stanzas each.

La creu dels vents. Barcelona: Premi ciutat de Barcelona, 1959, 70 pp.
   This long poem is written as a dialog between the city and the four cardinal winds. These winds are the spirit of the world, but also the spirit of the city: Barcelona. They draw an immense cross upon this large city. La creu dels vents presents an organic unity, but also with a large variety indispensable in any long poem.

Gent del nord. Barcelona: Club de novellistes, Editor Biblioteca catalana de novella, 1971, 173 pp.
   This novel is a sociological chronicle of a phenomenon that still is going on in Spain: the invasion of the Mediterranean coast every summer by thousands of tourists. The narrator studies the influence and the alteration of the traditional physiognomy of the coast during

this period of the year. Her general sympathy towards all the characters is remarkable, considering the theme of the novel.

Gent del Sud. Barcelona: Club de novellistes, Biblioteca catalana de novella, 1964, 198 pp.
    The novel is an historic testimony of the important phenomenon of immigration in Spain. It takes place in a small village in her native Pyrenees where two different mentalities are in conflict: the mountain people who are true to their traditions and the immigrants from the south, hungry and rootless. It is a novel of strong emotion.

Parèntesi. Barcelona: Nova Collecio LLetres, 67; Alberti, 1962, 154 pp.

Que s'ha fet d'en Pere Cots. Andorra: Novela popular, Alfaguara, 1966, 110 pp.
    In this novel of psychological analysis, a man, normal, simple and anodyne, disappears. With a rigorous objectivity, the author guides us through several episodes in order to explain the psychology of her character.
                                                                    CF

MANTUA, Cecília A.. See: ALONSO, Cecilia.

*MARCAL I SERRA, Maria-Mercè (1952-).
    A poet, born in Ivars d'Urgell, she studied philology at the University of Barcelona, and is now professor of Catalan language and literature at the Institut Rubió i Ors in Sant Boi de Llobregat. She participated in the founding of the "Llibres del Mall" collection in 1973 and in 1976 won the Carles Riba prize for her book of poetry Cau de Llunes. She has published poetry in various journals, and some of her lyrics have been sung by Marina Rossell, Ramon Muntaner, Maria del Mar Bonet and others. The motto from Cau de Llunes indicates her socio-political orientation: "A l'atzar agraeixo tres dons: haver nascut dona/ de classe baixa i nació oprimida/ I el tèrbol atzur de ser tres voltes rebel." ("I thank chance for three gifts: having been born a woman/ of the lower class and an oppressed nation/ and the turbid blue of being three times a rebel.")

Bruixa de dol. Barcelona: Edicions del Mall, 1979, ISBN 84-7456-082-9, 92 pp.
    A collection of poems and songs written between 1977 and 1979 in which the author finds her own voice while recovering some Catalan literary traditions. Images of witches, fairies, and other marginal people pervade this sensual and feminist poetry.

Cau de llunes. Barcelona: Aymà, 1977, "Ossa Menor," 76 pp.
    This collection of poetry won the Carles Riba prize in 1976; it is preceded by a drawing by Joan-Pere Viladecans and a poem by Joan Brossa. The poems were written between 1973 and 1976, and are divided into four thematic parts. The first and last sections, in very different styles, are love poems; in the last part the poet uses popular traditions which render very musical poetry. The second part is nourished by her socio-political attitude, and the third by her feminist commitment. The volume is currently out of print.

Sal oberta. Barcelona: Edicions del Mall, 1982, ISBN 84-7456-122-1,
100 pp.
   A collection of poems which includes "Freu," "Heura," "Set cançons
esparses i un romanç" and "Raval d'amor." It is another example of
the poet's insistence on speaking in her own voice, from her own
experience, from the point of view of a woman.

Terra de mai. Valencia: El cingle, "Papers erosius," 1982,
ISBN 84-7456-124-8, 37 pp.
   In this collection of 15 sextinas, the poet successfully uses the
medieval form for poetry with modern preoccupations and imagery.
While following the six-line, six-stanza verse form with a closing
tercet, the language and rhythm flow gracefully in this often sensual
poetry.

                                                                    KM

MARCO, Concha de (1916-).
   This writer's works include short stories, essays, and numerous
translations of art books. She has traveled throughout Europe and
America, and served as Visiting Professor at the University of Puerto
Rico. Although she was trained in the natural sciences, she is noted
for her poetic creation. In 1973 she was the recipient of the Premio de
la Crítica Juan Ramón Jiménez for her collection Tarot. While
married to Juan Antonio Gaya Nuño, she collaborated on travel guides
and wrote for Insula.

Acta de identificación. Madrid: Mediterráneo, 1969, 108 pp.
   The 56 poems which comprise this collection have a historical
basis which provides the foundation for dealing with modern problems.
Part I, "Mujer de Piedra" is a series of poems dealing with the Roman
conquest of Spain: celtíberos, Escipión, Numancia, Atalaya. Part
II, "Estación de metro sin parada" are love poems titled with Roman
numerals. Several speak of suffering, being a victim of a second
party, much in the same way as Spain was conquered completely by the
Romans. Part III is called "Dudresnaia Corallina."

Cantos del compañero muerto.

Congreso en Maldoror. Madrid: Biblioteca Nueva, 1970,
ISBN 84-7030-172-1, 123 pp.
   This poetry collection is comprised of I. Ponencias, and II.
Discusiones. The 29 poems from part I follow the ABC's: "A de
Ariadna," "B de Balística," "C de Calle," "CH de Chacal," "D de
danza, etc. The second 29 poems are réplicas, refutaciones,
impugnaciones, conclusiones, afirmaciones, discusiones,
contradicciones and contestaciones to the poems from part I. Some
of these change perspective or focus. Others elaborate different
ideas or ways of viewing a person or action.

Diario de la mañana. Madrid: Mediterráneo, 1967, 94 pp.
   This collection of 36 poems reads like a newspaper, with various
sections or headlines for titles which one sees everyday, such as
"Página en color: Gormaz," "Golpe de estado en Africa," "Vida
cultural," "Necrología," "El teatro," "El cine," "¿Está usted
satisfecho de su empleo?" and "Crucigrama." It begins with "Portada"
and ends with "Contraportada." The poems contained in this journ-

alistic piece react to or are motivated by headlines which very well could pertain to a 1967 daily newspaper.

Guía de Soria. Leon: Everest, 1971; 1976; 1978; 1980; 1981; ISBN 84-241-4386-8, 155 pp.

Hora 0. 5. Colección Poetas de Hoy, 45. Santander: La Isla de los Ratones, 1966, 54 pp.
   These 25 poems represent the poet's first published volume of poetry. The originality of the poems lies in their departure from contemporary issues or themes and their evocation of classical influences in form and theme. They represent an original viewpoint in the unexpected construction and twists given to old themes.

La mujer española del Romanticismo, estudios biográficos. Club Everest, v. 3-4. Leon: Everest, 1969, 2 v., ISBN 84-241-2807-9, 348 pp.

"Los niños en la pintura de Valáquez." In Varía Vazqueña. Tomo I. Madrid: Ministerio de Educación Nacional. Publicaciones de la Dirección General de Bellas Artes, 1960, pp. 352-364.
   This essay covers several aspects of children in Velázquez' paintings. The introduction speaks of the appearance of children in Spanish art. Part II deals with children in the religious paintings. Part III focuses on the royal children and the absence of their smile. Part IV discusses the portraits of the prince Baltasar Carlos. Similarly, Part V is about those of the infanta doña María Teresa de Austria. Infanta Margarita and Prince Felipe Próspero are the subjects of the last two subdivisions.

Una noche de invierno. Colección Adonais, 315. Madrid: Rialp, 1974 ISBN 84-321-1674-2, 79 pp.
   The 25 poems are structured in three parts to reinforce the theme of the passage of time. Poems with titles for each quarter hour between 6:00 and 12:00 (evening) are broken by an "intermedio" between 9:15 and 9:30. It contains two poems about Asturia women's lives bound by the rules of a cloister. The first person "yo" narrative voice prevails in reflections about time's fleeting nature, but becomes universal in the final poem, "Son las doce," which enumerates various life experiences throughout the world.

Tarot. Madrid: Mediterráneo, 1973?, 141 pp.

Veinticinco años de poesía femenina española. Caracas: 1969.

Urbión.
                                                                MDJ

MARCH, Susana (1918-).
   One of Spain's leading women poets, she is the author of several books of poetry, novels, and short stories. In addition, she has co-authored with her husband, Ricardo Fernández de la Reguera, a series of historical novels entitled Episodios nacionales contemporáneos. While not stridently feminist in tone, much of her work deals with women

and women's lives, and with themes which touch her own life as a woman, artist, and individual.

Algo muere cada día. Barcelona: Planeta, 1955, 257 pp.
This novel of a disintegrated man-woman relationship is seen from a feminine point of view, but not overtly feminist in tone. Like much of the author's work, it is critical of the social conventions (within a uniquely Spanish context) which compel individuals to adopt roles and live their lives within these.

Cosas que pasan. Barcelona: Planeta, 1983, 181 pp.
A collection of short stories, dealing with the lives of an assortment of characters, with particular importance given to the women figures. Many of the stories contain an element of violence which seems intrinsically connected to the male-female relationship portrayed. The author places emphasis on the traditional societal constaints on women at the same time that she examines the individual's ability (or inability) to break through them.

Poemas (1938-1966). Santander: Isla de los Ratones, 1966, 143 pp.
An anthology of selections from the poet's previous works (Rutas, 1938, La pasión desvelda, 1946, Ardiente voz, 1948, El viento, 1951, La tristeza, 1953). Most of the poems reflect a very subjective vision of major themes (i.e. death, time, aging, etc.) based on the poet's own experience of them. In general the works reveal a feminine consciousness in fundamental disaccord with societal mores and restrictive conventions.

DD

MARIÑO CAROU, María (1918-1967).
According to Uxio Novoneira, Mariño is the first Galician mystical poet. She is deeply concerned with the experience of death, and is close to the people's language and culture.

Palabra no tempo. Lugo: Celta, 1963.
A collection of deep, almost metaphysical poems. Prologue by Ramón Otero Pedrayo.

Verba que comenza. To be published in Vigo: Xerais.
Thirty-five unpublished poems, now appearing posthumously, present pessimistic, anguished poetry.

CNC & AM

MARTEL, Carmen (1915-).
A native of Cádiz, she received a degree in nursing and worked in several hospitals tending the wounded during the tragic years of Spain's Civil War. She has traveled extensively throughout Western Europe and was associated with Cádiz' Departamento de Artesanía de la Organización Sindical, during which time she organized several artistic exhibitions. Besides contributing numerous literary articles to respected journals she has received various literary awards for several of her more than 60 novels written for children.

Al rasgar el velo del pasado. Madrid: Pueyo, 1950, 172 pp.

¿Anclas?...¿Fortuna? Madrid: Pueyo, 1957, 135 pp.

Aquel marino de Cádiz. Barcelona: Bruguera, 1949, 159 pp.

Una aventura extraña. Barcelona: Bruguera, 1963, 128 pp.

Aventuras de Juanillo. Cádiz: Excelicer, 1941, 106 pp.

Bajo los pinos de Mallorca. Barcelona: Bruguera, 1958, 121 pp.

El broche de corales rosa. Barcelona: Bruguera, 1946, 191 pp.

Cambie por tu amor. Barcelona: Bruguera, 1967, 128 pp.

Concurso de novios. Madrid: Pueyo, 194, 189 pp.
Madrid: Pueyo, 1948.

¡Demasiado tarde! Madrid: Pueyo, 1956, 142 pp.

La estrella de rubíes. Madrid: Excelicer, 1948, 124 pp.

Gardenias en el ojal. Madrid: Pueyo, 1947, 187 pp.

La guerra a través de las tocas. Cádiz: Establecimiento Cerón,
1938, 208 pp.

Herencia guerrera. Madrid: Escelicer, 1961, 99 pp.

La Hostería del Duque. Madrid: Pueyo, 1948, 169 pp.

Isabel de Valderas. Córdoba: Oficinas y Almacenes, 1943, 246 pp.

Laura de Monteflorido. Madrid: Pueyo, 1946, 186 pp.

El Pierrot Rojo. Madrid: Pueyo, 1943, 205 pp.

La princesita de los brillantes. Madrid: Pueyo, 1942, 203 pp.
Madrid: Pueyo, 1945, 200 pp.

¿Quién fue él? Madrid: Pueyo, 1958, 125 pp.

Las vacaciones de María Rosa. Barcelona: Hymsa, 1949, 151 pp.

Vida íntima de Manuel de Falla y Matheu. Cadiz: La Voz, 1966,
273 pp.

Yo quiero ser futbolista. Bilbao: Paulinas, 1965, 206 pp.

Marineros de ocasión. Madrid: Escelicer, 1966, 163 pp.

Nieve y fuego. Madrid: Pueyo, 1956, 134 pp.

San José de Calasanz. Barcelona: Vilamala, 1963, 90 pp.

RK

MARTIN GAITE, Carmen (1925-).
Born in Salamanca, Carmen Martín Gaite first became known as a social realist writer and member of the "Generation of Mid-Century." Her fiction has explored not only neorealistic currents, but also avant-garde psychological and fantastic directions. She has won the Premio Café Gijón (1954), the Premio Nadal (1957) and the Premio Nacional de Literatura (1979). Martín Gaite is also an eighteenth century scholar (her doctorate is from the University of Madrid) as well as a contemporary literary critic, and has authored several books in each of these fields.

A rachas. Edited by Jesús Muñárriz. Madrid: Peralta, 1976, ISBN 84-85272-04-8, 74 pp.
This slim volume of poetry is divided into three sections: one presents the poems of the writer's youth, and the other two those of her early middle years. This time span, coupled with the absolute spontaneity of her verses, make the anthology a very personal record of Martín Gaite's thoughts over time. The verses in A rachas were not intended to be widely shared, and came to be published only through the persistence of editor Muñárriz. Not available.

Las ataduras. Barcelona: Destino, 1960, ISBN 84-211-1401-8, 195 pp. Contains the title novella and seven short stories. Paperback edition of novella only, with introduction by Ana María Moix, Barcelona: Barral, 1978.
Contains the title novella, which explores the question of commitments in a realistic narrative about a young wife and mother. The short stories "Tendrá que volver," "Un alto en el camino," "La tata," "Lo que queda enterrado," "La conciencia tranquila" and "La mujer de cera" also are included. The novella alone constitutes the slim paperback edition introduced by Ana María Moix, whose essay focuses more on the novella's introductory quotation from Kafka than on its text. Readily available.

El balneario. 1st ed., Madrid: Afrodisio Aguado, 1945, ISBN 84-233-0674-7. Contains the title novella and short stories whose number increases in subsequent editions. 2nd ed., paperback, Madrid: Alianza, 1968. 3rd ed., Barcelona: Destino, 1977, 186 pp.
Each edition of this anthology contains the sophisticated title novella, winner of the 1953 Premio Café Gijón. The first edition also contains the stories "Los informes," "Un día de libertad," and "La chica de abajo." The second edition adds to these "La oficina," "La trastienda de los ojos," and "Variaciones sobre un tema." The third edition further includes "Tarde de tedio" and "Retirada." Only the third edition is currently available.

El castillos de las tres murallas. Barcelona: Lumen, 1981, ISBN 84-264-3039-2, 84 pp.
The author's first novel for children is a lyrical fairy tale which follows most expected conventions, yet is unmistakably a creation of Carmen Martín Gaite. In the novel, a young girl and her mother are oppressed by a wicked father/husband, who eventually turns into a reptile. El castillos de las tres murallas commands the interest of both children and adults. Illustrations are by Juan Carlos Eguillor.

El cuarto de atrás. Barcelona: Destino, 1978, ISBN 84-233-0960-6,
211 pp.
Trans. The Back Room. Helen R. Lane, New York: Columbia University
Press, 1983, ISBN 0-231-05458-0, 210 pp.
    Winner of the 1979 Premio Nacional de Literatura, this novel has
occasioned the greatest critical response of any of the author's
works. The novel "writes itself" during the course of a night-long
conversation between a woman who represents Carmen Martín Gaite and
a mysterious male interviewer dressed in black. El cuarto de atrás
is a unique hybrid: a fantastic novel, and a realistic memoir of
growing up as a woman in Franco's Spain.

Cuentos completos. Paperback. Madrid: Alianza, 1978, ISBN
84-206-1704-0, 324 pp. 2nd ed., Madrid: Alianza, 1980.
    All of Martín Gaite's short stories to date are collected in this
anthology, which is prefaced by an introduction by the author. This
volume unites the collections El balneario and Las ataduras; no new
stories appear for the first time. Martín Gaite's novellas and short
stories are grouped here according to theme, rather than chronologically, and their continuity is underscored by the fact that early and
more recent short stories appear side by side.

Entre visillos. Barcelona: Destino, 1958, ISBN 84-233-0221-0,
260 pp. 7th ed., Barcelona: Destino, 1978.
    A major example of the neorealistic aesthetic of the Generation of
Mid-Century, this novel won the Premio Nadal of 1957. The novel
objectively traces a year in the life of an iconoclastic schoolgirl
in an unnamed provincial Spanish city, modeled after the author's
native Salamanca. Entre visillos has been noted for its extremely
realistic ("tape-recorded") colloquial dialogues, as well as for its
depiction of a bright postwar woman adolescent.

Fragmentos de interior. Barcelona: Destino, 1976, ISBN
84-233-0043-9, 202 pp.
    A fast-paced series of vignettes detailing the habits and
adventures of a well-to-do Madrid family and its household retinue,
set against the pulsating life of the city itself. Because in a
first reading the quick plot seems to detract from the novel's
acutely detailed panorama of contemporary urban life, Fragmentos de
interior should be considered "a novel to read twice."

Retahílas. Barcelona: Destino, 1974, ISBN 84-233-0995-9, 234 pp.
Paperback edition, Barcelona: Destinolibro, 1979.
    A night-long conversation, expressed through interlocking mono-
logues best perceived as verbal missives, constitutes the content and
form of this novel. One protagonist is a middle-aged woman, and the
other her young adult nephew. Retahílas demonstrates great rever-
ence for the spoken word, both in its premise (based on the conventions of oral discourse) and in its theme of language as savior.

Ritmo lento. Barcelona: Seix Barral, 1963, ISBN 84-233-0890-1,
291 pp. 2nd ed., in paperback and without Epilogue, Barcelona: Seix
Barral, 1969. 3rd ed., Barcelona: Destino, 1974.
    This novel has only recently been recognized as having been a

literary pioneer of the new social novel in Spain. Ritmo lento is a
complex, synchronic psychological exploration of the character of a
superior nonconformist young man, whose absolute morality precludes
successful adjustment to the world around him. The first and third
editions of the novel are identical, but in the second (paperback)
edition the work's Epilogue was excised by the author.

JLB

MARTIN VIVALDI, Elena.
    A lyrical poet inspired by Juan Ramón Jiménez, who has lived and
worked amid great recognition in her native Andalusia, Martín Vivaldi
may be considered provincial in the privileged non-pejorative sense
applied to Rosalía de Castro, and also in the sense of having lived in
an inner exile averted from political reality during the Franco years.
Her poetry, of which several volumes have been published, is in a free
verse of subtle fluidity with occasionally traditional forms (e.g.
sonnet) and expresses a woman's solitude through landscapes both
external and internal.

    Arco en desenlace. Granada, 1963, 86 pp.
        Poems.

    Cumplida soledad. 1953-1976. Granada: Secretariado de
    publicaciones de la universidad, 1976.
        In this volume, with poems different from those in Durante este
    tiempo, although overlapping them chronologically, Martín Vivaldi
    has found a mature elegiac tone so intrinsic to the Spanish tradition
    since Garcilaso, that of a woman for whom it is too late to reveal
    herself in love and who, inaccessible to others in her true being, is
    condemned to accept her exterior self. Strange though it may seem,
    this leads to inner peace and poetic self-reliance. Although there
    are new bold accents of color, especially in Sonetos en amarillo, she
    reveals herself above all as a great poet of the night (Nocturnos), a
    night "without lament" more human than day, in which life and death
    are peacefully united.

    Diario incompleto de abril. Homenaje a Gustavo Adolfo Bécquer
    (1947). Ed. Angel Caffarena. Cuadernos de María Isabel. Málaga:
    Librería Anticuaria El Guadalhorce, 1971.
        Written in Sevilla in 1947, these poems were not published until
    1971, by which time the author was well-known in her native Granada.
    The 17 texts in free verse, written during and addressed to the month
    of April, who personifies an exciting but elusive alter ego, perhaps
    a friend or lover, capture contradictory moods in dramatic monologues
    about nature (rain, orange blossoms, wind), of which often the poet
    becomes a part, as a rose, tree, or branch. However, joy and capric-
    iousness are invariably overshadowed by suddenly darkening landscapes
    painted in extinguished colors, whose melancholy effect is not unlike
    that of Bécquer's poetry, to whom the volume is dedicated.

    Durante este tiempo. 1965-1972. Barcelona: El Bardo, 1972.
        The three subdivisions of this volume indicate the main themes of
    Martín Vivaldi's oeuvre: Día a día resumes the meditation about
    daily existence in diary format; Paisajes suggests rain, ocean, and
    night landscapes that are internal as well; Las ventanas iluminadas

conjures the loneliness of a strangely timeless rather than stridently modern city. She dedicates the volume to her contemporaries,
the poets of the Generation of 1927, and it is in their company that
these texts, with their intensely personal vision of human space and
time, place her henceforth.

Primeros poemas (1942-1944). Málaga: El Guadalhorce, 1977.
Introduction by Fidel Villan Ribot.

UMS

*MARTINEZ I CIVERA, Empar Beatriu (1914-). Also: Beatriu Civera.
    A Valencian, she has worked in the world of fashion as well as in the
world of letters. As a child, she wrote "comèdies" which she, her
sister, and other friends presented. Educated in a nuns' school, she
considered life in the convent at one time, but married instead. She
edited the periodical La Voz Valenciana during the Civil War, and was
later chosen as Secretary General of the literary journal Lo Rat Penat,
the first woman to hold that position. As writers who have had an
impact on her work, she names Zola, Unamuno, Baroja, Sartre and de
Beauvoir. She has won various literary prizes.

La crida indefugible, 1969.

Una dona com una altra, 1961.
    Novel.

Entre el cel i la terra, 1956.
    Novel.

Vides alienes, 1975. Winner of the Víctor Català Prize.

KM

MARTINEZ VALDERRAMA, María Luz (1918-).
    A poet, short story writer and essayist, Martínez Valderrama was
born in Madrid. Her article on Gabriel Miró won the Segundo Premio
"Amigos de Gabriel Miró" in 1969.

La página de cada día. Madrid: Vassallo de Mumbert, 1972, 262 pp.
    This collection contains ten short stories, the prize-winning
essay on Miró "Por sendas de Gabriel Miró," a story "El anciano
señor en el humo dormido" based on a Miró story, and 17 articles
reprinted from newspaper columns. The latter deal with such subjects
as the author's neighborhood in Madrid, her garden, spring, summer,
vacation days and the kidnapping of a child. It contains a prologue
by José Luis Cano, praising her sensitivity, and drawings by Domingo
Viladomat. Available from Kent State University library.

Por mi solo camino. Madrid: Gráf. Carasa, 1973,
ISBN 84-400-6767-4, 94 pp.
    Poems.

CLG

MASOLIVER, Liberata (1911-).
    Masoliver is the author of several historical novels based on the
Spanish Civil War and a number of romances with sentimental and/or
religious themes. Her years of greatest productivity span the

mid-1950's through the early 1970's. Several of her novels appeared in
La Pensa of Barcelona. The action of her novels is often situated in
Catalonia or Equatorial Africa. Her docudramas of the Civil War,
Barcelona en llamas and La retirada brought some popular success, as did
her early jungle novels, Efún, Selva negra, selva verde, and La mujer
del colonial. Major preoccupations of this writer are: the inhumanity
of war; the universal need for human communication; the power of
spiritual faith. Masoliver is also the author of two religious texts,
Dios con nosotros and Estés donde estés, and La bruixa, a children's
short story in Catalan verse.

Barcelona en llamas. Barcelona: Barna, 1961, 235 pp.
    This novel was a finalist in 1961 for the Premio Seix Barral and
is Masoliver's first historical novel based on the Civil War. Isabel
is a Nationalist sympathizer who has been imprisoned by the militia
in Barcelona. When the charity of an old friend, a Republican, leads
to her release, she goes to live in a room attached to a miserable
cabaret whose star attractions are three scandalous "animadoras."
There Isabel meets a mysterious fugitive, Jaime Vargás. Her love
for the man, who is later taken off by the Republicans, sustains her
through the last year of the war. Months later, as she views a
post-war victory mass, she recognizes one of the officiating priests.
It is Jaime Vargás. Primary significance of this sentimental novel
is its depiction of daily life in war-torn Barcelona from a
Nationalist perspective. Paperback. Out of print.

La bruixa. Barcelona: Jaimes Libros, 1961, 31 pp. Illustrations by
Gloria Serra.
    La bruixa is a modern fairy tale for children written in Catalan
verse. Two children are carried off by the witch Pirulina whose
broom has crashed in their garden after a collision with a
helicopter. One fantastic adventure follows the next until the
children are reunited with their parents. Hardbound. Out of print.

Un camino llega a la cumbre. Barcelona: Peñíscola, 1966, 282 pp.
    The narrow trail that leads from Las Rocas to the tiny chapel high
in the mountains represents the difficult spiritual trek awaiting the
protagonist in this sentimental novel. Throughout the book Valentina's faith in the Virgin brings her to the chapel where she
communicates her needs to the Intercessor. When she is raped and
becomes pregnant, she tries to kill herself, but is stopped by her
childhood friend, Antonio. When he offers to marry her and be a
father to the child, Valentina's problems seem to be solved. But
Antonio's lack of sexual interest in her and his affair with a
debauched village woman make her life miserable and test her faith.
The ultimate reward of Valentina's patience and devotion is a recon-
ciliation with Antonio and an awakening of his romantic interest in
her. Paperback. Out of print.

Casino veraniego. Barcelona: Peñíscola, 1968, 208 pp.
    In this novela de ambiente y costumbres, Masoliver presents a
wealthy Catalan family on summer vacation at the Costa Brava. The
star of the novel is 17-year-old Carmina, who attracts a variety of
suitors: Jesús, the adolescent intellectual plagued by existentialist doubt; Quique, an awkward, arrogant señorito; and Ramón
Isern, married, middle-aged, and in unrelenting pursuit of Carmina.

Antonio, family friend/doctor, is the girl's real love, but pride and circumstances prevent her from revealing her feelings. The action culminates in Isern's attempted rape of Carmina. The potential disaster brings Antonio and Carmina together. Out of print.

Dios con nosotros. Barcelona: Jaimes Libros, 1970, ISBN 84-7091-150-3, 429 pp.
    In Dios con nosotros Masoliver reconstructs events in the life of Christ. Biblical text is followed by the author's interpretation. The prose style is informal and intimate. Paperback. Out of print.

Efún. Barcelona: Garbo, 1955, 248 pp.

Estés donde estés. Barcelona: Jaimes Libros, 1972, 76 pp.
    The spiritual advice in Estés donde estés derives from letters written in the early nineteenth century by the founder of a religious order dedicated to foreign missions. Masoliver echoes the priest's counsel to his followers and directs her message to Miguel, a young, distraught homosexual whom she has befriended. Her philosophy: with faith, perseverance, and divine assistance, one can transcend all carnal obstacles to achieve peace with God. Out of print.

Los Galiano. Barcelona: José Janés, 1957, 225 pp.
    The Galiano family is wealthy, culturally and socially well connected, but teetering on the brink of spiritual bankruptcy. The setting is Barcelona in the mid-1950's where young women ride Vespas, drink cuba libres, and listen to Count Basie. Young men do the same, as well as pursue women, write abstract poetry, and achieve literary prestige. Impotence, divorce, infidelity are some of the items addressed in the novel. Major themes are selfish vs. unselfish love; romantic illusion vs. reality; material wealth amidst spiritual poverty. Primary value of the novel is its usefulness as a novela de costumbres of the middle years of the Franco regime from an urban bourgeois perspective. Hardbound. Out of print.

Hombre de paz. Barcelona: Jaimes Libros, 1969, 279 pp.
    José Luis Valls is a surgeon in Barcelona during the Civil War. In his care is Cari, whose father has been executed by the militia. Both Cari (a Nationalist) and Valls (a Republican) are courageous and generous as they help the injured of both sides of the conflict, but the doctor, in a desperate moment, commits a perfect murder in order to save his sister's life. Preoccupied by guilt and the feeling that he has lost his faith, he is also haunted by his seemingly unrequited love for Cari. The narrative takes the form of Valls' post-war confession to a priest who absolves the man and advises him to declare his love to Cari (who does, indeed, love him). But before the tale can end happily, Valls dies in a car crash. Primary value of the novel is its description of daily life in Barcelona during the war. Paperback. Out of print.

Maestro albañil. Barcelona: Peñíscola, 1963, 231 pp.
    The setting is a shanty town on the edge of a wealthy resort in Catalonia. Maruja is a maid, and her husband Paco is a bricklayer, who, although happily married, still yearns for the child that Maruja

is unable to give him. When he returns from a long work detail in
the Pyrenees, he brings back a pregnant woman, Mazzantina, who is to
provide the couple with a child. Maruja's love and loyalty are
tested when she discovers that Paco is the father of the child and
when Mazzantina refuses to leave after the birth of the baby, even
though she neglects its care to pursue her own scandalous lifestyle.
But Maruja's patience and fidelity ultimately triumph. Mazzantina
leaves and the baby stays. Written in the future, the narrative has
both a hypothetical as well as definite quality. Realistic
description and dialogue. Paperback. Out of print.

Los mini-amores de Angelines. Barcelona: Jaimes Libros, 1972,
239 pp.
    This is a sentimental comedy of errors with a grim ending.
Angelines is a selfish upper-middle-class beauty whose romantic
indiscretions lead to disaster. After three years of marriage to
Fernando, she takes a lover, Arturo, who is her equal in sensuality
but her superior in intelligence and, more importantly, in morals.
Where Angelines' love is mere physical desire, Arturo's engagement is
one of the heart. When Fernando discovers the affair, he employs his
best friend, Jaime, to distract his flighty wife by courting her.
Eventually Arturo, enraged at being jilted, kills both Angelines and
the innocent Jaime. The author's antifeminist attitudes are clearly
stated in this novel. Paperback. Out of print.

La mujer del colonial. Barcelona: Barna, 1962, 323 pp.
    The value of loyalty and self-sacrifice is underscored in this
adventure novel set in Equatorial Guinea. When Clara's ailing,
impotent husband leaves for Spain, she remains behind to manage the
ranch until it can be sold at a fair price. A victim of passion, she
has a brief affair with Narváez, a wealthy, arrogant landowner. The
woman's sense of guilt and disillusionment is compounded when she
discovers that she is pregnant. She breaks with Narváez and has the
baby. Eventually she leaves the child with a deserving couple, makes
peace with God, and returns to her husband. Masoliver's familiar
themes of the flesh in conflict with the spirit and loyalty vs. amor
propio reappear in La mujer del colonial. Paperback. Out of print.

Nieve y alquitrán. Barcelona: Peñíscola, 1965, 150 pp.
    Camilo, scarred by physical and emotional deprivation, is the
town's marginated man. Natí is a neglected waif from an impoverished and decadent family. A friendship develops between the two
outcasts, but, as Natí blooms into youth, Camilo ages, and, because
of his own reclusive nature as well as his friendship with the girl,
he becomes a target for the cruel pranks of the townspeople. When he
discovers that his only human contact has fallen in love with a young
man, he hangs himself. The setting is the Costa Brava in the 1960's.
Themes of the individual in conflict with society; the universal need
for human contact and communication; the limits of human suffering
are all addressed. Paperback. Out of print.

Pecan los buenos. Barcelona: Peñíscola, 1964, 253 pp.
    This sentimental novel traces the evolution of two obsessions:
that of the male protagonist with a married woman and the woman's
obsession with her frustrated maternity. By Franco-era standards
María is a model wife, self-sacrificing, loyal, passive and devout.

It is not David's occasional affairs that move María to sin in
revenge. Rather, it is her discovery that before they married he had
contracted and been cured of a venereal disease which probably would
leave him sterile. María throws herself into the arms of the
novel's long-suffering protagonist, Víctor, best friend and business
partner of David. Later, the woman analyzes her selfish motives, is
repentant, and breaks with Víctor. The married couple is reunited--
David none the wiser about the details of María's pregnancy--and
Víctor is left to anticipate the birth of his "godchild." The
book's title suggests its main theme. Paperback. Out of print.

La retirada. Barcelona: Peñíscola, 1967, 302 pp.
    Via a nearly day-by-day account of the last year and a half of the
Civil War as experienced by two Republican infantrymen, La retirada
relates the retreat of Negrín's troops, the disintegration of the
army, and its unsympathetic reception in France. Antonio is a
courageous but reluctant draftee who must conceal the religious faith
that sustains him. His friend, Joaquín, is a disillusioned Party
delegate sent to spy on Antonio in the political purge of the last
years of the war. In spite of the abundance of stereotypes and the
book's predictable religious message (Joaquín undergoes a timely
conversion after his friend's death), it is an interesting novelized
account of the retreat and an effective commentary on the inhumanity
of war. Paperback. Out of print.

Selva negra, selva verde. Barcelona: Barna, 1959, 266 pp.
    The protagonist of this curious jungle novel is the Italian Etore
Ascari, whom the author describes as a highly principled adventurer,
whose "ideales políticos nacieron al estallar la guerra entre Italia
y Abisinia y murieron cuando asesinaron al Duce, su bandera"
("political ideals were born at the outbreak of war between Italy and
Abyssinia and died when they assassinated Il Duce, his standard
bearer"--trans. CLG). Masoliver recounts Etore's life among a tribe
of cannibals, his affair of the heart with Whuora, a village beauty
whose supposed rape by a gorilla has made her a pariah. After a
series of unlikely adventures, Etore leaves his benign captors with a
sense of relief that he left unconsummated his love for the African
woman. Paperbound. Out of print.

Telón. Barcelona: Jaimes Libros, 1969, 353 pp.

                                                                    BDM

*MASPONS I LABROS, Maria del Pilar (1841-1907). Pseud. Maria de
Bell-Lloch.
    A folklorist and novelist born in Barcelona, she was the sister of
Francesc Maspons, and was married to F. Pelay Briz. She contributed to
different Catalan newspapers such as "La Renaixença," "Lo Gay Saber,"
"La Ilustració Catalana," "La Veu de Montserrat" and "La Veu de
Catalunya." As a poet, she obtained two prizes in the 1875 and 1880
Jocs Florals (Catalan literary contest). Her style is very emotional
yet simplistic, which is due more to a lack of means than to her
intention.

    Elisabeth de Mur. Col.lecció La Novel.la Catalana, 12. Barcelona:
May 31, 1924. First edition 1880, 31 pp.
    The book consists of two legends in prose: "Elisabeth de Mur"

which gives the name to the book and "Els amors de l'esclava Afany".
The book has a portrait frontispiece.

Lectura Popular. Biblioteca d'autors catalans. Volum XV, Number
246. Barcelona: 1879?, Ilustració Catalana, 544 pp. Maspons i
Labrós, pp. 33-64.
    The book includes a few of the author's poems: "A la Verge
Montserrat," "Blanqueta," "Lo single del Vall-de-Ros," "Afany," etc.
All of them are already included in other books by the author.

Llegendes Catalanes. Barcelona: 1881, Tipografia Espanyola, 383 pp.
    The book is a compilation of 39 Catalan legends, among them "La
font de Sant Salvador," which is about the curative power of water;
"Lo cavaller del Mont-negre," "Guillem Berenguer comte d' Ausona,"
and "Nadal en Monmany," about a traditional shepherds' feast.

Montseny. Barcelona: Biblioteca de la Tomasa, 1890.
    A compilation of different legends related to the Mountain of
Montseny, the book is divided into six sections. The first four are
religious traditions. "Lo devantal" is about the prohibition of the
tree of paradise; "Las encantadas de la nit de Sant Joan" is the
punishment of ambition; "La sala" tells the story of a wealthy
youngster who turns to robbery due to a lack of religious beliefs;
"Sant Miquel del Barretons" the belief of guarding against headaches.
The fifth, "Montsoliu" talks about "lo dret del mal ús" (the right
of feudal lords to misuse their vassals). The last one, "Montsoliu
lo convit de las truytas" talks of a legendary road near the castle
that served for emergency escape or provided a way to go for food.

Salabrugas. Poesias Catalanas. Barcelona: 1874, Estampa de la
Reinaxença, 144 pp.
    Prologue by Joan Sardá. The verses are simple, reflecting her
emotions, full of delicacy and kindness. In her religious poetry,
she finds herself a little impeded but the poems never lack sincerity. Spontaneity and delicate simplicity are the two primary
qualities of her poetry, making up for the lack of grandiloquence.
Her style is natural with a popular tone and a facility of
expression. The book includes among others: "A la Verge Maria,"
"La Festa Major," and "Lo Single de Vall-de-Ros."

Vigatans i botiflers. Barcelona: 1879. 1st ed., 1878, Joan Roca
Bros., 182 pp.
    An inscription to Jacint Verdaguer is signed by the author. The
book is a historical novel about the loss of Catalan privileges and
rights. The death of the fighters for the independence of the
country is also treated.   VC-E

*MASSANES DE GONZALEZ, Maria Josepa (sometimes written as Josefa or
Josepha) (1811-1887).
    Born in Tarragona, she was a poet with a very firm scholarly
training. Her father, a military man, was pursued by the Conde de
España in 1827 and remained abroad until 1832. Besides Catalan and
Castilian, Massanés learned Italian and French. She started out
publishing her poems in several newspapers: "El Vapor," "El Guardia
Nacional," "La Religión." Her work appeared not only in national
newspapers, but also in foreign papers, especially the "Noticiero de 17

Ambos Mundos" and "El Periódico de EE.UU." She was a member of the
"Academia de las Buenas Letras." In 1840, with other Catalan poets, she
was selected to write for the Album, which was given to the king and
queen on their visit to Barcelona. Before dying, she submitted all her
work to the Biblioteca Museu Balaguer.

Flores Marchitas. Barcelona: Imprenta de A. Brusi, 1850, 324 pp.
    A compilation of some poems which had been published before in
newspapers. Many of them are personal addresses like "A mi esposo,"
"A mis lectores," "A la Sra. Da Dolores Botta," "A los Beneméritos
Cuerpos del Ejército Español," etc. The book is written in
Castilian.

Importancia de la perfecció dels brodats. Barcelona: Imprenta de
la Renaixença, 1881, 14 pp.
    An opening celebration speech on behalf of the Gimpera sisters'
needlework exhibition in 1881. The speech was a call for a regeneration of the crumbling Spanish industry, and its protection from foreign competition. The book concerns the history of needlework and
its importance since the times of the Holy Scriptures and Greek myth-
ology. It also expounds the artistic talent of the three Gimpera
sisters.

Lectura popular. Biblioteca d'autors catalans. Volum VI.
Barcelona: Ilustració Catalana number 91. 544 pp. Massanés de
González, Maria Josefa: 65-96.
    The book includes a few of the author's poems to show her literary
production. Some of the poems are: "La roja barretina catalana,"
"La creu del terme," "Lo dia dels difunts," "Creure es viure," etc.;
all of them included in other books.

Poesias. Barcelona: Imprenta de J. Rubió, 1841, 262 pp.
    A collection of poems in Castilian in a brilliant style, rich in
imagery, and full of the most moral principles. Two poems included
are: "Cataluña" and "El beso maternal." The latter was read in
honor of the poet at an 1838 session of "La Academia de Las Buenas
Letras." The government of New York had it translated to be taken
into consideration by the educational system.

Poesies. Barcelona: Ilustració Catalana, 1908, 158 pp.
    Compilation of 29 poems characterized by the beauty of their
imagery, tranquility and love of humanity which overflows each verse.
Some of the poems included are: "La creu del terme," "La roja
barretina," "Les dones catalanes," "Les festes Majors a Catalunya,"
"Ofrena a la Verge de Montserrat." The book was published
posthumously.

Respirall: Darreras Guspiras. A collection of Catalan poems.
Barcelona: Estampa Peninsular, 1879, 19 pp. See: Joan Roca i Bros.
Volúm Rimas, Barcelona, 1879.
    The book is a compilation of poems, among which are: "La roja
barretina catalana" written on the occasion of the arrival of the
victorious volunteers from Africa in the year 1860; "Creurer es
viurer," awarded a prize in the "Jochs Florals" at Barcelona in 1860,
and "La batuda de las olivas," which is a description of the Catalan
custom of olive harvesting.   VC-E

*MATHEU, Roser (1892-).
   Born in Barcelona and daughter of the poet Francesc Matheu, Roser
Matheu grew up in a social and familial climate very favorable to her
creativity. She participated in the famous contest "Jocs Florals" and
won several prizes. The physical and emotional endurance suffered by
the author during the Civil War influenced her work. Nevertheless, her
books are characterized by a great tenderness and humanism.

   Cançons de Setembre. Barcelona: La Revista, 138, 1936, 63 pp.

   La Carena. Barcelona: La Revista, 119, Editor Altes, 1935, 113 pp.

   Poemes a la filla. Barcelona: La Revista, Editor Arca, 1949, 90 pp.
      Through these poems, Roser Matheu expresses very intimate
   feelings; her personal ways of thinking and feeling. Without other
   objectives than to state some ethical values, she succeeds in
   communicating a general tenderness through her work.

   Poemes de la fam. Barcelona: Publicaciones Revista. Editor
   Barcino, 1953, 54 pp.
      The different impressions of the author during the Civil War made
   possible this book of poems. Matheu suffered physically and
   emotionally during this period and her poetry presents a different
   view from the official history of the war.

                                                                    CF

MATURANA DE GUTIERREZ, Vicenta (1793-1857).
   She is the best-known woman writer of the period of Ferdinand VII, a
king to whom she was always loyal. She was an intimate friend of
Amalia, the king's wife, and went into exile in France after Ferdinand's
death in 1833. Her husband lost his life fighting for the Carlist
cause. Her first novel appeared anonymously in 1825, but in her second
novel she identified herself, explaining that "el temor de singu-
larizarse, y la probable seguridad de atraer los tiros de la envidia y
la ignorancia" ("the fear of being singled out, and the probability of
attracting the malicious attacks of envy and ignorance") cause women in
Spain not to write. Although she often spoke out in favor of women's
rights in the prologues of her books, her works do not treat the plight
of women in early nineteenth-century Spain. She is remembered
principally for her poetry and for writing a very early prose poem.

   Ensayos poéticos. Madrid: Vergés, 1828, 106 pp.
      Contains 28 pastoral odes on love, nature, friendship, and
   morality, 20 sonnets on philosophical, moral, and historical topics,
   two satires, one on older women who try to act young and another on
   bullfights, and a number of other poems. At a time when Spanish
   poetry preferred the rigid meters of neo-classicism, she cultivated
   an impressive variety of verse forms, including letrillas, romances,
   liras, décimas and sonnets. In this she may be regarded as a
   precursor of the Romantic revolution in versification.

   Himno a la luna. Poema en cuatro cantos. Bayona: Duhart-Fauvet y
   Maurin, 1838, xv-71 pp.
      This long poem written in prose may well be one of the earliest
   manifestations of the genre in Spain. It is an impressionistic
   poem--Romantic in conception--in which she expresses the emotions and

ideas that the moon inspires in her. Throughout the poem a comparison is made between the sun as a man and the moon as a woman, often
extolling the virtues of the moon-woman. The fourth canto is political in that she laments the sad state of affairs in Spain after
Ferdinand's death. The prologue contains many autobiographical
details and also explains that she was inspired to write this hymn
after reading the Himno al Sol written in French by the Abbé de
Reyrac.

Poesías de la señora doña Vicenta Maturana de Gutiérrez. Paris:
Librería de Lecointe y Lesserre, 1841, 215 pp. 3rd ed., Madrid:
Santiago Aguado, 1859.
     The collection is divided into two parts, the first of which is
the poems of the 1828 Ensayos poéticos. Those of the second part
appear here for the first time. It begins with a sonnet on the death
of María Josefa Amalia, the wife of Ferdinand VII and a friend of
the poet; yet despite this somber introduction, the new poems are
mostly of a light humorous or satirical nature. For instance, in "La
mujer casera de mediana fortuna," she complains of the boring duties
of the housewife. The new poems have the same variety of meters as
the 1828 collection.

Sofía y Enrique. Novela original. 2 vols. Madrid: Vda. de
Villalpando, 1829, xv-158 and 120 pp.
     This novel, like others of its ilk written in the first half of
the nineteenth century, is a cross between the sentimental novel and
the Byzantine novel. Of the former it contains long, detailed
analyses of the psychology of love, and of the latter it employs an
intricate plot that includes separation of the lovers, shipwreck, and
a final, satisfactory reunion. Set during the era of Ferdinand VII,
it recounts some of the court intrigues and the incipient insur-
rection in the American colonies, but it contains surprisingly little
costumbrismo. Sofía's ambitious father is opposed to her marriage
to Enrique who, as a segundón, has no claim to his family's titles
or wealth, but his persistence and prudence prove him an upright man,
and the father realizes that happiness and virtue are more important
than wealth and social status.

Teodoro o El huérfano agradecido. Madrid: Vergés, 1825, 244 pp.
                                                                RR

MATUTE, Ana María (1926-).
     Contemporary Spanish novelist, writer of short stories and children's
literature, Matute has steadily amassed a series of prestigious literary
awards, among them the Premio Nadal. Part of the Generación de Medio
Siglo, she combines a committed attitude toward humanity and society
with a highly subjective, lyrical style. Major themes are the Civil
War, rites of passage connecting innocent childhood with later disillusionment, the modernization of biblical themes, and the passage of time.

A la mitad del camino. Barcelona: Rocas, 1961, 206 pp.
     This collection of personal essays, filled with nostalgic reminis-
cences, observations on human nature and intimate impressions of
objects, people, or nature is of interest primarily because it
contains many of the clearest statements of Matute's attitude toward
life, undisguised by fiction.

Los Abel. Barcelona: Destino, 1948, 227 pp. Barcelona: Destino,
1981, 84-233-1108-2, 244 pp.
     The author's first published novel received high honors from the
Nadal Committee. The memoir format lays bare the disintegration of a
family and the modernization of the Cain-Abel myth in the rivalry of
two brothers. The emotional impact is conveyed through the sister's
narration, which offers a penetrating psychological study as well as
a chronicle of her personal growth and goals.

Algunos muchachos. Barcelona: Destino, 1968, 84-233-0287-3,
165 pp. Barcelona: Destino, 1982, 84-233-1182-1, 170 pp.
     This excellent example of Matute's talents in the short narrative,
contains fine, although abbreviated, examples of her major themes:
lost childhood, the separation of the individual from society, the
recognition of injustice, the rebellion of the individual against the
status quo. Symbolism and some fantasy add an interesting dimension;
interior monologue enhances the interior realism.

El arrepentido. Barcelona: Rocas, 1961. Barcelona: Juventud,
1967, 84-261-0507-6, 154 pp.
     Matute's fourth collection of short stories continues many themes
from earlier works: childhood fantasy ("La luna"); disillusioned
adults ("El maestro"); the Civil War and social concerns ("El hermoso
amanecer"). Sentimentality overemphasizes the pathos of some
situations; the surprise ending reinforces the pessimism.

Caballito loco. Barcelona: Lumen, 1962, 84-264-3015-5, 94 pp.
Barcelona: Lumen, 1979, 84-264-3015-5, 94 pp.
     A story for children. Idealism vs. cruelty characterizes the
relationship of a horse and his master. The horse has many traits
reminiscent of the younger, idealistic protagonists of Matute's adult
fiction.

Carnavalito. Barcelona: Lumen, 1962. Originally included in a
volume with Caballito loco. Barcelona: Gaya Ciencia, 1981,
84-7080-162-7, 72 pp.
     A children's tale weaving allusions to the Civil War with the
innocence of children in search of a Land of Peace.

En esta tierra. Barcelona: Exito, 1955, 303 pp.
     An extensive revision of Las luciérnagas, unpublished because of
censorship problems. The Civil War shatters the comfortable life of
Soledad's family and opens a new world of different values for her.
Idealistic adolescents, the unhappy rite of passage to adulthood,
social injustice and disillusionment are recurrent themes in her
work, which includes interior monologue and flashbacks.

Fiesta al noroeste. Barcelona: Pareja y Borrás, 1959. Barcelona:
Destino, 1982, 84-233-1182-1, 170 pp.
     This prize-winning short novel is an excellent example of Matute's
narrative skills. With the stylized landscape of La Artámila as
background, powerful landowner Juan Medinao remembers his unhappy
childhood and obsessive attraction to his half-brother. The work
contains themes of Cain-Abel, loneliness, unhappiness and alienation,
social interest in the lower classes. The device of the Catholic

confessional adds an intimate tone of truth to the psychological
revelations.

Los hijos muertos. Barcelona: Planeta, 1958, 84-320-5483-5,
557 pp. Barcelona: Destino, 1981, 84-233-1149-X, 500 pp.
Trans. The Lost Children, Joan MacLean, New York: MacMillan, 1965.
      This ambitious novel describes several generations of a family
torn by conflicting values, personified in two couples. The Civil
War reinforces a sense of hopeless disillusionment and pessimism,
made more poignant by the contrapuntal alternation of past-present.
The prose is rich with symbolism, plastic and sensorial metaphors.
Premio Nacional de Literatura, 1958.

Historias de la Artámila. Barcelona: Destino, 1961, 84-233-0302-0,
168 pp.
      Twenty-two stories, set within the mythical region of Artámila,
describe less desirable facets of human nature, the frustration of
dreams, or a tragic event. Simple, unadorned prose, pervaded by a
note of suave melancholy, describes the tragic situations.

Libro de juegos para los niños de los otros. Barcelona: Lumen,
1961, 84-264-1001-X, 80 pp.
      Belying the title, this work is not a book for children, but a
series of pieces that combine characteristics of the essay, the
sketch and the short story. They describe the "games" of nameless
children which are not really games at all, but fantasy outlets for
their repressed envy, hatred and sense of deprivation. Matute's
strong social criticism is undisguised here, and reinforced by black
and white photographs.

Los niños tontos. Madrid: Arion, 1956, 56 pp. Barcelona:
Destino, 1981, 84-233-0958-4, 82 pp.
      Twenty-one short sketches, generally of a fantastic nature, deal
exclusively with children. Death or escape usually follows contact
with harsh reality, but the unpleasant truth is narrated with a
lyrical, metaphoric and understated style that contrasts sharply with
the content.

El país de la pizarra. Barcelona: Molino, 1961. Barcelona:
Lumen, 1978, 84-264-3577-7, 32 pp.
      Juvenile fiction, which combines her usual association of
childhood and fantasy in the land beyond the blackboard.

Paulina, el mundo y las estrellas. Barcelona: Garbo, 1960, 184 pp.
Barcelona: Lumen, 1981, 84-264-3027-9, 158 pp.
      Full-length juvenile fiction, it describes a young girl's
awakening to social injustice and poverty, and her idealistic
solution to the problem.

Pequeño teatro. Barcelona: Planeta, 1954, 272 pp.
Barcelona: Planeta, 1982, 84-320-0003-5, 288 pp.
      The title theme of "All the world's a stage" accompanies the plot.
An impressive stranger arrives at a little Basque town; his grandil-
oquent ways blind the inhabitants to the fact that he is a swindler.
Young, rebellious Zazu alone realizes the truth about him and the
hypocrisy and pretentiousness of the people. A certain lack of

narrative skill betrays the fact that this was actually written
earlier than her first published work.

La pequeña vida. Madrid: La novela del sábado, n.d.
    Later retitled "El tiempo" and included in the collection of the
same name, the novelette tells of the friendship of two unhappy
adolescents, and their tragic attempt to escape from the demands of
harsh reality.

El polizón del Ulises. Barcelona: Lumen, 1962.
Barcelona: Lumen, 1981, 84-264-3022-8, 126 pp.
    A children's story using some of the most poignant and recurrent
themes in Matute's literature: adventures culminating in the
realization that childhood has ended, often linked with interaction
with a disillusioned, alienated adult, this work is reminiscent of
some sections of Los hijos muertos.

Primera memoria. Barcelona: Destino, 1960, 245 pp.
Barcelona: Destino, 1982, 84-233-0736-0, 212 pp.
Trans. School of the Sun, Elaine Kerrigan, New York: Pantheon Books,
1963, 242 pp.
    The first novel in a trilogy collectively entitled Los mercaderes.
Using myth to reinforce unchanging patterns of behavior, Matute
modernizes the Cain and Abel theme and the betrayal of Christ to
structure the unhappy situation of young Matia, forced to live on an
island (Mallorca) with her grandmother and cousin Borja during the
Civil War. Their unjust betrayal of young Manuel truncates the
childlike innocence of youth, revealing reality in its most
unpleasant aspects. Feminist themes, social criticism, and a psychological study of disillusionment are underlined by an unusually complex style, rich with metaphors and the lyrical use of nature and
symbols. It won the 1959 Nadal prize.

El río. Barcelona: Argos, 1963, 172 pp. Barcelona: Destino, 1973,
84-233-0754-9, 198 pp.
    El rio closely follows the format of A la mitad del camino,
including the incorporation of some of the pieces from the earlier
work. Memories of childhood and the region are evoked by the
author's return to Mansilla de la Sierra, after it has been submerged
by a reservoir. Melancholy, resignation, nostalgia, and an emphasis
on the passage of time understandably structure the work.

El saltamontes verde. El aprendiz. Barcelona: Lumen, 1975,
84-264-8001-5, 96 pp. Barcelona: Lumen, 1982, 84-264-3001-5, 96 pp.
    Two works of juvenile fiction, each with a message clearly stated
within the story. El saltamontes is a talking grasshopper who has
stolen the voice of an orphan for the purpose of doing good for mankind. El aprendiz pits idealism vs. materialism; in it an old man
learns a lesson of love and disinterest.

Los soldados lloran de noche. Barcelona: Destino, 1964, 227 pp.
Barcelona: Destino, 1982, 84-233-0243-1, 230 pp.
    Manuel, first introduced in Primera memoria, reappears here.
Renouncing a sizeable inheritance, he makes a pilgrimage to learn
more about Jeza, a Christ-like figure killed during the Civil War.
He and Marta, Jeza's widow, speak of their past and the idealism of

Jeza. Both sacrifice their lives for what he represents. Matute's
ongoing themes of solitude, disillusionment, her penchant for mod-
ernizing Biblical myth (Christ, Cain and Abel), the use of retrospection, and the mixture of interior monologue with neorealistic
tchniques are evident here.

El tiempo. Barcelona: Mateu, 1957, 265 pp.
Barcelona: Destino, 1981, 84-233-1157-0, 259 pp.
   In her second collection of short stories, the subjects are
varied, the quality is uneven. Common themes connect them: Cain and
Abel, the passage of time, the disillusionment of life.

La torre vigía. Barcelona: Lumen, 1971, 84-264-2601-8, 237 pp.
Barcelona: Lumen, 1973, 84-264-4264-1, 238 pp.
   Using the chivalric novel as framework, Matute expresses her
ongoing concerns with disillusionment, solitude, and alienation.
Experimental techniques suggest affiliations with the New Novel in
Spain, but most are devices that have always been associated with her
highly personal style.

La trampa. Barcelona: Destino, 1969, 84-233-0627-5, 277 pp.
Barcelona: Destino, 1980, 84-233-1069-8, 277 pp.
   This final novel of the trilogy Los mercaderes returns to the
island of Primera memoria where the now-adult Matia and others
celebrate the grandmother's 99th birthday. Multiple viewpoints
interweave past and present, disillusionment and betrayal. A new
central character, Mario, touches most lives in some way, and his
terrible secret (as a child, he was tricked into revealing his
father's hiding place, thus causing his death) is a symbol of
everyone's betrayal. An air of fatality underlines the ultimate
desolation and resignation, and the one hope for the future--Matia's
son--commits an act of gratuitous self-sacrifice.

Tres y un sueño. Barcelona: Destino, 1961, 84-233-0182-6, 137 pp.
   This collection contains three stories of people (two children and
one adult who never realizes that she is growing up) who live apart
mentally or physically from the "real world," each participating in a
private world which reflects their inability to cope with adult life.
A large amount of fantasy and symbolism makes this work more difficult to interpret, but it accurately reflects Matute's opinions
concerning the separation between childhood and the adult world.
                                                              MEWJ

MAURA, Julia (1910-1970).
   Principally a dramatist, she is the most performed of the post-war
women dramatists in Spain. Her first play, La mentira del silencio
(1944), deals with such traditional themes as honor and el qué dirán.
Her final play, Jaque a la juventud (1965), initiates a new direction:
depicting Spain's new materialism and rapidly changing morality; this
work shows a much more contemporary focus in terms of situation,
character, and language.
                                                              PWO

MAYORAL DIAZ, Marina (1942-).
A Gallega from Mondoñedo (Lugo), she is Professor of Spanish
literature at the Universidad Complutense of Madrid and authority on the
poetry of Rosalía de Castro (La poesía de Rosalía de Castro, Madrid:
Gredos, 1974). Other critical works include: Análisis de textos:
Poesía y prosa españolas, 2nd ed. (Madrid: Gredos, 1977) and, in
collaboration with Andrés Amorós and Francisco Nieva, Análisis de
cinco comedias: Teatro español de la posguerra (Madrid: Castalia,
1977). Her short stories appear along with those of other contemporary
Spanish writers in anthologies published by the Confederación Española
de Cajas de Ahorros. Mayoral's novels revolve around the universal and
multifaceted theme of personal liberty and confine themselves to the
post-war era. Like her compatriots, Emilia Pardo Bazán, Ramón del
Valle-Inclán and Cela, she incorporates into her novels the legends and
customs of her native Galicia.

Al otro lado. Madrid: Magisterio Español, Novelas y Cuentos, 1981,
238 pp.
The novel develops on two levels: The conscious level represented
by the everyday reality of post-Civil War Spain, and the unconscious
level found on the other side, al otro lado, of that same reality.
On the first level, the protagonists suffer the effects of a society
closed to dialogue. On the second level, they have crossed over to
the other side of the mirror where legend, mystery, and magic replace
dogma, authoritarianism and moral taboos. It is this equilibrium
between banal reality and pure fantasy that gives the novel its
exceptional quality among those that comment on post-war and
preconstitutional Spain.

Cándida otra vez. Barcelona: Ambito Literario, 1979, ISBN
84-7457-047-6, 102 pp.
The early post-Franco years form the reference point of this
novella whose liberal protagonists view with ambivalence the passing
of the old régime that had given them their identity and raison-
d'être as the enlightened opposition. Superimposed on the socio-
historical background is a mystery whose solution comes at the end of
the story with the mentioning of the name of Cándida. Cándida
represents the progressive segment of Galician gentry and functions
as a counterpoint to contemporary Spain's indiscriminate sacrifice of
traditions on the altar of modernization. The work is a sincere,
non-modish look at change in Spain.

La única libertad. Madrid: Cátedra, 1982, ISBN 84-376-0329-3,
397 pp.
Within the gothic setting of Spain's isolated region of Galicia
unfolds the partially narrated, partially epistolary account of a
terminally-ill young woman who comes to grips with her sordid past
while in the process of writing the history of La Braña, her family
pazo or country manor. The cathartic effect of writing, the rescue
of individuality from the collectivizing tendencies of ancestral
traditions, and the establishing of one's own liberty, la única
libertad, are themes that provide this novel with a timeless and
universal appeal that transcends its feminist and regional
components.

DRG

MEDIO, Dolores (1914-).
Best known for her novels and short stories, her work is associated
with traditional realism and the social novel. Her talents were
confirmed by several literary prizes, among them the Premio Nadal.
Several books are distinctly autobiographical, with a young, observant
and analytical young woman as main protagonist. Others concentrate on a
character representative of the middle or lower class as well as an
individual in his own right. Her main themes deal with man's place in
society, his conflict with external and familial pressures, economic and
emotional deprivation.

Andrés. Oviedo: R. Grandío, 1967, 288 pp.
    A collection of short stories which received the Premio Sésamo,
all deal with children or adolescent boys placed in a sad or pathetic
situation. Poverty structures many of their lives, truncating their
childhood and forcing them to work at an early age. Some are lost in
a world of adult values; others suffer the unhappy transition between
childhood and adulthood. The subjective view of the characters
colors the situations with emotion; popular, lower-class speech gives
an air of documentary realism.

Atrapados en la ratonera: Memorias de una novelista. Madrid: Alce,
1980, 84-852-6237-9, 259 pp.
    The subtitle is self-explanatory. The title refers to the
novelist's experiences in her home city of Oviedo during the Civil
War. This is a good example of intrahistoria and the way great
events affect people who cannot control them.

El bachancho. Madrid: Magisterio Español, 1974, 84-265-7151-4,
182 pp.
    This collection offers stories previously published in near-
inaccessible magazines (and which are the usual realistic, emotion-
charged situations of lower-class protagonists) with several new
pieces. There is an obvious attempt at new subject matter (science
fiction in "Transposición;" the supernatural dimension in "Un
extraño viajero") but the interest in ordinary lives, the ironic or
surprise ending, and the basic realism of emotion are still present.
Introduction by Victor Alperi.

Bibiana. Madrid: Bullón, 1963, 84-7033-028-4, 354 pp.
Barcelona: Destino, 1967, 84-233-0277-6, 345 pp.
    The first novel of the trilogy Los que vamos a pie, the title
refers to Bibiana, an ordinary woman from a middle-class family,
whose existence is structured solely around her husband and children.
Medio uses her to comment on Spain's social structure, education and
human relationships, but Bibiana is a sympathetic character who lives
in her own right. Medio continues her chronicle of the middle class
(urban setting, daily routine), and her technique of quick, vividly
drawn sketches.

Compás de espera. Barcelona: Ediciones G.P., 1954.
    In Medio's first collection of short stories, most stories detail
pathetic situations of lower-class people, invariably "victims" of
the system or of the prejudices of others. The marked class
division, solitude, indifference toward one's fellow man, and
economic worries are constant themes in Medio's works.

Diario de una maestra. Barcelona: Destino, 1961, 233 pp.
Barcelona: Destino, 1976, 84-233-0180-X.
   Much of this work reflects Medio's own experiences and philosophy.
The novel deals with two aspects of Irene's life: Irene the teacher
(her work in a rural school, her views on education) and Irene the
woman (symbolized by her affair with her teacher). She demonstrates
the philosophy of love and good will as a way of life, with emphasis
on the development and maturation of Irene and special interest in
child/educational psychology.

El fabuloso imperio de Juan sin tierra. Barcelona: Plaza y Janés,
1981, 84-013-0324-9, 270 pp.
   Juan's return from America to his small town after an absence of
many years gives rise to a series of conjectures about whether or not
the apparently poor man is really wealthy, as he states. Colloqui-
lisms, regionalisms, interpolated stories of human interest and human
foibles, narrated mainly in conversational form, make the town come
alive.

Farsa de verano. Madrid: Espasa Calpe, 1973, 84-239-1542-5, 287 pp.
   Using the unanimist technique seen in El pez sigue flotando, Medio
presents a diverse group on a package vacation trip, each with his
own story, characteristics and thoughts interwoven. An unexpected
accident adds a note of tragedy to the novel of these ordinary
people. Realistic, minute descriptions narrated with sympathy and a
note of benevolent humor characterize this work.

Funcionario público. Barcelona: Destino, 1956, 84-233-0211-3,
252 pp.
   Pablo Marín, middle-class "everyman," works as a telegraph
operator in Madrid. Grim reality is offset by fantasies about a
mysterious woman whose diary he happens to find. Interior realism
allows self-presentation of character, complementing a realistic
portrayal of some of Spain's most pressing postwar problems: housing
shortage, economic hardship and exploitation, social and financial
pressures, the individual's changing place in society.

Mañana. Cinco Novelas. La novela del sábado, V. Madrid:
Cid, 1954.
   In this novelette narrating the attempts of a young woman to
change her monotonous, dehumanized existence, chance ruins an
unexpected opportunity for her to fulfill her life with a man.
Simple, concise presentation enhances the emotional impact. Medio
uses the ironic ending here and in other works to suggest the
character as victim.

El milagro de la Noche de Reyes. Burgos: Hijos de Santiago
Rodrigues, 1948.
   A story for children. The Three Kings arrive at a toy store; they
and the chidren listen to stories by the Dream Fairy. Simple
vocabulary; personification abounds; pleasant reading for young
people with lessons often contained within the tales.

Nosotros, los Rivero. Barcelona: Destino, 1953, 359 pp.
Barcelona: Destino, 1980, 84-233-1024-8, 360 pp.
   Lena Rivero returns to Oviedo, which she explores while reminis-
cing about her youth there. There is skillful interweaving of
fiction and history, of individual and social concerns, and of the
changes that progress brings to the traditional way of life. The
novel shows the influence of traditional realism and naturalism, with
particular inspiration in Clarín's La Regenta. There are also many
autobiographical elements. The novel won the prestigious Premio
Nadal.

La otra circunstancia. Barcelona: Destino, 1972, 443 pp.
Destino, 1973, 84-233-0750-6, 346 pp.
   The second novel of the trilogy Los que vamos a pie turns from
Bibiana to her husband Marcelo, and from the hard economic times
faced earlier to a more comfortable existence. The economic ease,
which parallels the historical circumstances of Spain, brings with it
other types of problems.

El pez sigue flotando. Barcelona: Destino, 1959, 84-233-0233-4,
252 pp.
   In unanimist style (a large number of characters presented in a
reduced area), the novel interweaves ten stories of tenants in a
Madrid apartment house. Fragmented linear stories give the illusion
of simultaneity, although a basic realistic intent underlines experi-
mentation. Common denominators of disillusionment, emotional or economic deprivation, and isolation underline their pathetic situations.

El señor García. La novela popular, No. 33. Madrid: Alfaguara,
1966, 130 pp.
   This novelette has some affinities with Funcionario público. An
office worker is led to believe that he will be promoted to office
head; news of this raises him considerably in the estimation of
colleagues and acquaintances. The next day he learns that the job
was given to a man with better connections. Temporal switches
heighten the emotion of anticipation (contrasts between his dull
existence, meager salary and his future enjoyment). The ironic
ending is typical of her literature, as is the choice of an
unimportant person as main character.

El urogallo. Gijon: NOEGA, 1982, 84-860-1506-5.
   A collection of three long stories, two of which had already been
published (Mañana and El señor García). In "El urogallo," a
Republican guerrilla is captured during the Civil War by using his
novia as bait in a trap, paralleling the vulnerability of the bird in
the title during mating season. According to the prologuist (Juan
Cueto Alas) this story was written during the Civil War but never
published because of censorship restrictions.

                                                                MEWJ

MELCON, María Luz (1946-).
   José María Martínez Cachero (Historia de la novela española entre
1936 y 1975. Madrid: Castalia, 1979, p. 284) considers her to belong
to the group of the "nueva ola" o "novísimos" according to José
Domingo's definition. She has also published poetry.

Celia muerde la manzana. Barcelona: Barral, 1972, 288 pp.
    A finalist for the Barral prize of 1971, it received the same
number of votes as the winner Haroldo Conte. It is about life in a
women's residence. There is a broad spectrum of characters: Sela
and Dorita, the lesbian lovers; Adela, the prankster; Celia, the
rebel; Esperanza, her friend; and the nuns. The novel is divided
into three parts: "Nochenegra" with an epigraph by Rimbaud,
"Fangodía" with another epigraph by Heraclitus, and an epilogue
"Rojoepílogo" with a quote from San Juan. There is an excess of
episodes and complications as if the author was trying to shock the
reader. The contrast and similarities between the nuns and the
students are interesting. It could be compared to Aguas muertas by
María Dolores Boixados.

                                                                    CA

MERCADER, Trina (1919-).
    Born in Alicante, Trina Mercader resided for 20 years in Morocco.
Called by some critics a "fundadora de poesía," she founded and
directed the journal Al-Motamid and a collection of books on poetry
entitled "Itimad." Mercader's first work, Tiempo a salvo, appears
equally hard to procure in Spain. It has been said that Mercader's
greatest satisfaction in life was meeting Vicente Aleixandre in 1953.
Mercader's poetry, as exemplified in Sonetos ascéticos, incorporates a
conceptual precision and rigorous form. The themes of life, death, and
God are treated separately, yet intertwine throughout the poems.

    Sonetos ascéticos, El Bardo, 73. Barcelona: Saturno, 1971, 63 pp.
        Directed by Jose Batlló, this work is a collection of 39 poems
divided both structurally and thematically into three parts. In Part
I (Vida), the narrator as earthy angel enjoys the perennial sadness
of nature as petals fall from the flower, as though from life itself.
The rain, symbolic of perpetual weeping, introduces Part II (Muerte)
in which the narrator transcends the earthly state of poverty and
affliction. Ultimately in Part III (Dios), she responds to an
infinite hope for a life after death. Commentaries are by Antonio
Carvajal and Federico García de Puñeda.

    Tiempo a salvo. Granada: 1956.
        Tiempo a salvo appeared as Mercader's first work. The work pre-
sents an autobiography of the poet's life prior to 1956. Poor dis-
tribution of the work accounts for its unavailability in both the
U.S. and Spain. A prologue by Pío Gómez Nisa precedes the autobiography.

                                                                    JSC

MIEZA, Carmen Farrés de (1931-1976).
    As a child she was separated from her family at the outbreak of the
Civil War. Her father escaped from Spain and settled in Mexico. Mieza
remained in Spain and completed her education as a schoolteacher. She
then joined her father in Mexico but returned to Spain in 1954. She
published two novels and several short stories, one of which won the
1960 story contest in "El Correo Catalán" of Barcelona. In 1965 she
established a publishing firm, Ediciones Marte. She committed suicide
in 1976 in Barcelona, the city of her birth.

La imposible canción. Barcelona: Plaza y Janés, 1962. Paperback edition. Barcelona: Bruguera.
This novel portrays the lives of five Catalonian exiles living in Mexico City. Once nurtured by their political ideals and their desire to return to a "free" homeland, they have sunk into a crippling abulia. Once politicians, they now, out of habit, attend dinners they hate, listening to empty rhetoric in which they no longer believe. Homesick, they cannot become integrated into Mexican life; and it pains them to watch their children becoming assimilated Mexicans. Only one of the younger generation wants to go to Spain and understand his background and comprehend his father's suffering. This is the same novel as Las Barreras, listed in Quien es quien en las letras españolas; it was never published under that title.

Una mañana cualquiera. Lérida: Prisma, 1965.
This is a study of the complex relationships between a late adolescent who comes from Spain to Mexico to visit her exiled father and his ignorant lower-class Mexican wife. The father, a doctor, has made a life for himself in a small jungle town, but he experiences the bitterness, desolation, weariness, solitude and isolation of exile. He envies his daughter because she is the one with a future, while he is already worn out; and he is as exiled from his daughter as he is from Spain. Having cut her ties with Spain, the daughter decides to follow her lover wherever his journalistic career takes him; she will be at home in the world. The novel won the Premio Urriza of the city of Lérida. Available University of Kansas library.

CLG

MILLAN ASTRAY, Pilar (1892-1949).
A novelist and dramatist, of conservative, upper-class family, with links to the military establishment, Millán Astray was imprisoned by leftists during the Spanish Civil War (1936-39). A certain popular success notwithstanding, she is significant largely because of being almost the only woman of her day writing theater under her own name in Spain. Her work seldom transcends the level of light entertainment, and is an embodiment of conventional values and conservative ideology.

Al rugir el león. Madrid: Sociedad de Autores Españoles, 1923, 48 pp. Madrid: Editorial Siglo XX, 1924, 35 pp.
Three-act play.

Adán y Eva. Madrid: Velasco, 1929, 72 pp.
Comedy in three acts by Guy Polton and George Middleton, adapted by Pilar Millán Astray.

Los amores de la Nati. Madrid: Sociedad de Autores Espanoles, 1931, 76 pp. Also published by Rivadeneyra, Madrid: 1931.
Sainete in three acts.

La casa de la bruja. Madrid: Sociedad de Autores Españoles, 1932, 76 pp.
Comedia popular melodramática en three actos.

Cautivas; 32 meses en las prisiones rojas. Madrid: Saturnino
Calleja, 1940, 243 pp.
   Memoirs.

La condesa Maribel. Madrid: E. de Miguel, 1942, 64 pp.
   Comedy.

Las dos estrellas. Madrid: Prensa Moderna, 1928, 45 pp.
   Novel; illustrations by Loygorri.

La Galana. Madrid: Prensa Moderna, 1926, 64 pp.
   Three-act comedy.

Las ilusiones de la Patro. Madrid: Sucesores de R. Velasco, 1925,
65 pp.
   Sainete in three acts.

El juramento de la primorosa. Madrid: Velasco, 1924, 68 pp.
2nd ed., "con un juicio de J. Benavente y unos versos de Eduardo
Marquina," 1925, 77 pp.

La llave de oro. Madrid: Imprenta Pueyo, 1921. With a portrait of
the author by José Clará.
   Novel.

Mademoiselle Naná. Madrid: Velasco, 1928, 79 pp. Also printed by
Rivadeneyra, Madrid, 1928.
   Sainete in three acts.

Magda la Tirana. Madrid: Velasco, 1926, 64 pp.
   Drama in three acts, in prose, with musical illustrations by el
maestro Serrano.

La mercería de la Dalia roja. Madrid: Sociedad de Autores
Españoles, 1932, 78 pp.
   Three-act comedy.

El millonario y la bailarina. Madrid: Sociedad de Autores
Españoles, 1931, 76 pp.
   Three-act play.

El ogro. Madrid: Galatea, 1921, 77 pp. Drawings by Martínez
León.
   Children's literature.

Pancho Robles. Madrid: Sociedad de Autores Españoles, 1926. Also
published by Velasco, Madrid: 1926, 64 pp.
   Three-act comedy.

El paso de las hortensias. Madrid: Gráfica Madrid, 1924, 74 pp.
   Three-act comedy.

Ruth la Israelita. Madrid: Velasco, 1923, 48 pp.
   Three-act comedy.

Teatro. Madrid: 1923-1942.
Volume of seven plays previously issued by various publishers.
Contains: Al rugir el león, El juramento de la primorosa, Pancho
Robles, La Galana, Mademoiselle Naná, La tonta del bote, La condesa
Maribel.

La tonta del bote. Madrid: Velasco, 1925, 70 pp. Also published by
Cisne, Barcelona, 1936.
Three-act comedy (sainete).

JP

*MINGUEZ, Nùria.

Una casa a les tres torres. Barcelona: Club, 1974.
Novel. Winner of the Premi Palma.

El crim d'una nit d'estiu. Barcelona: Hogar del libro, 1981.
Novel.

KM

MIRALLES, Josep. See: DOMENECH I ESCATE DE CANELLAS, Maria.

MOIX, Ana María (1947-).
Ana María Moix belongs to a generation of writers who are a product
of the Spain of the 1960's and the continual "Coca-Colization" of
Spanish society. Born into a conservative upper-class family in the
cosmopolitan city of Barcelona, she initially formed part of a group of
young poets who rejected realism and the world of logic and sought to
incorporate popular myths, commonplaces of language and the mass media
into their writings. Her works are particularly notable for their
poetic fusion of the real and the surreal and their biting parodies of
traditional Spanish values and sex-role stereotyping.

Baladas del dulce Jim, Colección El Bardo. Barcelona: Saturno,
1969, 64 pp.
Baladas del dulce Jim is a book of poetry, written primarily in
prose form, which utilizes popular films and songs as a backdrop for
the author's thematic presentation of betrayed lovers, assassins and
tragic stories of romance. In this work, Moix's images flow freely
as she moves comfortably and unceasingly between her renditions of
love and death. She creates a solitary world of shadows and sadness
in which the sentimental and the political are symbolically and
originally united in the embrace of Gustavo Adolfo Bécquer and Che
Guevara, which closes one of the sections of the work.

Ese chico pelirrojo a quien veo cada día, Palabra Seis. Barcelona:
Lumen, 1971, 155 pp.
This collection of short stories presents a fascinating amalgam of
the real and the surreal as Ana María Moix adopts a Kafkian pose and
transforms ordinary reality into bizarre phenomena. Vampires who are
humanized, children who become animals, babies transformed into
birds, men and women fused into one another, young girls obsessed
with cats--are some of the scenarios created by the author to
critique certain aspects of contemporary society and reveal the
hidden desire of human beings to transcend the limits of reason.

Julia, Nueva Narrativa Hispánica. Editorial Seix Barral, 1st ed.
1970; 2nd ed., 1972; 220 pp.
    Ana María Moix's first novel explores the inner conflicts
experienced by a young woman who relives, during one night of
insomnia, the main events which have shaped her life during the past
15 years. The author uses her character's interior monologue to
examine such themes as the quest for personal freedom in the
upper-class Barcelona milieu of the 1960's; the perpetuation of
traditional values and institutions in a society in rapid transition;
student rebellions. This novel is of primary importance for its
profound penetration of the female psyche and its subtle rendition of
the theme of lesbianism.

No time for flowers y otras historias, Palabra Menor. Barcelona:
Lumen, 1971/782, 62 pp.
    In this work, a hybrid of poetry and prose, Moix continues to
explore the same themes present in Baladas del dulce Jim. Through a
series of interior monologues, composed of often disconnected
thoughts, she creates a compelling, yet somewhat confusing portrait
of a young woman destined to die because of a lost love and nihil-
istic sense of life. Popular songs, quotes from Lorca and echoes of
Tennesee Williams' world form the backdrop of this text, which combines the hermetically personal with references easily identifiable
to the reader.

Walter ¿por qué te fuiste?, Hispanic Nova. Barcelona: Barral,
1973, ISBN 84-211-0255-9, 259 pp.
    In this novel, Ana María Moix uses a complex literary form to
continue her satire of the traditional bourgeois society of the
Barcelona of the 1960's and to present an audacious rendition of
human sexuality. Through the use of several narrative voices,
presented in the first, second and third persons, Moix delves into
the psyche of three main characters and develops their individual
tales of struggle with the existing order. Leftist politics, male
and female homosexuality, bisexuality and sodomy are some of the
themes treated both seriously and comically by the author in this
iconoclastic work.

                                                                LGL

*MONSERDA DE MACIA, Dolors (1845-1919).
    Born in Barcelona, Monserdà grew up surrounded by the books and
conversation of her bookbinder father and her well-read mother. She
first published poetry and articles on social issues in Castilian,
writing within the tradition of Catholic liberalism. In 1877 she began
to write poetry in Catalan, later contributing short novels, plays and
novels to the Renaixença literary movement. She continued to publish on
social issues affecting the working class, especially working women.
Monserdà is a major figure in early Catalan feminism. As a writer, she
helped move fiction by women into a realistic vein through the depiction
of contemporary social conditions.

Amor mana; comèdia en tres actes. In La Quiteria, 3rd ed.
Barcelona: Políglota, 1930, pp. 223-73.
    Published posthumously, Monserdà's third play and her only one in
prose was written in 1913, 37 years after her second play was staged.
It appears that Macià's opposition to her career as a dramatist

interrupted her writing of plays. Amor mana is closely related in
theme to her first novel, La Montserrat, treating the role of the
woman within and outside marriage, and contains some of the same
characters as the novel.

Buscant una ánima; novela de costums barcelonines. Barcelona:
Polìglota, 1919, 256 pp. 2nd ed., 1920. 3rd ed., 1929, 262 pp.
    Monserdà's last novel was published posthumously in the year of
her death.

Del Món. 2 vols. Biblioteca Popular de "L'Avenç," Nos. 88-89.
Barcelona: "L'Avenç," 1908, 228 pp. 2nd ed., Barcelona:
Polìglota, 1930, 238 pp. 3rd ed., Introducció i selecció de
Isabel Segura, Col.lecció Clàssiques Catalanes, No. 1, Barcelona:
laSal, edicions de les dones, 1983, 135 pp., ISBN 84-85627-20-2.
    These two slim volumes contain 12 short stories, most of which
focus on the figure of a woman, with half narrated in the first
person by a female narrator. The themes of isolation, marriage,
hollowness of contemporary values, and poetry versus reality affect
women ranging from a young servant girl to an elderly middle-class
widow. The 1983 edition with an introduction and bibliography by
Isabel Segura contains a selection of seven of the stories.

La fabricanta; novela de costums barcelonines (1860-1875). Illus.
Enrich Monserdà. Barcelona: Biblioteca de Francesch Puig, 1904,
250 pp. 2nd ed., Barcelona: Francesc Puig, 1908, 250 pp. 3rd ed.,
1935. 4th ed., Pròleg de Roser Matheu, Biblioteca Selecta, No. 461,
Barcelona: Selecta, 1972, 209 pp.
    Dedicated to the author's two daughters, the novel opens with a
citation from Fernán Caballero and a brief prologue. Set in the
Barcelona of the home workshop, the novel depicts the growth of the
small factory and the margination of women within the family unit,
while painting social customs in some detail. Daughter of a weaver,
the protagonist overcomes the handicap of marriage to a poor worker
by setting up and running her own loom, a feat she later duplicates
to rescue her husband's shop. A self-made woman who works in
isolation with self-abnegation, she represents the true values of the
culture. This is considered Monserdà's most powerful and best
realized novel.

La família Asparó; novela de costums del nostre temps. Barcelona:
La Renaixensa, 1900, 260 pp. 2nd ed., Barcelona: La Renaixensa,
1900, 256 pp. 3rd ed., Mataró: Imprenta Minerva, 1929, 287 pp.
    Monserdà's second novel was sufficiently popular to see two
editions in one year. Set in contemporary Barcelona and depicting
well-known figures, the roman à clef treats the egoistic materialism
of the elegant but amoral bourgeoisie. One entire chapter constitutes the male protagonist's inner monologue, in a technique which
relates to Monserdà's earlier interest in the theater.

Ma corona. Barcelona: 1877.
    A collection of seven short poems dedicated to Monserdà's
youngest daughter who died the same year, this volume is the first
published by the author in Catalan. The themes are sentimental and
religious. The collection received a prize in Certamen de Sants in
1878.

María Gloria, novel.la de costums barcelonines. Barcelona:
Llibrería Parera, 1917, 225 pp. 2nd ed., Barcelona: Políglota,
1928.
    Dedicated to Monserdà's granddaughter, this novel traces the
protagonist from her romantic dreaming as the pampered granddaughter
of a bourgeois but penniless family to her confrontation with
working-class reality as an orphan taken in by her old wet nurse.
Her marriage to a self-made member of the new middle class resolves
her need to support herself. The conditions under which working-
class women maintain themselves by sewing are treated in detail.

La Montserrat, novela de costums del nostre temps. Barcelona: La
Renaixensa, 1893, 302 pp.
Trans. Maria de M. V. de B. Biblioteca del Hogar, 2nd series,
Barcelona: Librería Católica, 1912, 225 pp.
    Monserdà's first novel breaks with her previous pattern of
publishing fiction in Castilian. The protagonist is the victim of
her future father-in-law's desire for wealth which leaves her a
spinster. The novel demonstrates the potential for living a useful
and happy life as a spinster. Narcís Oller wrote a letter praising
the novel, despite its split focus.

Poesies. Barcelona: Ilustració Catalana, 1911, 234 pp., 2 ff.
2nd ed., Barcelona: Antonio López, 1912, 234 pp.
    This second collection of Monserdà's poetry repeats some poems
from the 1888 collection but does not assemble all the poetry
published in the interim. Monserdà received many prizes for her
poetry in the Jocs Florals throughout Catalonia. Translations of the
volume have appeared in Spanish, German, French and Hungarian.

Poesies catalanes. Barcelona: La Renaixensa, 1888, 248 pp.
    The first collection of Monserdà's Catalan poetry, this volume
contains maternal, patriotic, intimate, historical, folkloric and
religious poems.

La Quiteria. Barcelona: Ilustració Catalana, 1906, 215 pp.
2nd ed., 2 vols., La Novela d'Ara, 13, Nos. 9-10, Barcelona: L'Avenç
Gràfic, 1925, 63 pp. and 64 pp. 3rd ed., La Quiteria. Amor mana,
Barcelona: Políglota, 1928, 273 pp.
    A foundling raised in rural Catalonia without love or education,
Quiteria learns self-worth and affection from a woman who visits the
village and takes Quiteria to Barcelona as her maid. The novel
opposes the life of a servant girl in Barcelona to marriage to a
villager. Although Quiteria initially longs for freedom and the
city, she chooses love and marriage. The role of the middle class
and the local priest in educating and counseling the worker is
fundamental.

Sembrad y cojereis, comedia en tres actos y en verso.
Administración Lírico-Dramática. Barcelona: Jaime Jepús, 1874,
64 pp.
    The play was performed in 1874 in Barcelona at the Teatre Romea.
It is written in verse.

Teresa o un jorn de prova; comèdia dramàtica en dos actes.
   Monserdà's second play, also in verse, was performed at the
Teatre Romea on February 24, 1876. Dedicated to Monserdà's mother,
the play treats the theme of maternal heroism.

                                                                MB

MONTERO, Rosa (1951-).
   Born in Madrid, Rosa Montero worked briefly in independent theater
before studying journalism and psychology. Since 1971 she has worked
with the media, especially the newspaper El País, where she was editor
of the Sunday literary supplement from 1980-1981. She won the Premio
Mundo for journalism in 1978 and the Premio Nacional de Periodismo in
1981. She is especially well known for her interviews, two collections
of which she has published: España para ti para siempre (1976) and
Cinco años de País (1982). A dedicated feminist, Montero deals with
women's issues both in her newspaper articles and her three novels.

   Cinco años de Pais. Madrid: Debate, 1982.
      Collection of interviews.

   Crónica del desamor. Madrid: Debate, 1979, ISBN 84-7444-023-8,
   276 pp.
      This first person narration is Montero's first novel. In it many
   feminist issues are presented, including contraception, abortion,
   fair pay and treatment in the workplace, and the single woman as
   parent. It also explores relationships between women friends, men
   and women, male homosexuals, and parents and a feminist daughter. It
   is important as a description of the Spanish society from a feminist
   perspective. Available in paperback.

   España para ti ... para siempre. Madrid: A. Q. Ediciones, 1976.
      Collection of interviews.

   La función Delta. Madrid: Debate, 1981, ISBN 84-7444-037-8,
   369 pp.
      Themes in this novel include death and dying and the relationships
   beween men and women. The technique used is a double diary. One is
   by a dying woman in her 60's, detailing her reactions to old age,
   death and dying, and her relationships with her one faithful friend.
   The dying woman also writes the other diary which examines in retrospect the crucial week of the premiere of her first movie as a
   director when she was 30 years old. In this second diary she also
   explores her relationship with several men, including two lovers.
   She also describes her fear of success and of failure as a professional person. The work is significant for its feminist themes and
   the self-conscious interrelationship between the two diaries as a
   literary technique. Available in paperback.

   Te trataré como a una reina, Biblioteca Breve 622. Barcelona: Seix
   Barral, 1983, ISBN 84-322-0441-2, 245 pp.

      Montero's third novel is a portrait of the seamier side of Spanish
   society: the low-rent apartments, rundown clubs, and the Barrio
   Chino specializing in drugs and prostitution. Several representative
   individuals are shown in their desperate loneliness and longing to
   escape their spiritual and/or economic poverty. That escape is

embodied in the neon palm trees and boats of the "Tropicana" bar
sign. Like the sign, the wished-for paradise also proves to be
false. A well-written, very pessimistic portrait. Available in
paperback.

EDM

*MONTORIOL I PUIG, Carme (1893-1966).
Born in Barcelona, she dedicated her early years to music. Her
contact with letters began when she translated Shakespeare, Pirandello
and Baring into Catalan. She wrote poetry, novels and theatre, the
latter being her most successful effort. Her literary career began
late; her first play was published when she was 37, a period which
coincided with the liberties of the Second Republic. She participated
in women's associations and was president of the Lyceum Club. She never
wrote again after the Civil War. Her silence was a result of the
political situation created by the Franco dictatorship which prohibited
Catalan and confined women to their homes.

L'abisme. Barcelona: Llibreria Millà, col. Catalunya Teatral, no.
43, 1933, 44 pp.
L'abisme; L'huracà. Barcelona: LaSal, edicions de les dones,
col.lecció Clàssiques Catalanes, no. 2, 1983, 119 pp.
Her first play, this work is in three acts and was premiered
January 20, 1930 at the Teatre Novetats in Barcelona. It deals with
mother-daughter relationships, showing the complexity of the
affection between daughter and mother ranging from love to hate. The
press reacted strongly to this play; there was a division of opinion
among critics. Some were scandalized by the demythification of
motherhood implicit in the work.

Avarícia. Barcelona: Llibreria Millà, col. Catalunya Teatral,
no. 96, 1936, 48 pp.
This play was presented at the Teatre Novetats in Barcelona on
February 26, 1936. In it the author analyzes the capital vice of
avarice, the crazed passion for money. It is the only occasion in
which this author deals with the theme of father-children relationships. It is the least successful of her works.

Diumenge de Juliol. Barcelona: Edicions de la Rosa dels Vents,
1936, 124 pp.
A collection of stories written between 1921 and 1936, "Diumenge
de Juliol" is the title of one story. The book has no thematic
unity. The ten stories are dated at different locations in
Catalonia; it is likely that her summer voyages around the Catalan
provinces and to London inspired her to write these stories. The
work went unnoticed because it was published three months after the
outbreak of the Civil War.

L'huracà. Barcelona: Llibreria Millà, col. Catalunya Teatral,
no. 70, 1935, 42 pp.
L'abisme; l'huracà. Barcelona: laSal, edicions de les dones, col.
Clàssiques Catalanes, no. 2, 1983, 119 pp., pròleg d'Albina
Fransitorra.
This play premiered January 25, 1935, during the season of the
Oficial de Teatre Català, at the Poliorama Theatre in Barcelona.

It deals with the theme of incest between a mother and her son and
unveils the most hidden and publicly censured aspects of mother-son
relationships. The conservative sector bitterly attacked the author
for having dealt publicly with the theme of incest. The work should
be republished.

Teresa o la vida amorosa d'una dona. Barcelona: Llibreria
Catalònia, 1932, 245 pp.
   This author's most important novel addresses the problem of the
married woman who separates from her husband and begins a new life,
with work playing the role as liberator of women since it means
economic independence. Maria-Antònia Oliver wrote an excellent
article on this work, which appeared in Avui March 25, 1979.
For its merit and easy readability, the work should be republished.

ISS

*MONTSENY, Federica (1905-).
   Very active in the Republic, she also wrote several books on
political subjects and collaborated in periodicals, both in Castilian
and in Catalan. She wrote a novel entitled Cent dies de la vida d'una
dona.

KM

MORA, Constancia de la (1906-).
   Granddaughter of statesman Antonio Maura, de la Mora grew up among
the Spanish gentry. After her first marriage failed, she scandalized
Spanish society by leaving her husband and breaking family ties. From
the beginning of the Second Spanish Republic, she sympathized with the
Left. Both she and her second husband, the Republican military officer,
Ignacio Hidalgo de Cisneros, were anti-Franco activists during the Civil
War. de la Mora worked with foreign journalists reporting on the war
until victory was certain, at which time she fled from Spain.

Doble esplendor. Autobiografía de una aristócrata española,
republicana y comunista, 1938? Recent edition: Barcelona: Critica,
1977, ISBN 84-7423-028-4, 467 pp.
American edition: In Place of Splendor. The Autobiography of a
Spanish Woman. New York: Harcourt, Brace, 1939, 433 pp.
Mexican edition: Doble esplendor. Mexico: Atlante, 1944.
   In Place of Splendor is an autobiographical text of both literary
and socio-historical value. As an historical text, it supplies an
abundance of information about early twentieth century Spain and the
Spanish Civil War from the viewpoint of a woman. Themes include
primary education of women, motherhood, Church repression of young
women, marriage, divorce, feminism, women and politics, women and
law. It includes a glossary of names. The English edition is out of
print. A Spanish paperback edition is widely available in Spain. Of
interest to historians, Women's Studies students and to the general
public interested in Spain.

SMG

*MORLIUS, Remei (1854-?).
   Poet, born in Barcelona. She published a book of verse called
Poesies, with no date.

KM

MORO, Eduarda.
Born in Toledo, Moro has written articles, poetry and criticism for various Spanish and foreign periodicals.

Contorno mío. Madrid: Agora, 1960, 39 pp.
In this collection of 24 poems, several of them sonnets, traditional in style and form, the tone generally is one of nostalgia and melancholy; and there is a feeling of emptiness. "Un tranvía que no se llama 'Deseo'" laments Mays and Aprils left behind and emphasizes words which denote loneliness, immobility and death. "Hoy te llamabas" is an ode to Toledo which evokes the pleasures as well as the sadness and quiet of the city. Available from the University of Toledo, Ohio library, the book contains a drawing of Moro by Ricardo Zamorano.

Este sol que me habla. Madrid: Ed. Aleto, 1958, 41 pp.

El tiempo me lee en voz alta. Colección Alrededor de la Mesa, 1960.
Poetry.

CLG

MULDER DE DAUMER, Elisabeth (1904-).
Born in Barcelona, her mother was South American and her father came from Holland. Her cosmopolitan and refined education, her travels and sophistication set her apart from most other Spanish writers who remained in Spain after the Civil War. Her novels tend to be exotic and introspective, centered on upper-class characters. Her technique is traditional, enlivened by excellent studies of the emotions.

Alba Grey. Barcelona: José Janés, 1947, 182 pp.
2nd ed., Madrid: Aguilar, 1950.
This escapist novel begins its narration in the mansion of a dying marquis, and ends in a convenient marriage after touring Egypt. There are some references to social inequality in Italy, but in general, a mannered style and a contrived story line predominate. Included by Entrambasaguas in vol. XI of his Mejores novelas contemporáneas.

La canción cristalina. Barcelona: Cervantes, 1928, 96 pp.
Fifty-two lirical poems dealing mostly with music and water. Of interest only to Mulder scholars.

Crepúsculo de una ninfa. Barcelona: Surco, 1942.
This lyrical novel is about a woman in love with a man who is incurably sick.

Los cuentos del viejo reloj. Barcelona: Juventud, 1941.
2nd ed., 1959, 127 pp. Illustrations by J. Junceda.
Short stories for children.

Una china en la casa y otras historias. Barcelona: Sucre, 1941, 122 pp. Illustrations by Solá Andreu.

Día negro. Serie Novelistas de Hoy, Obras Inéditas, No. 21.
Madrid: Rollan, 1953, 78 pp.
This is a short novel about a handsome, middle-aged, rich man with

blue eyes. His wife has been bedridden for many years. The narrator
follows him during a day of temptations and pessimism, of memories of
past lovers, and shows his final return home to his now dead wife.
The novel is a good psychological study plus an excellent portrait of
the clients of coffee houses, in pp. 25-29. Of interest to scholars
studying this period of Spanish literature.

Embrujamiento. Barcelona: Cervantes, 1927, 176 pp.
    Poems.

Eran cuatro. La Novela del sábado, año 2, No. 73. Madrid:
Tecnos, 1954, 64 pp.
    After the war a mother visits important people and places in the
lives of her four dead sons. The four sons, an aviator and a soldier
on the Nationalist side, a spy for the Nationalists, and an anarchist
on the Republican side, die just before the war is over. The
mother's attempts at conciliation fail, and she becomes mad and dies.
This novel forms part of a movement in the early 1950's, represented
by Gironella, to reexamine the Civil War from a less partisan point
of view.

Este mundo. Colección Sirena. Barcelona: Artigas, s/f 1945?,
315 pp.
    Six short stories: "Al sol," "Ruptura," "La pesca del salmón,"
"Paulina y el capitán," "El magnífico rústico," and "La gloria de
la Lebrija." The first two are interesting studies of the psychology
of love and estrangement.

Flora. La Novela del sábado, año 1, No. 27. Madrid: Tecnos,
1953, 62 pp.
    This novel, centered on the dreams spurred by the possible sale of
a house, with a Countess and a scorching end, does show some of the
economic anguish of post-Civil War Spain and the land speculation
that helped establish new fortunes. A hybrid novel, the exploration
of covetousness and sexual passion barely raises it beyond pure
scintillating entertainment.

La historia de Java. Barcelona: Juventud, 1935, 59 pp.
2nd ed., Barcelona: Juventud, 1943, 70 pp. 3rd ed., Madrid:
Arion, 1961, 64 pp. Illustrations by J. Narro. 3rd ed. has
illustrations by Antonia Dans.
    A story for children about the life of a wild cat.

Las hogueras de otoño. Barcelona: Juventud, 1945.
    This novel about a crisis in the love of a mature upper-class
couple is of sociological value for the study of the period.

La hora emocionada. Barcelona: Cervantes, 1931.
    Poems.

El hombre que acabó en las islas. Barcelona: Apolo, 1944, 309 pp.
2nd ed., Barcelona: Plaza y Janés, 1966, 206 pp.
    The novel is divided into four parts. The first, and by far the
best, could be described as tremendista and has many details
surprisingly similar to Carmen Laforet's Nada. The second part takes
place in Stockholm, and derives into Romantic or even Gothic models.

The third and fourth part see the hero renounce fortune and civilization in order to find quesionable contentment in far-away islands.

Luna de las máscaras. Barcelona: AHR, 1958, 222 pp.
    The novel centers on the thoughts of the participants in a car
accident. It describes a love triangle, formed in part by a great
actress and a famous sculptor. It is one of Mulder de Daumer's best
work, and a contrast to similar studies of Mediterranean resorts done
by García Hortelano and Goytisolo, as well as to portraits of
artists done by Fernández Santos. Of interest to scholars
interested in the novels of the 1950's.

Las noches del gato verde. Coleccion Pez Luna. Salamanca: Anaya,
1963, 71 pp.
    A short story about a child who has many animals, hides a serpent
in the attic, and befriends a green cat. The text is accompanied by
illustrations by Asunción Balzola. Clear prose, and a good example
of children's literature.

Preludio a la muerte. Barcelona: Apolo, 1946, 162 pp.
    This novel tells the story of two women, one of them from the
United States, who become friends and rivals while studying in
Switzerland. The ending is unusual for novels of the period. Many
good insights into friendship and love make this Mulder de Daumer's
best novel.

Sinfonía en rojo. Barcelona: Cervantes, 1929(?), 177 pp.
    The book contains 74 poems, preceded by an introduction by María
Luz Morales, who calls Mulder de Daumer "musa atormentada y
crepitante. They are mainly derivative poems about loneliness and
passion.

Una sombra entre los dos. Barcelona: Edita, 1934, 230 pp.
    Her first novel, written to defend a thesis, has been considered
an important feminist statement.

El vendedor de vidas. Barcelona: Juventud, 1953, 192 pp.
    This novel tells the story of an astrologer who sees his own
death. The narration is well structured and the atmosphere of
post-Civil War Spain is described with somber and effective details.
                                                              RDP

MULET, María (1930-).
    Mulet was born in the province of Valencia and has served as Director
of the Escuela de Orientación Marítima in Cullera (Valencia). She is
a novelist and poet, writing some of her poetry in the Valencian
dialect.

Amor, la misma palabra. Valencia: Prometeo, 1969, 302 pp.
    In this novel several married couples represent restless young
Spaniards of the 1960's. The women have difficulties relating to
their husbands, but when they have affairs, the novel degenerates
into the tone of a novela rosa. Available Kent State University
library.

<u>Nada al cor</u>. Valencia: 1973, ISBN 84-400-6966-9.
   Poems.

CLG

MUÑOZ ORTIZ, Sofía (1938-).
   Born in Barcelona, she teaches business school and has published in
Spanish and Latin-American journals. Besides her published novel, she
has written a dozen unpublished plays and is working on a book of
stories, <u>Historias de mi abuelo</u>.

<u>La pendiente</u>. Barcelona: Rumbos, 1961.

UMS

*MUR, Mireia (1960-).
   Born in Molins de Rei (Baix Llobregat), Mur teaches Catalan and is
active in the theater. She is studying Catalan Philology at the
University of Barcelona.

   <u>A despit del rei</u>. Barcelona: Mall, 1982, ISBN 84-7456-121-3, 52 pp.
      Her first book of poetry, this collection is structured around
   Ovid's <u>Metamorphosis</u> as it progresses from a false theatrical world
   to the poet's search for reality and truth. Some of her images are
   quite striking, such as in the closing poem of the book: Roja la
   lluna / amb dents de llet que es claven./ La nit s'atura. (The moon
   is red with teeth of milk that bite. Night stops.)

KM

*MURIA I ROMANI, Anna (1904-).
   Born in Barcelona, she studied at the Institut de Cultura i
Biblioteca Popular de la Dona. Her first newspaper article appeared in
the magazine <u>La Dona Catalana</u> in 1927, and from that time on she was
involved in extensive collaboration in many publications of the time.
She was very active politically from 1930 to 1939, a militant in Acció
Catalana Republicana, Esquerra Republicana de Catalunya and Estat
Català, on whose central committee she was a member during the War. On
January 24, 1939, she left Barcelona for France, where she met Augstí
Bartra, whom she married in October of the same year. Their transat-
lantic exile began in 1940, first in the Dominican Republic, then Cuba
and finally in Mexico where they lived until 1970, when they returned to
Catalonia. Murià stands out as a novelist, but also as a writer of
children's books and for her studies of the poetry of her husband.

   <u>Aquest serà el principi</u>. Barcelona: in press, 1985, 500 pp.
      The work is divided into three historical periods: the
   proclamation of the Second Republic and the Civil War, exile and a
   return to Catalonia. The work, which is very complex, is the major
   opus of this author. In it she gathers all her vital experiences,
   dividing them among different characters. There is no one character
   who represents Anna Murià, but all of them form a part of her life.
   The complexity comes from the fact that there is no narrator to
   explain the story; rather the characters all speak for themselves.

Joana Mas. Barcelona: Llibreria Catalònia, 1933.
    In this story of a young woman who falls in love with and marries
a man much older than herself, and quite well off, the situation
represents her greatest life aspiration. But the author presents us
with another character who contrasts with the protagonist, a woman
who is single, and economically independent. She works and has a
very unstable sentimental life. Murià tries to show two clearly
different models of women's lives, but she doesn't succeed in
analyzing either of them in depth.

La Peixera. Barcelona: G.S.E.C., 1938, 243 pp.
    This is the story of a young man condemned to earn his living as a
clerk in a sad office, from which he can only see the sky through a
tiny opening, and quartered by iron bars. The tedium and boredom of
each day are exactly like the day before and the day that will
follow, until the protagonist decides to put an end to the situation.

Res no és veritat, Alícia. Barcelona: Antonio Picazo, 1984,
158 pp.
    The book ends with an excellent autobiography of the author. The
narration in the work is of a love, never confessed, between brother
and sister. The author presents the characters who will intervene in
the novel in each chapter, focussing on a female figure, the sister,
who, in the presence of another woman, sentimentally linked with her
brother, also falls in love with another man, in whom she tries to
find the virtue of her brother. Literary criticism in Barcelona
totally ignored this novel when it came out.

                                                              ISS

N

NADA, Sor.
   A nun of the seventeenth century who wrote under this pseudonym, her
identity has not been established but her manuscripts suggest that she
was from Andalucía due to the s/c alternation in her handwriting. MS
12959/26 also reveals that she wrote at the request of a Superior,
"Mandame v(uestra) P(aternida)d," and that she was new to the order,
"escrivi por entretenimiento siendo resien profesa en la relijion."
("I write for entertainment, having recently professed religion.")

   Esplicacion sobre en que consiste la paz del Alma. Quartillas a un
   Alma que padese soledad interior. Madrid: Biblioteca Nacional,
   MS 12959/28 (7 leaves in quarto) (Letra del siglo XVII).
      After defining such peace, the manuscript assumes the dialogue
   form under the subtitle "Divino enquentro de Dios y el Alma en la
   soledad." The Soul expresses her concerns and Jesus responds:
   constancy on the difficult road of suffering, belief in his example
   and fidelity to his Blessed Mother will bring peace to the soul.
   This is the most fervent of Sor Nada's manuscripts.

   Mandame v P$\underline{d}$ que le de clave en que consiste un verdadero Amor de
   Dios. Madrid: Biblioteca Nacional, MS 12959/26 (9 leaves in quarto)
   (Letra del siglo XVII).
      This is the only manuscript from the Biblioteca Nacional that
   bears the signature of Sor Nada. In the discourse on the title
   subject the author uses the dialogue form in which she, the Soul, and
   Jesus respond to one another. She desires to know how to win eternal
   love and Jesus replies, using the example of his own life and the
   image of the firmly rooted tree.

   Pintura del propio Amor. Madrid: Biblioteca Nacional, MS 12959/27
   (10 leaves in quarto) (Letra del siglo XVII).
      Sor Nada discourses on self-love, using the image of a face.
   Comparing that face to the devil himself, she goes on "painting" the
   evil and ugliness of each part of the physiognomy, eyes, nose, teeth,
   etc. She is not sure of declaring the full extent of the evil of
   self-esteem and explains that it is urgent to avoid it so that the
   soul does not fall to hell.

   Quartillas a un Alma que padese soledad interior. MS 12959/28.
      This text does not have a separate MS number because it is part of
   "Esplicacion sobre en que consiste la paz del Alma." The "Quartillas" are octosyllabic quatrains numbered by the author 1 to 13.

In these verses the soul is suspended in air, tormented by and
chained to the world. Likened to a cicada, she hopes to take flight
to be fulfilled by the Love of her divine Spouse.

GM

NARCISA.

According to Serrano y Sanz (q.v.), Narcisa is the pseudonym of a
poet from Granada. Also, by scanning the list of contributors in
Pellicer's Anfiteatro (see: Pellicer de Ossau y Tovar, José.
Anfiteatro de Felipe el Grande. 1631; rpt. Cieza: A. Pérez Gómez,
1974, ISBN 84-400-6910-3, 80 leaves), it might be concluded that she was
of Madrid society since she associated with the nobles and the most
prestigious literati in the court of Felipe IV, King of Spain,
1605-1665.

Epigrama LXIII, "Feroz aplauso, Vencedora Fiera ..." in Anfiteatro de
Felipe el Grande.
Narcisa's sonnet is part of this very rare book, now available in
reprint, originally published to commemorate a feat of bullfighting
performed by Felipe IV. In this volume are collected verses by great
and minor poets of the time. Narcisa's poem (fol. 44r) addresses the
bull that gave glory to the king.

GM

NARVION, Pilar (1927-).

Pilar Narvión was born in Alcañiz (Teruel). She holds a Degree of
Licenciate in Philosophy and Letters from the University of Madrid. She
has been granted several literary awards such as "Cuentos de La Felguera
y Juventud" and the award "Víctor de la Serna" for journalistic
excellence. She is Professor of Journalism at the University of Madrid.
She has been a press correspondent in France and in Italy.

Historia de un perro borracho. Barcelona: La Caracola, 1959, 189 pp.
This is a delightful fiction work. The plot is the relationship
and the adventures of a boy, Peladilla, and his dog, Flechote. What
stands underneath the plot is the life of a small Spanish rural town
as seen through the eyes of Peladilla. The narrative style is simple
enough for children yet elegant enough to please the educated adult
reader. The author dedicates it to adolescent boys and girls.
Touches of humor, philosophy and poetry are interspersed through the
story. The book is sparsely illustrated in full color. Out of
print. Available only through interlibrary loan.

MCJ

NAVIA Y BELLET, Francisca Irene de (1726-1786).

Born in Turin, daughter of don Alvaro de Navia y Osorio, Marqués de
Santa Cruz (soldier, diplomat, and author), and educated in Spain,
Francisca demonstrated unusual aptitud, especially for languages. She
married the Marqués de Grimaldo, a soldier and diplomat. Highly
regarded by contemporaries for her piety as well as intellectual gifts,
she composed verse in Spanish and Latin, made numerous translations of
Latin and French poetry, and perhaps wrote plays and other works, but
burned them all shortly before her death, in a spirit of modesty and
humility. Only a Latin poem composed at age 16 has survived.

Memorial literario, VIII (1786), 67 ff. (Includes a brief biography
of the author.) Reproduced in part by Diego Ignacio Parada, in
Escritoras y eruditas españolas (Madrid: M. Minuesa, 1881), pp.
147-50. "Italia sibi gratulator de adventu serenissimi Philippe
Borbonii, eumque ut properet invitat" ("Italy congratulates herself
on the arrival of His Most Serene Highness Philip of Bourbon, and
urges him to make haste").
    This poem, which survived because it had already been published in
the Memorias de Trevoux (March, 1742), is typical laudatory verse.
It celebrates in 52 dactylic hexameters the arrival of Prince Philip
(the future Felipe V) in Italy in 1702, and expresses the hope that
he will bring an end to internal strife. The Latin is academically
correct and conforms to the classical rules of syntax and prosody,
but, as is typical of "Jesuit" Latin, it is lifeless and without
inspiration. There are numerous misspellings and misprints in the
reproduction by Parada.

RL

NELKEN Y MAUSBERGER, Margarita (1896-1968).
    Nelken, an outstanding feminist writer, politician and art critic,
was born in Madrid, where she studied painting, music, sociology, and
literature. She served from 1931-1936 in the Cortes Constituyentes for
the Spanish Socialist Workers' Party. She was a member of the Communist
Party during the Civil War, but left the Party in exile. In Mexico she
was the highly-respected art critic for Excelsior. Besides two novels,
books on women, politics and art, she wrote for Las Españas, Cuadernos
Americanos and many other publications. Her sister was the actress
Magda Donato.

    Carlos Mérida. México: UNAM, 1961, Dirección de Publicaciones,
    Coleción de arte, 9.

    La aventura de Roma. La Novela de hoy: ano 2, núm. 40. Madrid:
    Sucesores de Rivadeneyra, 1923, 60 pp.

    Carlos Orozco Romero. Trans. Irene Nicholson. México: Mexicanas,
    1951, 21 pp.
    Carlos Orozco Romero. México: UNAM, 1959, 145 pp. (UNAM,
    Dirección de Publicaciones, Colección de arte, 7).

    La condición de la mujer en España. Barcelona: Minerva, 1922?,
    280 pp. Madrid: CVSA Ediciones, 1975, ISBN 8435400328, 237 pp.
        Nelken's book provides an early and significant analysis of
    feminism in Spain. She includes two lectures on feminism that she
    gave at the Ateneo Español December 21, 1918 and January 2, 1919.
    The appearance of the book caused a great scandal in Spain because of
    her frank manner in discussing all kinds of problems of women in
    Spanish society: working conditions at home and outside of the home,
    maternity, prostitution, powerlessness in legal matters. Available
    in paperback and of general interest.

    Las escritoras españolas. Barcelona-Buenos Aires: Labor, 1930,
    235 pp.

    Escultura mexicana contemporánea. México: Mexicanas, 1951, 39 pp.
    (Enciclopedia Mexicana de Arte, 11.)

El expresionismo en la plástica mexicana de hoy. México: INBA, Departamento de Artes Plásticas, 1964, 297 pp.

Historia del hombre que tuvo el mundo en la mano, Johann Wolfgang von Goethe. México: Secretaría de Educación Pública, 1943, 118 pp.

La Mujer, conversaciones e idearioby Santiago Ramón y Cajal. Ed. Margarita Nelken with a foreword written by her. Buenos Aires: GLEM, 1941, 167 pp. Buenos Aires: GLEM, 1944, 154 pp.

La mujer ante las cortes constituyentes. Biblioteca para el Pueblo IV, No. 10. Madrid: Castro, 1931?, 106 pp.

Un mundo etéreo: La pintura de Lucinda Urrusti. 1st ed., Sep Setentas, 275. México: Secretaría de Educación Pública, 1976, 158 pp.

Por qué hicimos la Revolución. 2nd ed., Barcelona: International Publishers, 1936?, 283 pp. 3rd ed., Barcelona: Europa-América, 1936?, 283 pp.
    Nelken dedicates this book to her comrades, Socialists, Communists and union workers who were victims of the repression of the Revolutionary Movement of October 1934. In the book she combines a history of Spanish workers before the 1930's with an eye witness account of the events in the 1930's. She tries, she points out in the preface, to let the facts speak for themselves rather than taking a "literary" approach to the events. In spite of new leadership in Spain, workers in the tradition of centuries continued to be the underdogs. Of interest to scholars.

Primer frente. Mexico: Angel Chapero, 1944, 77 pp.

La trampa del arenal. Novela. Madrid: Librería de los sucesores de Hernando, 1923, 253 pp.

Tres tipos de Virgen: Fray Angélico, Rafael, Alonso Cano. Madrid: Imp. de la Ciudad Lineal, 1929, 122 pp. México: Secretaría de educación pública, 1942, 69 pp.

EMD

OJEDA, Pino (1916-).
  Born in El Pakmar de Teror (Las Palmas), this writer is highly
gifted. She has written theater, narratives, novels and poetry. She
also is an accomplished painter. However, her published work in book
form is made up of only three titles. As a poet, Ojeda contributes to
contemporary Spanish poetry with a highly lyrical and passionate voice
that speaks, in a poignant way, of the human condition. Her sincerity
and her expressiveness make her poems powerful, particularly her last
book where she reaches her greatest poetic maturity so far.

  Como el fruto en el árbol. Madrid: Rialp, S.A., 1954, 82 pp.
    With this book that received the second Adonais poetry prize for
1953, Ojeda's verse acquires a depth and an expressiveness not
attained in her first book of poems. Her command of poetic
expression is now mature and very much her own, without other
influences. Her vision goes beyond personal biography and becomes
universal. Ojeda's poetic meditation reaches deep into the com-
plexities of existence. This is, no doubt, her best book of poems.

  Niebla de sueño. Madrid: Ediciones de la Revista Mensaje, 1947,
145 pp.
    In this first book of poems, Ojeda, very much influenced by Juan
Ramón Jiménez, speaks about love but not as a universal reflexion,
rather, as a personal experience that produces in the poetess a
varied range of feelings: sadness, nostalgia, joy, hope, pain. This
clearly autobiographical work shows, nonetheless, a highly lyrical
poet full of passion. The book contains a photograph of the poetess.

  La piedra sobre la colina. Las Palmas de Gran Canaria: Tagoro,
1964, 33 pp.
    Love is also the central theme of this second book of poems but
the treatment of it differs from the first. The biographical aspects
have been transcended. The poetess, talking as a narrator, rather
than in the first person, tells of the depth of love, of its infinite
force and of its power. Love makes the lovers as forceful and
resistant as the stone where they reclined talking about love. The
poetic language has now acquired uniqueness and perfection. This
book received the poetry prize "Tomás Morales" for 1956.
                                                              AMF

*OLEART DE BEL, Maria.

M'empasso pols quan beso la terra. Palma: Moll, 1983.
Poetry.

KM

*OLIVER, Maria-Antònia (1946-).
Born in Manacor, Majorca, Oliver delves with mastery into her magical
island heritage as a source for much of her fiction. In addition to
novels and short stories, she has written TV screenplays, literary
criticism, and travelogues. She has also translated a number of authors
from English to Catalan, notably Virginia Woolf, whose work has had an
important impact on Oliver's own imaginative writing. She is married to
writer Jaume Fuster.

Coordenades espai-temps per guardar-hi les ensaimades. Barcelona:
Pòrtic, "Cristalls," 1975, ISBN 84-7306-141-1, 55 pp. The story is
reprinted in Figues d'un altre paner.
Her only work with an autobiographical basis, this long short
story, as well as its enigmatic title, were inspired by a dream which
brought the author back to her childhood in Manacor. The dreamlike
quality of the prose is reinforced in this small volume by the
imaginative drawings of artist Josep Maur Serra.

Crineres de foc. Barcelona: Laia, 1985, ISBN 84-722-587-9, 296 pp.
Using a contrapuntal technique, interweaving two related stories
together, Oliver explores the need for self-identification in women
and in peoples. Estel grows up along with her town, el Claper, and
both struggle to hold on to their visions, dreams and identities.
Once again, Oliver defies the classifications of prose fiction in
this epic, science fiction, fantasy, psychological novel.

Cròniques de la molt anomenada ciutat de Montcarrà. Barcelona:
Edicions 62, "El Balancí," 1972, 203 pp.
A novel in the form of a family chronicle which predicts social
destruction, this work uses as a source and lyrical element the
popular sayings and songs of Majorca, in an island version of magic
realism. There is a linear progression in the fragmented narration,
showing us three generations of linked families as concentric
circles. Complete with adventures in America, incestuous relationships and the transformation of a tranquil though sometimes stifling
Majorca into a tourist haven, the novel ends with a vision of its
destruction by the mythical creatures from the "rondalles."

Cròniques d'un mig estiu. Barcelona: Club Editor, "El club dels
novel.listes," 1970, ISBN 84-7329-017-8, 269 pp. 2nd ed., 1983.
This is a coming-of-age novel of an adolescent boy with a background of the destruction of Majorca by the tourist invasion. The
protagonist is shifted abruptly from a sleepy, rural ambience and
innocence to a sophisticated and decadent tourist hotel and his
sexual awakening. The narration is from the point of view of the
boy, whose physical trauma parallels his own loss of innocence as
well as that of his homeland.

Estudi en lila. Barcelona: Magrana, 1985, ISBN 84-7410-189-1,
198 pp.

A detective story by genre, feminist in its point of view, this novel addresses the problem of rape and its aftermath. The author contrasts the reactions of two victims: a very young and vulnerable Majorcan and a fashionable fortyish antique seller. A female detective, Majorcan as well, weaves the two other women together as they try to cope with their respective feelings of shame, fear, guilt and helplessness on the one hand, and outrage and vengeance on the other.

Figues d'un altre paner. Palma de Mallorca: Moll, "Raixa," 1979, ISBN 84-273-0269-X, 206 pp. Prologue by the author.
   A collection of short stories written earlier, with an explanatory prologue by the author. "Muller qui cerca espill, les mans s'hi talla I" later evolved into a TV screenplay, while "M'han florit ametllers a les butxaques" and "Litografia de Montcarrà" are embryonic for later novels. "Muller qui cerca espill II" is an extremely lyrical story based on the unexplained disappearance of a neighbor of the writer's in-laws. In addition to the intrinsic worth of the stories, the time lag between them and the prologue makes this collection very useful for understanding the evolution of this writer. "Coordenades espai-temps per guardar-hi les ensaimades" was also published on its own.

Punt d'arròs. Barcelona: Galba, 1979, ISBN 84-7136-239-2, 119 pp.
   Oliver's most urban novel and also her most clearly feminist to date. Beginning with a quotation from Virginia Woolf, some of whose work she translated into Catalan, Oliver acknowledges her debt to the English writer. The story is of a woman who searches for her identity, realizing painfully that she must choose solitude in order to find it and thus earn her freedom. Using the image of a "padrina" knitting, Oliver addresses a myriad of issues of interest to feminists while capturing the monotony of the routines and repetitions of daily life, brought into a coherent whole through the point of view of the protagonist.

El vaixell d'iràs i no tornaràs. Barcelona: Laia, "Les Eines," 1976, ISBN 84-7222-614-X, 203 pp.
   Beginning with a rhyming fairy-tale motif, this novel moves back and forth from an elaborate and magical tale of adventures with giants, rose-colored robots and other mythical beings to dreamlike philosophical monologues which offer a counterpoint to events in the narration. Using the voyage-as-life metaphor in an original way, Oliver presents a microcosm of society in which a strong woman solves difficult problems, and a few like-minded people work together, while the majority act in conformity without questioning anything.

Vegetal i Muller qui cerca espill. Barcelona: La llar del llibre, "Nova terra," 1982, ISBN 84-7279-125-4, 115 pp. Prologue by author.
   Two TV screenplays. The prologue explains her transition from writing fiction, a solitary occupation, to writing for television, a necessarily collaborative work. "Vegetal" deals with the problem of older women in society and their feelings of uselessness, and "Muller qui cerca espill," which evolved in changed form from the first of two short stories by the same name, addresses the very limited choices open to women, with the stagnation and frustration which inevitably result from a lack of meaningful personal development.

KM

ONTIVEROS, María.

   Agua de Mar. Madrid: Gíaficas Nebrija, 1951, 162 pp. Prologue by
   José María Peman.
      Poetry.

                                                                        CLG

*ORRIOLS, Maria Dolors (1914-).
   Born in Vic, she has written novels and short stories.

   Calvacades. Barcelona: Aymà, 1949.
      Stories.

   Contradansa. Barcelona: Pòrtic, 1982.
      Novel.

   Cop de Porta. Barcelona: Pòrtic, 1980.
      Novel.

   Petjades sota l'aigua. Vic: Eumo, 1984.

   Reflexos. Juris, 1951.

   Retorn a la Vall. Juris, 1951.

                                                                         KM

ORTIZ SANCHEZ, Lourdes (1943-).
   Born in Madrid, she studied Liberal Arts, and currently teaches at
the School of Dramatic Art. She writes often for newspapers and
magazines on literature, sociology and art. A prolific and diversified
author, she is included in Ymelda Navajo's Doce relatos de mujeres
(Madrid: Alianza, 1982) as one of the new women writers who started to
publish after 1970. She has also translated books from French, and
edited and provided an introduction for a collection of Mariano José de
Larra's Artículos políticos.

   La caja de lo que pudo ser. Serie Unos Cuantos Cuentos. Ills. by
   Montse Ginesta. Madrid: Altea, 1981, ISBN 84-372-1535-8, 28 pp.
      A children's book with originality and imagination, its theme is
   peace in history. It tells the story of a child who can change
   historical events by pressing on a little box that was given to him
   by a strange being. The illustrations by Montse Ginesta are
   eye-catching. Like other contemporary novelists--Ana Maria Matute,
   Jesús Fernández Santos--Lourdes Ortiz has written for children.

   Comunicación crítica. Cuadernos de la Comunicación, 5. Madrid:
   Pablo del Río, 1977, ISBN 84-7430-009-6, 159 pp.
      Essays on literary criticism.

   Conocer Rimbaud y su obra. Colección Conocer, 28. Barcelona:
   Dopesa, 1979, ISBN 84-7235-427-x, 125 pp.
      Essays on Rimbaud.

   En días como éstos. Colección Sibyla. Madrid: Akal, 1981,
   ISBN 84-7339-529-8, 120 pp.
      In this, her latest novel, the author stays away from the

so-called "feminine" topics. The theme here is violence. The main
characters are three men: Carlos, Toni and Jorge, who are
terrorists, fugitives from the law. The predominant narrative
technique is the interior monologues of Toni, the protagonist.
Divided in three parts, the first deals with the men's flight; the
second centers around the peaceful life in Toni's family farm and the
third returns to the life of the terrorists. The action moves
swiftly in a dramatic and compact novel that captivates the reader's
attention. The title indicates the contemporaneity of its theme.

Luz de la memoria. Colección Manifiesto. Madrid: Akal, 1976,
ISBN 84-7339-154-3, 214 pp.
     The title is based on a quote from Cernuda: "Tú, rosa del
silencio, tú, luz de la memoria." It has a strong, masculine tone;
there is nothing in the novel to indicate that its author is a woman.
The vocabulary, for example, has profanity and some vulgar terms.
The style is experimental. Narrated in second person, it can be difficult to follow at times. It has the characteristics of a structural novel according to Gonzalo Sobejano's definition. It pertains
to the generation of the 1970's and its youth. They cannot rid
themselves of their bourgeois morals despite their experimentations
with sex and drugs. The protagonist, Enrique García Alonso, is in a
psychiatric hospital after a crisis (Enrique has lost his voice,
which is ironic since he never had a say anyway). The rest of the
novel consists of a futile attempt to assimilate him into society.

Las murallas de Jericó. Poesía Hiperión, 23. Madrid: Peralta,
1980, ISBN 84-8527-54-4, 91 pp.
     A farce in three acts and a prologue, the book is billed on the
cover as a "scenic poem." There are symbolic characters in the
prologue: Razonable y Nadie, but the protagonists are Andrés y
María, who appear in the first act. There are some historical
characters as well: Rimbaud, Celine, Malraux, Trotski and Stalin,
who join in the second act. The play has an intellectual tone due to
its existential theme, the reference to the Bible, evident in the
title, and the presence of literary and political figures.

Picadura mortal. Club del Crimen. Madrid: Sedmay, 1979,
ISBN 84-7380-393-0, 190 pp.
     A good example of a detective story, or, as it is labeled on its
jacket "novela negra." A female detective, Barbara Arenas, is called
to investigate the disappearance of a businessman in the Canary
Islands. In a very subjective manner, the detective herself tells
the story of her case. And her personality comes through: A
liberated woman, who uses her gun, has casual encounters and is
intelligent. It presents a picture of life of the very rich and
their shady deals in drugs and crime. The use of suspense is
effective; all the characters are suspects until the end.

Urraca. Metropoli de novela. Barcelona: Puntual, 1982,
ISBN 84-86057-01-9, 206 pp.
     In this historical novel based on Queen Urraca (1109-1126) of
Castilla and León, the mother of Alfonso VII, the structure is a
dialogue--which turns into monologue at times--that the imprisoned
queen has with the monk who brings her food. Against the backdrop of
the historical facts, stands out the personality of the queen, her

strength and ambition. The archaic language helps to recreate the
medieval time period. The novel was finished with a grant from the
Fundación Juan March.

CA

OSORIO DELGADO, Amalia (1918-).
   Born in Bande, Orense, she is a teacher with a degree in public
relations. She has received prizes for poetry, short stories and
journalism in Spain and Italy and has also written film scripts and
three unpublished plays.

   El loco de los grillos. Madrid: Kaliope, 1952.
      Novel.

UMS

P

PALENCIA, Isabel de (1872 or 1878 or 1881-196?) (<u>Who's Who in America 1978</u> does not list a date of death).
Palencia was born into the prominent Oyarzábal family of Málaga, and her mother was a Scottish Protestant. She received a convent education in French and English and spent time in Great Britain. She was the founder and principal writer of the women's journal, <u>La Dama</u>, the first of its kind in Spain; a translator of contemporary English and American literature; correspondent for Laffan News Bureau, <u>Standard</u> and <u>Daily Herald</u> of London; and a daily columnist for <u>El Sol</u>. Active in the theater, she married Ceferino Palencia, writer, artist and son of a playwright. As the Republic's expert on women, children, education and slavery, she became Spain's envoy to the League of Nations. In 1936 she was appointed Ambassador of the Spanish Republic in Sweden, and she explained the Popular Front position in Canada, the United States and in the British House of Commons. In 1939 she went into exile in Mexico. Palencia also published memoirs, historical essays, children's literature and a book on Spanish regional costume.

El sembrador sembró su semilla. Madrid: 1928.
This fictional treatment of heredity and reproduction is the author's first novel. Palencia had first become interested in questions of sexuality and reproductive theory, a controversial theme widely discussed at the time, when she translated Havelock Ellis into Spanish several years before. The novel follows the models of nineteenth century Realism, especially of Pérez Galdós, and of Unamuno's philosophical and psychological character studies, joining both in their aim to awaken the consciousness of the Spanish people.

Diálogos con el dolor. Ensayos dramáticos y un cuento. México: Leyenda, 1945.
These lyrical introspective one-act plays are written in intensely psychological quasi-monologues, in which the central character, most often a woman, struggles to come to terms with loss and affliction (e.g. blindness, death, solitude), in accordance with the author's belief, rooted in a life full of struggle and grief, that suffering is a crucial aspect of being human. Although published first during her exile, some of the dramatic sketches were originally performed in Madrid during the early 1930's in a lay theater directed by Pío Baroja and were destined to be taken to culturally remote areas after a hoped-for Republican loyalist victory.

En mi hambre mando yo. México: Libro Mex, 1959.
    The autobiographically inspired novel of an upper-bourgeois
Madrid-Málaga family follows the fate of its members as they become
involved in and divided by political struggles between loyalist
Republicans and Falangist rebels in the 1930's. The development of
the central character, Diana, from an apolitical nubile debutante
into the committed wife of a young Republican permits the author to
capture with physical and psychological immediacy a crucial phase of
twentieth century Spanish history.

                                                                    UMS

*PALER, Enriqueta (1842-1927).
    Poet, born in Figueres.

Poesies. Lectura Popular no. 258.

                                                                     KM

*PALMA, Felip. See: VENTOS I CULLELL, PALMIRA.

PALOU, Inés (1923-1975).
    Inés Palou's death by suicide brought to an end a troubled life and
an all-too-brief literary career. Palou broke the law and served a
prison sentence. Her two novels are, to some extent, autobiographical.
The first deals with conditions in a women's prison, the second with a
group of bank robbers. Her characters live in a "No Exit" kind of hell.
They are not totally responsible for their crimes, but they must pay for
their anti-social acts. The novelist's strengths lie in her ability to
explore character within a novelistic structure which enhances theme.

Carne apaleada. Barcelona: Planeta, 1975, ISBN 84-320-5330-9,
332 pp. Subsequent edition, Colección popular Planeta No. 73, 1978.
    The despair and degradation of a women's prison is the theme of
this first novel by a writer whose own life included a prison
sentence. The somewhat autobiographical nature of the novel affects
the distance which exists between the narrator/author and her
characters. The prisoners are seen as victims of a society which has
impeded their natural social development and made of them anti-social
creatures whose actions must be punished. The female prisoners are
seen in contrast to representatives of the social order. The novel
makes a plea for social reform which would aid individual development
and obviate the need for retribution.

Operación dulce. Barcelona: Planeta, 1975, ISBN 84-320-5343-0,
233 pp. 2nd and 3rd eds., 1975.
    Five people plan and execute a daring robbery. The novel focuses
on the relationships among the five, on the reasons they lead a life
of crime and on what happens to each after they successfully rob an
armored car. Although the narrator alludes to factors which may
cause good people to engage in criminal acts, she is equally fervent
in her belief that every criminal must pay for her/his crime. Only
one of the group is apprehended by the authorities, but none truly
escapes. There is no clear conclusion to the novel, a fact which
heightens the reader's certainty that the fear, remorse and anger
which individual characters feel will never end.

                                                                    KHC

**PALLARES, Pilar (1957-).
Born in Culleredo, La Coruña, she is a secondary school professor of Galician literature. Her works can be situated in the most recent generation of Galician poetry in which references are no longer of a social nature as in preceding generations. This new direction begins with Con pólvora e magnolias by Méndez Ferrín, a major figure of Galician literature. Her formative context is constituted by readings of Portuguese poetry in particular, plus French and other foreign poets (Hölderlin, Neruda). The author now has clear the intention of writing feminist poetry, although initially it was not a conscious goal. Historically her work appears in post-Francoist process, when Galician culture and national awareness reappear with force. She was awarded the "Poesía Nova o Facho" and "Esquío" prizes. She has published poems in a number of Galician journals, among them Grial, Nordés, Coordenadas, Dorna, and Festa da palabra silenciada.

De Amor e Desamor I. A Coruña: Ediciós do Castro, 1984, ISBN 84-7492-220-8, 192 pp.
De Amor e Desamor II. A Coruña: Ediciós do Castro, 1985, ISBN 84-7492-237-2, 180 pp.
These volumes, edited by Sada, contain poems by Pallarés on pages 89-103 and 89-92 respectively. Both volumes contain a foreword and an explanation of Pallarés' poética.

Entre lusco e fusco. Sada, A Coruña: Ediciós do Castro, 1980, ISBN 84-7492-030-2, 94 pp.
This love poetry is of intimate orientation and experiential qualities. Nevertheless, the emotional dimension melds with a profound presence of Galicia, establishing a primary, basic commitment to her country. In this way, Pallarés' individual feelings possess a collective base and become a restatement of the central questions in Galician social poetry. In this work, however, there are none of social realism's standard subjects. It is too early to assess the significance and socio-historical importance of Pallaré's poetry, except that it can already be affirmed that she has established a place for herself in future studies of Galician literature. Paperback.

Sétima soidade. Colección Esquío de Poesía. Ferrol: Sociedade de Cultura Valle-Inclán, 1984, ISBN 398-1130-6, 41 pp.
The experience of love is a road to reaching world vision. She shows love as miracle, as discovery of realities in themselves surprising. Solitude has decisive importance and Galician reality appears as dematerialized presence. A work of great formal perfection which reveals a dense literary formation, this poetry springs from what is lost or missing; the author would like to create poems in which silences are as important as words. Her poetic goal points toward equanimity and purity. Paperback.

                                                                    KNM

*PAMIES I BERTRAN. Teresa (1919-).
Born in Balaguer (Lleida), she is the daughter of a farmer who was poor and a militant political activist. At 11, she began working in a sweatshop. An autodidactic teenager, she was soon correspondent for the revolutionary press. After the Spanish Civil War she was exiled in Mexico, where she studied journalism; she lived 12 years exiled in

France and 12 in Czechoslovakia. In 1957 she was awarded the President
Companys Prize in the "Jocs Florals" in Marseille. Her work should be
considered by all researchers in contemporary social and political
history.

Amor clandestí. Barcelona: Galba, Col. Els ulls, no. 3, 1976. 2nd
ed. 1976. 3rd ed. 1980. 4th ed. 1982. ISBN 84-85952-10-3, 238 pp.
    This is a love story that confirms both the attitudes and the
contradictions of a militant political woman. The novel deals with
the life of such a woman during the years when the private life of
political people was strongly affected by the political circmstances
of the moment. The woman's thoughts and feelings are printed with
normal printing characters; the narrative of actual facts is printed
in script. There is in this novel an intensity of feeling and an
absence of sentimentality that delight the reader. The book is
divided into five parts. Paperback.

Aquell vellet gentil i pulcre. Palma de Mallorca: Moll, Biblioteca
Raixa 113, 1978, ISBN 84-273-0247-9, 217 pp. 2nd ed. 1982.
    The novel is divided into seven chapters. The story is presented
through the thoughts and actions of several characters, combining
flashbacks with contemporary events, and developing a complicated and
interesting plot. Life in post-war Barcelona, degradation and misery
brought by defeat, the power of Nazi refugees in Spain and their
infiltration in the French underground and survival in post-war
France are points extremely well presented. Paperback.

Busque-me a Granada. Barcelona: Destino. Col. El Dofí. 1980,
ISBN 84-233-1091-4, 141 pp.
    The narrative develops around a journey to the south of Spain;
during the journey, every stop is savored and every character opens
up an avenue of unknown possibilities. A Catalan woman is fascinated
in Granada by traditions and political feelings completely foreign to
her; characters, legends and historical anecdotes transform the
journey into an adventure of the mind. Sources of documentation are
presented with the author's critical appraisal; historical enigmas,
that constitute a story within a story, are accurately studied, often
with strong emotion. Paperback.

Cartes al fill recluta. Barcelona: Pòrtic, Col. Llibre de butxaca,
no. 127, 1984, ISBN 84-7306-221-3, 133 pp.
    The book is written in epistolary style. The letters are written
by a woman to her son in the military service, but the narrative is
developed on two levels; one is formed by letters written at regular
intervals of time; the other level is formed by one very long letter,
posterior in time to the others, and appearing in fragments after
each one of the "regular" letters. This long narrative is written
during the night of February 23, and includes factual notes about the
failed military coup in Spain. The novel incorporates a chronicle of
a very crucial moment of Spain's contemporary history, narrated by a
woman whose husband and son are placed in the center of it.
Paperback.

Crònica de la vetlla. Barcelona: Ed. Selecta, Col. Antilop, n. 6,
1976, ISBN 84-298-0602-4, 232 pp.
    This novel should be considered as the introduction to all the

other writings of the author. The book describes the local events in
her native city, Balaguer, during the last years of the first dictatorship that Spain suffered in this century. The hope created by
the new Republican regime, the deep-rooted differences between rich
and poor and, dramatically, between the liberal right wing and the
workers' leftist parties are all personified in lively characters and
an exciting narrative that takes the reader to the beginnings of the
Spanish Civil War. As in most of Pàmies' books, the title is
especially accurate. Paperback.

Cròniques de nàufrags. Barcelona: Destino, Col. El Dofí, 1977,
ISBN 84-233-0703-4, 193 pp.
    Through letters written by 25 women and 15 men, the author builds
the stories of 40 people who are survivors of a terrible "shipwreck."
They are post-war people, of all ages, and this is a chronicle of
their efort to survive with dignity, in spite of individual circumstances. This is not a political book; it is a real and stimulating
testimony of a real and devastating period of contemporary life in
Europe and elsewhere. Paperback.

Dona de pres. Barcelona: Proa. Biblioteca a Tot Vent. Ed. Joan
Oliva, 1975. 2nd ed. 1976. ISBN 84-209-4521-8 (paperback),
84-209-4522-6 (hard cover), 226 pp.
    This is a social novel describing the moral and physical suffering
of women whose husbands were in jail because of political ideas. It
is an excellent study of the two main characters: Neus, the wife,
the "dona" of the title, and Rafael, her husband. Neus is strong and
courageous; Rafael, selfish and self-centered. The novel shows the
development of Nora's consciousness and rejection of the traditional
ideas taught to her in her childhood in a religious school. A good
study of different kinds of women confronting the same situation, and
a somewhat metaphysical line of thought, this is a universal novel.
It contains a prologue by Domènec Guansé.

Gent del meu exili. Subtitle "Inoblidables." Barcelona: Galba/
Sagitario. 1st ed. 1975. 2nd ed. 1976. 3rd ed. 1976. ISBN
84-7136-188-4, 169 pp.
    From her years of political exile, Pàmies selects several
characters, the "unforgettable" of the subtitle. Through their lives
Pàmies shows that anguish and pain are found everywhere. Some of
her characters will remain forever with the reader: the woman whose
son was exterminated by the Nazis when he was three years old,
leaving her in a strange world of her own; the two French sisters in
Mexico, so devoid of hope that cancer seems a soft liberation;
Mauricette and her loneliness, all of them linked by a background of
despair and inherent goodness. This is a social document, strongly
presented, with a characteristic note of down-to-earth humor in the
epilogue. Paperback.

Massa tard per a Cèlia. Barcelona: Ed. Destino. Col. El Dofí,
1984, ISBN 84-233-1312-3, 204 pp.
    The novel deals with the search for clues to the suicide of
Cèlia, a main character around whom the action is developed. The
investigation of facts and opinions are the elements of a mystery
novel, although this is not exactly what the reader finds. There is
the description of Slovakia today and its contrast with the country

that emerges as seen by the people who knew Cèlia; the same contrast
is found in the different versions given about Vilko Koralis,
Cèlia's lover in the past. There are excellent studies, given as
interior monologues, of different people: the husband, the son, the
friend, the neighbor...The suicide is not explained, but the reader's
interest is caught all the way. Paperback.

Matins de l'Aran. Barcelona: Pòrtic, Col. El brot., no. 14, 1982,
ISBN 84-7306-0184-5, 179 pp.
    The book is formed by ten stories that develop in ten different
villages in the Valley of Aran. The stories are only linked by the
beautiful landscape and by the author, visiting the villages. Some
of the stories are left without apparent ending, reflecting the life
of everyday people. Some of the characters are farmers and woodsmen
of the area, some are summer visitors; some are old and some are
young; sometimes animals and plants seem to be the center of the
action. There is humor and irony in the book, and the pleasure of
discovery seems to be alive in every page. Paperback.

Memòria dels morts. Barcelona: Planeta, Col. Ramon Llull, Serie
Novel.la, 1981, ISBN 84-320-3505-X, 212 pp.
    As in most of Pàmies' books, there is a political background;
politics here, however, is only a point of departure for a strong
denunciation of women's situation. Pàmies' style is always clear
and realistic, but she introduces here an element of imaginative,
almost fantastic, quality: the book begins with a meeting of the
author with her dead mother in a misty landscape. The author takes
the reader through a world full of the "necessary lies of the living"
by means of the truth spoken by the dead, the only ones with freedom
of speech since they do not need anybody nor have they anything to
hide. In spite of this setting, the book is a lucid and realistic
exposition of feminist values. Paperback.

Quan érem capitans. Subtitle: "Memorias d'aquella guerra."
Barcelona: DOPESA, Col. Pinya de Rosa, 1974, ISBN 84-7235-186-6,
174 pp. 1st ed. with complete original text. Barcelona: Ed. Proa,
Bibl. A tot vent, n. 212, 1984, ISBN 84-7588-013-4, 214 pp.
    The Spanish Civil War is seen through the eyes of an enthusiastic,
dedicated socialist young woman. Main personalities of the time in
the world of politics, business and the arts are artistically mixed
with the narrative. The anguish of the last days of the war and the
painful escape through the French borders are very well described.
The poems to the devastated soil of Catalonia and a personal remembrance of Paul Robeson are described with poignancy. Paperback.

Quan érem refugiats. Subtitle "Memories d'un exili." Barcelona:
DOPESA, 1975, ISBN 84-7235-228-5, 190 pp.
    Narrative describes the tragic situation of women in refugee camps
and prisons in France; there is an especially dramatic scene of an
abortion performed in the prison cell. Divided into five parts:
1. the refugees' camp; 2. stay in Paris and jail there; 3. dramatic
description of pain and anxiety of life in exile and the suffering of
life in Catalonia; letters from exiles; 4. exile in France and on the
ship to South America; 5. Dominican Republic and Cuba; life under
Trujillo; political situation with Spain as an ally of Germany and
Italy and Nazi domination in France and Ethiopia. Paperback.

Rosalia no hi era. Barcelona: Destino. Col. El Doff. 1982,
ISBN 84-233-1210-0, 167 pp.
    The author travels to Galicia in summer, 1981. As the title
implies, she searches for Rosalía de Castro and places one of that
poet's best known poems, "La negra sombra," at the beginning and
throughout the book. Rosalía's life is recreated in these pages
through her words and thoughts, the tragic life of a woman of strong
spirit. There are strong feelings of feminist conviction in the
author's treatment of the anguish of Rosalía as woman and as mother
and of her role in a culture and language as oppressed and
ill-treated as the author's own. Paperback.

Si vas a París, papà... Barcelona: Hogar del libro, Col. Nova
Terra, no. 22. 1st ed. 1975. 2nd ed. 1976. 3rd ed. 1982. ISBN
84-7279-127-0, 191 pp.
    The narrative is centered in May, 1968 in France. The book has a
more mature perspective than some of her other politically oriented
works, but it is again expressed with forceful conviction. It
presents a good analytical description of the French ideals and
thoughts in 1968 and contemporary Catalan crisis and conflicts. The
constant mixture of reality, and real and imagined people gives the
book rhythm and strength. Paperback.

Testament a Praga. Prize JOSEP PLA 1970. Barcelona: Destino, Col.
El Doff. 1st ed. 1971. 2nd ed. 1971. 3rd ed. 1973. 4th ed. 1976.
 5th ed. 1979. ISBN 84-233-0764-6, 220 pp.
    This ambitious and controversial book relates experiences of exile
in Paris and Prague. Loneliness of exile is combined with honest
revision of socialist theory after the Russian invasion of Czechoslovakia in 1968. The book is divided into four parts: in the first
and second, fragments of her father's memories alternate with the
author's recollection of the father's death and contemporary events.
In the third part only the author speaks and the fourth consists of
two letters from the father, both answering his daughter and
re-creating parts of his life. There is strength in these letters,
and longing for the native land he will never see again.

Va ploure tot el dia. Barcelona: Edicions 62 s/a; Col. El Balancí,
88. 1st ed. April 1974. 2nd ed. June 1974. 3rd ed. December 1974.
ISBN 84-297-0987-8, 176 pp.
    The novel is dedicated to "all those exiles who cannot, dare not
or do not want to go back home." Divided into three parts, the book
presents the thoughts and emotions of a Catalan woman returning after
30 years of political exile. Only 24 hours separate the first and
the last pages, but there are constant flashbacks brought on by
association of ideas due to the questioning by police. The background of the falling rain gives a dramatic feeling of the loss of
youth passed in exile and a special awareness of the fact that many
myths and beliefs have also been destroyed. Paperback.

Vacances aragoneses. Barcelona: Destino, Col. El Doff, 1979,
ISBN 84-233-0990-8, 201 pp.
    At first glance this book may seem the description of a summer
vacation in the mountains of Aragó. People living in the valleys
and near the streams, however, are the subject of the book. Their
stories are sometimes overwhelming, as happens with the description

of the retarded little girl; sometimes they are as peaceful as the
countryside, with the village priest in the center of the story.
There is tenderness and humor, too, in the constant reminder of the
limitations that age imposes in the author herself, and in her
companion.

MM

*PAPIOL I MORA, Maria Angels.

Amor amb majúscula. Barcelona: Autor, 1978, ISBN 84-400-4294-9,
78 pp. Prologue by Joan Pelegrí i Partegàs.
      A young Catalan, Marc, goes to London, abandoning family, home and
fiancée. His religious faith keeps him from madness. Descriptions
of nature underscore the states of mind of the characters.

Entre mimosas. Barcelona: 1979.
      Novel.

KM

PARDO BAZAN, Emilia (1851-1921).
      Born in La Coruña to a noble family, she enjoyed all the privileges
of a precocious only daughter. Although she received only the standard
education provided to females of her class, she read, as an adolescent,
all the great writers of the period. Later she taught herself Italian,
French and German so she could read the great writers of those languages, and she also published translations. At age 15 her parents
afianced her to don José Quiroga, and they were married in 1869. She
first became known in the literary world with her critical essay on
Feijoo. She then wrote articles for magazines and soon began the first
in an interminable series of literary polemics with fellow writers.
Menéndez Pelayo, Zorrilla, Galdós and Clarín were among her friends,
and she supported the ideas of Giner de los Ríos. Her interest in
science and pedagogy prompted her interest in krausismo. After travels
in France and her reading of Zola, she published in 1883 La cuestión
palpitante, the highly controversial essay which is often credited with
introducing Naturalism to Spain. It also may have precipitated the
separation from her husband. There followed a very fecund period of
novels, stories, articles, lectures and travel. A feminist, she particularly wrote about the education of women. Although she was never
elected to the Real Academia, she was appointed the first woman
professor at the Universidad Central. This prolific writer is second
only to Santa Teresa as the best-known woman writer of Spain, and
undoubtedly remains the most widely read.

CLG

Belcebú. 1912.
      Belcebú deals with maleficence and witchcraft, pioneering the
esperpento genre later established by Valle-Inclán. The setting is
the familiar Galicia, but the time is during the kingdom of Carlos
II, who was known as the "bewitched." This short novel has a
capricious structure but is beautifully written in the prevalent
modernistic style of the time.

Bucólica. 1884.
      This novelette is written in autobiographical style as a series of
letters to depict realistically and dramatically the Galician

ambiance of the countryside. Joaquín, aspiring to be a judge,
details to a Madrid friend his failure to achieve marriage with a
peasant girl who finally decides for one of her own kind.

Cada uno....
    It is a short novel and the expression of a case of conscience. A
man meets unexpectedly a boyhood friend in a monastery. Enrique
confesses his turbulent past and the reasons which led him to become
a monk. Pardo Bazán portrays in him a Christ figure who expiates
the sins of the dissolute society of S***.

El Cisne de Vilamorta. 1884.
    A triangular relationship, and the psychological implications that
such a relationship entails, form the central theme of this novel.
Leocadia, a school teacher, full of romantic ideals, and Nieves, the
sophisticated city wife of the grand old man of local politics, Don
Victoriano, compete for the favors of Segundo, the village poet,
known as El Cisne. Nieves, however, is merely relieving her boredom
by mesmerizing Segundo, and when Don Victoriano dies, she drops him.
Broken hearted, the poet emigrates to America, in turn breaking Leocadia's heart and prompting her suicide. Although the three characters are not well-defined, they, rather than their environment, so
typical in most of Pardo Bazán's novels, take center stage in this
one.

Una cristiana. 1890.
    Carmen, a young spirited woman, marries Felipe, a repulsive old
man. The narrator is Salustio, his nephew, who comes to their wedding and instantly falls in love with the delicate Carmen. He moves
in to share their household. Why did Carmen marry Felipe? Can she
love him? Does she love Fr. Moreno, her constant spiritual advisor?
Or does she love Salustio? The novel is concerned with Salustio's
search for the answers to these questions. Although she is seemingly
a devoted wife and paragon of Christian virtues, when Salustio falls
seriously ill, Carmen cares for him tenderly. He is more perplexed
than ever. The answers to his questions come in the sequel, La
prueba. In this novel, Pardo Bazán seemingly rejects materialisic
psychology and affirms the basic irrationality of human behavior.

La dama joven. 1885.
    This novelette is a story of ambition and dreams versus common
sense. An older and frustrated sister takes motherly care of a young
one who is very attractive and has a good future as an actress.
Instead of imposing her will for a life of theatrical fame, the old
sister lets the young one choose married life with an ordinary man
she loves.

Doña Milagros. 1894.
    Benicio Neira, a gentle, weak man, and his wife, the strong-willed
Ilduara, have 12 children, each with a different character. Benicio
narrates the story; his salary cannot cover their needs. Doña
Milagros, a wealthy and childless neighbor, has a big heart and would
help them, but Ilduara's unreasonable hatred prevents it. After a
stormy scene with Milagros, she has a fit and dies, leaving Benicio
to cope with the financial and educational problems of raising the
family. His only comfort is the chaste friendship of Milagros, but

this is ruined by malicious gossip which causes Benicio to avoid her.
Doña Milagros demonstrates her innocence, and when she moves to
Barcelona with her military husband, Benicio presents her with his
baby twins. This simple account, in the style of a chronicle, is one
of Pardo Bazán's most delightful novels.

Dulce Dueño. 1911.
    In this story within a story, two erudite men, a pious priest and
an old freethinker, are the mentors of Lina, a rich and spirited
young woman. The priest reads to her the life of St. Catherine of
Alexandria as a model to imitate. She is beautiful, talented and
original but she is undecided whether to choose a religious life in
the convent or a mundane life with the wooers who surround her: a
pedantic, middle-class young man, a sensuous vagabond (her cousin),
and the audacious son of an ex-minister. After many escapades and
trials Lina chooses to go to her Sweet Lord (Dulca Dueño) and toils
in a madhouse to serve Him, to the bewilderment of all who admired
her. As with most of Pardo Bazán's novels, this one is naturalistic
in the details, but psychological aspects predominate, leading to a
spiritual ending.

Finafrol.
    It is a realistic and dramatic novelette of Galician ambiance. It
portrays rustic outcasts and features loutish yokel speech. The
abandoned child Sidora grows up to be a fine flower--Finafrol--in a
society of tramps led by a blind old man who enslaves her. Through
virtue, beauty and a stroke of luck she is about to escape and marry
a wealthy young man, but fate does not bend and tragedy ensues.

Una gota de sangre.
    The narrator, Mr. Selva, is openly accosted at the theater by a
man vaguely familiar, on whose shirt he notices a fresh drop of
blood. On his way home he discovers a body near his apartment.
Suspected by the police, Selva launches a private search for the
killer. Mystery and suspense with a great deal of intrigue are added
ingredients to Pardo Bazán's naturalistic view of society in this
short novel.

Insolación. 1889.
    Madrid is the setting for this novel which presents the relation-
ship between a respectable young Galician widow named Asís and the
tawdry Andalusian, Pacheco. Without knowing each other well, she
accepts his invitation to attend the Feria of San Isidro, where she
is carried away by the holiday atmosphere and the wine. The ensuing
chapters describe the continuous efforts of Asís to forget Pacheco,
in which she does not succeed; her feelings overcome her inhibitions;
she sleeps with him and decides to marry him. The story is told by a
narrator with conflicting points of view: sympathetic yet ironic,
with the novelist's point of view remaining ambiguous. Here and in
Morriña, published together, Pardo Bazán places her characters in a
new setting and portrays their nostalgic feeling towards Galicia.

La madre Naturaleza. 1886.
    In the continuation of Los pazos de Ulloa, the illegitimate young
Perucho and Manolita, the legitimate daughter, unaware of their paternal kinship, fall in love incestuously which we are made to feel

is inevitable. Perucho and Manolita consummate their love in all
"natural" innocence under a symbolic "tree of knowledge," only to
find themselves cast out from a society unmoved by their human tragedy. People compound the crime by condemning Manolita to expiate her
fall in a convent and Perucho to despair. Nature is presented as an
overpowering and hypnotic force which crushes Perucho and Manolita.
Their love is sunken in a lush, vital, even sensual background to
such an extent that this novel is accepted as the author's zenith as
a "paisajista." It is certainly considered one of her best.

Memorias de un solterón. 1896.
     This continuation of Doña Milagros is primarily the story of the
widower Benicio Neira and his large family, as seen by Mauro Pareja,
their unrepentant bachelor neighbor. We hear of various problems in
Benicio's household, particularly Rosa's flirtation with the landlord
and Argos' with Mejía, the Governor of Marineda. The two girls are
dishonored and Benicio, with unexpected vehemence, runs Mejía
through with his sword. Although Mauro has no intention to marry, he
is caught up in the trials of the family and is attracted and finally
entrapped by Feíta, the most spirited of the 11 daughters of
Benicio. The novel's happy ending is a reversal of the author's
previous naturalistic pessimism.

Misterio. 1903.
     It is a historical novel filled with international intrigue
tracing the wanderings across Europe of the enigmatic French Dauphin,
son of Louis XVI. Pardo Bazán imagines that he survived the
mistreatment received from the barbarian Swiss shoemaker in whose
care he was left. Using the alias Guillermo Dorff, Louis XVII set
out to recover his throne, helped by his beautiful daughter Amelia
and the young nobleman, Renato de Giac, who loved her. Renato became
convinced that Dorff was the Dauphin by reading his "Memoires," which
form a story within the novel. Against them are Louis XVIII, uncle
of the Dauphin, and Baron Lecazes, implacable enemy of the aspiring
Prince. It is a belated historical romance (folletín) full of
surprises, assassinations, and mysteries, only saved from the
heaviness typical of such works by Pardo Bazán's masterful style.

Morriña. 1889.
     Esclavitud, a Galician girl, the illegitimate daughter of a priest
and a woman of easy morals, goes to Madrid to escape the shame of her
origins. She works for Doña Aurora, a widow from Galicia with whose
son, Rogelio, she falls in love. When the mother discovers the
liaison, she is determined to break it up by sending the girl to work
in another house and her son away to Galicia. As a last desperate
attempt to hold Rogelio, Esclavitud gives in to him in vain. The
novel ends with his departure on the train while Esclavitud, feeling
totally abandoned, separated from her natural surroundings and filled
with "morriña"--extreme anguish--commits suicide. The character of
the novel is naturalistic-deterministic.

Obras completas. Madrid: Aguilar, 1947. 2nd ed. 1964. 3rd ed.,
first reprint 1973. ISBN 84-03-00985-2. Vol. I and II: Preliminary
study, notes and preambles by Federico Carlos Sainz de Robles. Vol.
III: Introduction, bibliography, selection of critical material,
prologue, classification of stories, notes and appendices by Harry L.

Kirby, Jr. The three volumes contain 20 novels: Pascual López
(Autobiografía de un estudiante de Medicina) 1879; Un viaje de
novios 1881; La Tribuna 1882; El Cisne de Vilamorta 1884; Los pazos
de Ulloa 1886; La madre Naturaleza 1887; Insolación 1889; Morriña
1889; Una cristiana 1890; La prueba (Segunda parte de "Una
cristiana"); La piedra angular 1891; Doña Milagros 1892; Memorias de
un solterón 1894; El tesoro de Gastón 1897; El Niño de Guzmán
1897; El saludo de las brujas 1898; Misterio 1903; La quimera 1905;
La sirena negra 1908; Dulce dueño 1911; 13 cuadros religiosos; 544
short stories, classified by the editors into such categories as
"Cuentos de la vida moderna," "Cuentos de épocas pasadas," "Cuentos
de Galicia," "Cuentos de humor y tristeza," "Cuentos de fantasía,
"Cuentos de amor y pasión," "Cuentos de Navidad y Año Nuevo,"
"Cuentos de la tierra," "Cuentos trágicos;" 7 plays; literary
criticism.

Los pazos de Ulloa. 1886.
    Father Julián is a village priest who strives to bring order and
civilization to the manor of Ulloa, in a remote corner of Galicia.
He encourages its Marquis, Don Pedro Moscoso to abandon Sabel, his
mistress, and marry his cousin Nucha. When Nucha bears him a girl
and not the expected son, the Marquis soon returns to his sinful
involvement with Sabel. Nucha becomes increasingly anxious about her
situation and the safety of her daughter. She begs Father Julián to
help her escape, but, when the two are caught conferencing together,
the priest is expelled from the manor, and Nucha dies soon after.
Widely considered Pardo Bazán's best novel, it is a naturalistic-
psychological portrayal of the Galician country and its people,
anguished by traditions and strong religious ties.

La piedra angular. 1891.
    The setting for this novel of ideas is Marineda, Pardo Bazán's
fictional name for her home town of La Coruña. The brutal murder of
a man by his wife and her lover create the situation. In the
foreground are the public executioner, Juan Rojo, his son Telmo and
the philanthropic educator--doctor, Pelayo Moragas, an opponent of
capital punishment. He sets out to understand Rojo, a man who clings
to his duty in spite of being despised by society and losing his wife
and the respect of his son. The doctor convinces Rojo to refuse to
execute the criminals and give up his profession; in return, his son
will be cared for and educated. Having lost everything which gave
his life a purpose, it is not surprising that Rojo ends his own life.
While Pardo Bazán is obviously against capital punishment, she is
equally sympathetic with the executioner, in this case the victim.

La Quimera. 1905.
    Silvio Lago, the protagonist, is a painter just returned from
Argentina without the riches he had expected. He is of modest
country origin, but youthful and talented and has an unbounded
ambition to be immortal, which is his chimera. Through his painting
he becomes acquainted with beautiful and influential women: Clara,
the sensual; Espina, the boldly expressive; and Minia, the comforting
and serene helper. With their aid, he triumphs, but like the
mythical glauco, slaying the chimera does not bring him happiness.
In this symbolic novel Pardo Bazán departs further from naturalism.

It is her last major work and depicts the aristocratic society of Galicia and Madrid which the author knew so well.

La sirena negra. 1908.
　　Death, symbolized as a siren, is calling Don Gaspar de Montenegro, whose aging heart is divided among various women, his sister, mother, an English governess, the mother of Rafaelín. He is a boy whose tragic end finally breaks the spell of the siren, and saves Montenegro's life. With the Madrid turn-of-the-century background the novel is a masterful description of the protagonist character. The book is available in hardback, but paperback is readily available in the Colección Austral for classroom use.

La Tribuna. 1882.
　　It is the story of a mildly revolutionary working girl named Amparo who is seduced by a young officer who then refuses to marry her because of her lower class standing. The background in which the novel is set is the upheaval following the 1868 Revolution which brought about the first Spanish Republic. Amparo works in a cigarette factory where she fights social injustice, which she blames on the middle and the upper classes. She is loved by Chinto, a poor devil who is socially her equal, but below her personal standards. She is well-read and articulate and speaks out to persuade the illiterate and frightened masses to rise for the revolution. The day her son by the officer is born yelling, is the day the new-born Republic is greeted by a group of the most convinced cigarette makers who yell out together: Viva the Republic! Pardo Bazán's revolutionary theories of naturalism, published the same year, are strictly implied in this novel.

Un viaje de novios. 1881.
　　The newlyweds, Miranda and Lucía, daughter of a rich merchant, go to France on their honeymoon. He misses the train in one of the stations while she is asleep. Distraught by his strange absence, Lucía is consoled by the gentle Artegui, traveling in the same compartment. This sensitive young man is quite a contrast to old Miranda, whose reappearance stops the growing involvement. Toward the end of the novel, Artegui, cast into deep melancholy by his mother's death to the extent of considering suicide, providentially re-encounters Lucia, who saves him. He urges her to run away with him, but her pregnancy and loyalty to the husband prevails. The novel is written in the naturalist style and highlights the controversy of La cuestión palpitante in which the author was then involved.

AR

PAYA MIRA, Carmen (1918-).
　　Born in Monóvar, Alicante, she graduated with a licenciatura de filosofía y letras. As a pianist and writer, she has combined her talents in the unique form of lecturing on music while performing. Her tours have taken her through Spain and various foreign countries. She has received various prizes in music and literature and published a novel.

Aventuras de un hombre tímido en París. Editorial Pueyo.

UMS

*PAZOS I NOGUERA, Maria Lluisa.

Devastació - Gresol de nit. Barcelona: 1980.
Poetry.

El joc dels jocs les raons. Barcelona: 1978.

KM

**PENAS, Anxeles (19?-).
Born in La Coruña, where she teaches Castilian language and
literature at a public high school, she is bilingual, and writes in
Galician and Castilian.

Con los pies en la frontera. La Coruña: Moret, 1976.
A collection of poetry, rather experimental in form and content.

CNC & AM

*PENYA d'AMER, Victòria (1827-1898).
A poetess, she was born in Ciutat de Mallorca. Sister of Pere
de'Alcàntara, she married Pere Nicolau. She took part in the first
Jocs Florals and obtained a prize. Her lines range from popular and
familiar to moralizing and religious tone. She contributed to different
magazines: "Lo Gay Saber," "La Renaixença," "La Ilustració Catalana,"
etc. As editor she worked for "La Ilustración Católica" and "El
Pensil del Bello Sexo." She was an honorary member of La Academia de
Las Buenas Letras de Barcelona in the year of 1872.

Amor de Mare. 4 pp.
The poem was awarded a prize in the Jocs Florals in 1865.

Manat d'homenatge a Victòria Penya d'Amer. Ed. Esteve Albert i
Corp.
The book includes a poem of Penya: "Anyorança." The plot of the
poem deals with the arrival of a knight from a faraway place. It
relates the wife's solitude and sorrow due to longing. Finally she
dies because of the nostalgia for her husband.

Poesies. Barcelona: Ilustració Catalana, 1909, 233 pp.
This posthumous compilation of 58 poems bears a religious tone.
Some of the poems included are: "A la poesia," "Al Sagrat cor de
Jesus," "Al Sagrat cor de Maria," "A la Verge de Montserrat," etc.
Lines show a lovely and tender soul. Penya d'Amer falls in love with
folkloric and everyday life, which is portrayed through fine
language. Editing by F. Mateu and preface unsigned.

Poetas Baleares.S.XIX. Poesias de autores vivientes. Estampa de
Pere Joseph Gelabert 1873. 269 pp. Victoria Penya, p. 247.
Four of the poems of the poet are included in the book:
"Anyorança" "En Josepet," "Amor de Mare," and "A la Verge Maria."
The poems are in both Catalan and Castilian.

Els Poetes Romantics de Mallorca. Recull antlògic amb una
introducció i comentaris, edited by M. Sanchis Guarner. Biblioteca
"Les Illes d'Or" No. 40-41. Palma de Mallorca: Moll, 1950, 286 pp.

The book includes on pp. 113-123 three of Penya d'Amer's poems:
"En Carles de Viana i Na Blanca de Navarra," "Lo meu niu" and "Lo bon
Jesuset."

VC-E

*PESSARRODONA I ARTIGUES, Marta (1941-).
She was born in Terrassa (Barcelona), the only child of a middle-
class couple. She attended the Universidad de Barcelona where she
specialized in history and Romance languages. She has been writing
poems since she was 12 years old. She used to write in Spanish until
1964, when she adopted Catalan as her literary language. Some of her
poems are written in English. She was a Lecturer in Spanish at the
University of Nottingham from 1972 to 1974. She writes in many
newspapers and periodicals. Some of them are: Camp de l'Arpa, Dones en
lluita, Avui, El Pais, L'avenç, etc.

Berlin Suite. Barcelona: Mall, 1985.
     In this short volume, Pessarrodona continues developing elements
seen in earlier works, and makes progress toward new goals in her
poetry and humanism.

A favor meu, nostre, edicions de les dones. Barcelona: Ed. La Sal,
1982, ISBN 8485637113, 74 pp.
     Collection of poems divided in six sections and epilogue. The
edition was prepared by Esther Tusquets. It belongs to a series of
books dedicated to women. The first section is called: "A favor
nostre," and the author dedicates it to other women writers who
encountered many problems writing and publishing. Most of her poems
deal with an old love. There are nostalgic feelings and a great deal
of sadness. Available in paperback, but very hard to find.

Memòria. Barcelona: Lumen, Paraula menor, 1979, ISBN 8426428622,
58 pp.
     This collection of poems is divided in two groups. There is a
prose epilogue. The first part, named "Memòria" concentrates on
winter. There is a nostalgic feeling. The author misses her own
land where winters aren't as cold. There are constant references to
the past and the emptiness of winter. In the second part, there is
no winter now, and the author concentrates on the new spring and the
rainy afternoons that inspire good writing. In the epilogue we learn
that the author is in London, and she remembers her youth. There are
many biographical references. It is summer now, and she misses the
Mediterranean Sea. Available in paperback, but difficult to find.

Poemes 1969-1981. Prologue by R. Pinyol-Balasch, drawings by Josep
M. Subirachs. Barcelona: Edicions del Mall, 1984, 221 pp., ISBN
84-7456-182-5.
     A collection from previous works, including Setembre 30, Vida
privada, Memòria i, A favor meu, nostre. There is a prologue by R.
Pinyol-Balasch, "Agraiments i apologies" by the author, an epilogue
of new works, and drawings by Josep M. Subirachs.

Setembre 30. Barcelona: Ed. Ariel, 1969.
     The title of this work appears in one of the poems of the second
part of Memòria where it is followed by a parenthesis that says
"provisional title." The poem talks about the feeling of love she

felt earlier. She says it made her feel very much alive, even though she wants to deny it now.

Vida privada. Barcelona: Lumen Paraula menor, 1972, ISBN 8426428517, 58 pp. 3rd ed., Barcelona: Lumen, 1973.
     Collection of poems with a prologue, written by the author herself, and an epilogue. Pessarrodona mentions how poetry is a kind of striptease. Her poems in Vida privada show us her attitude toward her surroundings. The prologue is a series of unconnected sentences where we can find a wide variety of subjects, from political connotations to erotic feelings, anguish, disgust for her city, etc. In some of the poems we see the problem of political persecution of poets and also there are references to the truth of the old poets in the poem "The old masters." Available in paperback.

MLG-E

PINAR, Florencia (15th century).
     Beyond her name and the fact that three of her poems appear in fifteenth and sixteenth century cancioneros (the Cancionero of the British Museum, the Costantina, and the General) little else is known of Florencia Pinar. Since the Cancioneros in which her work appears are not easily accessible, see: Alan Deyermond, "The Worm and the Partridge: Reflections on the Poetry of Florencia Pinar," Mester (Los Angeles), 7(1978), 3-8. The poems, "!Ay! que ay quien más no vive," "Destas aves su nación," and "Ell amor ha tales mañas" treat the theme of love, contain plays on words, and employ concrete imagery. Pinar's use of animal imagery in the opinion of A. Deyermond makes her "poetry strongly sexual in nature" (Spain's First Women Writers, in Women in Hispanic Literature, ed. Beth Miller, Berkeley, Los Angeles, London: Univ. of California Press, 1983, p. 50).

MM

*PLA, Walda (1913-).
     A novelist from El Masnou, she wrote Salt d'euga (1962) and Amarga joia (1968).

KM

*PLANELLES, Neus.

Llepolies i pastissos. Barcelona: Edhasa, 1981, 96 pp.

KM

POMAREDA DE HARO, Joaquina (1912-).
     This author writes for a number of publications and is primarily known as a short story writer. She also contributes to radio programs in Albacete, where she was born and now resides.

El actor y sus personajes. Albecete: A. González, 1967, 114 p.
     A collection of aphorisms, narrations and poetry.

CLG

*POMPEIA, Núria (1938-).
     Born to a Barcelona bourgeois family and raised during the Franco regime amid post-war conflicts and repression, she is primarily a journalistic cartoonist who contributed regularly to the periodical Triunfo, and later became managing editor of a weekly, Por Favor.

The only woman in Spain to become well-known as a cartoonist, she has
worked in both Castilian and Catalan, usually producing works of a
mixed-genre or transitional nature, between graphic and literary, a
blend of text and cartoons: Maternasis (1967), Y fueron felices
comiendo perdices (1970), Pels segles dels segles (1971), La educación
de Palmira (1972), and Mujercitas (1975). Her only exclusively verbal
book to date is Cinc cèntims (1891), a short-story collection. Her
themes are predominantly feminist.

   Cinc cèntims. Barcelona: Edicions 62, 1981, ISSB: 84-297-1710-2,
   189 pp. Twelve short stories: Un sopar de duro, Els aparadors,
   Activitats culturals, L'ordre i el matrimoni, Dissetè segona ema,
   Guanyem la llibertat, Objectes perduts, Tallar, rentar i Marcar, Un
   fe divisions, La generacio perduda, Endevina endevinalla, "Mirall
   endins de l'aigua del meu somni".
   "Five Cents" is Pompeia's only exclusively verbal text to date, a
dozen short stories written in vivid, precise and colloquial Catalan.
Common to all the stories is the feminist viewpoint, her character-
istically satiric sense of humor, and the critique of upper-class or
bourgeois life and values. Subjects range from a drunken dinner
party to weekend rituals and outings of the well-to-do, pseudo-
intellectual pursuits and pseudo-artistic collections to sexist
education. Other feminist themes include the view of matrimony as a
paternalistic despotism, politics within marriage, disappointment of
women's hopes for liberation under one regime and then another.
Pompeia underscores the lack of real change beneath the appearance of
modernization and progress.

   La educación de Palmira. Barcelona, 1972.
   Cartoons and text. Pompeia's most famous cartoon character,
Palmira is a sort of Lucy (from the "Peanuts" strip), who is
well-known to newspaper readers throughout the Spanish-speaking
world. In this integrally conceived volume on her upbringing, the
author shows how traditional education deforms the female's natural
impulses and intellect, and sets the stage for future conflict and
alienation.

   Maternasia. Barcelona: Kairós, 1967.
   Cartoons. Relying heavily on visual media, Pompeia offers a
graphic history which communicates the changes in a woman's body and
her life which come about with motherhood.

   Mujercitas. Barcelona: Kairós, 1975, 144 pp.
   Cartoons and text. "Little Women" provides a compendium of the
themes of four earlier collections of cartoon-text blends, combining
hilarity and incisive satire in an indictment of those sectors and
attitudes of society which contribute to changing the active,
creative, adventurous, spontaneous, rebellious, exploring girl-child
into a passive, submissive, inhibited, dependent, comforming and
boring woman. From Victorian morality and Biblical justifications of
male domination to the emphasis on beauty and sexuality, sexist-role-
typing and the romantic dream of "happily ever after," she juxtaposes
traditional stereotypes with feminist reality, making her points with
humor and insight.

Pels segles dels segles. Barcelona: Edicions 62, 1971. 157 pp. illustrations. Castilian translation by Jordi Teixidor.
   In her first work in Catalan, which incorporates a larger admixture of text with her satiric cartoons, Pompeia continues the feminist thematics of her earlier books, reinforcing the message of Y fueron felices... ("happily ever after"). Contrasting the masculine and feminine views of woman's lot "for hundreds of centuries," she undertakes a task of consciousness-raising which both undermines the notion that marriage is the sole goal of a female's life and the justification that "that's the way it has always been."

Y fueron felices comiendo perdices. Barcelona: Kairós, 1970, 279 pp. Cartoons and text. Texts in Spanish, Catalan, or French.
   Using the Spanish equivalent of "and they lived happily ever after," Pompeia satirically undercuts the standard middle-class dream of romantic love and marriage. "And They Were Happy Eating Partridges" confronts the myth of the supposedly blissful wife and mother with the everyday realities which constitute life once the honeymoon is over.

JP

PORTAL NICOLAS, Marta (1930-).
   Marta Portal was born in Nava (Asturias) and studied in Colombia on a Fundación Juan March fellowship. She has been a journalist and professor of literature on the Facultad de Ciencias de la Información. She has written short stories, essays and literary criticism as well as novels. There have been numerous translations of her works, and one won the Italian Premio Adelaida Ristori in 1975.

A ras de las sombras. Barcelona: Planeta, 1968.
   Novel.

A tientas y a ciegas. Barcelona: Planeta, 1966. 26th ed. 1979.
   Portal's first novel won the 1966 Premio Editorial Planeta. The protagonist is a rarity, a woman who, at age 30, decides to return to the University to finish her degree. Previously living in an egocentric environment of comfort, she had been frigid, resenting her unfaithful husband's showing her off as a beauty. She awakens to sensuality and awareness of her body and has an affair with her professor; however tradition prevents her from considering the possibility of leaving her husband, and she returns to the marriage, determined to be more giving and to have children. While Sara's return to University is unusual in Spanish society, and her attempt to find independence and more self-fulfillment is exemplary of some awakening that was occurring in the 1960's, the novel's ending is complete capitulation to traditional societal attitudes.

El buen camino. Barcelona: Planeta, 1975.
   Novel.

Ladridos a la luna. Barcelona: Plaza y Janés, 1970.
   This novel introduces a married woman who has been having an affair. Through the course of a sleepless night she decides to end the affair.

El maíz, grano sagrado de América. Madrid: Instituto de Cultura
Hispánica, 1970.
   Historical, linguistic and literary study.

El malmuerto. Barcelona: Planeta, 1967.
   Short novels.

Proceso narrativo de la Revolución mexicana. Madrid: Cultura
Hispánica, 1977.
   Study of the contemporary Mexican novel.

La veintena. Madrid: Magisterio Español, 1973.
   Stories.

CLG

**POZO GARZA, Luz (1922-).
   Born in Ribadeo (Lugo), she studied teaching, piano and Romance
philology. A renowned poet of both Galician and Spanish, she has
published such works as "El vagabundo," "Cita en el viento," and "O
paxaro na boca," in addition to Concerto de outono and Ultimas
palabras/verbas derradeiras. Her poetry abounds in a lyricism,
spontaneity and style of a testimonial character. She co-directed the
journal Nordés and belongs to the Académica Correspondiente a la Real
Academia Gallega and is a professor of Spanish Language and Literature
at the Instituto Nacional de Bachillerato-Masculino de la Coruña.

Concerto de outono. La Coruña: Ediciones de Castro, Serie Liminar,
1981, 89 pp.
   Concerto de outono presents a collection of poems by the author
written entirely in Galician.

Ultimas palabras/verbas derradeiras. La Coruña: Moret, Nordés
Colección de Poesía, 1976, 95 pp.
   In this work, the poet presents a series of symbolic connotations
in an effort to exteriorize a situation in which words alone seem
inadequate. The title suggests this attention to "palabras," in
which she progresses thematically from the initial idea of "menos
palabras cada día" ("fewer words each day") to a semantic analogy
full of reiteration of the word "nada." The latter further
intensifies her predominant theme of nihilism. According to Tomás
Barros in the work's prologue, there is a gradual transition from
beginning to end toward a pathetic tone that eventually becomes an
"unsuspected limitation."

JSC

**PRIETO ROUCO, Carmen (1901-).

Horas de frebe. Poesías galegas. Monólogos representabres.
Villalba: El Progreso Villalbés, 1926; 2nd ed. "correxida e
aumentada," 1928.
   Some of this descriptive, "costumbrista" poetry has a mild
political orientation. Other poems are full of subjective lyricism
in Rosalía de Castro's style.

CNC & AM

PUERTOLAS VILLANUEVA, Soledad (1947-).
She was born in Zaragoza and studied journalism. Later, she received an MA in Spanish literature at the University of California in Santa Barbara. At present, she writes literary criticism in the newspapers. She is one of the writers in Doce relatos de mujeres edited by Ymelda Navajo, Madrid: Alianza, 1982.

El bandido doblemente armado. Madrid: Legasa, 1980, ISBN 84-85701-06-2, 140 pp. 2nd ed., Biblioteca de autores españoles, Madrid: Trieste, 1984, ISBN 84-85762-32-0, 150 pp.
The first edition of this book won the "Premio Sésamo" in 1979. It is a beautiful book. Divided in ten chapters with titles, each could be read independently as a short story. The key element of the novel is the narrator, a young man, who tells candidly of his relationship with the Lennox family. The characters are well defined: la señora Lennox, her husband, James, the oldest, Terry, the narrator's friend, Eileen and Linda. The theme is friendship and trust; the title is symbolic.

Una enfermedad moral. Biblioteca de autores españoles, 1. Madrid: Trieste, 1982, ISBN 84-85762-06-1, 163 pp.
A collection of short stories which, according to the author's preface, all have in common a moral problem. "Un país extranjero" is the story of an older lady who rides to town in the bus and after an incident becomes withdrawn. In "La indiferencia de Eva," a novelist--not the author, by her own admission--flirts with a radio announcer. A very intimate, original story. Other stories are: "Koothar," "Contra Fortinelli," "La llamada nocturna," "En el límite de la ciudad," "La orilla del Danubio," and "Una enfermedad moral" which titles the book. The last one, "El origen del deseo" is the only one which is autobiographical. These short stories show great diversity in place and time.

El Madrid de La lucha por la vida. Hechos y palabras, 3. Madrid: Helios, 1971, 136 pp.
Dedicated to Carlos Blanco Aguinaga, it is a literary essay on Pío Baroja.

                                                                CA

PUNCEL REPARAZ, María (1927-).
Known primarily as a writer of theater works for children, the author has also published biographies of saints and other figures and one volume of poetry, Poema en quince cuadros (La Coruña, 1955) and a book of practical ideas for the home (Madrid: 1972).

                                                                CLG

QUEIZAN, María Xosé (1938-).
   Born in Vigo, where she teaches Galician language and literature at a
public high school, she is a feminist and politically involved. She has
published many articles and essays (A muller en Galicia, 1977;
Recuperemos as mans, 1980), as well as many uncollected poems and short
stories.

   Amantia. Vigo: Edicións Xerais, 1984.
      A feminist novel, the action occurs at the time of the Roman
   colonization of Galicia.

   A orella no buraco. Vigo: Galaxia, 1965. 2nd ed. 1984.
      "Objectalist" novel, influenced by the French Nouveau Roman.
                                                             CNC & AM

QUIROGA, Elena (1921-).
   One of the major women novelists of post-war Spain, Quiroga first
achieved national recognition by winning the Nadal Prize for 1950. In
1983 she became the second woman elected to the Spanish Royal Academy.
Her major works are characterized by their use of stream of consciousness and their probing psychological analyses. Frequent themes include
the causes and effects of the Civil War, the sociological reality of
Galicia, the problem of growing up female, and women's lives.

   Algo pasa en la calle. Barcelona: Destino, "Ancora y Delfin," no.
   102, 1954, 220 pp. (In Las mejores novelas contemporáneas, ed.
   Joaquín de Entrambasaguas, vol. 12, Barcelona: Planeta, 1971.)
      The author's first "Faulknerian" novel is one of her major works,
   particularly important for its penetrating analysis of the psychological effects of divorce in a society that had abolished divorce
   retroactively. Set in the 1950's, the novel, through a multi-
   perspective, stream of consciousness technique traces the lives of
   the various characters, emphasizing the years of the Second Republic
   when Spain had a model divorce law. This represents a daring
   approach to a subject held taboo under the National Catholicism of
   Franco Spain.

   La careta. Barcelona-Madrid-México: Noguer, 1955, 213 pp.
   Madrid: Ediciones del Centro, 1974, 194 pp. Prólogo de M. E.
   Coindreau, ISBN 84-7227-005-X.
      One of Quiroga's major works and perhaps her most effective use of
   stream of consciousness, this novel is deeply rooted in existential

philosophy. Moisés is an alienated protagonist who has never overcome the psychological damage from the death of his parents in the
Civil War. The novel tentatively explores a number of taboo topics,
including the atrocities commited by both sides in the war, sexuality, the ineffectiveness of the Catholic Church, and religious prejudice. It is also highly critical of the so-called bridge generation.

Carta a Cadaqués. Santander: Imprenta Bedia, 1961, 12 pp.
    Privately printed poetic work, written as a thank you to friends
who allowed her the use of their home on the Costa Brava while she
was writing one of her novels. Copy available in the Biblioteca
Nacional in Madrid.

La enferma. Barcelona-Madrid-México: Noguer, 1955, 243 pp.
    A penetrating psychological analysis of various women's lives, it
focuses primarily on an unnamed narrator and Liberata, the sick woman
of the title. The narrator's journey to a Galician fishing village,
where Liberata has lain motionless and silent since abandoned by her
childhood sweetheart, presents the opportunity for self-awareness.
There is interesting use of stream of consciousness and of a multi-
perspective technique in recounting the story of Liberata and the
other villagers.

Envío al Faramello. Madrid: Raycar, 1963, 13 pp.
    Privately printed poetic work, including photographs. Written in
tribute to a family friend in Galicia during his terminal illness.
Copy available in the Biblioteca Nacional in Madrid.

Escribo tu nombre. Barcelona-Madrid: Noguer, 1965, 678 pp.
    The second work in the Tadea trilogy, this novel--Quiroga's
longest--examines in detail the experiences of a young girl in a
Catholic boarding school during the Second Republic. The convent
school is treated as a microcosm of the greater society. The
backlash against a Mother Superior's liberal views anticipates the
Civil War itself. An effective cry for freedom, the novel also
daringly introduces the subject of female sexuality. One of her
major works, it was chosen to represent Spain in the first international Rómulo Gallegos novel contest.

Plácida, la joven y otras narraciones. Madrid: Prensa Española,
1956, 186 pp. Includes Plácida, la joven, Trayecto uno (originally
published in "La Novela del Sábado," no. 2, 1953) and La otra ciudad
(originally published in "La Novela del Sábado," no. 35, 1953).
Barcelona-Madrid: Noguer, 1970, 206 pp.
    Three short novels, closely related in style and technique to the
longer works of the same period. Trayecto uno reflects the current
of social realism in vogue in Spain in the early 1950's. La otra
ciudad is a transitional work, combining social realism with
subjective, psychological analysis. Plácida, la joven, written in
1956, is typical of Quiroga's mature psychological works. Like La
enferma it contrasts the feelings and experiences of a narrator from
the city and those of a Galician villager.

Presente profundo. Barcelona: Destino, "Ancora y Delfin," no. 416,
1973), ISBN 84-233-0772-7, 168 pp.
    One of the author's major works, particularly important for its

analysis of women's lives, it juxtaposes the stories of two suicides, that of an older Galician woman who is cast aside by her husband and children and that of a cosmopolitan young divorcee who, separated from the child she loves, drifts into the drug culture. It creates counterpoint between these characters and two liberated women, as well as a counterpoint between the urban center and Galicia, and reflects existentialist philosophy and stream of consciousness.

La sangre. Barcelona: Destino, "Ancora y Delfin," no. 76, 1952, 346 pp. Barcelona: Destino, "Destinolibro," no. 136, 1981, ISBN 84-23-1121-X, 346 pp.
    Like Faulkner's Absalom, Absalom!, this novel traces several generations of a family, culminating in the end of the family line. The setting is Galicia, and the time extends to the period preceding the Spanish Civil War. The most innovative aspect of the novel is the choice of narrator: a chestnut tree. From its vantage point outside the ancestral home, the tree recounts only what it sees and understands. The result is an effective ironic distancing.

La soledad sonora. Madrid: Espasa-Calpe, 1949, 265 pp.
    A promising but immature first novel, La soledad sonora is of interest primarily for its introduction of characters and themes that relate to Tristura, one of Quiroga's major works. A melodramatic love story is played against the historical background of Civil War and volunteer participation of Spaniards on the Russian front. Out of print and not available in American libraries.

Tristura. Barcelona-Madrid: Noguer, 1960, 282 pp.
Titled: Secreto de la infancia. Novela de una niña. México: Diana, 182, ISBN 968-13-1347-X, 282 pp.
Reissued: Barcelona: Plaza y Janés, 1984, 266 pp.
    Winner of the Premio de la Crítica for 1960 and one of the author's major works. From the perspective of a little girl, it reflects the social and religious hypocrisy of a middle-class family in Santander in the 1930's and effectively develops the themes of absence and silence. It contrasts Tadea's experiences in Santander with the relative freedom of Galicia. First in a projected trilogy, the novel is important for its impeccable style and its vivid portrayal of growing up female in a particular environment.

La última corrida. Barcelona: Noguer, 1958, 226 pp.
    Quiroga's only novel set outside the regions with which she is most familiar (Galicia, Madrid, Santander), this work evokes the arid plain of La Mancha and the world of the bullfight. A third person narration generally views the three bullfighters from without, but the flow of time, from a brief period in the fictive present to an extended remembered past, and the use of multiple perspectives are related to her other novels of the 1950's.

Viento del Norte. Barcelona: Destino, "Ancora y Delfin," no. 58, 1951, 278 pp. (In Colección Premio Nadal, vol. 3, Barcelona: Destino, 1970. Barcelona: Destino, "Destinolibro," no. 198, 1983, ISBN 84-233-1138-4, 278 pp.)
    Nadal Prize-winning novel set in rural Galicia, its linear structure and traditional narrative form in combination with setting led critics erroneously to label it "nineteenth century." The novel

is known for its penetrating psychological study of authentic Galician characters during the pre-Civil War period. Poetic style, and themes of orphanhood, loneliness, and social class distinctions relate it to later novels. Not one of author's major works, it still is her most popular.

PZ

R

RAFAEL MARES KURZ, Carmen de (1911-). Pseud. **Carmen Kurtz.**
   Though from Barcelona, Kurtz writes exclusively in Spanish. She is
an award-winning writer of novels and short stories for both adults and
children (Premio Ciudad de Barcelona, 1954; Premio Planeta, 1956, among
others). At least six movies have been based on her juvenile novels.
Her works have an international perspective: two ancestors were Catalan
emigrants who married women from the U.S., and Carmen married a
Frenchman and lived in France between 1935 and 1943. Her works are more
personal than those of her contemporaries of the Generation of 1954;
effects of war on individuals, relationships between men and women, and
the influence of one's family heritage are common themes in her works.

   Al lado del hombre, Colección Autores Españoles Contemporáneos.
Barcelona: Planeta, 1961, 289 pp. Barcelona: Planeta, 1968, same
collection. Barcelona: Planeta, 1973, Colección Autores Españoles
e Hispanoamericanos, ISBN 84-320-5286-8, 276 pp.
   This is a novel of approximately cyclic form, beginning on a
Wednesday morning, then retracing the events of the previous day and
night until the present. On a train trip from Bilbao to Barcelona, a
young woman becomes acquainted with a middle-aged man. Upon their
arrival in Barcelona, they have a one-night affair. Themes include
the search for self, the romantic experiences of one's youth, and
one's first sexual experience.

   Al otro lado del mar (Sic transit, I). Barcelona: Planeta, 1973,
ISBN 84-320-5286-8, 277 pp.
   This first novel in the trilogy Sic transit introduces the reader
to three generations of the individualistic Roura family and to their
history. Through the doctor-narrator's psychological study of the
grandfather and his children, the theme and problems of aging and old
age are explored, including the guilt and conflicts of the offspring
when the father can no longer care for himself. The title refers to
the ancestors of the family who lived in the Americas and to the desire of the grandson to leave Spain. Possibly available in hardback.

   Las algas. Barcelona: Planeta, 1966, 402 pp. Barcelona: Plaza y
Janés, 1979. Colección El Arca de Papel, ISBN 84-01-41154-8, 312pp.
   This novel treats two interrelated themes. The theme of country
versus city has been expanded to include a confrontation of authenticity with artificiality. While the Costa Brava town of Sescalas
experiences moral and ecological destruction by tourism, the narrator's true, devoted love for a woman from Sescalas is also destroyed

by a woman tourist from the city. Available in both hardback and paper.

El becerro de oro. Barcelona: Planeta, 1964, 379 pp. 2nd ed., Barcelona: Planeta, 1967. Barcelona: Plaza y Janés, 1979, ISBN 84-01-43603-6, 314 pp.
This novel explores the worship of money as the "root of all evil," thus the reference to a golden calf, a false deity. For the few happy characters in the book, money is not an obsession. Most of the problems of the other characters are caused by money or the lack thereof. Available in hardback and paper.

Cándidas palomas. Barcelona: Bruguera, 1975, ISBN 84-02-04420-4, 192 pp.
This short novel about the friendship between a middle-aged woman and a 12-year-old girl is, in fact, an appreciative portrait of Spanish pre-adolescents of the 1970's: their spontaneity, their lack of inhibitions, and their joie de vivre. It also explores the advantages and the loneliness of being unmarried at age 50, and the critical decision whether to accept a proposal of marriage at that age. It won the Premio Ciudad de Barbastro. Available in hardback.

El desconocido. Barcelona: Planeta, 1956, ISBN 84-320-5112-8, 326 pp. Ten printings, the most recent in 1976. Also in Premios Planeta, 1955-1958, Barcelona: Planeta, 1979.
This novel explores the theme of waiting, the effects of 12 years of absence. Antonio Rogers volunteers for the Spanish army to Russia (1942), but is taken prisoner in a Russian concentration camp, 1942-1954. This is an aspect of Spanish history seldom treated in novels of the period. It is narrated from two points of view-- Antonio's and his wife's--their waiting, reunion, and the disillu-sionment due to the fact that they have changed. She views her husband as a stranger, "un desconocido." The novel won the 1956 Planeta Prize. José María Gironella wrote a short prologue to the Premios Planeta edition. Available in hardback.

Detrás de la piedra. Barcelona: Timón, 1958, 282 pp. Madrid: Bullón, 1963, 283 pp. Colección Libros Reno, Barcelona: Plaza y Janés, 1975, ISBN 84-01-43481-5.
This novel presents the stifling, boring provincial life in Spain. The first person narrative is written by a non-conformist middle-class industrial engineer while he is in jail for a crime he did not commit. Set in the late 1940's, the novel presents the themes of prison life (though no political prisoners are specifically men-tioned) and self-delusion. The crisis of being imprisoned awakens the narrator's consciousness to his meaningless existence. "Piedra" in the title refers to the walls of the prison as well as to any social or psychological barriers to self-fulfillment. Paperback.

Duermen bajo las aguas. Barcelona: Planeta, 1954, ISBN 84-320-5110-1. Barcelona: Planeta, 1961. Manantial Series, Barcelona: Plaza y Janés, 1976, ISBN 84-01-46057-3, 312 pp.
In this, her first novel, Carmen Kurtz gives a first-person narrative of the dreams of a young woman for a different life. She is not satisfied with her life as a housewife in France. The effects of World War II on her and on her husband are also shown. One of the

changes is her loving another man while still loving her husband. It
also explores the love of a mother for her child. Many parts of the
novel are autobiographical. Winner of the Premio Ciudad de
Barcelona, 1954, the novel is available in paperback.

En la oscuridad. 1963.
    Finalist in the Premio Café Gijón competition. Unavailable for
review.

En la punta de los dedos. Barcelona: Planeta, 1968, 374 pp.
    This novel reiterates several themes common to Kurtz's novels:
old age, frustration of living in the Spanish provinces, and
loneliness. The frustration of an unhappy marriage and the search
for real love are also explored. The structure is especially
interesting: one character meets another in the street and the
reader follows that new character until another is met or telephoned.
The whole town, therefore, is the protagonist though the omniscient
narrator concentrates on a nucleus of about one dozen people.

Entre dos oscuridades. Barcelona: Planeta, 1969, 285 pp.
Colección Libros Reno, Barcelona: Ediciones G. P., 1979, ISBN
84-01-43609-5, 249 pp.
    The two principal themes of this novel are death and the
circumstances in life which make death a welcome alternative. The
beginning and ending chapters describe the death throes and eventual
death of an executioner, who is remembering five of his victims. The
five middle chapters describe the lives and crimes of those people
executed. In every case the criminals are victims of circumstances
which, they are convinced, can be changed only by murder. There is
some social commentary but the novel is more important as a
psychological study. Available in hard cover and paperback.

Oscar Cosmonauta. Barcelona: Juventud, 1962, 172 pp. 2nd ed.,
1967. 3rd ed., 1975.
    This juvenile novel was a finalist in the Premio Lazarillo
competition of 1963 and received an honorable mention for the Hans
Christian Andersen Prize in the same year. This book begins the long
series of adventure novels about a 12-year-old Catalan boy, Oscar,
who combines reality and fantasy. On Mars, Oscar learns of the
dangers of xenophobia and government oppression--this was written
during the Franco regime. The boy learns on the planet Telo to
respect tolerance. Other messages are warnings about atomic energy
and nuclear war. It is didactic yet enjoyable.

Oscar Espeleólogo. Madrid: Cid, 1966.
    In this children's novel, children learn about spelunking,
archaelogical discoveries, and prehistory. There is also the message
that crime does not pay. Not readily available.

Oscar Espía Atómico. Barcelona: Juventud, 1963. 2nd ed., 1966.
3rd ed., 1975.
    Themes in this children's adventure novel include the dangers of
nuclear energy and the bomb; importance of loyalty to friends. In a
combination of realism, fantasy, and intrigue, blueprints for a new
weapon will be stolen if Oscar (age 12) and his friends do not catch
the thief. Not readily available.

Oscar y el Yeti. Madrid: Cid, 1964.
   A children's adventure novel, its theme is tolerance and
appreciation of other cultures.   A secondary message is that poverty
does not preclude love and happiness in one's family. It is
dedicated to Juan Pablo Goicoechea Matute, son of Ana María Matute,
"que tanto se parece a Oscar." Not readily available.

Piedras y trompetas, ilustrado por Odile Kurz. Barcelona: Noguer,
1981.
   This is a collection of children's stories. Themes include: how
writing began, prejudice, avarice. The message that females should
lead full lives, and not be hampered by stereotypes and tradition is
also found here. Beauty in actions rather than physical beauty is
also extolled. Not readily available.

El regreso (Sic transit, III). Barcelona: Planeta, 1976,
ISBN 84-320-5351-1, 277 pp.
   The third volume in the trilogy Sic transit continues the history
of the Roura and Robert families from their descendants' "return" to
Spain until the present day. It is narrated by Ricardo, the grandson
of the narrator of the second volume. Ricardo has learned from two
generations who regret not expressing their love for their family.
While reviewing and compiling his grandfather's notes, Ricardo
defines and discovers himself. The family cycle begins again as
Ricardo prepares to journey to America to visit his father. Excellent style and psychological analysis are evident throughout the
trilogy. Available in hard cover and paperback.

Siete tiempos. Barcelona: Plaza y Janés, 1964, 319 pp.
   This collection of 27 short stories is divided into seven
"tiempos" or periods of time, some of which also represent themes.
The major themes are death, poverty, love, alienation or loneliness,
and the suffering caused by war. Many also portray village life--its
conformity and the importance of appearances--and those who rebel
against it. Not readily available.

El último camino, Colección Leopoldo Alas, 22. Barcelona: Rocas,
1961, 186 pp. Colección Libro Amigo, 447, Barcelona: Bruguera,
1976, ISBN 84-02-04934-6, 185 pp.
   This collection of short stories is united by the theme of the
bitterness or loneliness of one's later years and the theme of death.
Often the "last road" mentioned in the title is death. In "Los
ángeles se equivocan" an old man feels that the angels have erred in
leaving him alive while his younger friends and family members die.
In "El gamberro" an old artist who is very poor sees his masterpiece
in an exhibition, but is sent away when he insists on touching the
sculpture. Poverty of old people is portrayed repeatedly. Paperback.

El viaje (Sic transit, II). Barcelona: Planeta, 1975,
ISBN 84-320-5327-9, 290 pp.
   This novel is the second volume of the trilogy Sic transit and
explores the psychological and social history of two Catalan
families, the Rouras and the Roberts. This volume explores the
generation which immigrated to the United States and Cuba and their
children born in the New World. It also has historical interest,

giving an outsider's view of the Civil War of the United States and
the conflict over Cuba. Available in hardback.

La vieja ley. Barcelona: Planeta, 1956, 304 pp. 2nd ed., 1967.
    The title refers to "una vieja ley ... que nos obliga a amar, a
ser amados" ("an old law ... which obligates us to love, to be
loved"). If we love one who ignores us or ignore one who loves us,
this is the source of loneliness. The major themes are: the search
for love and happiness, the stifling provincial world of a young
Spanish bourgeois woman in the 1920's through the 1940's, and her
rebellion against that world. An interesting study in perspective,
the novel's first four chapters are written from the point of view of
the four men who care for Victoria; the last six chapters and a short
epilogue are written by Victoria in the first person. Hardback. Not
readily available.

EDM

*RAGUE-ARIAS, Maria-Josep (1941-).
    Collaborator in several periodicals, she has written non-fiction
books in Castilian and a novel in Catalan. She is a member of the
newly-formed group "Mujeres y teatro" whose goal is to encourage women's
participation in all aspects of theater.

    I tornarà a florir la mimosa. Barcelona: 62, 1984,
ISBN 84-297-2183-5, 114 pp.
    The stories in this collection are varied in style and theme. The
author addresses in a very straightforward way the difficult issues
of rape and suicide, as well as those of love, desire, and
motherhood. A pervasive attitude of the author that links them
together is that a love that "no té braços" is what counts--love
must mean freedom. And there is hope, as the title so lyrically
suggests.

KM

*REINA DE MALLORCA (1313-1346).
    Milà i Fontanals identified this poet as being Costança d'Aragó,
daughter of Alfons el Benigne of Catalunya-Aragó and sister of Pere III
el Ceremoniós. She married Jaume III of Majorca. According to Martí
de Riquer, the identity of La Reina de Mallorca could be hidden under
the person of Violant de Vilaragut, the second wife of Jaume III de
Majorca.

    EZ EU AM TAL QU'ES BO E BELH. See: Castellet, J.M., i Molas, J.
Antologia General de la Poesia Catalana. Barcelona: Edicions 62,
1979, ISBN 84-297-1525-8, 298 pp. La Reina Costança de Mallorca,
pp. 25-26.
    The book is a brief example of Catalan poetry since the XIII cen-
tury. It includes the best literary productions of Catalan poetry.

    Manat d'homenatge a La Reina Costança de Mallorca. Barcelona:
Esteve Albert, 1975, ISBN 84-400-8371-8, 64 pp. La Reina Costança de
Mallorca, pp. 5-8.
    The book includes her poem "EZ YEU AM TAL QU'ES BO E BELH."

VC-E

*REQUESENS I DE LIORI, Estefania (?-1549).
     Born in Barcelona, she wrote a series of 90 letters to her mother
describing daily life and details of the society of which she was a
member. The letters were written between 1534 and 1540, and published
in 1942.

                                                                    KM

RESINO DE RON, Carmen.
     She began publishing poetry in literary journals while studying
history at the University of Madrid, after which she resided for some
time in Switzerland, where she became interested in the theatre.
Returning to Spain in the late 1960's, she wrote plays to be produced by
independent theatre groups. She has also written several novels, as yet
unpublished. At present she teaches history in Gijón, Spain. Her work
reflects her interest in contemporary feminist issues as well as the
historian's sense of perspective.

     El presidente (Tragedia en tres actos). Madrid: Quevedo, 1967,
     212 pp.
          A three-act, quasi-historical tragedy set in medieval Scotland,
     the central theme is a search for true democracy. It is a study of
     personal and political idealism manipulated by an ambitious man's
     will to power. A secondary theme concerns the ambiguous role of
     women in the affairs of state. Use of historical setting or figures
     was a frequent censorship-evading device among playwrights in Franco
     Spain. Out of print.

     Ulises no vuelve. Madrid: Instituto Internacional de Teatro, 1983,
     65 pp.
          The Ulysses/Penelope/Telemachus myth is destroyed in this
     contemporary, psychological drama which reflects problems of the
     upper-middle class: the trauma of divorce and the rebelliousness of
     the young. The play derives its main interest from the development
     of two types of emotional conflict, marital and generational, within
     the family. The colloquial dialogue and social theme of the play
     recall the works of the so-called "Realist Generation" of Spanish
     playwrights.

                                                                    HC

*RIERA GUILERA, Carme (1948-).
     She was born in Majorca and lived on the island as a child and later
moved to Barcelona to attend the Universidad de Barcelona. She studied
Filosofía y Letras, her area of specialization being Spanish literature
of the Golden Age. She received a degree as Licenciada en Filología
Hispánica. She is currently working as a professor of Spanish language
at the Universidad Autónoma de Barcelona and also teaches in a high
school. She publishes in many journals and periodicals and has written
a study of Ramón Llull.

     Epitelis tendríssims. Prologue by Aina María Sureda. El Balancí.
     Barcelona: Ed. 62, 1981, ISBN 84-297-1785-4, 120 pp.
          In this collection, with a prologue by Ana María Sureda, there
     are seven stories. The first one has an English title: "As you like,
     darling." The book is a little different from other works by Riera.
     Here we have a group of stories with a humoristic tone and very
     erotic. It is a more open form of narration and takes us into the

senses of the characters. The language has erotic and pleasurable connotations. Easily available in paperback.

Jo pos per testimoni les gavines. Barcelona: Laia, 1977, ISBN 84-722-427-9, 69 pp. 12th ed., 1983.
   Collection of 12 narrations divided in two parts. Part one has the title: "Sòta el signe d'una memòria impenitent." Part two is named: "Bisti de càrrega." The narrations are written with a prose that is very close to lyric speech. Everything is centered on the relationships of female characters. Riera uses a very subjective perspective dealing with her characters. We find in this work many reminiscences of her other collection of narrations: Te deix, amor, la mar com a penyora.

Palabra de mujer, bajo el signo de una memoria impenitente. Prologue by Guillem Frontera. Barcelona: Ed. Laia, 1980, ISBN 84-7222-987-4, 202 pp.
   This is the Spanish translation of some of the narrations of Carme Riera, included in her two books: Te deix, amor, la mar com a penyora, and Jo pos per testimoni les gavines. It has a subtitle: "Under the symbol of an unrepentant memory," which is taken from part one of Jo pos per testimoni les gavines. There is a very melancholic tone in these narrations. They are very subjective. We find frequent references to the sea and other places where the author spent her youth.

Una primavera per a Domenico Guarini. Barcelona: Ed. 62, 1981, ISBN 84-297-1676-9, 190 pp. 6th ed., 1981.
Una primavera para Doménico Guarini. Trans. Luisa Cotoner.
Barcelona: Norte, 1981.
   This novel won the 1980 Premi Prudenci Bertrana. In three parts and an epilogue, it concerns Domenico Guarini, who assaulted the painting "La Primavera" by Botticelli. A Catalan woman reporter goes to Florence to attend his trial and sends reports back to her paper, La Nació. The case becomes part of her life when she discovers that she is starting to solve some of her personal problems along with Guarini's case. It is interesting to observe the combination of colloquial, formal and journalistic style. Available in paperback.

Te deix, amor, la mar com a penyora. Prologue by Guillem Frontera.
Barcelona: Laia, 1975, ISBN 84-7222-420-1, 119 pp.
20th ed., Barcelona: Laia, 1983.
   Collection of short stories. The book is divided in three parts.
1) I a trenc d'alba sempre enyor l'amor, 2) Balcons de tristos somnis, 3) Recomença la dança. In these narrations the author shows us that she is a free writer. The characters act as free people who cannot be part of the conventional society or who refuse the pre-established rules. The narration that names the book tells the story of an adolescent love. The sea was a witness of this love. There are many references of Riera's birthplace, Majorca, and the city. The book is available in paperback. There are 20 editions. Easy to find in bookstores and libraries.

                                                                    MLG-E

RINCON, Maria Eugenia (1926-).
    She was born in San Esteban de Gormaz (Soria). Her poetry deals
mainly with the all encompassing theme of love. Love towards the lover,
love towards the son and love towards the father. In other words, love
is the leitmotif for the meditation of Rincón and through it she will
try to find the meaning of existence. The presence or the absence of
love conforms the driving force of this poetry of obvious autobiographical connotations. The directness of expression and the always well-
contained emotion are two main aspects of the poetry so far published by
Rincón. Her own personal history is the inspiration for her poetry.

    Boca sin tiempo. Provincia, Colección de Poesía, León, 1974, ISBN
    84-00-04073-2, 96 pp.
        In this book of poems Rincón's main theme is: love. The book
    tells a love story that goes from the beginning of the relationship
    to the separation and death. Beyond the possible biographical
    aspects of the book, the importance of it is the way the theme is
    treated. Love is the all-powerful and all-important experience of
    life, and through it, time and death are conquered. Another aspect
    in the development of the theme of love is the characterization of
    the lover (the man), at certain times, as a child needing the care
    and protection of his counterpart (the woman). In this way, then,
    the portrayal of the lover could have only been done by a woman poet.
    Available in paperback, includes biographical note.

    Frontera de la sombra. Madrid: Cultura Hispánica, 1973, ISBN
    84-7232-209-2, 158 pp.
        This book of poems is a meditation on death, life and the passing
    of time. The poet utilizes the death of her own father as the
    vehicle of her reflections about childhood, memories, time,
    friendship, love; in short, death as the central motif of the
    book--the death of a loved one--is the starting point for Rincón's
    meditation. The tone is never dramatic nor desperate, yet, beneath
    the serene countenance of the poems, a deep feeling of anguish
    gravitates powerfully. Rincón writes a poetry almost devoid of
    imagery but, nonetheless, very expressive and emotional.

    Tierra secreta. Valencia: author's own edition, 1962, registration
    number 7136-1961, 82 pp.
        In this first book of poems by Rincón, there are two main themes:
    love and maternity. The poet sings the joy of love and the pain of
    separation. Love, then, is an experience that produces sadness and
    happiness. The theme of maternity appears as an experience that
    liberates the poet from her isolation. In love the complete union
    between the two lovers is impossible, whereas in maternity, the union
    is possible. Maternity, then, appears as the all-encompassing and
    profound human experience. The book contains a preface by Rafael
    Ferreres. Available in paperback.
                                                                    AMF

RIVERA TOVAR, Anunciación (1919-).
    Born in Madrid, she has worked for the government and on newspapers
and magazines.

    Agua estancada. Madrid: Librería de Ferrocarriles, 1963, 382 pp.
    Novel.

Desde mi farol. Madrid: Ed. Gráficas, 1968.
    This collection of novels, short stories, prose poems and poetry
includes: Escenario, 160 pp.; Un hombre a la deriva, 260 pp., and
Agua estancada, 382 pp.

Escenario. Madrid: 1961, 164 pp.
    Short stories, poems and essays.

Un hombre a la deriva. Madrid: Librería de Ferrocarriles, 1963,
260 pp.
    Novel.

La otra guerra de la posguerra. Madrid: Gráficas Yegües, 1968,
230 pp.
    Novel.

Verdades y fantasías. 188 pp.
    Short novel, poems, prose poems.

                                                                    CLG

ROCABERTI, Isabel de (1551-1624). Hipólita de Jesús.
    She entered the monastery when she was 11 and became a Dominican nun
at 16. She taught herself Latin and became well known as a cultivated,
wise, and extremely intelligent person. Most of her work is devoted to
the description and analysis of mystical experiences, written at the
request of her confessor. An unsuccessful attempt to obtain her
beatification took place in 1676. Her works were published by her
nephew, Archbishop Juan Tomás de Rocaberti.

    Libro de su admirable vida y doctrina, que escribió de su mano.
    Valencia: Francisco Mestre, 1679-1685. Ed. by Juan Tomás de
    Rocaberti. Four vols. 351, 279, 348, and 590 pp.
        The first volume contains an engraving that claims to be her true
    portrait. With the exception of the first pages of the first volume,
    Rocaberti uses the third person narrative to refer to her life. She
    describes with vivid images her mystical experiences and allows
    interesting insights into the life of a monastery. She reminds the
    reader of Sor Juana Inés and Saint Teresa of Avila, but her voice is
    unique.

                                                                    RDP

*RODOREDA I GURGUI, Mercè (1909-1983).
    A native of Barcelona, where she collaborated on many periodicals
before the Civil War, she developed her career as a narrative writer
during her exile in Geneva. She has been recognized as one of the
greatest Catalan writers, and her works have received the most important
prizes of Catalan literature: Creixelles (1937), Víctor Català (1957),
Premi d'Honor de las Lletres Catalanes (1980) and Ciudad de Barcelona
(1981). In her novels and short stories, women are confronted with both
their family life and the political reality of Spain. The result is a
very personal and profound meditation about the human condition.   AC

    Aloma. Original version not published, 1937. Revised version.
    Barcelona: Edicions 62, 1969. Reedited in Obres Completes.
    Barcelona: Edicions 62, 1976-1978, Vol. I.
        The first of Rodoreda's novels (1937), although not published

until 1969, Aloma contains the most characteristic elements of the
author's style. It is a narration inscribed in the pre-war years of
Barcelona. Rodoreda develops here an acute exploration of daily life
with very poetic language. Aloma, a character who is at the same
time weak and full of strength, lives in an aggressive world vividly
in contrast with her peaceful attitude toward living.   AC

El carrer de les Camèlies. Barcelona: Club dels novel.listes, 1966.
In Obres Completes. Barcelona: Edicions 62, 1976-1978, Vol. II.
   This novel is very much related to La Plaça del Diamant. Both
works portray women of extraordinary sensuality. El carrer de les
Camèlies tells the story of Cecilia, her ideas of the world, her
frustrated love affairs, her solitude. However, in spite of those
similarities, El carrer adds new elements to the narrative of
Rodoreda: there is a more detailed study of the picaresque and also
a different presentation of the theme of love.   AC

Jardí vora el mar. Barcelona: Club dels novel.listes, 1967.
In Obres Completes. Barcelona: Edicions 62, 1976-1978, Vol. II.
   In the whole of the literary production of Rodoreda, this is an
atypical novel; the main character is not a woman but an old male
gardener, who tells from outside the story of a love triangle. This
device, the introduction of a narrator inside the novel, gives the
opportunity for an objective approach to the topics that Rodoreda
uses. Nevertheless, it is possible to find in this work the
nostalgia, tenderness and sense of tragedy peculiar to the author.
Jardí is also atypical because it is not intended to be a realistic
novel, in the way that La Plaça del Diamant and El carrer de les
Camèlies are, for example.   AC

La meva Cristina i altres contes. Barcelona: Edicions 62, 1967.
In Obres Completes. Barcelona: Edicions 62, 1976-1978, Vol. II.
My Christina and Other Stories. Trans. and with an introduction by
David H. Rosenthal. Port Townsend, WA: Graywolf Press, 1984.
   This collection of short stories can be characterized for its
inherent unity. The language is more dense than in other works by
Rodoreda; the book is built not upon descriptions, but upon
suggestions or allusions. The stories are not realistic, but rather
imaginative; in a way, they create a new reality in which humankind
moves toward a pantheistic death.   AC

Mirall trencat. Barcelona: Club Editor, 1974.
   This novel is more complex than any other of Rodereda. It does
not deal with a main character, but with the history of a family from
the beginning of the century until the years after the Civil War.
The world depicted here is sophisticated, full of refinement, and the
language used to describe it is rich and, one could say, baroque.
The most relevant topic of the book is death; it is seen with
desolation and impotence, but also related to magic.   AC

La Plaça del Diamant. Barcelona: Club dels Novel.listes, 1962.
Reedited in Obres Completes. Barcelona: Edicions 62, 1976-1978,
Vol. I.
La Plaza del Diamante. Trans. Enrique Sordo. Barcelona: EDHASA,
1965.
The Pigeon Girl. Trans. Eda O'Shield. London: Deutsch, 1967.

The Time of the Doves. Trans. and introduction by David Rosenthal. New York: Taplinger, 1983.
    Rodoreda's best known novel, it has been translated into several languages. As in previous works, we find an apparently simple description of daily life, in this case from the point of view of Natàlia, a lower-class woman. The novel deals with her life, destroyed both by war and her husband. It is a very brave approach to these themes, frequently neglected. Together with the richness of ideas goes a remarkable use of language, which make La Plaça del Diamant a classic in Spanish literature. This novel is the basis of a film by the same name.   AC

Semblava de seda i altres contes. Barcelona: Edicions 62, 1978.
    This book is another collection of stories, some of which had already been published separately in several literary magazines. It continues the tradition of La meva Cristina i altres contes, and is full of lyricism and fantasy. There is also an interest in themes like love, death, solitude, etc. already seen in other books written by Rodoreda, although here they are treated with a profound density.
                                                                        AC

Quanta, quanta guerra. Barcelona: Club Editor, 1980.
    The first novel by Rodoreda which has a male protagonist, its structure is that of a Bildüngsroman, or apprenticeship to life. In the literary tradition of the voyage as life, Adrià learns the lesson of the importance of solidarity. With the war in the foreground of the novel throughout, it is the vision of a mother carrying her dead child, refusing to believe he is dead, that represents a turning point for Adriá. Adriá returns home at the end, and we are left with the hopeful image of a rising sun.   KM

Viatges i flors. Barcelona: Edicions 62, 1980.
    Some of these stories were written in Geneva during Rodoreda's exile, and some in Romanyà, Spain. They are all narrated with great fantasy and imagination, and, although humor is combined with a pathetic tone, a deep pessimism pervades the whole work. Pessimism is a vital attitude that leads in these stories to a need to escape. AC

Vint-i-dos contes. Barcelona: Selecta, 1957. Reedited in Obres Completes. Barcelona: Edicions 62, 1976-1978, Vol. I.
    The Víctor Català Prize winner in 1957, Vint-i-dos contes shows a great variety of narrative techniques, but an impressive thematic unity. In these 22 short stories, women seem to have the same problematic relationships with the world as Aloma. The difference is that the society here reflected is that of the Spanish post-war. With this work, written in a very reflective tone, begins the so-called mature period in Rodoreda's writing.   AC

*ROIG I FRANSITORRA, Montserrat (1946-).
    Born in Barcelona, Montserrat Roig graduated in 1968 from the University of Barcelona, where she later taught. A well-known journalist and television interviewer, Roig has published several collections of her interviews as well as a study of Catalans in Nazi concentration camps, a report on Leningrad during World War II, and a book of feminist essays. Between 1970 and 1980 she wrote in Catalan a collection of short stories and four novels, all of which appeared in

Spanish translations from 1980 to 1983. Her journalistic training is reflected both in her literary style and the strong sense of contemporary chronicle found in her fiction.

L'hora violeta. Barcelona: Edicions 62, "El Balancí," 1980, ISBN 84-297-1667-X, 232 pp. Reprinted in 1980 and 1981, same series. La hora violeta. Trans. Enrique Sordo. Barcelona: Argos Vergara, 1980, ISBN 84-7178-398-3, 269 pp.
   The fictional biographies of the Miralpeix and the Ventura-Claret families from her previous novels are blended with political and feminist considerations. Roig includes a variety of sexual relationships with greater frankness than in her previous works, attesting to the increase in personal freedom in Spain after the death of Franco. Roig continues to present a collection of portraits of unfulfilled and frustrated females and to favor a disjointed narrative structure incorporating diaries written by her characters.

Molta roba i poc sabó. Barcelona: Selecta, 1971. Barcelona: Edicions 62, "El Cangur," 1978, ISBN 84-297-1386-7, 186 pp. Reprinted in the same series at least five times. Aprendizaje sentimental. Trans. Mercedes Nogués. Barcelona: Argos Vergara, 1981, ISBN 84-7178-328-2, 198 pp.
   A collection of short stories with a prologue by Joan Fuster dated 1978 and two brief biographical commentaries prepared by the author. Almost all of the stories are preceded by quotations taken primarily from foreign authors. Despite these and other indications of cosmopolitanism, Roig writes a documentary of contemporary Spanish society. She collects a series of fictional chronicles on the banal Barcelona middle class and its stagnating young adults bred during the Franco regime. The introduction to love announced in the book's title fails to provide her protagonists with any sense of meaning for their lives.

L'òpera quotidiana. Barcelona: Planeta, "Ramon Llull," 1982, ISBN 84-320-3508-4, 210 pp. La ópera cotidiana. Trans. Enrique Sordo. Barcelona: Planeta, 1983, ISBN 84-320-7164-1, 223 pp.
   As in a musical opera, the characters of this novel pronounce arias and cavatinas and start duets in an attempt to tell their life story and divulge their intimate feelings. They are for the most part people who through love try to escape from their boring and unsatisfactory daily existence. Roig creates one of her most fully developed male characters. Unlike her female creations, he is unable to surrender himself to love with total devotion. The disparate personal stories are held together by the recurrent conversations between Horaci Duc and his landlady Patricia Miralpeix.

Ramona, adéu. Barcelona: Edicions 62, "El Balancí," 1972. Barcelona: Edicions 62, "El Cangur," 1976, ISBN 84-297-1221-6, 166 pp. Ten reprintings by 1981. Ramona, adiós. Trans. Joaquim Sempere. Barcelona: Argos Vergara, 1980, ISBN 84-7017-978-0, 190 pp.
   Using third-person narration and a diary format, Roig interweaves the stories of three women sharing the same name and born into three successive generations of the same family. The family structure allows the author to record three different periods in Catalan

history while at the same time examining the consistencies and changes among the lives of separate individuals. The youngest Ramona dares to rebel against the social conventions of her class and the posture of passivity of her elders but not without realizing the new problems that emancipation brings. A strong sense of sociological document underlies the entire novel.

El temps de les cireres. Barcelona: Edicions 62, "El Balancí," 1977, ISBN 84-297-1282-8, 240 pp. Nine reprintings by 1981.
Tiempo de cerezas. Trans. Enrique Sordo. Barcelona: Argos Vergara, 1980, ISBN 84-7017-854-7, 245 pp.
   Roig continues the family saga she began in her previous novel. Here the author's interest centers upon a 40-year-old woman's return to the family she ran away from 12 years before. Mixed feelings of apprehension and affection converge as the protagonist observes her various family members, who, for differing reasons, remain distant strangers to her. Roig paints a melancholy picture of a set of psychologically lost people for whom the happy "time of cherries" of the book's title has disappeared.

                                                                CGB

ROMERO SERRANO, Marina (1908-).
   Born in Madrid, Marina Romero was educated at the Instituto Escuela. With a degree from the Escuela Normal de Maestros and a Smith College scholarship, she went to the United States in 1935, where she earned an M.A. at Mills College and taught at Douglass College from 1938 until 1970. Her early poetry--Poemas "A" and Nostalgia de mañana--reflects the heavy influence of the Generation of 1927, especially Pedro Salinas, in its rhetorical and lyrical playfulness and neo-popular strains. In Presencia del recuerdo, Midas and Sin agua, el mar, significantly, all written in exile though published in Spain, Romero attains a greater luminosity and depth through a simplicity of style in this most personal and intimate of poetry. Her last books have been written for children. The poet now resides in Madrid.

   Alegrías. Poemas para niños. Preface by Eugenio Florit.
   Salamanca: Anaya, 1972, ISBN 84-207-0884-4, 150 pp. Madrid:
   Escuela Española, 1980, ISBN 84-331-0111-0, 55 pp. (a selection of 1972 ed.).
      Dedicated to all children, "para que sigan soñando" ("so they may keep on dreaming"), this illustrated collection of poems focuses on the child's love for animals. Using techniques of repetition, alliteration and similar sounding phonemes unconnected semantically, the poet suggests the delightfully irrational and imaginative world of childhood. The clarity and lightness of line--"¡¡Puertas del aire, abrid las alas!!" ("Doors of air/open your wings!!"), she writes--further Romero's invention of a child-like language.
   In December 1979, 20 of these poems were adapted by composer Antón García Abril as a "Cantata- Divertimento" (at the Teatro Real de Madrid) for the International Year of the Child (see RCA, Long Play, Emisión por Radio Nacional, 1982).

   Campanillas del aire. Poemas para niños. Madrid: Escuela
   Española, 1981, ISBN 84-331-0141-2, 48 pp.
      Thirty poems for children, previously published in the 1972 collection Alegrías. Sample titles are: "Elefante," "Toro,"

"Gavilán," "Gato Montés," "Búho," "Caracol," and "Delfín," each
one dedicated to well-loved figures of literature and fantasy and
other inventions (the Ugly Duckling, Martín Fierro, Ali Baba, etc.).
With a prologue by the author, in which she writes, "Para vosotros
todos, chicas y chicos, y hasta para los grandes, la alegría y el
gozo de estos poemas para que sigáis soñando" ("For all of you,
boys and girls, and even adults, the happiness and pleasure of these
poems so that you may contine to dream"). Illustrated. Paper.

Midas. Poema de amor. Madrid: Insula, 1954, ISBN 84-7185-057-5,
82 pp.
    Midas, though composed of 53 separate poems, may be read as a
single, long poem. It begins with "Oro," a canticle to the full and
joyous possesion of love. But it ends with the melancholy "Ya no sé
qué decir," the last step of an inner voyage through passion and its
loss. Though the sense of plenitude disappears in Midas--"Ya no
sabré las calles/sin tu andar" ("I will no longer know the streets/
without your step")--in the concluding lines, the poet preserves
through language itself the essence of her experience: "Ya quedas
para siempre/creado en mi palabra,/y no habrá lenta gota/que logre
emanciparte" ("You remain forever/created in my word/and there will
be no slow drop/which can succeed in freeing you"). Paper.

Nostalgia de mañana. México: Rueca, 1943, 89 pp.
    Poems written between 1930 and 1943. The first group (1930-35)
displays a lightness of touch and playfulness of rhythm and word
which probably reflect the influence of the Generation of 1927. In
the second group (1938-43), we sense a deepening of tone and feeling,
anticipation Midas and Presencia del recuerdo. Love and its absence
are expressed temporally as the desire to write "un presente/que no
existe" ("a present/which does not exist"), and reiterated by the
poet's projecting herself into a future "con fuerza de presente"
("with the force of the present").

Paisaje y literatura de España. Antología de los escritores del
98. Estudio preliminar y fotografías en color de Marina Romero.
Prólogo de Julián Marías. Madrid: Tecnos, 1957, ISBN
84-309-0313-5, 430 pp.
    This is an early example of the attempt to fuse literature and
accompanying color photographs into a single aesthetic experience.
The experiment, says Julián Marías in his prologue, "El paisaje y
la imaginación exacta," is fraught with implicit difficulties, but
the photographer/writer manages to capture the spirit of the
Generation of 1898 (selected are Unamuno, Azorín, Baroja, Antonio
Machado, Valle-Inclán, Juan Ramón Jiménez, and Juan Maragall)
through a pictorial feel for specific landscapes. In her "Estudio
preliminar," Romero remarks that the book also responds to deeply
felt pedagogical needs. Winner of the Premio INLE.

Poemas "A". Madrid: Asociación de Alumnas de la Residencia. Imp.
S. Aguirre, 1935, 34 leaves, n. pag.
    Her first book of poetry, now extremely rare, was written at the
height of the poesía pura of Guillén and other poets of the period.
It delights in a kind of verbal virtuosity, while at the same time
exploiting the simplicity of popular rhythms and imagery. The
serious themes as the passing of time and personal grief. Some of

these poems were later collected in <u>Nostalgia de mañana</u>.

<u>Presencia del recuerdo</u>. Madrid: Insula, 1952, ISBN 84-7185-063-X,
98 pp.
    Dedicated to the memory of Pedro Salinas, this book of poems also
reveals Salinas' influence in its style and themes. Written with de-
ceptive simplicity and clarity, the poems abound with tightly constructed paradoxes redolent of <u>La voz a ti debida</u> and other Salinas
works, such as "mi querer no queriendo," "y tú no estás, estando,"
and "la muerte/te hace más presente." Major themes are time and
death, the memory of lost love, and the poet's solitude. Paper.

<u>Sin agua, el mar</u>. Madrid: Agora, 1961, 55 pp.
    Consisting of 33 pieces numbered backwards, this is a collection
of intensely wrought, <u>intimiste</u> poems in which the writer's
out-of-synch feelings with the world are balanced by the need to
reach out toward both the human and the divine. Working along
traditional lines in her view of life as a form of dying--"Esta
prolongada muerte,/o esta acortada vida"--("this prolonged death/or
this life cut short")--Romero establishes a parallel paradox as well
about existence as "este estar sin ser." Seeking communication
beyond herself, she discovers that "el hombre no dialoga," that "dos
y dos/son cinco ..." ("two and two/are five") in human relationships.
The last poem, written as a prayer, reflects and summarizes her
anguish and despair. Paper.

                                                                    NMV

ROMA, Rosa (1940-).
    Born in Valencia, Romá is best known for her 1971 critical study of
Ana María Matute (Madrid: EPESA). She has also adapted novels for
television.

<u>La maraña de los cien hilos</u>. Barcelona: Destino, 1976.
    This novel follows its female protagonist through school, growing
up, and marriage, through flashbacks and interior monologue.

<u>Mujer, realidad y mito</u>. Barcelona: Plaza y Janés, 1979.
    With as much breadth, if not as much scholarship, as Simone de
Beauvoir, Romá analyzes the history and character of women,
attitudes toward them, and their role in society, particularly their
place in contemporary Spanish society. The chapter titles indicate
the subjects treated: for example, "La feminidad como ente
literario," "La inevitable penuria," "En busca de un salario," "La
mujer como productora de arte," "Devoradora maternidad," "No hay que
perder la esperanza." Romá discusses the inadequate education
received by Spanish girls; they are educated to "be women," not to
freely choose a career. There is also a brief survey of laws
specifically in reference to women. Paperback.

                                                                    CLG

ROMO ARREGUI, Josefina (1913-).
    Josefina Romo has spent her entire career between her poetry and her
academic research, publishing several anthologies and monographs of
Spanish writers and volumes of her poems. She received a doctorate from
the University of Madrid in 1944 for her prize-winning dissertation on
Gaspar Núñez de Arce. While still living in Spain, she contributed to

the work of the Consejo Superior de Investigaciones Científicas (including the Cuadernos de Literatura Contemporánea) and founded and edited the literary magazine Alma. Since the 1950's she has been a Spanish literature professor at the University of Connecticut and is a past-president of the Academia de la Lengua Española de Nueva York.

Acuarelas, no venal. Madrid, 1935.

Aguafuertes y otros poemas, no venal. Madrid, 1940.

Autoantología. New York: Academia de la Lengua Española de Nueva York, 1968, 117 pp.

Cántico de María Sola. 1946-1948. Edición de lujo limitada y numerada. Madrid: J. Romo Arregui, 1950, 59 pp.
   Cántico de María Sola, named for the first entry of this collection, is divided symmetrically into nine cánticos, nine sonetos and nine poemas. "María Sola" is Romo herself speaking in the first person, often in the form of an interior dialogue. Companionless, childless and friendless, her parents dead and her siblings estranged, she finds herself profoundly alone (hence, sola) in these melancholy poems. Of particular interest is her poem "Ciudad" in which she describes her paseo through a foreign city, probably New York, a city which was to loom large in her future.

Elegías desde la orilla del triunfo. New York, 1964.

Isla sin tierra. New York, 1955.

Larga soledad definitiva. Ensayos. (In preparation in 1979 - no confirmation of publication.)

La peregrinación inmóvil. Versos de _____; ilustraciones de Josefina Brú. Madrid: Talleres de Gráfica Universal, 1932, 82 pp. Reprinted 1934?
   Romo explains in her preliminary poem that this "peregrinación inmóvil" describes her flights of imagination. The book, with prologue by Rafael Villaseca, is divided into five sections titled jirones, místicas, romancillos, pétalos and tríptico romántico. As these titles suggest, her poems are intensely personal, always melancholy, sometimes fanciful and often religious, which find their reflection in images from nature. Here is an example:
   Llevo dentro del alma un amor a las cosas,
   que es la esencia suprema de mi amor a la vida
   mientras haya jazmines y pomas olorosas,
   !qué importa que la dicha para mí esté perdida!
   (I carry within my soul a love of things,
   which is the supreme essence of my love of life
   while there are jasmines and sweet-smelling apples
   what does it matter that happiness for me is lost!

Poemas de América. Madrid, 1967.

Romancero triste, no venal. Madrid, 1936.

NJM

*ROSSELLO I MIRALLES, Coloma (1875-1955).
She wrote <u>Valledemossines</u> (1911), a series of "quadres de costums."
She also wrote two unpublished plays; <u>Asprors</u> (in Catalan) and <u>Salve
Regina</u> (in Castilian).

KM

*RUBIES, Anna (1881-1963).
Born in Port de la Selva, she wrote stories for children and
collected legends from her area.

KM

RUBIO GAMEZ, Fanny (1948-).
A poet, she holds a Doctorate in Romance philology and is Professor
of literature at the Complutense University in Madrid. She lectures and
writes on Spanish poetry.

<u>Comentarios de texto</u>. 1976.

<u>Hiperión</u>. 1977.

<u>Primeros poemas</u>. 1966.

NLB

RUBIO Y LOPEZ GUIJARRO, María del Carmen (1915-).
Born in Ibi, Philippine Islands, of a Spanish father and an American
mother, this poet and novelist has collaborated on several literary
magazines such as <u>Gemma</u>, <u>Clarín</u>, and <u>El Erîa</u>. She is an honorary
member of the Centro Cultural Literario y Artístico AGA de Aranguren
(Vizcaya). When the Civil War began, she was a <u>maestra nacional</u>, and
the school where she taught was burned to the ground. Her literary
concerns are the Civil War and its devastating effects (particularly as
seen from the point of view of the victors), conjugal and family life,
particularly the conflict between generations, and the maintenance of
existing social structures. Favorite themes are the need for
resignation in the face of disappointment and pain, and acceptance of
one's destiny. Her writing is somewhat didactic and has a strong
spiritual orientation.

<u>Extraña noche de bodas</u>. Aranguren, Vizcaya: El Paisaje, 1981,
ISBN 84-85956-08-7, 75 pp.
A short novel set in Madrid and Toledo, the sentimental story of
romantic intrigue takes place in the present, but is rooted in the
Civil War and its aftermath. A friendship between Diana and Lita,
two bourgeois women, frames the story of Lita's relationship with
Juan Antonio whose betrayal by his bride on their wedding night provides the story's title. His erratic behavior and mysterious past
confuse and intrigue Lita, but all obstacles preventing their union
are eventually swept aside by circumstances, and they are able to
marry and form the home they have both longed for. Sympathy for the
male protagonist, unquestioning acceptance of the double standard and
code of honor lead to a predictable ending.

<u>Hojas sueltas que lleva el viento</u>.
Poetry.

<u>Margarita y sus problemas</u>.

Una mujer maltratada por el destino.

Por los senderos de la vida. Madrid: Artigrafia, 1977,
ISBN 84-400-3926-X, 77 pp.
    A collection of 46 poems dedicated to their majesties the King and
Queen of Spain, to the exiled, and to peace. The introductory poem
exhorts the reader to utilize the brief time allotted to human beings
on earth in the practice of Christian ideals. Varied themes: war
and peace, love and disillusionment, life's brevity, suffering and
sublimation, the cycle of life and death, nature, children.

El precio del perdón. Bilbao: Editores Comunicación Literaria de
Autores, 1981, ISBN 84-228-0190-6, 176 pp.
    In this novel set at the beginning of the Civil War, Cristina is
an unhappily married woman who loses her maids when they go into the
mountains to fight with the Republicans. Before she had married Juan
Armengol, an aviator, she was involved with Fernando, who then
married Elena, Cristina's friend. Later on, Cristina learns that
Juan and Elena are having an affair, but she's so happy with her
children, that she suffers silently until she learns that her husband
has abandoned her and sent their eldest sons, Alfonso and Andrés, to
Russia. Her efforts to recover her children are finally rewarded
several years after the war when Juan, who has been living in Mexico
with Elena and their children, sends for Alfonso and Andrés. Their
father, who can't bear to see them motherless, and plagued by the
guilt of having abandoned them, finally grants permission to Elena to
leave Spain and join the boys in Colombia, where he has sent them to
avoid an unpleasant confrontation between his former and present
wives. All conflicts are resolved at the end, and all is forgiven
and forgotten, as Alfonso announces his engagement to Luci, a young
Spanish woman he had met in Russia.

La rebeldía de los hijos. Historia de una familia (1936-1966).
Aranguren, Vizcaya: El Paisaje, 1982, ISBN 84-85956-41-9, 154 pp.
    The plot of this novel set during the Civil War and after is
narrated through the diary of Elena, a young woman whose family is
living in Madrid at a refugee center with several other families,
which consist solely of women and children, as all adult men are
either fighting or missing. The plot centers around Elena's
clandestine relationship with Alberto, a young militiaman whom she
marries when she becomes pregnant before the end of the war. Neither
Elena's nor Alberto's mother accepts their union at first, but as
time goes by, these conflicts are resolved. The story traces Elena's
reactions to the war, the birth of their eight children, including a
deformed child who later dies, and the development of her relationship with her husband and children. Themes are the ignorance of the
Spanish people with respect to the politics of the Civil War, the
day-to-day physical and emotional deprivation and anxiety caused by
the war, the insecurity of its aftermath, the impatience of the young
and their unwillingness to postpone gratification of their natural
desires, the importance of parent-child communication and mutual
understanding. This novel was awarded the "El Erfa" prize in 1981.

Relatos de una prisión. Madrid: published by the author, 1982.
                                                            PTI

S

*SAAVEDRA, Anna Maria de (1905-).
  Born in Vilafranca del Penedès, she has published poetry in periodicals such as Hèlix, L'amic de les arts, La revista, Revista de poesia.

KM

SABUCO DE NANTES BARRERA, Oliva (1562-ca. 1622).
  Born in Alcaraz (Albacete), daughter of Bachiller Miguel Sabuco and his first wife, Francisca de Cózar, she was married to Acacio de Buedo at age 18, but used her two baptismal godmother's last names. The coexistence of contemporary educated women makes her case unusual only in that her field was medicine. In another sense, her controversial work is unique. Nueva Filosofía and Vera Medicina give the author as Doña Oliva Sabuco. However, several male historians in this century claim that the first book was written by her father who signed with his daugh- ter's name "to give her honor." Allusions regarding Vera medicina center on her possible Moorish blood, which make historians' claims of the godfather's authorship--himself reputedly Moorish--more incomprehensible. Given the persecution of women, "moriscos," and false physicians in sixteenth-century Spain, these arguments raise additional questions not answered to date.

  Nueva filosofía de la naturaleza del hombre. Ed. Pedro Madrigal con privilegio. Madrid: 1587. Ed. Pedro Madrigal, Madrid: 1588. Ed. João Lobo D'Albito, Imprenta de Fructuoso Lourenço de Basto, Braga: 1620. Ed. Martín Martínez, incomplete edition, Madrid: 1728. Ed. Rivadeneira, Biblioteca del P. Rivadeneira, Obras escogidas de filósofos españoles, vol. LXV, selected chapters, Madrid: 1847. Ed. Dr. Guardia, incomplete edition in French, Paris: 1886. Ed. Octavio Cuartero, Imprenta de Ricardo Fé, Madrid: 1888, 437 pp.
  The work is divided in four "coloquios" where three shepherds argue the merits of empirical training and self knowledge against Galenic, Hippocratic and Arabic theories. In addition to a Preface stressing the value of knowledge and ethical behavior, there is a dedicatory letter to King Philip II and another to the Count of Barajas soliciting protection against plagiarists. A Glossary in Latin and in two parts titled "Dicta Brevia" recapitulates the work. It is in the dedication to King Philip where we find: "As unusual and new is this book as it is it its author." Some modern historians claim that it was written by her father. The first two chapters establish the cosmological framework of human existence. The third and fourth directly deal with medical issues. More intuitive than

strictly scientific, these chapters are observations on nature, anatomy, nutrition, laws, and social structure. Of interest to scholars, particularly medical historians.

Vera medicina y vera filosofía, oculta a los antiguos, en dos diálogos. Ed. Pedro Madrigal, Madrid: 1587. 2nd ed., Pedro Madrigal, Madrid: 1588. 3rd ed., Ed. João Lobo D'Albito, Imp. de Fructuoso Lourenço de Basto, Brago: 1620. Last known edition, Ed. Octavio Cuartero, Imp. de Ricardo Fé, Madrid: 1888.
    Divided into 25 small chapters in dialogue form, it is a polemical attack on contemporary medical practices and theories. Possibly this work, included in most editions as part of the Nueva filosofía (pp. 222-344), was considered by its author as a separate one. Vera medicina enjoyed a revival in the nineteenth century that recognized its pioneering hypotheses about the physiology of the nervous system which predate Bichat, George Enst, Warton, Charles Lepois, and others. Perhaps the work's greatest contribution is the discovery, albeit not systematized, of the psychosomatic relationship between passions and emotions. It is also a striking document about the Spanish society as it was in the second half of the sixteenth century. Some male historians recently claim that this book was written by Doña Oliva's godfather because "it couldn't have been written by a woman." Of interest to scholars, feminists and historians.

PFCG

SAENZ-ALONSO, Mercedes (1917-).
    From a noble family of San Sebastián, Sáenz-Alonso credits her lettered father as her mentor. Her studies in Filosofía y Letras were interrupted by the Civil War. She began as a journalist then went on to write post-war realistic novels. Best known for her book on Don Juan, she is also a professor (U. Navarra) and international lecturer (art, history, literature), literary critic, founder of radio programming, director of cultural and professional organizations (often in her home region) and newspaper correspondent. She has won prizes for her essays, criticism, short stories, and journalism.

Altas esferas. Barcelona: L. de Caralt, 279 pp.
    During World War II, Loretta Sheridan, a minor character in Bajos fondos, moves through a troubled Europe with undercover agents and the elite, making her way to high places. Embittered by the misery she suffered as a child, she betrays England and commits parricide. The author acknowledges the critical help of Cela and others in her dedication. The theme of home and family prevails. Available in a few U.S. libraries.

Bajos fondos. Barcelona: L. de Caralt, 1949, 291 pp.
    Set in London before World War II, this first novel of Sáenz-Alonso takes place in a poverty-stricken neighborhood. Four very different family groups live in the same building, giving the work its labyrinthine collection of characters, some of them monstrous. Altas esferas is the companion piece to this work. As in all her novels, the theme of the family is dominant. Very hard to find.

Breve estudio de la novela española. San Sebastián: Caja de Ahorros Provincial de Guipúzcoa, 1972, 157 pp.
    Critical study.

Del Bósforo a Gibraltar. San Sebastián: Agora, 1963, 108 pp.
    Travel book.

Del Molino al Minarete. Madrid: Afrodisio Aguado.
    Travel book.

Don Juan y el donjuanismo. Madrid: Guadarrama, 1969, ISBN
84-250-0089-0, 330 pp. (Punto Omega; Colección universitaria de
bosillo, 89) "Apéndice;" Don Juan y su interpretación en la
música, por Javier Bello Portú.
    The author calls this work an "essay" and considers it her best.
In 38 chapters of objective and erudite examination she deals with
all that Don Juan encompasses--in Spain and other countries--
resisting previous definitions of the phenomenon. Her thesis is that
he is a vital force, an intelligent and recklessly brave man who is
directed toward woman as the destiny of his existence. Winner of the
Premio Guipúzcoa, 1969. Readily available. Paperback.

Hekate.Noche.Muerte.Mujer. Ed. Seminarios-Hora H.
    Study of witchcraft.

La pequeña ciudad. Barcelona: L. de Caralt, 1952, 222 pp.
    A small-town, middle-class pharmacist is driven by his
disproportionate aspiration to succeed as a writer and is almost
destroyed by failure. His upper-class friend, a painter, accepts the
same frustration with resignation. The novel is centered around the
family. Available in a few U.S. libraries through OCLC.

La Poesía Pre-renacentista española. Ed. Nacional.
    Critical study.

El tiempo que se fue. Barcelona: L. de Caralt, 1951,
ISBN 84-217-1542-9, 437 pp.
    Set in San Sebastián, it is a novel of the evolution of customs
and way of life that affects a noble Basque family. While the
destruction of war is in part the cause for this change, the author
sees a greater menace in the alteration and possible collapse of the
institution of the home. The world can regain its vanishing
spirituality by recalling the home as the site of love and moral
principles. Her prologue calls this novel a "canto" to the home of a
time that once was. Forward by José Berruezo. Recent ISBN
indicates availability. Also in some U.S. libraries.

                                                              GM

SAEZ DE MELGAR, Faustina (1834-1895).
    She became a widely known writer for her newspaper articles and
stories in El trono y la nobleza, La antorcha, La época, La guirnalda,
La mujer, and El correo de la moda where her controversial story La cruz
del olivar first appeared (1867). She was the founder and editor of La
violeta (1862-1866), La canastilla de la infancia and Paris charmant
(sic)(1884). Her writings exuded a highly sentimental and romantic
style atacked by Pérez Galdós, who wrote a parody of her novel in La
desheredada.

    La cruz del olivar.
        Once upon a time an old childless couple, the servant guardians of

a duke's castle, found a baby girl abandoned in a mud puddle near the
Cross of the Olive Grove (title of the story). She was given the
name of María and although raised in poverty and distress she became
a virtuous, beautiful lady. While she was expected to marry Manolo,
a peasant, she meets the son of the Marquis of Torrente whom she
adores in secret. At the end of the novel it is discovered that
María is the child of the count of Silo, Lucía, who had been
kidnapped by some gypsies and abandoned by the cross of the olive
grove. She marries the marquis and they live happily ever after.
Published in an annex of Anales Galdosianos, 1980, the novelette
is of interest to scholars and those fond of romantic stories.

AR

*SALES FOLCH, Núria (1933-).
   Poet from Barcelona, she has published Exili a Playamuertos (1961)
and Història dels mossos d'Esquadra (1962).

KM

SALISACHS, Mercedes (1916-). Pseud. María Ecín.
   Born in Barcelona, this Catalan author studied business in the
Escuela de Comercio and married in 1935. Under the pseudonym María
Ecín, her first novel was published in 1955 (Primera mañana, última
mañana). The following year she was a finalist for the Premio Planeta,
as she was again in 1973. Her most famous novel, La gangrena, won the
same prize in 1975. In addition she has won the Premio Ciudad de Barcelona (1957) and the Premio Ateneo de Sevilla (1983). Other important
commercial and critical successes include La presencia and La sinfonía
de las moscas. Many of her novels have been translated into English,
French, Italian, German, Portuguese, Finnish, and Swedish.   EDM

   Adagio confidencial. Barcelona: Planeta, 1973, ISBN 84-320-5288-4,
   269 pp. Finalista Premio Planeta 1973. 1st ed. in Popular Planeta,
   Barcelona: Planeta, 1976, ISBN 8432021237, 209 pp. 2nd ed., 1977.
   3rd ed., 1982.   EDM

   Carretera intermedia. Colección gigante. Barcelona: Luis de
   Caralt, 1956, 223 pp. Colección Autores españoles e hispanoamericanos, 2nd ed., Barcelona: Planeta, 1969, 285 pp. 3rd ed., Barcelona: Planeta, 1969, 284 pp. French translation.
      This novel was a finalist for the Premio Planeta. Set on the
   Riviera, it is the story of Bibiana, a homely woman of 40, who has
   just recovered from a nervous breakdown suffered after the tragic
   accidental death of her child and the subsequent abandonment by her
   husband. She was also abandoned by the man she loved, who, because
   of religious scruples, did not sexually consummate that love.
   Bibiana is a unique protagonist for the period in that she has a
   profession; she is a chemist; but, although her profession played
   some role in her past--her husband accused her of neglecting their
   child for her laboratory--it is not important in the action of the
   narrative. There is more concern with the depiction of her loveless
   marriage, of her earlier reluctance to embark on an affair, and on
   her awakening to sex at a mature age.   CLG

   El declive y la cuesta. Barcelona: Planeta, 1962. 2nd ed., 1966,
   300 pp.   EDM

Derribos. Barcelona: Argos Vergara, 1981.
    Salisachs subtitles this volume of memoirs, "Crónicas íntimas de
un tiempo saldado" and dedicates it to her grandchildren. She
reflects on her childhood, her family, her early development as a
writer, the dictatorship of Primo de Rivera and the advent of the
Republic. In the preamble she comments that she has selected only
those moments of her life which left her "marked," small moments of
everyday life which impressed her, rather than attempting a serious
study of an epoch.   CLG

La estación de las hojas amarillas. Barcelona: Planeta, 1963,
479 pp. 2nd ed., 1964, 494 pp. 3rd ed., 1968, 443 pp. 4th ed.,
Barcelona: Argos Vergara, 1980, ISBN 8470179314, 381 pp.
La Saison des Feuilles Mortes. Trans. France: Robert Laffont,
1965.   EDM

La gangrena. Autores españoles e hispanoamericanos. 1st ed.,
Barcelona: Planeta, 1975, ISBN 8432053422, 535 pp. Premio Planeta,
1975. 2nd ed., 1983. Colección Popular, Barcelona: Planeta, 1981,
ISBN 84-320-2193-8, 445 pp.   EDM

Los que se quedan. Barcelona: Juventud, 1942, 190 pp.   EDM

Más allá de los rafles. Colección gigante. Barcelona: Luis de
Caralt, 1957, 204 pp. Grandes clásicos contemporáneos, 47, Madrid:
Círculo de Amigos de la Historia, 1977, ISBN 8-422-50144-9, 244 pp.
                                                                 EDM

Una mujer llega al pueblo. Colección ómnibus, 11, Barcelona:
Planeta, 1957, 517 pp. Premio Ciudad de Barcelona. 4th ed., 1968,
518 pp. Colección Popular Mayor, Barcelona: Planeta, 1977, ISBN
8432027057, 382 pp. 2nd ed., 1981.
The Eyes of the Proud. Trans. by Delano Ames, London: Methuen,
1960; New York: Harcourt, Brace, 1960, 302 pp.
A Mulher que voltou. Portugal: Estudios Cor, 1960.
Eine Frau Kehrt Zurük. Hamburg: Nannen-Verlag, 1963.   EDM

Pasos conocidos: Dos novelas y nueve relatos. El reloj de sol, 3,
Barcelona: Pareja y Borrás, 1958, 255 pp.   EDM

La presencia. Barcelona: Argos Vergara, 1979, ISBN 847017818,
301 pp. 9th ed., 1982.   EDM

Primera mañana, última mañana. Colección gigante. Barcelona:
Luis de Caralt, 1955, 421 pp. 2nd ed., Los libros de la veleta, 2,
Barcelona: Nauta, 1968, 480 pp. Barcelona: Planeta, 1984,
ISBN 843204234X, 435 pp.   EDM

El proyecto y otros relatos. Barcelona: Planeta, 1978,
ISBN 8432053740, 235 pp.   EDM

La sinfonía de las moscas. Barcelona: Planeta, 1982,
ISBN 84-320-5554-9, 327 pp.   EDM

La última aventura. Colección Autores españoles contemporáneos.
Barcelona: Planeta, 1967, 317 pp. 2nd ed., 1969, 317 pp.   EDM

Colección Popular Planeta, 71, Barcelona: Planeta, 1978, ISBN
8432021806, 212 pp. 2nd ed., 1981, 212 pp.   EDM

Vendimia interrumpida, Colección españoles contemporáneos.
Barcelona: Planeta, 1960, 410 pp. 2nd ed., 1962. 3rd ed.,
Barcelona: Argos Vergara, 1982, ISBN 8471783606.
Vendemmia Interrotta. Trans. Italy: Editrice Internazionale, 1963.
La vendange interrompue. Trans. France: Robert Laffon, 1962.   EDM

Viaje a Sodoma. Barcelona: Planeta, 1977, ISBN 8-432-05369-4,
286 pp. 4th ed., 1978.   EDM

El volumen de la ausencia. Barcelona: Planeta, 1983, ISBN
84-320-5559-X, 302 pp. Premio Ateneo de Sevilla, 1983.
     This novel, which was on the best-seller list in Spain late in
1983 and early in 1984, tells the story of a middle-aged woman who
has just been told that she has a terminal illness. In a walk
through the streets of Barcelona, she evokes memories of her past and
plans how she will live to the fullest her few remaining months of
life. The omniscient narrator alternates with the directly quoted
thoughts of the protagonist. Many times external stimuli--las
Ramblas, an avenue--stimulate the memories. This work is often
considered one of the best by the author, especially in its
psychological portrayal. Available in hardback.   EDM

*SALVA, Maria Antònia (1869-1957).
     She belongs to the "Escola Mallorquina," a version of Catalan Modern-
ism but with marked local characteristics. Her poetry is mostly inspired by the Majorcan landscape and folklore and is concerned with
lyrical descriptions of an idyllic country life in a timeless world,
without ideological preoccupations or insoluble dilemmas. Her ideology
evolves within a constrained Catholic orthodoxy. Her style was influenced by Verdaguer, Costa i Llobera and Mistral, whose works she translated to Catalan.   ASR

Al cel sia! Barcelona: Edhasa, 1981, ISBN 84-350-0327-2, 165 pp.
Prologue by Xesca Ensenyat, choices by Miquel Angel Botella.
     This collection, gathered by Miquel Angel Botella, contains
various pieces from previous works, including Espigues en flor, El
retorn, Llepolies i joguines, Cel d'horabaixa and Lluneta del pagès.
There is also an index of titles, and one which lists the first line
of each poem. The book is available, easy to use, and the choices
are excellent.   KM

Antologia poètica. Ed. Josep Carner. Biblioteca Selecta de Poesia,
No. 232. Barcelona: Selecta, 1957, 212 pp.
     A good representative selection of poems by Josep Carner. Car-
ner's preface contains one of the most interesting and revealing
literary commentaries ever made on Salvà. It includes some prose
pieces and a selection of her translations of Mistral. Paperback.
                                                                   ASR

Cel d'horabaixa. Vol. 4 of Obres de Maria Antònia Salvà. 6 vols.
Majorca: Moll, 1948-55, 148 pp.
     This book marks a point at which the poet reaches artistic
maturity, the poetry becomes artistically more assertive and less

emotional, without changes in theme, style or technique. Most poems
were written during the 1930's and 1940's. They are a mixture of
subjects typical of Salvà: religious events, country life and
salutations to friends or relatives.   ASR

Entre el Record i L'Enyorança, Proses i memòries. Vol. 6 of Obres
de Maria Antònia Salvà. 6 vols. Majorca: Moll, 1948-55, 167 pp.
   Her only work in prose, it is a reflection on her previous poetry
and, for this reason, very revealing. She explains her inspiration
in peasant culture, with its "glossing" tradition, in her ancestors
and their home. She recognizes the influence of M. Costa i Llobera
and Verdaguer. Some pieces are autobiographical. Even in prose, her
writing maintains a lyrical tone, a simple style and a wide range of
vocabulary.   ASR

Espigues en Flor, Poesies. Ed. Josep Carner. Barcelona: Impremta
Altés, 1926, 214 pp.
Espigues en Flor. Vol. 1 of Obres de Maria Antònia Salvà. 6 vols.
Majorca: Moll, 1948-55, 258 pp.
   Some of these poems appeared first in Poesies. They are organized
by their theme: Personal feelings, flowers and vegetation, elegies,
religion, etc. They are simple but exquisite poems inspired by her
surroundings, in the same style of Poesies. This book includes her
"Poema de l'Allapass," her longest, a poem of epic tone about her
ancestry, and "Camí d'Orient," her only work considering a landscape
outside Majorca. Preface by Josep Carner. Appendix of Majorcan
words at the end.   ASR

Llepolies i Joguines. Palma de Majorca: Biblioteca "Les Illes
d'Or," 1946, 110 pp.
   This work is divided into two sections: one (Llepolies) deals
with sweets and delicacies from Majorca, and the other (Joguines)
with children's games and toys. They are short colorful poems of
folkloric interest, with no other pretention than to reflect poetically those two aspects of everyday life. In spite of their simplicity, the poet attains in them a high degree of lyrical excellence.
                                                              ASR

Llibre de poesies de Maria Antònia Salvà per servir de lectura a
les escoles de Catalunya. Ed. Consell de Pedagogia de la Diputació
de Barcelona, Mancomunitat de Catalunya. Barcelona: Impremta Casa
de Caritat, 1918.
   This is an edited version, comprising a selection of her early
works. The poems are organized according to their degree of language
difficulty and they are meant to be read by school children. The
Catalan has been normalized. It has a grammatical appendix to be
considered in relation to the poems.   ASR

Lluneta del Pagès. Vol. 5 of Obres de Maria Antònia Salvà. 6
vols. Majorca: Moll, 1948-55, 174 pp.
   Her previous themes reappear in this book: light lyrical pieces
on country life and scenes, religion and salutations. The section
"Guerra i post-guerra" reflects her views on the Spanish Civil War.
She visualizes it as a conflict between religious and non-religious
factions rather than on human or political terms. The war imposed a
new theme on Salvà, but she dealt with it without departing from her

local setting or modifying her literary style.   ASR

Maria Antònia Salvà. Ed. Tomàs Garcés, Sèrie "Els Poetes
d'Ara." Barcelona: Lira, 1923, 59 pp.
    A small pocket edition belonging to a collection of contemporary
poets, it is a selection extracted from Poesies. The spelling has
been changed to make it conform to the rules of the "Institut
d'Estudis Catalans." Preface by Tomàs Garcés, based on the
commentary by M. Costa i Llobera on Poesies. Available in some
libraries.   ASR

Poesies. Ed. Dr. Michael Costa, Sèrie Estampa de les Filles de
Maria. Palma: Joan Colom, 1910, 157 pp. First published 1903.
Both editions available only in some libraries.
    Her first imaginative publication is a collection of poems written
throughout her life up to 1903. The poems are presented in four
sections according to their theme: personal feelings, country life,
religion and miscellaneous. They are lyrical poems reminiscent of
Catalan Modernism, inspired by the most menial things but very
subtle. Preface by Miguel Costa i Llobera. Some of these poems will
reappear in future publications.   ASR

El Retorn, Poemes. Barcelona: Lluís Gili, 1934, 135 pp. Most
recent edition: El Retorn. Vol. 3 of Obres de Maria Antònia
Salvà. 6 vols. Majorca: Moll, 1948-55, 176 pp.
    In this work, she looks back with nostalgia, hence the title
"retorn." It is divided into three sections according to the poem's
theme: childhood and her life in the country, her manor and the land
of her ancestors, and miscellaneous. All these subjects are stylized
into pure lyrical expression with a melancholic and personal tone.
Appendix of Majorcan words at the end.   ASR

SALVADOR MALDONADO, Dolores (1938-). Pseud. Salvador Maldonado.
    Better known as a scriptwriter for T.V. and cinema, Lola Salvador
combines this activity with a vocation for traditional novel writing and
has produced two novels. The consequences of the Civil War are discern-
ible in her view of life; she is mostly a self-educated woman who as a
young girl left Spain for France and Belgium. Since her return she has
worked for Spanish Radio and Television; she also does journalistic work
for some magazines. Among her numerous scripts for T.V. is Juan Soldado
which won the Prague Award for T.V. productions in 1974, and El crimen
de Cuenca, prepared with Juan A. Porto for Pilar Miro's noted film.

El crimen de Cuenca. Barcelona: Argos Vergara, 1981, ISBN
84-7017-808-8, 154 pp. From first edition to 1984 there have been 18
editions of the book. There exist two other works with this same
title; they are both versions of the movie script co-authored by Lola
Salvador and Juan Antonio Porto Alonso: Madrid: Copyservice
Parking, 1979, and Madrid: Incine, 1979.
    This work shows a combination of historical research, which tran-
scribes documents from the famous trial of Belmonte (Cuenca), with a
reconstruction of the characters and situations written in a novelistic fashion. The result is an absorbing account of a judicial error
first denounced by El Sol in 1926, prompted by the reappearance of
the supposed victim. The suffering of the indicted peasants, the
coldblooded civil guards who extracted their confession, the

petulance of the judge, the indifference of the priest and corruption of the cacique, come out in a vivid narration. There is an appendix, a chronological table, and a bibliography.

...mamita mía, tirabuzones. Barcelona: Planeta, 1981,
ISBN 84-320-4176-9, 187 pp.
   This novel is mostly autobiographical. Constructed with a chrono-logicaly altered pattern (it has a direct circularity at the begin-ning and end), it is in its actual narrative technique quite tradi-tional in its employment of the confessional third person. It shows an effort on the part of the narrator-author to rid herself of memo-ries of an unhappy, orphaned childhood during the first half of the Franco years. The novel belongs to the self-exploratory trend ob-servable in many authors after the establishment of democracy in Spain.

M-EB

*SANCHEZ-CUTILLAS I MARTINEZ, Carmelina (1927-).
   Born in Madrid, but with close ties to Valencia, she studied Filosofia i Lletres, and as a writer, has divided her attention between the history of Valencia during the Middle Ages and works of literary creation--poetry and narration.

Conjugació en primera persona. 1969.
   Poetry.

Els jeroglífics i la pedra de Rosetta. Valencia: Eliseu Climent, 1976.
   Poetry.

Llibre d'amic e d'amada. Valencia: Torres, 1980.
   Poetry.

Matèria de Bretanya. Valencia: Eliseu Climent, 1976, 1980, 1982, ISBN 84-85211-11-1, 196 pp.
   Fictionalized and lyrical memoirs, with a prologue by Pere Maria Orts i Bosch. The author draws a series of vignettes based on childhood memories to paint the society of the late 1920's and early 1930's in a small town. Winner of the Andròmina Prize in 1976.

Un món rebel. 1964.
   Poetry.

KM

SANT JORDI, Rosa de. See ARQUIMBAU, Rosa Maria.

SANTA TERESA, Sor Gregoria Francisca de (1653-1736).

Poesias de la Venerable Madre Gregoria Francisca de Santa Teresa. Carmelitas Descalza en el convento de Sevilla, en el siglo Dola Gregoria Francisca de la Parra Queinoge. Paris: J. Claye, 1865.
   Part of the Hispanic Society of America collection, 613 W. 155th Street, New York, NY 10032. Manuscript may be available in microform; contact Dupre Library, U. of SW La., Lafayette, LA 70504.

MBM

*SANTAMARIA I VENTURA DE FABRIGUES, Joaquima (1854-1930).
Pseud. **Agnes de Valldaura.**
   Born in Barcelona, Santamaria published under her pseudonym, being
best known for her collections of religious traditions, Tradicions
religioses de Catalunya (1877 and 1925), a work which received a prize
in the Certamen de la Joventut Catòlica in 1877. Numerous editions
exist, including a translation into Spanish (1925). She contributed to
newspapers in Buenos Aires and to "La Llumnera" in New York. Her
contribution to the debate over women is the essay Breus consideracions
sobre la dona (1882).

   Fullaraca; prosa y vers. Barcelona: Estampa Peninsular, 1879, 231
   pp.
      A collection of poems and prose pieces.

   Ridolta. Aplech de poesías. Barcelona: Roca, 1882, 53 pp.
      A collection of poetry.

                                                                    MB

SANZ CUADRADO, **María Antonio** (1914-).
   Holder of a Doctorate in Romance philology, Sanz Cuadrado, who was
born in Madrid, has taught language and literature. Primarily a poet,
she has also written critical works and biographies of Spanish literary
and political figures. She has also written works for children and many
magazine articles. Also an artist, one of her books contains her
drawings.

   Dios creciente. Màlaga: Librería Anticuaria El Guadalhorce, 1965,
   75 pp. Ed. by Angel Caffarena.
      Poems.

   Mientras el sol gira. Màlaga: Cuadernos de María José, 1966.
      Poetry.

                                                                    CLG

SAU SANCHEZ, Victoria (1930-). **Victoria Sau.**
   Since 1975 Victoria Sau has been actively engaged in the feminist
movement as a writer, public speaker, and Professor of Psychology at the
Universidad Central de Barcelona. The author of Manifiesto para la
liberación de la mujer, Mujer: matrimonio y esclavitud, Mujeres
lesbianas, La suegra, and El diccionario ideológico feminista, Sau
acknowledges the impact of Simone de Beauvoir and Betty Friedan on her
own writing, yet describes her feminist position as "teórica e
independiente." In addition to her career as a writer, Sau is a
practicing psychologist in Barcelona and the founder of El Seminario
Permanente de Investigación de la Nueva Psicología de la Mujer.

   Aprende a cocinar sin errores. Biblioteca "llave." Barcelona:
   Aura, 1977, ISBN 84-214-0120-3, 174 pp.

   El baúl viajero. Drawings by Antonio Ayné, Cuentos Toray.
   Barcelona: Toray, 1973, ISBN 84-310-0473-8, 163 pp.

   El catalán, un bandolerismo español. Barcelona: Aura, 1973,
   ISBN 84-214-0080-0, 296 pp.

La decoración del hogar. ABC de las Artes Caseras. Barcelona:
Toray, 1967, 144 pp.

Un diccionario ideológico feminista. Totum Revolutum. Barcelona:
Icaria, 1981, ISBN 84-7426-072-8, 277 pp.
   Sau's objective in Un diccionario is to redefine from a feminist
perspective significant terms regarding family relationships, sexuality, and power, all basic to understanding woman's historical domination by man. The author describes her work as an act of "feminismo
científico...que por mi parte consiste en la aplicación del método
del materialismo histórico al análisis de las relaciones mujer-
hombre para tratar de dar a partir de las mismas una 'explicación'
científica de cualesquiera otras relaciones humanas, o sea, del
mundo. ("Scientific feminism...which, for my part, consists of the
application of the method of historical materialism to the analysis
of woman-man relations, to try to give them a scientific 'explanation' like any other human relations, that is, of the world.")
Contains a prologue, index, and extensive bibliography. Paperbound.

La duquesa resfriada. Leyenda rusa. Ill. by Rosa Galcerán, Cuentos
"Azucena." Barcelona: Toray, 1973, ISBN 84-310-0880-6, 144 pp.

El globo. Drawings by Antonio Ayné, Cuentos Toray. Barcelona:
Toray, 1973, ISBN 84-310-0476-2, 156 pp.

Historia antropológica de la canción. Impacto Literario, vol. 3.
Barcelona: Picazo, 1972, 282 pp.

Manifiesto para la liberación de la mujer. Libro Amigo, vol. 341.
Barcelona: Bruguera, 1975, ISBN 84-7175-077-5, 383 pp.
   This work is as much an exhaustive socio-historical study of women
as it is a political manifesto. Marriage and family, incest, virgin-
ity, adultery, and prostitution are all examined from a feminist perspective. Sau studies the origin and current status of female arche-
types such as la soltera, la bruja, la profetisa, la frígida, la
devoradora del hombre, and acknowledges woman's victimization by the
patriarchy while exhorting the former to renounce the role of accom-
plice in her own exploitation. Contains prologue, index, and bibliography. Paperbound.

Mujer: matrimonio y esclavitud. Colección Apogeo, Serie
Testimonio. Madrid: Júcar, 1976, ISBN 84-334-8002-2, 159 pp.
   Sau criticizes marriage as an economic, sexual, and social
institution in which woman is the politically disenfranchised
partner. The book begins with a concise definition of terms, a
survey of the history of marriage, a statistical review of woman's
role in the institution, the current status of marriage, and a
critical look to the future. "Mientras los individuos no sean libres
como tales individuos--entiendo por libertad la posibilidad plena de
realización personal para todos y cada uno de los ciudadanos, y sin
que la de ningunos de ellos se obstenga por la explotación de
segundas personas--no se puede prever cómo será en el futuro la
unión intersexos, pues todos los modelos conocidos hasta ahora no
están basados en la libertad, sino en la esclavitud." ("As long as
individuals are not free as individuals--by freedom I mean the
possibility of full personal realization for each and every citizen,

without that of any being based on the exploitation of others--we cannot predict what the union between sexes will be in the future, as all models known until now are not based on liberty, but on slavery.") Prologue, index, and bibliography. Paperbound.

Mujeres lesbianas. Colección Lee y Discute. Madrid: Zero-Zyx, 1979, ISBN 84-317-0526-4, 102 pp.
This is a concise historical analysis of lesbianism within a political context. Sau identifies critical ideological differences between male homosexuals and lesbians, underscores the relationship between feminism and lesbianism, and presents the lesbian perspective as a powerful political alternative. "El lesbianismo cuestiona los valores que forman parte de la heterosexualidad, el matrimonio, la familia, la dependencia de la mujer respecto al hombre, la materni- dad y los papeles masculino y feminino. Cuestiona, por lo tanto, indirectamente, el propio sistema económico." Published by Zero-Zyx as part of the series "Biblioteca Feminista" directed by Anabel Gonzàles. Contains prologue, index and bibliography. Paperbound.

El secreto del emperador, adapt. de una leyenda yugoslava. Illus. by Rosa Galcerán, Cuentos "Azucena". Barcelona: Toray, 1973, ISBN 84-310-0878-4, 143 pp.

Sectas cristianas. Barcelona: Aura, 1971, 279 pp.

La suegra. Barcelona: Ediciones 29, 1976, ISBN 84-7175-099-6, 241 pp.
The author scrutinizes a bitter cycle. As a young girl, one is seduced by the myth of romantic love which ultimately demands the female's unqualified commitment to the male, whose primary objectives are gratification and freedom. As the bride's hope gives way to the wife's disillusionment, the woman seeks her razón de ser in the role of mother. But, when her dependent charges mature and marry, the woman must face what Sau calls "el último acto: la quema de la bruja." As a mother-in-law, woman is anathema. "Puede que la tol- eren, pero no la querrán. Aún en el caso de una mujer determi- nada la quieran su yerno o yerna, en tanto que suegra es una mujer despreciada." Sau examines the socio-historical and popular literary image of the mother-in-law, the traditional rivalry with the daughter-in-law, the case of the regressive, dependent son, and "la terrible pareja: la suegra y el yerno." The cycle repeats itself with each new generation. Prologue, index, and bibliography. Paper.
BDM

SEDANO, Dora (1902-).
She was born into an upper middle-class family in Madrid. Although she wrote some narrative and poetry, she produced principally plays as an adult. Frequently working in collaboration, she wrote approximately 15 plays, performed in Madrid in the 1940's and 1950's. Her works, primarily domestic comedies or political melodramas, reflect her conservative ideology.

La diosa de arena (with Luis Fernández de Sevilla). Proscenio, #9. Madrid: Artes Gráficas, 1952, 62 pp.
This political melodrama reflects the conservative position of the Franco regime. A young woman brainwashed by evil communists even- tually sees the light after her marriage into a pious Catholic

family. Published only in paper. Available only through libraries
with the "Proscenio" collection.

Mercaderes de sangre. Madrid: Afrodisio Aguado, 1945, 270 pp.
    This is a melodramatic novel set in Paris at the time of the
Spanish Civil War. Here the "good" traditional Spaniards are contrasted to Spanish communist "traitors." Unavailable for purchase
and available in very few libraries in the United States. Of
interest to researchers of rightist Civil War novels or those
interested in women's literature.

Nuestras chachas (with Luis Tejedor). Biblioteca Teatral, #170,
Madrid: Arba, 1953, 54 pp.
    This bourgeois domestic comedy portrays through caricature and
farce the servant problem. Don Juanism is winked at, and the values
are those of the conservative Spanish bourgeoisie of the 1950's.
Paperback. Available only through libraries holding the "Biblioteca
Teatral" collection.   PWO

SEGOVIA RODRIGUEZ, María Paz. Pseud. Paz de Castilla.

Como un secreto. Madrid, 1952.
    This novel is dedicated "To the suffering youth of today's world,
who, with their effort and sacrifice, have strewn the turbulent and
episodic present era with moving examples." Available U. of Southwestern Louisiana library.
                                                                  CLG

*SERRA, Maria Girona.

Records i anhels. Bilbao: La Gran Enciclopedia Vasca, 1978.
    Poetry.
                                                                  KM

*SERRAHIMA, Núria (1937-).
    Born to a bourgeois family in Barcelona, Serrahima began life under
traditional and conservative auspices. Her early education, up to age
14, was in a private convent school. She then abandoned formal education to devote herself intensively during five years to studying
painting under Ramón Rogent. Shortly before her father's death in
1958, she turned to literature, and after another apprenticeship, produced her first novel in Catalan, Mala guilla, a finalist for the 1973
"Josep Pla" Prize in Catalan literature. In the last years of the
Franco regime, the "boom" in vernacular literatures had not gathered
impetus so she was one of a handful of women choosing to write in
Catalan. L'olor dels nostres cossos (1982) is a collection of three
novellas united by feminist themes.

Mala guilla. Barcelona: Edicions 62, 1973, "El Balancí,"
ISBN 84-297-0866-9, 196 pp.
    The autobiographical content frequent in first novels appears both
on the socio-historical level (where reflections of the adolescent's
personal experience in tense post-war readjustments under the Franco
regime form the context), and on a more personal, individual level,
since the author's late father is an important source of inspiration.
Paralleling events in her life (the 14-year-old protagonist decides

to quit school), the novel portrays those formative influences which combined to repress and limit female students and abort artistic or literary interests, independence, and self-expression: continual insistence on sin and confession, distant memories of World War II, fear of her grandparents, a frustrating of her preferences for the country over the city, and labeling of her as "bad" because of innocent mischief, youthful vitality and spontaneity.

L'olor dels nostres cossos. Barcelona: Edicions 62, 1982, "El Balancí," ISBN 84-297-1901-6, 172 pp.
   Three novellas are united by common feminist themes, the use of a first-person narrative point of view and a feminine protagonist. In the title story (The Smell of Our Bodies), the married narrative consciousness reflects upon conjugal life during a sleepless night beside a snoring husband, anguished by her need for self-esteem, paternalistic tyranny, the disillusionment of romantic love, her economic dependence and love for her children, which force her to reject separation and suicide. Negres moments d'Emma (Emma's Dark Moments) sketches the repressions which have made an asthmatic invalid, almost a cripple, of Emma, who has retreated from solitude, sexual exploitation and personal frustration into extreme neurotic passivity. Amants strikes a happier note, as a liberated woman runs through the alphabet of initials she has assigned her lovers past and present.
                                                                      JP

SERRANO, Eugenia (1918-).
   A graduate of the University of Madrid, Serrano has contributed essays and stories to newspapers and magazines and has worked as a journalist. She has also written radio scripts. She won the Premio Artes y Letras for short stories in 1943 and is the author of two biographies, including one of Winston Churchill.

Chamberi-Club; Perdimos la primeravera. 1953.
   Novels.

Pista de baile. Madrid: Bullón, 1963.
   This novel is a reflection of the rootlessness of young people of the 1960's. Constanza, an artist whose world is comprised only of brief relationships, surrounds herself with bohemians, alcoholics, homosexuals and drug addicts. Constanza makes her own way in the world and is independent; yet she realizes that she is sometimes like a sheep, following the fads of her friends because she cannot tolerate solitude. Concerned that at 30 she is aging and will lose her young lover, she notes that her communist friends already seem half-dead. The dance floor of the title symbolizes youth and budding eroticism; and Constanza feels herself slipping off that precarious surface.

Retorno a la tierra. 1945.
   Novel.

                                                                      CLG

SIGEA DE VELASCO, Luisa (circa 1530-1560).
   A classical scholar and author of various poems, letters and dialogues in Latin and Spanish, she was an active participant in the intellectual life of the court of Doña María in Lisbon, where she was

recognized as an expert in Greek, Latin, and Hebrew literature. Her
work reflects her classical erudition as well as a fundamental
disillusionment with the intrigue and hypocrisy of court life.

Ad Augustissimam Eamdem (Mariam Infantem) Sintrae Descriptio Poetica,
per Loisam Sygeam Toletanam. Paris: Juan Nicot, 1566.
Apuntes para una biblioteca de escritoras espanolas. Ed. Manuel
Serrano y Sanz. Madrid: Biblioteca de Autores Espanoles, 1975, Tomo
270, pp. 404-405.

Duarum virginum colloquium de vita aulica et privata. Copied in
1552. Entire dialogue reproduced in Apuntes para una biblioteca de
autoras espanolas. Ed. M. Serrano y Sanz. Madrid: Biblioteca de
Autores Espanoles, 1975, Tomo 270, pp. 419-471.
    This is a lengthy disquisition on the advantages and disadvan-
tages of both court life and rural life in the form of a dialogue
between two young girls. The author calls upon her extensive
knowledge of Greek and Hebrew writers on the subject and provides a
full list of these sources at the beginning of the work. The work is
of interest to students of classicism in sixteenth-century Spain.
There is no existing Spanish translation.

Poesias castellanas. In Apuntes para una biblioteca de autoras
espanolas. Ed. Manuel Serrano y Sanz. Madrid: Biblioteca de
Autores Espanoles, 1975, Tomo 270, p. 408.

Sintrae descriptio poetica.
    This work is a description of the natural splendor of Cintra,
Portugal. Bucolic in tone, it is full of mythological allusions
which reveal the extent of the poet's classical culture. A Spanish
translation is found in Menéndez Pelayo, Estudios poéticos.
Madrid: Imprenta Central, 1878, pp. 95-101. Also in Serrano y Sanz,
Biblioteca de Autores Españoles, t. 270, pp. 403-404.

                                                                    DD

SILVA Y COLLAS, Micaela de (1809-1884). Pseud. "Camila Avilés."
    Although born in Oviedo, Micaela Silva y Collás lived first in
Barcelona and later in Madrid, where she studied languages and the
masterpieces of Spanish literature. Numerous newspapers published her
poems under her pseudonym "Camila Avilés" but she is best remembered
for her satire Un novio a pedir de boca, a translation of Manzoni's El
cinco de mayo and a volume of collected poems. According to poet Miguel
Angel Príncipe (1861), she might have become famous had she not been so
modest about publishing her works.

Emanaciones del alma, colección de poesías. Madrid: Imprenta y
Librería de los hijos de Vázquez, 1885, 268 pp.
    Silva's poems, many written under her pseudonym "Camila Avilés,"
were gathered from her numerous collaborations in newspapers and
magazines and published posthumously in one volume.

Un novio a pedir de boca, sátira. Madrid: Imprenta de M. Campo
Redondo, 1963, 14 pp.
    This satire in verse is composed of 35 octavas reales in which the
author's persona, Petra Ceballos, describes in first person what her
prospective suitor should be like. Besides listing such characteris-

tics as honesty, fidelity, modesty, decency, etc., she also declares
what kind of man she finds undesirable: gambler, dandy, glutton,
womanizer, spendthrift, foul-mouthed lout and wife-beater. Sadly,
she laments, she is destined not to marry, for the virtuous man does
not exist and the other type is all too numerous. But, on the other
hand, she concludes laconically: "Me llaman alma en pena, pero
!cuerno!.../ Más vale el purgatorio que el infierno!!" ("They call
me a soul in Purgatory, but my goodness!... Purgatory is better than
Hell!!")

NJM

*SIMO I MONLLOR, Isabel-Clara (1943-).
Born in Alcoi (Valencia), she received her Bachelor's degree in Philosophy from the University of Valencia. She participated in early
nationalist groups of Catalonia. Simó has taught throughout Catalonia,
as well as working as a journalist. She started the weekly paper
Canigó in 1972 and directed it for more than ten years. In 1978, Simó
received the "Víctor Català" prize for her collection of stories, Es
quan miro que hi veig clar. She is working on another collection called
"No m'escanyis, amor."   TMM

Es quan miro que hi veig clar, Col.leccio Antilop 22. Barcelona:
Selecta, 1979, ISBN 84-298-0455-2, 199 pp.
   Each of the six short stories in this collection deals with daily
problems of people. The author takes a close look at the pressures
of adolescence, old age and the new independence of women. A leitmotif of the conflict between Castilian and Catalan is apparent
throughout the collection. The language is current Catalan, with in-
terjections of the Valencian dialect. Simó has a very human insight
into the sentiments of modern Catalonia, and this work is an aid to
the understanding of the contemporary, middle-class Catalan character. Winner of the Premi Víctor Català, 1978. Paperback.   TMM

Idols. Barcelona: Magrana, 1985, ISBN 84-7410-187-5, 264 pp.
   The male protagonist of this novel, Bru, is a lucid and rational
young student who nevertheless falls into the trap of trying to solve
personal and philosophical problems by changing locations. The title
is from Novum Organon by Francis Bacon, from which a dedicatory
paragraph is quoted, explaining the various prejudices, or mindsets,
from which we can suffer, and which keep us from thinking clearly.
Bru is held for a time by his tumultuous relationship with the
troubled and troubling Ruth, but he finally opts for Maria Dolça,
whose name is somewhat significant.   KM

Júlia, Les Ales Esteses, 12. Barcelona: Ediciones de la Magrana,
1983, ISBN 84-7410-122-0, 243 pp.
   Júlia is a factory worker in nineteenth-century industrial Alcoi,
Valencia. She is able to rise above her class through her strong
character and a wealthy marriage, yet it is clear by the examples of
the conflicts between factory workers and the owners, that her case
is singular. The actual story takes place over a span of 22 years,
but gives a history of the more important events, as far back as 20
years before. Had the term been known in the nineteenth century,
Júlia would have been considered a feminist. The story is written
in the Valencian dialect, but is easily understood. Paperback.   TMM

SINUES Y NAVARRO (DE MARCO), María del Pilar (1835-1893).

An ardent advocate of the cult of domesticity, María del Pilar Sinués wrote highly successful, moralizing, romanticized novels about (in)famous women. She believed she had a mission to educate Spanish women, which she did, albeit from the bourgeois, Catholic point of view. In spite of her moralizing, her own life was far from the happy endings she often described in nearly 100 novels and many more articles. A victim of her own romantic ideas, she married José Marco sight unseen in her native Zaragoza. After their disastrous marriage ended, she lived by her writing, including editing the newspaper El ángel del hogar.

A la luz de una lámpara, colección de cuentos morales. Madrid: Imprenta Española, 1862, 192 pp. Another printing, 1866. 2nd ed., Madrid, 1872. 3rd ed., Madrid, 1873. 4th ed., Madrid: G. Hernando, 1876, 176 pp. 6th ed., corregida, Madrid: Establecimiento Tipográfico de Alvarez Hnos., 1889, 175 pp. 7th ed., cuidadosamente corregida, Madrid: V. Suárez, 1921, 175 pp.

A la sombra de un tilo. Madrid, 1862.

A río revuelto, novela original. Madrid: 1866.

La abuela, narración. Madrid: Oficinas de La Ilustración Española y Americana, 1878, 409 pp. 2nd ed., Madrid: V. Suárez, 1899.

Agustina de Aragón, romance histórico. Barcelona?: J. M. Ayoldi, 187-?.

Las alas de Icaro, novela. Valenica: Piles, 1872. 2nd ed. published with Premio y castigo. 4th ed., Madrid: V. Suárez, 1903, 218 pp.

Album de mis recuerdos. Memorias de una joven de la clase media. Madrid: Moro, 1862.

El alma enferma, novela original. Madrid: 1865. 3rd ed., Madrid: J. A. García, 1882. Another ed., Madrid: Librería General de V. Suárez, 1910.

El almohadón de rosas, novela original. Madrid: Imprenta Española, 1864, 263 pp. Also published in Dramas de familia, v. 2, Madrid: A. Jubera, 1885.

La amiga íntima, novela original y El palacio de los genios, leyenda fantástica. Barcelona: Manero, 1878, 240 pp. Another edition Madrid: Librería General de V. Suárez, 1908, 249 pp.

Amor y llanto. Colección de leyendas históricas originales, Madrid: 1857. 2nd ed., Madrid: Imprenta de T. Núñez Amor, 1857, 260 pp. Another ed., Leipzig: F. A. Brockhaus, 1867, 288 pp. 4th ed., Madrid: V. Suárez, 1898, 430 pp.

El ángel de las tristezas. Madrid: 1865.

El ángel del hogar, estudios morales acerca de la mujer. Madrid: 1862. Another ed., México: Imprenta de J. Barbedillo, 1876. 7th ed., "cuidadosamente corregida y considerablemente aumentada," Madrid: Administración, 1880?. Another ed., Madrid, 1881. 8th ed., Madrid: V. Suárez, 1904.

Los ángeles de la tierra. Madrid: Imprenta de los hijos de J. A. García, 1891, 369 pp.

El becerro de oro, narración. Barcelona: Manero, 1875, 340 pp. Another ed., Madrid: Librería General de V. Suárez, 1910, 222 pp.

El camino de la dicha. Cartas a dos hermanas sobre la educación. Madrid: 1868.

Cantos de mi lira. Colección de leyendas en verso, Madrid: Imprenta de T. Núñez Amor, 1857, 259 pp.

Celeste, novela. Madrid: 1863. Also published in Dramas de familia, v. 2, Madrid: A. Jubera, 1885.

El cetro de flores y El castillo, la aldea y el palacio, colección de leyendas basadas en las obras de misericordia. Madrid: Tello, 1865.

Combates de la vida, dos novelas originales. Madrid: Establecimiento Tipográfico de M. Minuesa, 1876, 398 pp. 3rd ed., Madrid: Administración, 18--, 421 pp.

Cómo aman las mujeres. Madrid: Administración de J. Roldán, 1889?, 322 pp.

Cortesanas ilustres, leyendas históricas. Madrid: 1878.

Cuentos de color de cielo. Madrid: Leocadio López, 1867, 383 pp.

Cuentos de niñas. Barcelona: Bastinos, 1879, 192 pp.

Damas galantes, historias de amor. Madrid: L. López, 1878, 376 pp.

La diadema de perlas. Novela histórica original. 2nd ed., Madrid: Imprenta de La Península, 1857, 119 pp. First ed. published as the folletín in Las Cortes. Another printing 1863.

Doña Urraca (from her Galería de mujeres célebres?). Doña Urraca, Queen of León and Castile, an historical romance of the middle ages, English trans. by Reginald Huth, Bath: Wilkinson Bros., 1880.

Dos venganzas. Novela histórico-original. Madrid: Imprenta Española, 1862.

Dramas de familia, v. 1. Madrid: Imprenta de la viuda e hijos de J. A. García, 1883. V. 2, Madrid: A. Jubera, 1885.

Las esclavas del deber, leyendas históricas. Madrid: S. Calleja,
1878, 351 pp.

La expiación, novela original. Barcelona: Manero, 18--.

La familia cristiana. La corona nupcial, novela original. Madrid:
A. Pérez Dubrull, ed., 1871.

Fausta Sorel, novela original. Madrid: 1861. 2nd ed., Madrid: V.
Suárez, 1902.

La flor de Castellar. Published with Premio y castigo. Barcelona:
1866.

Flores del alma. Poesías. Barcelona: Establecimiento Tipográfico
de Narciso Ramírez, 1860.

Galería de mujeres célebres, leyendas originales, 15 v. Madrid:
1864-1869.

La gitana, novela original. Barcelona: Manero, 1878, 268 pp.

Glorias de la mujer, leyendas originales. Madrid: S. Calleja, 1878,
456 pp.

Una herencia trágica. Madrid: Imprenta de la viuda e hijos de J.
A. García, 1882, 360 pp.

Hija, esposa y madre, cartas dedicadas a la mujer acerca de sus
deberes para con la familia y la sociedad. Madrid: Imprenta de los
hijos de García, 1863. 2nd ed., Madrid: Aribau, 1877, 430 pp.
3rd ed., Madrid: 1883. 5th ed., Madrid: V. Suárez, 1904. Another
ed., Bogotá: Mundial, 194-?, 459 pp.

Una hija del siglo, novela original. Madrid: Imprenta de El Correo
de las Antillas, 1873, 200 pp. Also published in Combates de la
vida, Madrid: Establecimiento Tipográfico de M. Minuesa, 1876.

Una historia sencilla. Barcelona: Manero, 1886.

Isabel; estudio del natural. Madrid: Imprenta de los hijos de J. A.
García, 1888, 410 pp.

El lazo de flores. Published in Narraciones del hogar, Madrid: A.
Jubera, 1885.

La ley de Dios, colección de leyendas basadas en los preceptos del
decálogo. Madrid: Imprenta de Rivadeneyra, 1858, 400 pp. 2nd ed.,
Madrid: Imprenta de Nieto, 1859. Another ed., Madrid: 1866. 8th
ed., Madrid: V. Suárez, 1904, 240 pp. 9th ed., Madrid: V.
Suárez, 1911.

Un libro para las damas. Madrid: Aribau, 1875, 392 pp.
Another ed., Madrid: Aribau, 1878, 392 pp.

Un libro para las madres. Madrid: Oficinas de La Moda Elegante
Ilustrada, 1877, 406 pp. 2nd ed., cuidosamente corregida, Madrid:
A. Jubera, 1885.

Luz y sombra. 2nd serie. Leyendas originales. Madrid: S. Calleja,
1879, 331 pp.

Margarita, novela original. 2nd ed., Madrid: T. Núñez Amor, 1857,
219 pp. 1st ed.? 4th ed., Barcelona: Manero, 1877. Another ed.,
Madrid: V. Suárez, 1913.

Los mártires del amor, leyendas originales. Madrid: 1879, 356 pp.

Mecerse en las nubes. Published in Combates de la vida. Madrid:
Establecimiento Tipográfico de M. Minuesa, 1876.

La misión de la mujer, novela original. Barcelona: Manero, 1886.
Another ed., Madrid: V. Suárez, 1908.

Morir sola, narración. Madrid: B. N. Giménez, 1890, 467 pp.
Another ed., Madrid: V. Suárez, 1910.

La mujer en nuestros días; obra dedicada a las madres y a las hijas
de familia. Madrid: Sáenz de Jubera Hnos., 1878, 218 pp.
Reprinted by same publisher in 1910, 208 pp.

Mujeres ilustres, narraciones histórico-biográficas. Madrid:
Establecimiento Tipográfico de Alvarez Hnos., 1884.

Narraciones del hogar. Madrid: 1862. Another ed., v. 1, Madrid:
A. Jubera, 1885; v. 2, Madrid: V. Suárez, 1885. Another ed.,
Madrid: V. Suárez, 1908.

Un nido de palomas, novela original. Madrid: Imprenta Española,
1865, 268 pp. Another ed., Barcelona: S. Manero, 1877, 279 pp.
Another ed., Madrid: J. M. Faquineto, 1889, 312 pp.

No hay culpa sin pena. Novela Original. Madrid: Imprenta
Española, 1864, 235 pp. 4th ed., aumentada.

Novelas cortas. Madrid: J. Roldán, 1890, 366 pp.

Páginas del corazón. Madrid: Establecimiento Tipográfico de
Alvarez Hnos., 1887, 415 pp. Another ed., Madrid: J. A. Faquineto.

Palmas y flores, leyendas del hogar. Madrid: Librería General de
S. Calleja, 1877, 308 pp.

Plácida, un drama de familia. Barcelona: S. Manero, 1877, 288 pp.
Another ed., Madrid: J. M. Faquineto, 1880, 307 pp.

Premio y castigo, comedia en tres actos y en prosa, imitación del
teatro extranjero por los Sres. V. y S. y L. Madrid: 1858.

Premio y castigo. Novela original. 2nd ed., Madrid: J. Peña,
1857, 163 pp. 1st ed.? Published with La flor de Castellar,

Barcelona, 1866. 4th ed. published with Las alas de Icaro (2nd ed.),
Madrid: V. Suárez, 1903, 218 pp.

La primera falta, novela original. Barcelona: Manero, 1879, 230 pp.
Another ed., Madrid: V. Suárez, 1908, 197 pp.

Querer es poder, novela original. Madrid: Imprenta Española, 1865,
235 pp. Another ed., Barcelona: Manero, 1877, 280 pp. Another ed.,
Madrid: V. Suárez, 1908.

La rama de sándalo. Novela original. 2nd ed., Madrid: Imprenta
Española, 1862, 245 pp. 1st ed.? Also published in Narraciones del
hogar, Madrid: A. Jubera, 1885.

Reinas mártires. Madrid: 1878, 436 pp.

Rosa, novela original. 3rd ed., Madrid: Imprenta de La Península,
1857, 142 pp. Another ed., 1864. 4th ed., aumentada, plus Flor de
oro, leyenda original, Madrid: Moreno, 1865, 232 pp. Another
combined ed., Madrid: V. Suárez, 1907, 218 pp.

La senda de la gloria, novela original. Madrid: Imprenta Española,
1863. 2nd ed., aumentada y corregida, Madrid: Oficinas de La Moda
Elegante Ilustrada, 1880, 389 pp.

El sol de invierno, novela. Madrid: Imprenta Española, 1863.
2nd ed., corregida y aumentada, Madrid: Oficinas de La Moda Elegante
Ilustrada, 1879, 366 pp. Another ed., Madrid: Librería General de
V. Suárez, 1916, 415 pp.

Sueños y realidades. Memorias de una madre para su hija. Madrid:
Imprenta Española, 1865.

Tres genios femeninos, leyendas originales. Madrid: S. Calleja,
1879, 435 pp.

El último amor, novela original. México: Tipografía de J. M.
Aguilar Ortiz, 1872, 180 pp.

Veladas de invierno en torno a una mesa de labor, Colección de
leyendas. Barcelona: Manero, 1866.

Verdades dulces y amargas; páginas para la mujer. Madrid: García,
1882, 364 pp. 2nd ed., Madrid: V. Suárez, 1898, 398 pp.

La vida íntima. Correspondencia de las familias del gran mundo.
En la culpa va el castigo, novela original. Madrid: Imprenta de
Aribau, 1876, 416 pp. 2nd ed., Madrid: Oficinas de La Ilustración
Española y Americana, 1878, 416 pp. 3rd ed., Madrid: Imprenta de
los hijos de J. A. García, 1891, 449 pp.

La vida real. Alegrías y tristezas de una familia. Estudio social.
Madrid: Imprenta y fundición de los hijos de García, 1884, 391 pp.
Another ed., Madrid: V. Suárez, 1913.

La virgen de las lilas, novela original. Madrid: 1863.
2nd ed., Madrid: Imprenta Española, 1865, 224 pp.   NJM

SORIANO, Carmen.
   Soriano is a writer from Alicante.

   Hombres desnudos. Madrid: Prensa Española, 1974,
   ISBN 84-287-0287-X.
   A finalist for the Premio Alfaguara, this novel treats the
disfigurement of the Spanish Mediterranean coast by the construction
of large hotels and tourist apartments. A group of neighbors lose
their homes as a result of the greed of a construction promotor who
has no conscience. Soriano's theme is that the desire to get rich
quick results in dehumanization.

                                                                    CLG

SORIANO JARA, Elena (1917-).
   Born in Fuentidueña de Tajo (Madrid) of ruined Andalusian gentry,
she is a novelist of realist and intellectualist predilection who shows
psychological insight in female characters. Author of a novel, Caza
menor (1951) and a trilogy, Mujer y hombre (1955), she has also written
numerous articles, collaborated on Indice and was the founder and
director of El Urogallo.

   Caza menor. Madrid: La Nave, 1951, 398 pp. Madrid: Prensa
   Española, 1976, ISBN 84-287-0397-3, 310 pp.
   The first novel by the author has a country setting with great
detail of local customs, revealing a first-hand knowledge of the
described region and giving to the narrative a characterization of
"costumbrismo." The main characters are the parents and their three
sons, to a lesser degree the wife of one of the brothers. After she
dies tragically, fleeing from her husband's home and the carnal
desires of his two brothers, the house and the whole family
disintegrate, engulfed in the effects of the Civil War as well as
because of the weakness of the clan. In spite of some imbalance in
the development of characters, the novel is a very meritorious
contribution to literature.

   Espejismos. Madrid: Calleja, 1955, 212 pp., v. 2 of Mujer y hombre.
   The theme of this novel is the conflicting relationship of a
couple in their forties after long years of marriage. The action
occurs in the brief span of time during an operation to which the
wife is subjected. Husband and wife reflect on the years lived
together; she to regret her fading youth and the loss of the hold
that she used to have on him; he to consider the effects that the
passing of time has on their mutual feelings, and his need to evade
himself through a liaison with a younger woman. There is introspective vision by means of monologues and a skillful capture of the
feminine temperament.

   Medea 55. Madrid: Calleja, 1955, 258 pp., v. 3 of Mujer y hombre.
   This novel is a parallel in modern times to the classic drama, as
the title anticipates. Here love has the character of egotistic
eroticism, uncontrollable and self-centered passion, in itself
destructive and tragic. The theme, although somewhat contrived by
its dependence on the classical myth, is rich in narrative devices:
stream of consciousness, flashback technique. The stormy love of
Daniela-Medea and Miguel-Jason takes them from Spain through Europe
and finally to South America (unknown to Elena Soriano but skillfully

dealt with). The death of their short-lived daughter turns Daniela
into the destruction of Miguel's newfound love.

Mujer y hombre. Trilogía. 3 vols. Madrid: Calleja, 1955.
V. 1 La playa de los locos. V. 2 Espejismos. V. 3 Medea 55.
    The three narratives that constitute this trilogy are not mutually
related but have different characters, independent setting and plot.
However, there is an underlying common theme in the three volumes
since all of them deal with three aspects of the conflictive nature
of love. The author shows that her potential as a novelist is well
developed.

La playa de los locos. Madrid: Calleja, 1955, 200 pp. V. 1 of
Mujer y hombre.
    Publication of this novel encountered difficulties with censorship
and was only authorized to circulate in a very limited way. In
summer 1984 a new edition was being prepared. In this volume love
has a nostalgic character, being an idealized feeling stretched over
the years. Narrated in retrospect as an epistolary monologue, the
names of characters never appear. Twenty years later the narrator
returns and tries to reconstruct the love that for two decades has
been tormenting her, finally coming to the realization that he is
dead and to the recognition of her own solitude. The work exhibits
psychological depth, a poetic approach to an evocation and good
insight of feminine mystique.

                                                                      PS

SUAREZ DE DEZA, María Isabel (1920-).
    Born in Argentina of a Spanish family, she came to Madrid at age 12,
graduated from the central university (in Filosofía y letras), married
a Spaniard, and feels completely Spanish. Although principally a dramatist, she has written television scripts and contributed many articles
to newspapers. Her three plays, performed in the 1950's, are poetic and
imaginative. They are available in paper only through libraries.

    Buenas noches. Colección Teatro, # 19, Madrid: Alfil, 1952, 52 pp.
        In a play somewhat reminiscent of Casona, a young bride is per-
    suaded to play a brief role with the village madman. The play deals
    with honor, guilt, dreams, and role playing and is of interest
    primarily to specialists in contemporary Spanish theater.

                                                                      PWO

SUAREZ DEL OTERO, Concha (1908-).
    Suárez was born in Luarca, Asturias. She received her bachillerato
in Oviedo and her doctorate at the University of Madrid where she held a
cátedra in Spanish literature. Although she began her literary career
early with two novels, Suárez spent nearly 20 years (1930-1949) without
publishing any works. Since that lapse, however, she has continued to
produce significant works that are uniformly divided in four genres:
novels, poetry, essays, and short stories. As a critic, she has collaborated with various journals, including ABC, Blanco y negro, and La
Estafeta Literaria. Suárez has been nominated for and received
numerous literary awards. Her literature evinces a polished, classical
style, with a certain tendency toward the unusual and/or abnormal.

Mabel. Madrid: Biblioteca Patria, 1928.
Suárez del Otero's first novel, Mabel, was written during its
author's adolescence. The novel takes place in an Asturian village,
and relates the life of María Isabel Salazar (Mabel), a young school
teacher. Mabel comes from a prominent family that has faced ruin-
ation. She takes refuge in the countryside and adapts well to rural
life, finding peace, happiness, and love. Mabel won the Premio
Biblioteca Patria in 1928. According to the author no known copies
exist as it is out-of-print and unobtainable.

Me llamo Clara. Madrid: Quevedo, 1968, 289 pp.
For many critics this "novel within a novel" is Suárez del
Otero's best work of fiction. The first part of the novel includes a
significant portion of an autobiographical novel written by the protagonist in exchange for a money advance she has received from a
publisher-friend. She has turned to fiction as a last resort, after
losing her teaching job. Suddenly, in the midst of her novel, Clara
takes a position with a Madrid travel agency as a tour guide in Europe. Me llamo Clara then proceeds to relate the adventures of Clara
in numerous European countries, including an ill-fated romance that
ends with her renouncing marital plans and returning to Spain.
Suárez's style is clear and unencumbered by literary brushwork. The
structural twists of the narrative serve the novel's desired impact
well.

Mi amiga Andrée. Madrid: Afrodisio Aguado, 1954, 169 pp.
Mi amiga Andrée is a collection of ten short stories, four of
which were previously published in La vida en un día. The themes
and narrative style of the latter are continued in Mi amiga Andrée.
Suárez stresses the existential plight of women in search of
security and happiness. Although the various settings move from the
commonplace to the rarified, the author maintains strict contact with
real people and their concerns.

Satanás no duerme. Madrid: Prensa Española, 1958, 199 pp.
Satanás no duerme is a curious novel that relates the lives of
six high school students from Madrid who, upon graduation in June,
1936, swear an oath to reunite ten years hence, in 1946. The novel
then proceeds to trace the careers and loves of these six friends,
following them through the ravages of the Spanish Civil War and the
post-war period. Numerous unexpected twists develop in the
narrative. On the day of reunion, not surprisingly, the formerly
close friends discover that time has taken its toll and little if
anything now bonds them as a group.

La vida en un día. Madrid: S. Aguirre, 1951, 215 pp.
A collection of 12 short stories, La vida en un día established
its author as a master storyteller. The work was a finalist for the
Premio Alvarez Quintero (Spanish Royal Academy). Most of the stories
evidence a decidedly feminine point of view. Love, loneliness, and
family are unifying themes. Noteworthy is Suárez's tendency to portray suffering and unusual characters. The dreams and disappoint-
ments of women in Spanish society, poignantly depicted by the author,
are couched in what are almost invariably stories with a surprise
ending.

Vida plena. Madrid: Afrodisio Aguado, 1949, 115 pp.
    Vida plena is a collection of 70 poems divided among three
distinct sections: "Paisajes y sueños," "Amor," and "Plenitud."
The three divisions correspond, as the author explains, respectively
to formative periods in her life: 1928-31, 1931-42, and 1936-49.
Manifesting a penchant for classical style (including the cuaderna
vía), Suárez moves from idyllic, somewhat naive poetical allusions,
to a mature and incisive view of humanity: its triumphs and sufferings. In short, the arrangement of poems traces Suárez's own
internal evolution from adolescence to adulthood.

Vulgaridades. Madrid: Mujeres Españolas, 1930.
    Vulgaridades, a novel of adolescence, takes place in Asturias. It
relates the story of two friends, Carmen and Marta. The two girls
are dreamers who see their dreams transformed by reality into something completely different, but perhaps better than that which they
had dreamed. (Annotation provided by Concha Suárez del Otero.) The
only known existing copy belongs to the New York Public Library.

                                                            SLS

*SUÑOL, Cèlia (1899-).
    A novelist born in Barcelona, she is the first woman writer to break
the silence imposed by the Franco dictatorship, winning the first Joanot
Martorell Prize in 1948. Her youth was marked by tuberculosis: first
her own, then her husband's, who died just a few years after they met,
and finally, her son's. She remarried, had a daughter, and was widowed
again after a few years. She had to work to support her children, in a
bar, sewing and doing translations. Her experience working in a bar resulted in a novel Bar which the Franco censorship would not allow to be
published because it ended with the suicide of the protagonist. Suñol
considered literature a pleasure rather than an occupation. Though she
knew her talent, she left it aside to dedicate herself to her children.
Her blindness has prevented her from writing for the last 20 years.

L'home de les fires i altres contes. Barcelona: Selecta, Biblioteca
Selecta, no. 71, 1950, 191 pp.
    A collection of some of her stories, with no thematic unity. The
title story is the most successful of the selection. It combines a
story about a person who goes from fair to fair selling his products
with the explanation of her own difficulties in writing because of
domestic duties. She feels like writing but she has to make the beds
and scrub the bathroom, but then she realizes it's lunchtime and she
has to prepare the meal, and so on, until night falls and she is so
overwhelmed by domestic work that she postpones literary creativity
for a better time. All the stories in the book are based on her life
experiences. The work would be an excellent choice for republication
for classroom use.

Primera part. Barcelona: Col.lecció literària Aymà, 1948, 232 pp.
    This novel won the Joanot Martorell Prize in 1947. It was the
first time the prize was given after the Civil War. Primera Part is
a fictionalized autobiography. In it she describes the atmosphere of
Barcelona in the early years of the century, her contacts with the
feminist movement, her illness and her trip to a health spa in Davos,
Switzerland. There she met the man she would marry, who also
suffered from tuberculosis, which would claim his life a few years

later. From that moment, the author-protagonist's existence centers
on the relationship with her ill husband, which resulted in a
profound psychological crisis. The description of this crisis is one
of the book's most interesting moments. It has not been republished,
and some of its chapters would be appropriate for classroom use.

ISS

*SUQUE I D'ESPONA, Carme.

De la mar i del bosc. Barcelona: la Galera, 1980.
    Stories.

KM

*SUREDA, Emflia (1865-1904).
Majorcan poet.

Poesies mallorquines. 1905.

KM

SZEL, Elisabeth (1926-).
    Szel was born and raised in Budapest, Hungary, where she earned
considerable recognition as a prima ballerina and a decorated film-maker
and a scriptwriter. In 1956, along with many fellow Hungarian artists
and intellectuals, she took refuge in Spain, where she still lives. Her
artistic endeavors have turned to literature, and she is currently
considered one of Spain's leading woman narrators. Much of Szel's
narrative deals with her native Hungary; however, she has also written
poignantly about her adopted country. Her works are concerned primarily
with social and political issues. Szel's ability to produce original
works in Spanish, for her a foreign language, has prompted one critic to
suggest a parallel between Szel and Joseph Conrad.

Balada de cárceles y rameras. Barcelona: Luis de Caralt, 1975,
ISBN 84-217-2139-9, 330 pp.
    Balada de cárceles y rameras approximates the traditional Spanish
picaresque novel. It relates the life of Virgil Vasilescu, a habit-
ual criminal from Transylvania. Utilizing first person narration, an
alienated pícaro, episodic structure, and black humor, Szel takes
the reader on a fast-paced, outrageous adventure throughout Europe,
Africa, and the United States. The novel's time line moves from the
early 1900's to an undetermined point after World War II. As the
title suggests, a significant portion of the action takes place in
the numerous prisons visited by the protagonist. In fact, Szel seems
intent on documenting and comparing prison life in various countries.

La casa de las Chivas. Barcelona: Planeta, 1972, ISBN
84-320-5264-7, 261 pp. Note: This book is sometimes erroneously
catalogued in libraries under the name of Jaime Salom who, curiously,
holds the copyright.
    Based on Jaime Salom's award-winning play of the same name, La
casa de las Chivas is a penetrating psychological study of the
effects of war upon both soldiers and civilians. Set in a provincial
Spanish town during the last months of the Spanish Civil War, the
novel examines a family whose house has been occupied by friendly
troops. While war rages on the nearby front, internal conflicts
unfold within the household. Sex, hunger, and faith are central

themes that inform the tension-ladened plot. Noteworthy for its
apolitical stance (the novel was published during the Franco era), La
casa de las Chivas nonetheless poses salient questions concerning the
Spanish Civil War and its participants.

La mujer del armiño. Spanish trans. by León Klimovsky. Madrid:
E. Gimenez, 1962, 277 pp.

No apta para menores. Barcelona: Luis de Caralt, 1975, ISBN
84-217-4128-4, 325 pp.
    No apta para menores is a complicated novel that chronicles the
vicissitudes of Hungary and its people from the beginning of Soviet
occupation at the close of World War II till the Hungarian uprising
of 1956 and its subsequent aftermath. Szel admirably portrays the
ambience of repression and fear that plagued her countrymen at the
hands of Stalinist puppets. Her tone is accusatory and condemnatory.
Filled with intrigue and political machinations, Szel concentrates on
the Hungarian youth who participated in and suffered from their
abortive attempt for freedom. Undoubtedly much of the novel's matter
is autobiographical, since the author lived the very historical
events treated in No apta para menores.

Operación noche y niebla. Spanish trans. by León Klimovsky.
Madrid: Escelicer, 1961, 239 pp.

Prohibido nacer. Barcelona: Luis de Caralt, 1969, 309 pp.
    Prohibido nacer is a collection of four narrations whose unifying
theme is birth control. "Babi, creadora de ángeles" is a tale
concerning the disconcerting life of an aged midwife who specialized
in abortions. "Vada, hijos, ninguno" is a fascinating novelette
situated in sixteenth-century Hungary during the Turkish occupation.
Szel gives a lucid historical account of a dreary era which includes
a sympathetic treatment of abortion as a means to dignity. "Borbala,
hijo único" relates the background and subsequent trial of a
midwife-abortionist. Finally, "Animalis vitae, Humanea vitae" is a
kind of short history of birth control ranging from ancient times to
the present and, interestingly, into the future via science fiction.

Ven a morir en Amsterdam. Barcelona: Luis de Caralt, 1981, ISBN
84-217-1567-4, 281 pp.
    Totally congruent with Szel's great interest in contemporary soci-
etal problems, Ven a morir en Amsterdam centers on the issue of drug
abuse and its tragic results. Although the novel's action is situated, at times, in England and Amsterdam, the bulk of the narrative
occurs in Madrid and specifically treats the question of illegal drug
activity in post-Franco Spain. The problem is viewed through a variety of perspectives, including the police, youth, the families of
drug users, and international traffickers. There are abundant doses
of violence, illicit sex and perversion that inform the dark under-
side of a seamy world. In spite of the ragged topics, Ven a morir en
Amsterdam is probably Szel's best novel with regard to structure and
narrative technique.

                                                              SLS

TARGIONI, Lodoni Eduarda (1936-).
   Targioni was born in Turin, Italy of an Italian father and American
mother. She studied in Italy, the United States, Morocco and Spain and
now resides in Spain, where she has pursued a career in journalism. She
has published six novels and has written screenplays and radio and
television scripts.

   Los amorales. Barcelona: Planeta, 1971, 293 pp.
      Novel.

   El precio de un hombre. Barcelona: Planeta, 1972, 360 pp.
      A political novel, the characters suffer the turbulence of life
   under a dictatorship. The narrator, an Italian businessman, must
   adapt his principles to attain his goals; Nicky, a Hungarian Jew,
   finds that women are his downfall; Marco uses his sister's relationship with the "Chief" to get ahead. Set in Italy before and during
   World War II; international cast also travels to Madrid and Lisbon.
   Available Kansas City, Kansas Public Library.

                                                                    CLG

TERESA DE JESUS (1515-1582).
   Teresa de Cepeda y Ahumada was born and educated in Avila. From an
early age, she was fond of reading books of chivalry and saints' lives.
At 19, she became a Carmelite, but falling ill, went to stay with an
uncle who introduced her to mystical literature. This struck a chord in
her, but she did not start to express her own ideas in writing until the
age of 47. She was well read in the ascetical mystical Spanish and
foreign--widely translated--literature of the 50 previous years. All
her writing had an immediate application: the Carmelite nuns she sedu-
lously strived to reform. Her life as well as her doctrines received
the canonization of the Church, but not before overcoming stiff opposition from various segments of society, notably the Inquisition.   AR

   Avisos.
      A collection of two/four-line maxims.   AR

   Camino de perfección. 1583.
   The Way of Perfection. Trans. E. Allison Peers, Garden City, NY:
   Image Books, 1964, 280 pp.

Constituciones.
This work presents the regulations of daily life for Santa
Teresa's nuns.   AR

Cuentas de conciencia. 1560-81.
These are intimate reports on events in Santa Teresa's life and
the lives of others close to her.   AR

Epistolario.
Teresa wrote innumerable letters of which some 500 are conserved
and have been published. These letters occupy more pages than all
her other works combined. Some are short, some long; a few are
bureaucratic, but the majority are a personal reflection of her
character. The letters to her family show preoccupation for their
welfare. The letters to the aristocracy and highly placed officials
of the government, including King Phillip II and various members of
his household, manifest her shrewdness and diplomatic talent in
protecting and preserving her reforms. Many other letters were
written to her nuns, regarding matters of the convent, and to
confessors and spiritual directors to uphold her ideas.   AR

Exclamaciones.
These exclamations are fervid prayers to God and Christ, pleading
for help in her miseries.   AR

Libro de las Fundaciones.
The Book of the Foundations continues her autobiography, but it
deals primarily with details of her reformation of the Carmelites.
Teresa reveals in confessional intimate style the peripeties of the
foundation of her 18 convents from 1567 to 1572 throughout various
points of the peninsula: especially interesting were Medina,
Valladolid, Toledo and Salamanca. The foundations of Andalucía
required special tact and effort due to personality conflicts and
distance: Beas, Sevilla, Caravaca. She then returned to the north
and was able to create new foundations in Palencia, Soria and Burgos.
This narrative was started in 1573 and finished just a few days
before her death.   AR

Libro de su vida.
The Life of Teresa de Jesús. Trans. E. Allison Peers, Garden City,
NY: Image Books, 1960, 397 pp.
The Life of Saint Teresa of Avila, Including the Relations of Her
Spiritual State. Trans. David Lewis, Westminster, MD: Newman, 1962.
                                                                CLG

Meditaciones sobre los Cantares.
The Meditations on the Canticle are short reflections on a few
passages (1,1; 1,2; 2,3-4; 2,5) of the Song of Songs. The book is a
pretext for Teresa to discourse on profound themes of spirituality
dear to her heart. She places the peace of the soul in the kiss of
God, but the soul is to avoid all attachments to riches, praises and
honors. The soul will then be in the perfect freedom of the spirit
which is the highest gift of God. At that stage, a divine friendship
is developed, and the soul remains in a prayerful quietude where the
union with God is consummated. The soul receives the bountiful love

of God and stays in perfect contemplation of the divinity to the
extreme of wishing to die without dying.   AR

Moradas.
Interior Castle. Trans. E. Allison Peers, Garden City, NY:
Doubleday, 1961, 235 pp.
     More specifically called Moradas del castillo interior (Mansions
of the Interior Castle). Widely considered a masterpiece of mystical
literature, it is Teresa's final work. Man's spiritual life is
compared to the interior of a castle in which seven mansions are
found. Through intensifying prayer, the soul moves from one mansion
to another getting ever closer to God who dwells in the innermost
center. This journey has three stages: purgative, illuminative and
at last unitive in which the consummation of the union with God is
achieved. Each of the castle quarters is marked by a particular
evolution of prayer with its consequent impact upon every facet of
the individual's life.   AR

Obras completas. Madrid: Aguilar, 1974.
Complete Works. Trans. E. Allison Peers, London: Sheed and Ward,
1946.
     The most recent one-volume edition of Santa Teresa's complete
works contains a preliminary study by Luis Santullano and an essay on
Santa Teresa's style by Ramón Menéndez Pidal. The contents include
the Vida de Teresa de Jesús y algunas de las mercedes que Dios le
hizo, Relaciones espirituales, Camino de perfección, Castillo
interior, o las Moradas, Conceptos del amor de Dios, Exclamaciones,
Libro de las Fundaciones, Constituciones, Modo de visitar los
conventos de las Carmelitas Descalzas, Avisos para sus monjas,
Respuesta a un desacío espiritual, Vejamen dado a varios escritos
sobre las palabras "Búscate en Mí," 32 poems and the Epistolario.
The Peers English translation is a three-volume work containing the
same works as the Aguilar edition with the exception of the
Epistolario. Peers provides helpful introductions to each work and
extensive notes.   CLG

Poesías.
     There are 33 poems of very popular and simple tone written for
various occasions: religious festivities, family celebrations and
the lyrical expression of her own feelings.   AR

Visita de descalzas.
     The work presents some 50 recommendations for those visiting Santa
Teresa's convents of Discalced Nuns.   AR

TORRE, Josefina de la (1910-).
     One of only two women recognized in Gerardo Diego's anthology as a
Generation of '27 poet (see also Ernestina de Champourcin), Josefina de
la Torre experimented with many art forms--instrumental and vocal music,
acting and theater production, radio and recitation, and writing,
chiefly poetry. Her older brother, Claudio de la Torre (1902), a
dramatist, poet, and novelist, encouraged her literary activity and both
made friendships with other Generation of '27 poets, among them Rafael
Alberti (who dedicated an alexandrine sonnet to Claudio in Marinero en
tierra) and Pedro Salinas, who greatly influenced Josefina's poetry and
wrote the introduction to her first book. Her early poetry, principally

free verse, exemplifies the tendency among Grand Canary Island lyricists to employ ocean themes and imagery. Some discrepancy exists concerning her birthdate, either 1907 or 1910.

Marzo incompleto. Colección de San Borondón. Las Palmas de Gran Canaria: Imprenta Lezcano, 1968, 58 pp.
   First published in the magazine Fantasía, the poems of Marzo incompleto long for an earlier, incomplete spring, while recognizing the completion of life. Retrospective glances reveal personal alienation, time preoccupations, unfulfilled love, wistfulness for unknown, unborn children, and the contemplation of and preparation for death. Technically naked--lacking complex metaphors, rhyme symmetry, and poetic devices--these seemingly cathartic verses undress the emotions, baring suffering, alienation, sadness, and desolation. Several of the 350 numbered-edition copies are available in U.S. libraries including Kent State University library.

Memorias de una estrella. La novela del sábado, año 2, num 87. Madrid: Cid, 1954, 80 pp.
   After a 24-year silence, Memorias de una estrella appeared as a "novel-of-the-week" in a subscription series. Written in memoir-fashion, the tale chronicles a pretty-but-superficial girl's pursuit of stardom, only to give way, abruptly, to housewifery in the suburbs. Both the title piece and the second selection, "En el umbral" are actually short stories which yield to stereotypes and have only slight character development or thematic content. The book may be found at Michigan Graduate School library.

Poemas de la Isla. Barcelona: Imprenta Altés, 1930.
   Probably the best poetry of her early years, Josefina's Poemas de la isla is characterized by a tone and attitude of frank spontaneity and flirtatious vigor and exuberance. As in her first book, a predilection for free verse predominates, with nature themes and attention to metaphors. The book is difficult to find in the U.S., but perhaps may be located by writing León Sáchez Cuesta, librero, Calle Serrano 29, Madrid 1.

Versos y Estampas. Octavo suplemento de Litoral. Málaga: Imprenta Sur, 1927, 68 pp.
   Published in 1927 when Josefina was still a teenager, Versos y Estampas is dedicated to her older brother, Claudio, who encouraged her writing. Its seven-page long, fairy-tale prologue, "Isla, pre-ludio, poetisa," by Pedro Salinas spins a symbolic fantasy fable which alludes to an island (her native Grand Canary), a girl (Jose-fina) and the prelude or incipient stages of her poetic inspiration transported by a grand, mythical eagle. The book's pages alternate "versos" and "estampas," giving it a "practice notebook" quality as though its author were undertaking writing exercises. The "estampas" are vignettes, written in a flow-of-consciousness fashion, which re-late childhood remembrances of places, games, and outcasts or margin-of-society characters. The alternating poems, "versos," although not carefully crafted and often incomplete, consistently strive for descriptive nature images, almost always the ocean, and creative metaphor making. A signed copy is located in Cornell library.

JBL

TORRE VIVERO, Carmen de la (1931-).
A poet in Madrid, she is Professor of declamation. She is a lecturer and magazine contributor. A book of poems and novel are in preparation.

Capas españolas y Glosas poéticas de los refranes de la capa. 1965

En las orillas de un lago. 1952, 64 pp.
   Here the poetry is of a love viewed with both nostalgia and disillusion. Images are drawn principally from nature. The poetry shows influences of Bécquer and Lorca and often uses traditional verse forms of the romance, the seguidilla, and the sonnet. Prologue by Juan de Contreras. Not widely distributed in the United States but is available through interlibrary loan.

Eternidad. Gráficas Valera, two editions.

Parajes líricos. Madrid: Samarán, 1963.
   The poetry displays nostalgia for love and for historic Spain, especially that of Castilla and Andalucía. Images are drawn from nature and from Spanish places of interest. There are influences of Cervantes and the Golden Age and traditional verse forms, including couplets, quatrains, and romances. Prologue by J. Alvarez Sierra. Not widely distributed in the United States but is available through interlibrary loan.

Poemas a Madrid. Madrid: Gráficas Cinema, 1970.

Presentimientos. Madrid: Martín y Macías, 1977, ISBN 8-48526-303-0.
                                                                NLB

*TORRES, Narcisa (18th century). Also: **Rosa Trincares.**
   She wrote poems praising the work of poet Carles Ros (1703-1773); including sonnets for "Práctica de Ortografía para dos idiomas, castellano y valenciano" and "Tratat d'adages" and a ballad in "arte mayor" for "L'Epítome del origen y grandeza del idioma valenciano."
                                                                VC-E

**TORRES, Xohana.
   Torres is a versatile writer who has published poetry, two plays and a novel. Her last known work and first novel Adiós María won the 1970 Premio "Galicia" awarded by the Centro Gallego de Buenos Aires.

Adiós, María. Buenos Aires: Galicia, 1971, 177 pp.

Do sulco. Vigo: Galaxia, Illa nova, no. 2, 1957, 69 pp.

Un hotel de primeira sobre o río. Vigo: Galaxia, 1968, 90 pp.

A otra banda do íberr. Vigo: Galaxia, 1965, 96 pp.
                                                                KHC

TROITIÑO, Carmen (1918-).
   Born in Guadalajara to a middle-class family from Galicia, she grew up in Madrid and graduated from the central university with a degree in history. She worked with the experimental theater in her student days and later directed works (principally the more demanding foreign ones)

in national theaters. She attempts certain innovative techniques in plays that probe serious questions of human motivation.

Pandereta. Madrid: C. Bermejo, 1949, 142 pp.
    Play in the experimental vein that probes tourist Spain. Laziness, drunkenness, and general intellectual superficiality are portrayed very negatively. Little-known work of interest primarily to those researching lesser-known figures. Preface. Available in libraries.

Pasiones. Madrid: Escelicer, 1952, 96 pp.
    A rural melodrama of violent passions and contrasts of character, the play suggests that destiny is rooted more in primitive urges than in rational choices. It favors balance and criticizes extremes. Preface. Available in libraries.

Si llevara agua. Colección Teatro, #139. Madrid: Alfil, 1956, 76 pp.
    Psychological drama borders on melodrama, and is reminiscent at times of Echegaray's El gran Galeoto and Benavente's Los intereses creados. A woman with a questionable past must defend herself when her brother-in-law is found dead in her home. Available in libraries and only in paperback. Of interest to researchers in contemporary Spanish theater.

Y los hijos de tus hijos. Colección Teatro, #203. Madrid: Alfil, 1958, 52 pp.
    The studious son of a wealthy prostitute is rejected by his upper-class sweetheart when her family learns of his origins. He then turns to a young woman from a background similar to his. The play suggests that societal prejudice, like heredity and environment, determine one's fate. Available in paperback only through libraries. Of interest primarily to specialists in contemporary Spanish theater.
                                                                    PWO

TUSQUETS, Esther (1936-).
    Though Esther Tusquets has played a very active role in recent Catalonian literary culture, serving as director of Editorial Lumen since the early 1960's, her own creative debut did not come until 1978 with the publication of El mismo mar de todos los veranos. Her production, which to date includes a novelistic trilogy and one volume of related short stories, focuses upon woman's existential margination and quest for authentic personhood within the restrictive bourgeois context of post-Civil War Spain.

El amor es un juego solitario. Barcelona: Lumen, 1979, ISBN 84-264-1953-X, 150 pp. 2nd ed., May 1979. 3rd ed., Oct. 1979. 4th ed., March 1980.
    In the second volume of her novelistic trilogy, Tusquets creates a closed universe centering around the experiences of a middle-aged protagonist and her two adolescent lovers. In a desperate attempt to escape both the tedium of her role as bourgeois housewife and mother and her fear of the aging process itself, Elia becomes the apex of a love triangle which affords her a vicarious sense of happiness and fulfillment through the emotional responses of her young lovers. Neither heterosexual nor homosexual love prove to be effective

antidotes to the existential dilemma of middle age. Paperback and
hardback editions are available.

El mismo mar de todos los veranos. Barcelona: Lumen, 1978, ISBN
84-264-2958-5, 229 pp. 2nd ed., Sept. 1978. 3rd ed., Feb. 1979.
4th ed., Oct. 1979. 5th ed., May 1980. 6th ed., April 1983.
    In this, her first novel, Tusquets employs literary and
mythological allusion to explore the middle-aged female's quest for
meaning and fulfillment beyond the confines of the traditional
patriarchal institutions of marriage and motherhood. Of particular
interest are the author's overt treatment of the lesbian theme and
her analysis of the mother-daughter relationship within the confines
of a restrictive bourgeois Catalan context. The work is available in
both hardback and paperback editions.

Siete miradas en un mismo paisaje. Barcelona: Lumen, 1981, ISBN
84-264-2960-2, 249 pp.
    A collection of related short stories, Tusquets' most recent work
focuses upon the female growth process at seven critical moments in
the life experience of a member of the Catalonian bourgeoisie. Of
particular interest are Sara's introduction to heterosexual and,
later, homosexual love, her growing awareness of social injustice,
and the subordination of her own needs and interests to those of
family and class. The work is available in both paperback and
hardback editions.

Varada tras el último naufragio. Barcelona: Lumen, 1980, ISBN
84-264-2956-4, 271 pp. 2nd ed., 1980.
    The trilogy begun in 1978 is completed with this novel which
continues to explore the experience of the alienated middle-aged
female. Unable to accept the dissolution of a marriage envisioned as
ideal, the protagonist retreats into an interior fantasy world which
threatens to destroy her. This experience is repeated in the marital
crisis of her closest friend. Unlike the protagonists of Tusquet's
two earlier novels, these women are able to reconstruct their lives,
offering in the process, contrasting solutions to the problems of
marital infidelity and solitude. Both hardback and paperback
editions are available.

                                                            LL-B

U

UCEDA, Julia (1925-).
  Born in Sevilla, Uceda received her doctorate from the Universidad de
Sevilla, with a thesis on José Luis Hidalgo. She taught at Michigan
State University from 1966 to 1973, then returned to Spain. After a
brief stay in Ireland, she now resides in Galicia. Considered, chronologically, a member of the Generation of the 1950's, she nevertheless
possesses a poetic voice and spirit of her own, which makes her difficult to categorize. Her poetry, which is intimate and strange and yet
never forgets the social context, has gravitated increasingly toward the
metaphysical and existential. She has also writen critical studies on
the poetry of Jorge Guillén and José Luis Hidalgo; and is currently
considered one of the most significant poetic voices in Spain.

  Campanas en Sansueña. Madrid: Dulcinea, 1977. Col. Dulcinea, 8.
  ISBN 84-400-3701-5, 61 pp.
    The title of this collection, which clearly recalls Luis Cernuda's
  "Resaca en Sansueña" and "Ser de Sansueña," also reflects a
  Cervantine view of reality as illusion, illusion as reality, in
  Uceda's poems. Written in Ireland (and Spain), they nevertheless
  double back like ghosts to another space, another time, as for
  example in the bitter and intensely crafted "España, eres un largo
  invierno." Death, time and identity seem to fuse in these poems, and
  in the end, only the light--"Luz: tan sólo en ella creo," she
  writes in the last poem, "Libertad de la luz"--paradoxically, has
  substance for this visionary poet. Paper.

  Extraña juventud. Madrid: Rialp, 1962. Col. Adonais, no. 203.
  ISBN 84-321-1532-0, 55 pp.
    Finalist for the Adonais Poetry Prize of 1961. The dedication--
  "Al hombre de mi tiempo"--reveals the social (and implicitly
  political) intentions of this book, in which the poet denounces the
  repressive and unjust political system, the inequalities, and the
  feeling of collective and individual alienation of her time and
  place. But in other poems, there is a distinct existentialist edge,
  as the poet questions her own sense of authenticity and identity,
  pressured by mortality itself. The language--"Julia Uceda, qué has
  hecho de tu sombra," ("what have you done with your shadow?") she
  writes--is intense and strong. Paper.

  Mariposa en cenizas. Prólogo de Manuel Mantero. Arcos de la
  Frontera: Alcaraván, 1959, 45 pp.
    In her first book of poetry, Uceda deals with the themes of love,

death and alienation. Taking the title from a line of Góngora's
Soledades, she sees her death as one which "aún no está madura"
("is not yet ripe") in God's fields, in the poem "Mariposa en
cenizas." Although most of the volume is love poetry, the reader
will also find poems like "La extraña," in which the poet senses she
has somehow been cut off from some other, prior existence. Her
poetry, as Manuel Mantero observes in the prologue (pp. 9-10), seems
to arise out of a deep and spontaneous well of mystery. Paper.

Poemas de Cherry Lane. Madrid: Agora, 1968, 45 pp.
     These 14 poems, written in free verse, reflect in large part the
poet's residence and experiences in the United States. As she
addresses a silent friend and listener named Charlie, Uceda further
explores the themes of personal identity and death, often intimately
entwined in her poetry. There is something of the hallucinatory,
akin to José Hierro's alucinaciones, to be found here, especially in
"Cita con una sombra." Her vision of reality is simply but
profoundly expressed in this line from "Condenada al silencio":
"Nada más natural. Nada más misterioso." Paper.

Sin mucha esperanza. Madrid: Agora, 1966, 74 pp.
     Divided into two parts, "Los símbolos" and "Los mitos," and
prefaced by the poem "Anánke," this volume of poetry treats
feelingly such themes as loss of identity and freedom, alienation,
lost childhood, exile and death. Particularly poignant are the poems
"Eterno oleaje" and "Una patria se ve desde la cumbre," in which
images of inner and outer exile from "an impossible country"--"'Ya
llegamos/a la patria.' Y jamás/será la patria" ("Now we return/to
the homeland/ and it will never/be the homeland")--are juxtaposed.
Traces of José Luis Hidalgo occasionally surface in her treatment of
death and God, as in "Hay un rostro detrás de la sombra" and the
last poem, "'No Trespassing'." Paper.

Viejas voces secretas de la noche. El Ferrol: Esquío-Ferrol, 1981.
Col. Esquío de Poesía, 6. ISBN 84-86046-00-9, 40 pp.
     Uceda divides this latest collection of poetry into five parts:
"Viejas voces secretas de la noche," "Orden del sueño," "Poemas
limítrofes," "Los dioses difíciles," and "Tregua." The intimate
and very personal character of her poetry turns markedly metaphysical
here--a tendency already noticeable in Uceda's early work--as the
poet seeks revelation in darkness, in the night which possesses its
own light, its own knowledge, or as she puts it, "la noche es
caminar/buscando ángulos de luz" ("night is out walking/searching
for angles of light"). Paper, in print.

NMV

UCETA, Acacia (1927-).
     Uceta was born in Madrid and received an education in the fine arts.
Her poetry has appeared in numerous anthologies as well as the collec-
tions listed below and has been translated into Portuguese, French,
Italian and English. Among the prizes awarded her work are the Elisa
Soriano, Contraluz, Fray Luis de León, Ciudad de Cuenca, Amigos de la
Poesía de Valencia and the Virgen del Carmen. She has received grants
from the Juan March foundation and the Spanish Ministry of Culture. Her
short novels have also received the Sésamo and Café Gijón prizes.

Al sur de las estrellas. Cuenca: Colección "Gárgola," 1976.
    Poetry.

El corro de las horas. Madrid: Colección "Agora," 1961.
    Poetry.

Cuenca, roca viva. Cuenca: Colección "Los Pliegos del Hocino,"
1980.
    Poetry.

Detrás de cada noche. Madrid: Nacional, 1970, 79 pp.
    This volume of poetry was the result of a 1968 grant from the
Fundación Juan March. Although divided into five sections, "La
mañana," "Mediodía," "La tarde," "La noche," and "... Y otra vez el
alba," the poems form a whole. The poem is a hymn to hope, which
human beings must conquer and hold onto in order to justify each
moment of their existence. Despite death, shadows and terrible
winters, the poet is astonished to find herself still alive; but her
face is lifted up.

Frente a un muro de cal abrasadora. Cuenca: El Toro de Barro, 1967.
    Poetry.

Una hormiga tan sólo. Madrid: Aguilar, 1967.
    Novel.

Intima dimensión. Madrid: El Toro de Barro, 1983, ISBN
84-85339-47-9, 59 pp.
    The three sections, "Esfera," "Círculo," and "Espiral," contain
12 poems each. The poet expresses her optimism and happiness. She
crosses over obstacles and dominates her own life. Uceta received a
fellowship from the Ministerio de Cultura to work on this book.

Quince años. Madrid: El Español, 1962.
    Short novel.

                                                                    CLG

URRETAVIZCAYA, Arantxa.
    One of a small group of authors to write in Basque. She has written
poetry and stories, as well as a non-fiction book, La conquista de
Albania (with Antton Olariaga).

    Zergatik Panpox? Donostia: Hordago, 1980?
    Catalan edition translated by Josep Daurella: Zergatik Panpox?
    Per què, menut? Sant Boi de Llobregat: Mall, 1982.
        The interior monologue of a young mother struggling to support
    herself and her son, this poignant book brings to life the pain of
    abandonment and solitude felt by a male-oriented, traditional woman.
    Even after several years, she wishes for el Txema, wanting to believe
    that his return would solve everything, but knowing it is not
    possible. The first person stream of consciousness format gives a
    look inside the mind of an unhappy, unliberated woman who has not yet
    seen and appreciated her own strength and beauty.

<u>Maitasunaren magalean</u>. San Sebastian: Gipuzkoako Aurrezki Kutxa
Probintzialaren Argitarapenak, 1980?
   Poetry.

<u>Aspaldian espero zaitudalako ez nago sekulan bakarrik</u>. Donostia:
Erein, 1980?

KM

VALDERRAMA, Pilar (1892-1979).
Poet and dramatist, she was born in Madrid. In her autobiography, published after her death, she declared she had been the secret platonic love of the poet Antonio Machado. She was married and had a son and two daughters but, after discovering her husband's infidelity, she sought in her poetry and in Machado's friendship the happiness she could not find in her marriage. The following four volumes of poetry were published in her life: Las piedras de Horeb (1922), Huerto cerrado (1928), Esencias (1930) and Holocausto (1941). None of the above books are available. Her dramatic poem titled "El tercer mundo" was published with two other works by women authors in the volume titled Teatro de mujeres. Tres autoras españolas.

> Sí, soy Guiomar. Memorias de mi vida. Barcelona: Plaza & Janes, 1981.

> "El tercer mundo." In Teatro de mujeres. Tres autoras españolas. Madrid: Aguilar, 1934, pp. 87-137.
>   Classified as a dramatic poem by its author, and as a comedy by the author of the prologue, Cristóbal de Castro, this drama has two acts in prose and one act in verse. The drama exploits the problem of the love triangle and the four different levels of reality, dream, will and artistic creation in which the characters choose to exist. The main theme is the woman's unhappiness at the level of reality and her escape to the level of dream and illusion in order to fulfill her desires.

EP-H

*VALENTI, Helena (1940-).
A native of Barcelona, from a bourgeois family background, Valentí grew up in post-war Spain under the Franco regime, at a time when tensions and repression were the norm. Escaping from restrictions and narrowness, she lived and studied in England, obtaining her Doctor of Literature degree from Cambridge University. She married an Englishman (a relationship which eventually ended in divorce). During a bohemian life in London (1968-1973), she was active in the women's liberation movement there. She returned to Catalonia in 1974, living for a time in Barcelona. Her first book, L'amor adult (1977) is a collection of thematically related short stories. Before publishing her second book, the novel La solitud d'Anna (1981), she moved to the coastal village of Cadaqués. She has since returned to Barcelona.

L'amor adult. Barcelona: Edicions 62, 1977. "El Balancí."
ISBN 84-297-1332-8, 122 pp. Eleven short stories: L'amor adult, Els
fils, L'altre, Desarrelament, Llums a la ciutat, Visita a les
catacumbes, El vell Amos, El bosc, Monàrquic, La falta, and La
felicitat.
   The 11 short stories are replete with motifs obviously drawn from
close personal observation: the foreign female in England, the tolerant British husband, posters with women's liberation subjects, al-
cohol, unwanted pregnancies, numerous non-communicating marriages.
Marital hostility, frequent separations and aggressively unconventional sexuality as well as the ubiquitous "liberated" but alienated
female recur repeatedly. Both marriage and the various love relationships are portrayed as a struggle, a fear of commitment, of emotions, of domesticity. Concern with economic self-sufficiency for
the female is another reiterated motif. Homosexuality, bisexuality
and the ménage a trois all provide indications of the enchantment of
all with the mystique of their respective sexes and inability to
mature. Valentí's feminism is judicious, not aggressive or
tendentious.

La solitud d'Anna. Barcelona: Edicions 62, 1981. "El Balancí."
ISBN 84-297-1684-X, 117 pp.
   Novel. Valentí treats conflicts of a more philosophical nature,
in the vein of Ortega y Gasset, with existential overtones:
appearance vs. underlying realities, the individual vs. collectivity,
creativity vs. impotence, fulfillment vs. frustration, communication
vs. solitude. Many had already appeared in her earlier story collection; in this second work, she concentrates especially upon the
crisis of creativity, the frustration of affective and emotional
urges, and the sexual conflicts which result from the individual's
feeling of futility and impotence in face of the dehumanizing effects
of mass society, technological change and technocratic functions.
The world portrayed is one where the difficulty of self-affirmation
drives some to seek power or to abuse, while others become cruel and
infantile, or retreat into solitude and hide behind facades.

JP

VALLDAURA, Agna de. See: Santamaria i Ventura, Joaquima.

*VAYREDA, Maria dels Angels.

La boira als ulls. Barcelona: 1977.
   Poetry.

Els defraudats. Figueres: Empordá, 1980.
   Novel.

KM

**VAZQUEZ IGLESIAS, Purificación (1918-). Also: Pura Vázquez.
   This author of 15 volumes of poetry in Castilian and Galician has
been called the successor to Rosalía de Castro in the field of
twentieth-century Galician poetry. Her poems, articles, short stories
and criticism have appeared in journals and newspapers throughout Spain,
Portugal, Argentina, Ecuador and Venezuela, where she taught at the
University of Caracas. She is a correspondent of the Real Academia
Gallega de Artes y Letras.

Los Aldán Fueron a América.

Borboriños, contos galegos. Madrid: Colección Brais Pinto.

Columpio de luna a sol. Madrid: Colección Colegio Mayor para
Menores, Boris Bureba, 1952, 192 pp.
     This collection of children's poetry designed for classroom use is
divided into seven sections, each with its own theme, which may be
read in any order. The book is dedicated to all children and to
those who still have a child's spirit. The themes of school, games,
people, animals, landscapes and dreams correspond to each of the
poems: (1) "Dejad que los niños se acerquen a mí," (2) "Tú no
sabes leer," (3) "Al Corro Claro," (4) "María del Mar Venía,"
(5) "En su mundo, tan pequeño," (6) "Veo, vel... ¿qué ves?" and
(7) "Yo quiero dormir."

O Desacougo. Colección Salnés, 29. Vigo: Galaxia, 1971,
ISBN 84-7154-161-0, 86 pp.

Duas novelas galegas. Segundo Pereira and Augas Soltas. Orense:
La Región, 1978, ISBN 84-400-4409-7. 93; 86 pp.
     Segunda Pereira is a short novel which details the life of a
Galician family after their father, Segundo Pereira has left them.
The narrator addresses the narrative to Segundo Pereira as if it were
a letter he is to receive. Should he receive it, and indeed the
reader does not know if he does, it would represent, for him, a
psychological analysis of his life and the effect he has had on
others. Since this is not certain, it ends up being a psychological
unveiling of the narrator.

Fantasías infantiles. Orense: Autor, Apartado 272, 1980,
ISBN 84-300-3332-7, 66 pp.

Mañana del amor. Colección Tiempo Nuestro, 1. Barcelona: Surco,
1956, 81 pp.
     This collection of 47 poems dealing with individual pain and
suffering, the influence of the landscape on human existence, the
land and love is prefaced by an introduction, "Envío" by María Luz
Morales. In this piece, she likens Vázquez' poetry to that of
Rosalía de Castro, in her elaboration of the same themes and eternal
messages which she sends in verse. The five divisions of the book
are: (1) Resurrección, (2) Dulce Dolor de Amor, (3) Pleamar del
Gozo, (4) Cuerpo de Amor, and (5) Mañana del amor.

Maturidade. Centro Gallego de Bos Aires: Galicia, 114 pp.

Monicreques; teatro infantil galego. Orense: La Región, 1974,
ISBN 84-400-7141-8, 40 pp.
     This collaborative effort with Dora Vázquez contains two plays
for children suitable for classroom use. The first play, O paxaro
azul is credited to Pura, while the other one, O trasno enredador, is
Dora's. Both plays are acted with one set. Cast and scenes are
simplified. Both plays are one-act and contain three short scenes.
Directions for set, costuming and casting are clearly defined.

Oriolos neneiros: poesía infantil galega. Orense: La Región, 1975?, ISBN 84-4008-303-3, 102 pp.

Los poetas. Orense: Ayuntamiento de Orense, 1971, 128 pp.

Presencia de Venezuela. Caracas: Lírica Hispana.

Rondas de norte a sur. Versos prós menos da aldea. Orense: Caja de Ahoros Provincial, 1968, 68 pp.

A saudade e outros poemas. Colección Salnés, v. 11. Vigo: Galaxia, 1963, ISBN 84-7154-096-7, 70 pp.

Los sueños desandados. Madrid: Pequeñas editoriales, 1973, ISBN 84-300-5836-2, 82 pp.

Tiempo mío. Colección Palma, 4. Segovia: Casa Amigos de Antonio Machado, 1952, 98 pp.
   The main themes of this collection of 52 poems are the passage of time, women's identity, nature, and the establishment of a sense of personal time. This is especially evident in the title poem, "Tiempo mío." Death seems to pervade many of the poems, and is treated in 11 of the selections included in the chapter "Esa Muerte." Other chapters are "Umbral," "Latido," and "Allí en la Sombra."

MDJ

*VENTOS I CULLELL, Palmira (1862-1917). Pseud. Felip Palma.
   Publishing consistently under her pseudonym, Ventós lived throughout her life in Barcelona, although her works have a rural Catalan setting. She adapts a realism bordering on naturalism to a sentimental view of life, counterbalancing the implacability of nature with liricism and comic scenes. Ventós left several unpublished works on her death, including a series of rural sketches, Visions d'un pasatge.

Asprors de la vida. Biblioteca Popular de "L'Avenç," No. 28. Barcelona: "L'Avenç," 1904, 97 pp.
   Consisting of five short stories all set in rural Catalonia, this collection depicts the harsh human realities of village life. Clearly influenced by naturalism, Ventós treats the themes of evil, hatred, and egoism and the resultant solitude and despair of life's victims, all against the backdrop of an unresponsive natural world. Several stories are written largely in a colloquial dialogue form.

La caiguda. Biblioteca Popular de "L'Avenç," No. 64. Barcelona: Llibreria "L'Avenç," 1907, 92 pp.
   Combining sentimental themes and a realistic treatment of life with detailed descriptions of nature, this short novel set in rural Catalonia treats the solitude of the individual and the egoism of mankind within the cycle of human life and the natural world. The novel attempts to reconcile the harsh reality of rural life and the brutishness of human nature with a harmonic vision of the power of love. Ventós depends on coincidence to establish the cyclical nature of life.

L'enrenou del poble. Quadro de costums en un acte. Barcelona: Bartomeu Baxarias, 1909, 48 pp.

Performed at the Teatre Català (Romea) in Barcelona on May 8, 1909, this short play centers on the comic figure of the village bad boy who uses his feigned desire to leave town to bring about his marriage to the town beauty. The resolution is opposed by the wise mayor, the only character not taken in by the fool. Numerous popular types appear with much humorous dialogue as filler. The play appears to be the reworking of a folk tale in which appearances deceive and true love wins out over the power of money.

Isolats, drama de familia en tres actes. Barcelona: "L'Avenç," 1909, 113 pp.
    Staged on March 20, 1909 in the Teatre Català (Romea) in Barce-lona, the play depicts the conflicts between inheritance and passion in a rural bourgeois family. Torn between her attraction for her sister's husband and pressure to marry, the protagonist ultimately retakes control of her own life and opts for solitude. The theme of blindness precipitates the denouement. Village characters and much popular dialogue not related to the conflict add a comic dimension. The play combines costumbrismo, realism and sentimentality.

La força del passat, drama en tres actes. Barcelona, 1911.

MB

*VERGER, Maria.
    Poet from Alcudia (Majorca), she wrote Clarors matinals (1924), Tendal d'estrelles (1930) and L'estela d'or (1934).

KM

*VERNET I REAL, Maria Teresa (1907-1974).
    Born in Barcelona and best known for her novel Maria Dolors, she collaborated on several publications where she started to publish her first short stories. Her fiction is characterized by an intense study of feminine psychology. Half of her work is written in Castilian and the other half in Catalan. She belongs to the generation of Catalan writers who encountered difficulty diffusing their books in Catalan due to the political repression which characterized the period of 1936-1960. She also translated several books from English into Spanish.

Les algues roges. Badalona: Biblioteca "A tot vent," 72, Editor Proa, 1934, 256 pp.

Amor silenciosa. Barcelona: Central Catalana de publicacions, 1927, 198 pp.

El camí repres. Badalona: Biblioteca "A tot vent," 24, Editor Proa, 1930, 271 pp.

Elisenda. Barcelona: Biblioteca "Rosa dels vents," 85, Editor Quaderns literaris, 1935, 92 pp.

Estampes de Paris. Barcelona: Biblioteca "Rosa dels vents," 24, Editor Quaderns literaris 24, 1937, 63 pp.

Eulàlia. Badalona: Biblioteca "A tot vent," 7, Editor Proa, 1928, 276 pp.

Final i preludi. Badalona: Biblioteca "A tot vent," 63, Editor Proa, 1933, 279 pp.

Maria Dolors. Barcelona: Novela d'ara, 145, Editor L'avenc Gràfic, 1926, 64 pp.

El perill. Badalona: Biblioteca "A tot vent," Editor Proa, 1930, 245 pp.

Poemes. Barcelona: Publicacion La Revista, 65, 1929, 61 pp.

Presó oberta. Biblioteca "A tot vent," 36, Editor Proa, 1931, 254 pp.

                                                                CF

*VICENS, Antònia (1942-).
Born in Santanyí, Majorca, she has written several books of narrations and novels, and has won literary prizes in both categories.

Banc de fusta. Palma de Majorca: Moll, 1968.
    Stories, winner of the Premi Vida Nova.

La festa de tots els morts. Barcelona: Nova terra, 1974.

Material de fulletó. Palma de Majorca: Moll, 1971.
    Novel and stories.

Primera Comunió. Palma de Majorca: Moll, 1980.
    Stories.

Quilòmetres de tul per a un petit cadàver. Barcelona: Laia, 1982.

La santa. Barcelona: Laia, 1980, ISBN 84-7222-928-9, 103 pp.
Prologue by Josep Maria Llompart.
    The novel is written with a background of Vicens' own small town--the streets, plaza, and people who inhabit them. With a vision that seems to come from a semi-conscious state between sleeping and waking, Vicens nonetheless gives us a lucid critique of that microcosm of society which represents the universal.

39 graus a l'ombre. Barcelona: Selecta, 1968.
    Novel, winner of the Premi Sant Jordi.

                                                                KM

*VILA, Mercè (1902-).
Poet born in Barcelona, she wrote Les hores (1918), Flor de l'ànima (1929) and Fugaç resplendor (1955).

                                                                KM

*VILLAMARTIN, Isabel de (?-1877).
A poet mentioned in Los trobadors nous (1858) and Los trobadors moderns (1859). She wrote Clemencia Isaura (1859) and La desposada de Déu (1862).

                                                                KM

VILLARTA TUNON, Angeles (1921-).
Born in Belmonte, Asturias, she was educated in Switzerland. A prominent journalist, she has written novels, essays, poems and short stories. She directed the second series of La novela corta and edited the comic periodical Don Venerando. For Una mujer fea, 1953-4, she received the "Premio Fémina." In 1953 also appeared La taberna de Laura--Poemas del mar. She has also written the following novels: Un pleno de amor, 1942; Por encima de las nieblas, 1943; Muchachas que trabajan, 1944; Ahora que soy estraperlista, 1949; Con derecho a cocina, 1950. (These works are known through secondary sources; it is imposs-ible to secure them or to identify their publisher.)

Una mujer fea. Madrid: Calenda, 1954, 389 pp. Premio Fémina 1953; Serie Grandes Novelistas de Nuestro Tiempo.
Through a well-constructed simple plot this novel engages the reader in a crescendo of foreboding. Josefa, daughter of the shop-keeper in a hamlet located somewhere in Galicia or Asturias, marries Julián, the bastard son of the last nobleman of the region. The townspeople are a collective character. Womanhood is demanding a voice, but it is the voice of non-heroic individuals. An affinity with Casona is evident in terms of setting and character development. This is a fine novel that is hard to find except through interlibrary loan.

NH

*VILLENA, Isabel de (1430-1490).
A Franciscan abbess of the monastery of Trinity of València from 1462 to 1490, she was the illegitimate daughter of the nobleman Enrique de Villena, also a writer, who died when she was four years old. She was brought up in the Valencian court with her relative Maria de Castilla, married to King Alfons V of Aragon. Neither her mother nor the place where she was born is known. Her real name is Elionor Manuel de Villena. It was changed to Isabel de Villena when she became a nun. She lived during the most splendid period of Catalan letters. Only one of her works is known to us: Vita Christi, written in Catalan. She enjoyed great prestige because of her vast culture, the nobility of her family, and her work as abbess.

Vita Christi. R. Miquel i Planas, editor of the princeps edition of València, 1497. 3 volumes. An Editorial Note introduces the text (vol. 1, beginning), and four appendices follow with the "Memòria del editor de la Biblioteca Catalana al ilustríssim consell de la Mancomunitat de Catalunya. Barcelona, 1916-1918" (at the end of vol. 3). Barcelona: Biblioteca Catalana, 1916. Vol. 1, 360 pp; vol. 2, 412 pp., vol. 3, 404 - 20 pp. Not reprinted.
It has 241 chapters, written in Catalan and addressed to the nuns of her monastery. It belongs to the medieval genre of tales dealing with the life of Jesus Christ. It is based on the four gospels and some apocryphal traditions. The great quantity of quotations in Latin (above all, patristic) reveals her vast culture. Its interest lies in the detailed description of daily environments, aristocratic and popular (domestic customs, meals, costumes, jewels), and on the rare protagonism of women. It starts with the conception of Mary and finishes with her ascent to heaven. It is also interesting because of its use of popular language. The edition of Miquel i Planas is

out of print. Another edition by Albert Hauf (University of Wales)
will be published before 1987 in Barcelona.

RC

VINYES OLIVELLA, Cèlia (1915-1954).
She was born in Catalonia but lived in Majorca. As she wrote only
one book in Catalan, Del foc a la cendra (1953), she is best known for
her books in Castilian. She is considered one of the writers who reno-
vated poetry in Majorca of the post-war period. Nevertheless, she
suffered, as did many other Catalan writers, repression of the Catalan
language, being "forced" to write in Castilian in order to survive.
Her works in Castilian are:
Antología lírica 1976
Canción tonta del sur 1948
Canto 1964
Como el ciervo corre herido 1955
Palabra sin voz 1953
Tierra de sur 1945
Trigo del corazón 1946
Viento levante 1946

CF

VOYSON, Ana.
Born in Madrid, Voyson first published stories and articles under a
pseudonym. After the Civil War, her own name became prominent as a
writer of essays, biography and newspaper and magazine articles. During
the 1950's she published frequently in ABC. In addition to her stories
and short novels, she published four novels.

Una aventura en cinco días. Barcelona: Cliper, 1945.
Won a prize for short novel sponsored by the publisher.

Cuentos de misterio. Barcelona: Rumbos, 1952.
Psychological and science fiction stories.

El manuscrito del bisabuelo. 1947.
A novel inspired by a sixteenth-century sailor, it won the "Virgen
del Carmen" prize.

CLG

XENIA. See: Karr i Alfonsetti, Carme.

*XIRINACS I DIAZ, Olga (1936-).
   Very active in the cultural life of her native city of Tarragona, she
began writing when she was 14. It wasn't until 1971, however, that she
became known in literary circles. Since then she has won numerous
literary prizes for both prose and poetry. She believes writers have an
obligation to get closer to the public, broadening cultural fields as
much as possible, and that the money spent on war preparations should be
spent on cultural life. Some of her favorite writers are Proust,
Mament, Woolf, Weiss, Simenon and Beauvoir. In 1980 she formed the
group El nus with several other writers and artists to collaborate on a
work called Tramada, published by the Institut d'Estudis Tarraconenses.
She recently won the Premi Sant Jordi for a novel about the suicide of
Virginia Woolf.

   Al meu cap una llosa. Barcelona: Proa, 1985, ISBN 84-7588-045-2,
   233 pp.
      This winner of the "Sant Jordi" prize is a novel which recreates
   wartime England while it studies Virginia Woolf's suicide and
   comments on the news media. The suffering of the townspeople, their
   reaction to the drowning of Woolf, whom they barely knew, and the
   thoughts of the shadow of Woolf during the three weeks before they
   found her body contrast with the crisp, official version of the
   progress of the war heard on the BBC.

   Botons de tiges grises. Barcelona: Proa, 1977.
      A collection of her poetic production. Tarragona is a constant
   setting for these poems, which are impressionistic and intimate at
   the same time. The 31 poems tell of the adolescence of a girl in
   love with the sea, who discovers Love. The lyricism stands in stark
   contrast with background of the violence of the 1940's.

   Clau de blau. Tarragona: Institut d'Estudis Tarraconenses, 1978.
      Poetry.

   Interior amb difunts. Barcelona: Destino, 1983.
      With a background drawn from impressionist painters, this novel
   recreates a passionate time--the turn of the century--and tells the
   story of young lovers. Winner of the Premi Josep Pla.

Llençol de noces. Barcelona: Proa, 1979.
    Poetry.

Música de cambra. Barcelona: Destino, 1982.
    The author describes this novel as a book of memories into which
are woven a series of strange adventures.

Preparo el té sota palmeres roges. Barcelona: Vosgos, 1981.
    Poetry, winner of the Premi Caravel.la.

                                                                KM

Z

ZAMBRANO DE RODRIGUEZ ALDAVE, María (1907-).
Born in Málaga, María Zambrano was a student of José Ortega y
Gasset. She contributed to Revista de Occidente, Cruz y Raya and other
periodicals. Arriving in Mexico in 1939 she taught at the University of
Morelos, Michoacán. She later taught at the University of Havana and
the University of Puerto Rico, contributing to such magazines as Las
Españas, Romance, and Nuestra España. She has also lived in Italy and
France.

La agonía de Europa. Colección de Ensayos Breves. Buenos Aires:
Sudamericana, 1945, 159 pp.

Claros del bosque. 1st ed., Biblioteca Breve, 434. Barcelona: Seix
Barral, 1977, 159 pp.
    Essays.

La confesión: Género literario y método. Cuadernos de filosofía
de luminar, 8. México: 'Luminar,' 1943, 63 pp.

Dos fragmentos sobre el amor. Malaga: Besar, 1982, 33 pp.

La España de Galdós. Cuadernos Taurus, 30. Madrid: Taurus, 1959,
114 pp. Barcelona: La Gaya Ciencia, 1982, 148 pp.

España, sueño y verdad. Colección El Puente. Barcelona:
E.D.H.A.S.A., 1965, 216 pp. Barcelona: E.D.H.A.S.A., 1982, 253 pp.

Filosofía y poesía. Morelia, México: Publicaciones de la
Universidad Michoacana, 1939, 157 pp.

Hacia un saber sobre el alma. Biblioteca filosófica. Buenos Aires:
Losada, 1950, 165 pp.

El hombre y lo divino. Brevarios, 103. México: Fondo de Cultura
Económica, 1955, 295 pp. 2nd ed., Breviarios, 103, México: Fondo
de Cultura Económica, 1973, 412 pp.

Los intelectuales en el drama de España. Santiago, Chile:
Panorama, 1937, 50 pp. Textos recuperados, 4. Madrid:
Hispamérica, 1977, 208 pp.

Obras reunidas. Primera entrega: El sueño creador, Filosofía y poesía, Apuntes sobre el lenguaje sagrado y las artes, Poema y sistema, Pensamiento y poesía en la vida española, Una forma de pensamiento: La 'Guía.' Madrid: Aguilar, 1971, 370 pp.

Pensamiento y poesía en la vida española. "Conferencias 'La Casa de España en México,' 1939." México: La Casa de España en México, 1939, 179 pp.

El sueño creador: los sueños, el soñar y la creación por la palabra. Universidad Veracruzana. Facultad de filosofía, letras y ciencias, 28. Xalapa, Mexico: Universidad Veracruzana, 1965, 179 pp. I sogni e il tempo. Trans. Elena Croce. Quaderni di pensiero o di poesía, lv, No. 1. Roma: De Luca, 1960, 37 pp.

La tumba de Antigona. Colección mínima literaria. México: Siglo veintiuno, 1967, 90 pp. Litoral Iv, no. 121-123. Torremolinos: Litoral, 1983.

JED

ZARDOYA GONZALEZ, María de la Concepción (1914-). Pseudonym used before 1946: Concha de Salamanca. Pseudonym used after 1946 to present: Concha Zardoya.
    Born in Valparaiso, Chile of Spanish parents, Concha Zardoya returned in 1932 to Spain where she began her writing career with history readers for adolescents, and, in 1947, received her undergraduate degree in Modern Philology from the University of Madrid. In 1948, she moved to the U.S. and received her Ph.D. from the University of Illinois in 1952. Until 1977 she remained in the U.S. as professor of Spanish literature at Illinois, Tulane, California, Yale, Indiana, Barnard, and Massachusetts universities. She then returned to Madrid. One of the most widely known and prolific of contemporary Spanish women poets, her poetry presently numbers 18 volumes, for which she has won various prizes; she also has published extensive literary criticism and translations. Characteristics of her work include: "Theme" books wherein all the poems included are interrelated by subject and/or theme; poems with critical-subjective evaluations of art or poetry masterpieces; Spain as a prevailing theme; structural predisposition toward free verse or assonantal rhyme and questions. Her best works were produced in 1965-77; she is still active in poetic production and literary circles.

La casa deshabitada. Madrid: Insula, 1959, 147 pp.
    Reinforcing a recurrent theme of lacrimose solitude, these poems, dedicated to those who are alone, unite the poet's lonelinesses with those of all the lonely people. Found in most large University libraries.

El corazón y la sombra. Madrid: Insula, 1977, ISBN 84-7185-102-4, 110 pp.
    This 1975 winner of the "Premio Fémina de Poesía" is thematically important, for it chronicles the poet's self-exploration, auto-definition, and revelation as she seeks to define her existence and soul ("corazón") through her own history/intrahistory, symbolized by "sombra." The overleaves and prologue ("Intrahistoria") outline Zardoya's own opinion of what her poetic opus of 15 works represents. Stylistically, it is a return to

earlier free-verse and questioning techniques. Known location:
Love Library, University of Nebraska.

Corral de vivos y muertos. Buenos Aires: Losada, 1965, 148 pp.
    Spain and its people who are dead to liberty or alive only in
memory is the omnipresent, all-pervading subject of this mournful
poetry. Included are some poems written from 1939 to 1947 which had
been censored in Dominio del llanto. Attention to technical
details--assonantal rhyme, formal metering, poetic recourses, and
varied versification--distinguish it as one of her most notable
works. Available in most large University libraries.

Cuentos del Antiguo Nilo (Las dos tierras de Hapí). Madrid:
Aguilar, 1944. Colección Crisol num. 81, 470 pp.
    This, her only book of short stories, serves as a transition from
fictionalized historical pieces to lyric poetry. It is the last time
she uses the pseudonym Concha de Salamanca. These short stories set
in the country of the Nile River (Hapí), embellish myths and legends
of Egyptian gods and courtiers. Filled with exoticism, they imagine
a world of kingly ascendancies tempered by human nature and fatalism.
Available from Dartmouth library.

Debajo de la luz. Barcelona: Instituto de Estudios Hispánicos,
1959, 59 pp.
    A genuine tenderness of tone permeates this outward-looking book
where self-knowledge comes by discovering, loving, and accepting
one's own soul as it is reflected in the needs and people of the
external world. Stylistically, while replete with exclamation points
and questions, its running pen monologues tend to employ less
scholarly language, making the observations seem more sincere.
Although not published until 1959, it won the Premio Boscan of 1955.
Colorado and Illinois libraries have it.

El desterrado ensueño. New York-Madrid: Hispanic Institute in the
United States, 1955, 119 pp.
    Printed in Spain, this travelogue of dreamy memories of Spanish
cities is dedicated to exiled Spaniards. Exclamatory and
interrogatory sentences alternate throughout the free-verse poems
with the proposition that in remembrance there is hope. Located in
many University libraries, including Illinois and Colorado.

Diotima y sus edades (Autobiografía en cuatro tiempos). Barcelona:
Ambito Literario, 1981.

Dominio del llanto. Adonais 41. Madrid: Hispánica Adonais, 1947,
102 pp.
    This winner of the 1947 "premio accesit Adonais" is dedicated "to
all the beings who have suffered, in body and spirit, the rigors and
violence of this time," and, as such, emphasizes the dominant cry of
distressed and suffering peoples. These 11-syllable, unrhymed poems
repeatedly question the nature of death and of God. Painful themes
and subjects (dead children, disenterred bodies) and a mossy nature
which participates in man's desperation reappear in these verses to
both known and unknown fellow sufferers. Available from Alderman
library, University of Virginia.

Donde El Tiempo Resbala (Romancero de Bélgica). Montevideo:
Cuadernos Julio Herrera y Reissig, 1966, 54 pp.
    Subtitled "Romancero de Bélgica," dedicated to Belgian friends,
and inspired by her first trip to Belgium in 1959, Concha's small
volume portrays pleasant surroundings where time "slips away" on
watery canal streets. Flamenco vignettes and "art-work poetry" (this
time the flamenco unicorn tapestry) complete this volume in which her
newly developed preference for assonantal rhyme is reinforced.

Elegías. Caracas, Venezuela: Lírica Hispana number 214, Febrero,
1961, 96 pp.
    One of Concha's favorite formats is to combine literary criticism
with her own emotional reaction to other poet's works. More like
encomiums than elegies, these laudatory pieces praise and
rhetorically question such greats as Garcilaso, Quevedo, Unamuno,
Machado, Lorca, and (the longest poem) José Luis Hidalgo. Many,
particularly the familial elegies, are reprints from earlier books.
Despite its tiny size, the edition includes the author's picture and
biography, an introduction by series editor Conie-Jean Lobell, and a
reproduction of Zardoya's handwritten description of these as ashen,
dolorous elegies. Known location: Adelphi University library.

Los engaños de Tremont. Colección Agora. Madrid: Alfaguara, 1971
M2705.--1971, 203 pp.
    Printed on her fifty-seventh birthday, Los engaños de Tremont
explores Zardoya's theory of poetic reality where deceptions lie and
lay in every sector: Tremont-on-the-Common (Boston, Mass., where it
was written in 1970-71), and in the external and internal stimuli of
doors, mirrors, windows, art, music, blood, souls, god, death, and so
on. Even the structure of the poems which comprise this, her
longest, book deceives; all are "pseudo sonnets," properly metered,
but unrhymed, mirroring the deceptions of reality and the poet's
resultant illusion/disillusionment.

La hermosura sencilla. New York-Madrid: Hispanic Institute in the
United States, 1953, 165 pp.
    After receiving her Ph.D. at the University of Illinois (1952)
with a thesis "España en la poesía americana," Concha published her
first book of poetry written--with Whitmanesque tones--in the United
States. Located in Love library, University of Nebraska.

Las hiedras del tiempo. Madrid: Biblioteca Nueva, 1972,
M1.312-1972, 52 pp.
    According to the author's bibliografic note which closes this
volume, Las hiedras del tiempo--itself fragmented and
regrouped--contains poems which had originally belonged to Debajo de
la luz (1959) and others from 1966 as well as more recent poetry.
Thus, as a patchwork of earlier--sometimes rejected--poems, it is
retrospective, with the theme of "light" permeating the whole.
Located in most libraries.

Hondo Sur. El Bardo Colección de poesía número 43. Madrid: Ciencia
Nueva, 1968, B.5037-1968, 169 pp.
    Fresh experiences in the "Deep South" of the U.S., gleaned while
teaching at Tulane in Louisiana, inspire these heart-felt verses
about bogs, bayous, abandoned plantations, cotton fields, the black

and white human condition, and solidarity. Noteworthy because of its subject-matter and uncomplicated style--at times based on Negro proverbs and music--Hondo Sur portrays the scenery, emotions, and heroes of the southern microcosm. Includes a prologue by and picture of the author. Located in most University libraries.

"Lecturas juveniles" series. Madrid: Aguilar, 1943-1945, (approximate dates), 100 pp. per volume.

Under the pseudonym "Concha de Salamanca," Concha Zardoya began her literary career by writing 12 historical readers. Two series were published by Aguilar in the mid-1940s (probably from 1943-45-- precise dates are not printed in the books). To the first series, "Historias y leyendas españolas," Concha contributed Los siete Infantes de Lara, Abindarráez y Jarifa (El Abencerraje), El Doncel del Mar, Reina después de muerta (los amores de Doña Inés de Castro), El Caballero de Olmedo, Doña Juana la Loca, and El Correo Mayor (El Conde de Villamediana). For the second series "Historias y leyendas de Ultramar," (South American subjects), she wrote El Anahuac conquistado (Cortés y Vasco de Quiroga), El Inca Garcilaso, Sor Juana Inés de la Cruz (la décima musa), and La desolada Patagonia (la expedición de Magellanes). Partly imaginative, these profusely illustrated, fictionalized histories retell legends and tales of Spanish conquerors and New World events. Intended for adolescents, their grammar, sentence structure and vocabulary would be difficult for beginning readers. Most are available through U. of Illinois, Champaign or Dartmouth College libraries.

Manhattan y otras latitudes. Ferrol, Spain: Esquío, 1983, ISBN 84-86046-06-8, 55 pp.

Stereotyped scenes of urban blight and inhumanity in Manhattan, "artwork" poetry based on New York museum pieces and evocations of other U.S. and Spanish cities ("latitudes") make up this free-verse volume of travel souvenirs. Hard to locate, may be available from the Valle-Inclán society in Ferrol, which awarded it the Esquío prize in 1983.

Mirar el cielo es tu condena (Homenaje a Miguel Angel). Madrid: Insula, 1957, 113 pp.

Typical of Zardoya's fondness for writing poetry about great artists and their masterpieces, this work combines critical and emotional reactions. Located in Illinois University library.

Pájaros del nuevo mundo. Adonais XXVII. Madrid: Hispánica Adonais, 1946, 75 pp.

Birds of all shapes, sizes, guises, and habitats inspire the free-verse poems of Pájaros del nuevo mundo. Dedicated to Gabriela Mistral, who helped form Concha's "adolescent soul," they borrow many modernist devices--New World themes, metaphors of abundant nature, exuberant colors--and showcase a prowess for lush description. Part of a volume called "Las manos y los pájaros" which was never published. Her first poetry, it is nonetheless, among her best.

Los ríos caudales: Apología del 27. Madrid: CORCEL, 1982, ISBN 84-300-7173-3, 95 pp.

Prefaced by a quote from Jorge Manrique, these long, generally loosely structured poems dedicated to the Generation of '27--broadly

defined to include León Felipe--react both critically and
subjectively to the works of 19 poets who influenced and impressed
Zardoya and laid the foundation for current poetry and criticism.

Los Signos. Alicante: Colleción Ifach, 1954, 61 pp.
    Poetry. Located in Illinois University library. Winner of the
"Accésit del Ifach de Poesía," Alicante, 1952.

JBL

ZAYAS Y SOTOMAYOR, María de (1600-1650?).
    Little more than appears in Serrano y Sanz is known about the
biography of this noted novelist. She produced two collections of ten
novelas, each set into a common frame which is strikingly feminist.

Desengaños amorosos, Parte segunda del sarao y entretenimiento
honesto. Ed. Agustín G. de Amezúa. Madrid: Real Academia
Española, 1950, 461 pp.
Ed. Alicia Yllera. Madrid: Cátedra, 1983, ISBN 84-376-0435-4,
511 pp.
    Once considered the definitive scholarly edition, the 1950 edition
(now out of print), with an extensive introduction, has been
superceded by Yllera's 1983 edition. Hers is a meticulous scholarly
edition of the second part, with excellent introduction, notes and
bibliography.

Novelas. Ed. José Hesse. Madrid: Taurus, 1965, 122 pp.
    This volume contains a popular introduction of historical, not
scholarly, interest, with versions of "La burlada Aminta y venganza
del honor," and "El prevenido engañado." Paperback available but
not recommended because of the partial presentation of Zayas' work.

Novelas amorosas y ejemplares. Ed. Agustín G. de Amezúa. Madrid:
Real Academia Española, 1948, 423 pp.
    This edition contains an extensive introduction and biblio-
graphical appendix and is considered the definitive scholarly edition
of the first part, despite the fact that it is based on the second
1637 edition and the ending of "El castigo de la miseria" differs
from the first. Otherwise there is minimal textual variation from
the first editions of her works to the modern ones. Out of print.

Novelas completas. Ed. María Martínez del Portal. Barcelona:
Bruguera, 1973, ISBN 84-02-03059-9, 670 pp.
    The only complete popular edition of both parts, this volume is
based on the authoritative Amezúa editions, with introduction and
bibliography. Out of print.

Novelas ejemplares y amorosas o Decameron español. Ed. Eduardo
Rincón. Madrid: Alianza 109, 1968, 230 pp.
    This is a popular, not scholarly, edition of six novelas with
introduction and notes which is widely available but not recommended
because of the partial nature of the selection and the introduction.
It contains from the first part: "El castigo de la miseria," "La
fuerza del amor," "El prevenido engañado," "El desengañado amado y
premio de la virtud;" from the second: "La inocencia castigada,"
"Estragos que causa el vicio."

A Shameful Revenge and Other Stories. Ed. and trans. by John
Sturrock. London: The Folio Society, 1963, 200 pp.
    A rather free and flamboyant translation (but the only ones
available to date) of eight of Zayas' more exciting stories, it
contains two from the first part: "Forewarned but forestalled,"
"There always comes the reckoning;" and six from the second part:
"The ravages of vice," "An innocent punished," "A shameful revenge,"
"A traitor to his own flesh and blood," "No good comes from marrying
foreigners," "A mistake discovered too late." Out of print.
                                                          HPB

Appendix I

AUTHORS BY BIRTHDATE

14th Century
1313   López de Córdova, Leonor

15th Century
1430   Villena, Isabel de
1435?   Cartagena, Sor Teresa de
1475?   Galindo, Beatriz
?   Pinar, Florencia

16th Century
1515   Teresa de Jesús
1530?   Sigea de Velasco, Luisa
1551   Rocaberti, Isabel de
1562   Sabuco de Nantes Barrera, Oliva
1569   Caro Mallén de Soto, Ana
1570?   Luján, Micaela de
?   Requesens i de Liori, Estefania
?   Enríquez de Guzmán, Feliciana

17th Century
1600   Zayas y Sotomayor, María de
1602   Agreda, María de Jesús de
1615?   Carvajal y Saavedra, Mariana
1623   Abarca de Bolea, Ana Francisca
1649   Beneta Mas i Pujol, Margarida
1653   Santa Teresa, Sor Gregoria Francisca de
1662   Borbon, María Luisa
?   (H)enríquez, Cristobalina
?   Nada, Sor
?   Narcisa

18th Century
1726   Navia y Bellet, Francisca Irene de
1742   Hore y Ley (de Fleming), María Gertrudis de
1768   Gálvez de Cabrera, María Rosa de
1768   Guzmán y de la Cerda (y de Sousa), María Isidra Quintina de
1793   Maturana de Gutiérrez, Vicenta
1796   Böhl de Faber y Larrea, Cecilia
?   Torres, Narcisa

19th Century

1811	Massanés de González, Maria Josepa
1820	Arenal, Concepción
1923	Coronado, Carolina
1826	Grassi de Cuenca, Angela
1827	Penya d'Amer, Victòria
1834	Sáez de Melgar, Faustina
1835	Sinués y Navarro (de Marco), María del Pilar
1837	Castro, Rosalía de
	García Balmaseda (de González), Joaquina
1838	Caimari, Margalida
1841	Maspons i Labrós, Maria del Pilar
1842	Paler, Enriqueta
1845	Herreros i Sorà, Manuela de los
	Monserdà de Macià, Dolors
1847	Corral, Clara
1851	Acuña y Villanueva de la Iglesia, Rosario de
	Pardo Bazàn, Emilia
1852	Armengol de Badia, Agnès
1854	Morlius, Remei
	Santamaria i Ventura de Fàbrigues, Joaquima
1856	Gili i Güell, Antònia
1860	Gimeno de Flaquer, Concepción
1862	Casanova de Lutoslawski, Sofía
	Ventós i Cullell, Palmira
1865	Karr i Alfonsetti, Carme
	Sureda, Emília
1867	Denis de Rusinol, Lluisa
1869	Espina, Concepción
	Herrera Garrido, Francisca
	Salvà, Maria Antónia
1873	Albert I Paradis, Caterina
1874	Lejárraga, María de la O
1875	Rosselló I Miralles
1877	Domènech i Escaté de Cañellas, Maria
1881	Bartre, Llúcia
	Llorens i Carreras, Sara
	Rubiés, Anna
1882	Maeztu (Whitney), María de
1883	Bassa, Maria Gràcia (Gràcia B. de Llorens)
1886	Canalias, Anna
1891	Ballesteros de Gaibrois, Mercedes
1892	Ibars Ibars, Maria
	Matheu, Roser
	Millán Astray, Pilar
	Valderrama, Pilar
1893	Montoriol i Puig, Carme
1895	Jacquetti i Isant, Palmira (P. de Castellvell)
1896	Nelken y Mausberger, Margarita
1897	Kent, Victoria
1898	Canyà i Martí, Llucieta
	Chacel, Rosa
	Gay, Simona
1899	Arderiu i Voltes, Clementina
	Bertrana, Aurora
	Icaza, Carmen de

1899   Suñol, Cèlia
19th Century (Exact Date Unknown):
?   Dato Muruáis, Filomena
?   Echevarría, María Jesús
?   García de la Torre, Ana
?   Palencia, Isabel
?   Villamartín, Isabel de

20th Century
1900   Alfaro, María
          Crusat, Paulína
1901   Madera, Asunción
1902   Figuera Aymerich, Angela
          Lafitte Y Pérez del Pulgar, Maria de los Reyes
          Sedano, Dora
          Vila, Mercè
1904   Fariña e Cobián, Herminia
          Leon, María Teresa
          Mulder de Daumer, Elisabeth
          Murià i Romani, Anna
1905   Alonso i Manant, Cecília
          Champourcin y Moran de Loredo, Ernestina de
          Galvarriato, Eulalia
          Montseny, Federica
          Saavedra, Anna Maria de
1906   Mora, Constancia de la
1907   Conde Abellán, Carmen
          Vernet I Real, Maria Teresa
          Zambrano de Rodríguez Aldave, María
1908   Laborda Medir, Clemencia
          Romero Serrano, Marina
          Suárez del Otero, Concha
1909   Gutiérrez Torrero, Concepción
          Rodoreda i Gurgui, Mercè
1910   Arquimbau, Rosa Maria
          Leveroni, Rosa
          Maura, Julia
          Torre, Josefina de la
1911   Masoliver, Liberata
          Rafael Marés Kurz, Carmen de
1912   Franco, Dolores
          Pomareda De Haro, Joaquina
1913   Pla, Walda
          Romo Arregui, Josefina
1914   Martínez i Civera, Empar Beatriu
          Medio, Dolores
          Orriols, Maria Dolors
          Sanz Cuadrado, María Antonia
          Zardoya González, María de la Concepción
1915   Castroviejo Blanco-Cicerón, Concha
          Linares, Luisa María
          Martel, Carmen
          Rubio y López Guijarro, María del Carmen
1916   Calvo de Aguilar, Isabel
          Marco, Concha de
          Ojeda, Pino

1916	Salisachs, Mercedes
1917	Sáenz-Alonso, Mercedes
	Soriano, Carmen
1918	Abelló i Soler, Montserrat
	Bravo-Villasante Arenas, Carmen
	Capmany Farnés, Maria Aurèlia
	Fórmica Corsi, Mercedes
	Fuertes, Gloria
	Maluquer i Gonzàlez, Concepció
	March, Susana
	Mariño Carou, María
	Martínez Valderrama, María Luz
	Osorio Delgado, Amalia
	Paya Mira, Carmen
	Serrano, Eugenia
	Troitiño, Carmen
	Vázquez Iglesias, Purificación
1919	Doña Jiménez, Juana
	Hernán, Josita
	Mercader, Trina
	Pàmies i Bertran, Teresa
	Rivera Tovar, Anunciación
1920	Alberca Lorente, Luisa
	Cajal, Rosa María
	Suárez del Otero, Concha
1921	Carré Sànchez, María del Pilar
	García Rata, Felisa
	Laforet, Carmen
	Llorca, Carmen
	Quiroga, Elena
	Villarta Tuñón, Angeles
1922	Alós, Concha
	Huidobro, María Teresa de
	Pozo Garza, Luz
1923	Palou, Inés
1925	Beneyto Cunyat, Maria
	Forrellad, Luisa
	Martín Gaite, Carmen
	Uceda, Julia
1926	Albornoz, Aurora de
	García Diego, Begoña
	Gatell, Angelina
	Kruckenberg Sanjurjo, María del Carmen
	Matute, Ana María
	Rincón, María Eugenia
	Szel, Elisabeth
1927	López Sainz, Celia
	Narvión, Pilar
	Puncel Reparaz, María
	Sánchez-Cutillas i Martínez, Carmelina
	Uceta, Acacia
1928	Forest, Eva
1929	Julió, Montserrat
	Lacasa, Cristina
192?	Boixadós, María Dolores
1930	Albó, Núria

1930	Alvarez de Toledo, (Luisa) Isabel
	Anglada, Maria Angels
	Aguirre, Francisca
	Mulet, María
	Portal Nicolás, Marta
	Sau Sánchez, Victoria
1931	Andrés, Elena
	Mieza, Carmen Farrés de
	Torre Vivero, Carmen de la
1933	Sales Folch, Núria
1934	Barbero Sánchez, Teresa
	Cornet i Planells, Montserrat
1935	Falcón O'Neill, Lidia
1936	Targioni Lodoni, Eduarda
	Tusquets, Esther
	Xirinacs i Díaz, Olga
1937	Jiménez Faro, Luz María
1938	Diosdado, Ana
	Fagundo, Ana María
	Muñoz Ortiz, Sofía
	Pompeia, Núria
	Queizán, María Xosé
	Salvador Maldonado, Dolores
1939	Figuera Aymerich, Angela
1940	Janés, Clara
	Romá, Rosa
	Valentí, Helena
1941	Pessarrodona i Artigués, Marta
	Ragué-Arias, Maria-Josep
1942	Canyelles, Antonina
	Chordà i Requesens, Mari
	Escobedo, Joana
	Mayoral Díaz, Marina
	Vicens, Antònia
1943	Ortiz Sánchez, Lourdes
	Simó i Monllor, Isabel-Clara
1945	Fernández Cubas, Cristina
	Gómez Ojea, Carmen
1946	Canelo Gutiérrez, Pureza
	Ibañez Novo, Mercedes
	Oliver, Maria-Antònia
	Roig i Fransitorra, Montserrat
1947	Moix, Ana María
	Puértolas Villanueva, Soledad
1948	Riera Guilera, Carme
	Rubio Gámez, Fanny
1951	Ledo Andión, Margarita
	Montero, Rosa
1952	Ensenyat, Franxesca
	Marçal i Serra, Maria-Mercè
1953	Aritzeta i Abad, Margarida
1957	Pallarés, Pilar
1960	Mur, Mireia
20th Century (Exact Birthdate Unknown):	
?	Andréis, Ester de
?	Arenys, Teresa d'

?	Barberá, Carmen
?	Becker, Angélicka
?	Blanc de Panero, Felicidad
?	Cabré de Calderó, Maria
?	Cardona, Fina
?	Cartañá Domenge de S. de Ocaña, E.
?	Cistaré, Lali
?	Díaz de Sáez, Francisca
?	Echévarría, María Jesús
?	Fabregat i Armengol, Rosa
?	Ferran i Mora, Eulàlia
?	García Bellver, Carmen
?	Gefaell de Vivanco, María Luisa
?	Ginestà, Marina
?	González, Assumpta
?	Guasch, Maria Carme
?	Guilló Fontanilles
?	Heine, Ursula
?	Lacaci, María Elvira
?	Lafontana i Prunera, Maite
?	Martín Vivaldi, Elena
?	Melcón, María Luz
?	Mínquez, Nùria
?	Mora, Constancia de la
?	Oleart de Bel, Maria
?	Papiol i Mora, Maria Angels
?	Pazos i Noguera, Maria Lluisa
?	Penas, Anxeles
?	Planelles, Neus
?	Prieto Rouco, Carmen
?	Resino de Ron, Carmen
?	Segovia Rodríguez, María Paz
?	Serra, Maria Gerona
?	Soriano Jara, Elena
?	Suqué i d'Espona, Carme
?	Torres, Xohana
?	Urretavizcaya, Arantxa
?	Vayreda, Maria dels Angels
?	Vergér, Maria
?	Voyson, Ana

Appendix II
AUTHORS IN CATALAN

The following is a list of authors included in this bibliography whose works are exclusively or primarily in Catalan:

Abelló i Soler, Montserrat
Alacseal, Virgili (pseud. for
    Caterina Albert)
Albert i Paradís, Caterina
Albó, Núria
Alonso i Manant, Cecília
Anglada, Maria Angels
Arderiu i Voltas, Clementina
Arenys, Teresa d'
Aritzeta i Abad, Margarida
Armengol de Badia, Agnès
Arquimbau, Rosa Maria
Bartre, Llúcia
Bassa, Maria Gràcia
Bell-Lloch, Maria de (pseud. for
    Maria del Pilar Maspons i Labrós)
Beneta Mas i Pujol, Margarida
Beneyto Cunyat, Maria
Bertrana, Aurora
Cabré de Calderó, Maria
Caimari, Margalida
Canalias, Anna
Canyà i Martí, Llucieta
Canyelles, Antonina
Capmany Farnés, Maria-Aurèlia
Cardona, Fina
Cartañá Domenge de S. de Ocaña,
    Elvira
Català, Víctor (pseud. for
    Caterina Albert i Paradís)
Chordà i Requesens, Mari
Cistaré, Eulàlia
Civera, Beatriu (pseud. for Empar
    Beatriu Martínez i Civera)
Cornet i Planells, Montserrat
Denis de Rusiñol, Lluisa
Domènech i Escaté de Cañellas,
    Maria
Dracs, Ofèlia (name for collective
    of writers, mostly male)
Ensenyat, Franxesca

Escobedo, Joana
Fabregat i Armengol, Rosa
Ferran i Mora, Eulàlia
Gay, Simona
Gili i Güell, Antònia
Ginestà, Marina
González, Assumpta
Guasch, Maria Carme
Guilló Fontanilles, Magdalena
Herreros i Sorà, Manuela de los
Ibars Ibars, Maria
Jacquetti i Isant, Palmíra
Julió, Montserrat
Karr i Alfonsetti, Carme
Lafontana i Prunera, Maite
Leveroni, Rosa
Llorens, Gràcias B. de (pseud.
    for Maria Gracia Bassa)
Llorens i Carreras, Sara
Maluquer, Concepció i González
Màntua, Cecília A. (pseud. for
    Cecília Alonso)
Marçal i Serra, Maria-Mercè
Martínez i Civera, Empar Beautriu
Maspons i Labrós, Maria del Pilar
Massanés de González, Maria
    Josepa
Matheu, Roser
Mínquez, Núria
Miralles, Josep (pseud. for Maria
    Domènech i Escaté de
    Cañellas)
Monserdà de Macià, Dolors
Montoriol i Puig, Carme
Montseny, Federica
Morlius, Remei
Mur, Mireia
Murià i Romani, Anna
Oleart de Bel, Maria
Oliver, Maria-Antònia
Orriols, Maria Dolors

Paler, Enriqueta
Palma, Felip (pseud. for Palmira
    Ventós i Cullell)
Pàmies i Bertran, Teresa
Papiol i Mora, Maria Angels
Pazos i Noguera, Maria Lluisa
Penya d'Amer, Victòria
Pessarrodona i Artiguées, Marta
Pla, Walda
Planelles, Neus
Pompeia, Núria
Ragué-Arias, Maria-Josep
Reina de Mallorca
Requesens i de Liori, Estefania
Riera Guilera, Carme
Rodoreda, Mercè
Roig i Fransitorra, Montserrat
Rosselló i Miralles, Coloma
Rubiés, Anna
Saavedra, Anna Maria de
Sales Folch, Núria
Salvà, Maria-Antònia
Sánchez-Cutillas i Martínez,
    Carmelina
Santamaria i Ventura de Fàbrigues,
    Joaquima
Sant Jordi, Rosa de (pseud. for
    Rosa Maria Arquimbau)
Serra, Maria Girona
Serrahima, Núria
Simó i Monllor, Isabel-Clara
Suñol, Cèlia
Suqué i d'Espona, Carme
Sureda, Emília
Torres, Narcisa
Tròlec, Isa (pseud. for male writer
    Joan B. Mengual)
Valentí, Helena
Valldaura, Agna de (pseud. for
    Joaquima Santamaria i Ventura)
Vayreda, Maria dels Angels
Ventós i Cullell, Palmira
Vergér, Maria
Vernet i Real, Maria Teresa
Vicens, Antònia
Vila, Mercè
Villamartín, Isabel de
Villena, Isabel de
Xènia (pseud. for Carme Karr i
    Alfonsetti)
Xirinacs i Díaz, Olga

Appendix III
AUTHORS IN GALICIAN

The following is a list of authors included in this bibliography whose works are exclusively or primarily in Galician:

Corral, Clara
Dato Muruáis, Filomena
Fariña e Cobián, Herminia
Heine, Ursula
Herrera Garrido, Francisca
Kruckenberg Sanjurjo, María del Carmen
Ledo Andión, Margarita
Mariño Carou, María
Pallarès, Pilar
Penas, Anxeles
Pozo Garza, Luz
Prieto Rouco, Carmen
Queizán, María Xosé
Torres, Xohana
Vásquez Iglesias, Purificación

TITLE INDEX

C

W

About the Editor

CAROLYN L. GALERSTEIN is Dean of the School of General Studies and Associate Professor of Comparative Literature at the University of Texas at Dallas. In addition to her numerous published articles, she has co-authored *Women and Public Policy* and edited Carmen Laforet's *Un noviazgo*.